On Law, Politics, and Judicialization

On Law, Politics, and Judicialization

Martin Shapiro
and
Alec Stone Sweet

OXFORD
UNIVERSITY PRESS

OXFORD
UNIVERSITY PRESS

Great Clarendon Street, Oxford OX2 6DP

Oxford University Press is a department of the University of Oxford.
It furthers the University's objective of excellence in research, scholarship,
and education by publishing worldwide in

Oxford New York

Auckland Bangkok Buenos Aires Cape Town Chennai
Dar es Salaam Delhi Hong Kong Istanbul Karachi Kolkata
Kuala Lumpur Madrid Melbourne Mexico City Mumbai Nairobi
São Paulo Shanghai Singapore Taipei Tokyo Toronto

with an associated company in Berlin

Oxford is a registered trade mark of Oxford University Press
in the UK and in certain other countries

Published in the United States
by Oxford University Press Inc., New York

British Library Cataloguing in Publication Data
Data available

Library of Congress Cataloging in Publication Data
Data available

ISBN 0-19-925647-0 (hbk)
ISBN 0-19-925648-9 (pbk)

1 3 5 7 9 10 8 6 4 2

Typeset by Newgen Imaging Systems (P) Ltd, Chennai, India
Printed in Great Britain
on acid-free paper by
Biddles Ltd.,
Guildford & King's Lynn

To Barbara and Martha

Acknowledgments

I am not by nature much of a collaborator. Alec has been the moving force behind this volume and has done a disproportionate share of the work in bringing it to fruition. Recently I have had occasion to reflect on how much of my scholarly life has been determined by the opportunities offered me by other people. I quickly came to a list of over 30, including Alec, but no one would be willing to read such a long list. I would, however, like to acknowledge those responsible for major redirections in my work. Sam Krislov, Antonin Scalia, and Lief Carter moved me into writing about administrative law, and the former Dean and the Assistant Dean of my law school, Sandy Kadish and Jan Vetter, into teaching in that area. Fred Greenstein drew me into writing on comparative law. I am deeply indebted to Mauro Cappelletti and Joseph Weiler for my initial forays in European Union matters and to Anne-Marie Slaughter, Joe, Renaud Dehousse, and Yves Meny for my subsequent re-entry. Alfred Aman recruited me into the globalization campaign and Harry Scheiber into its contract battalion.

The publishers who have allowed us to reproduce articles are acknowledged separately, in the text.

Martin Shapiro
February 2002

The research published in this book was supported in part by grants awarded by the US National Science Foundation, the US National Endowment for the Humanities, the Institute for Global Peace and Conflict Studies of the University of California-Irvine, the Institute on Global Conflict and Cooperation of the University of California-San Diego, and the Center for German and European Studies of the University of California-Berkeley.

Many months of work went into preparing the diverse elements of this manuscript for publication. I thank Margaret McCown (my graduate student assistant at Nuffield College), Ms Lin Sorrell and Ms Emma Hunter (of the secretarial staff at Nuffield College), Hannah Driscoll and Michael James (Oxford University Press) and Barbara Shapiro for their help with scanning, formatting, and copy-editing texts, chasing down lost references, and many other important, but often mind-numbing, tasks.

Martha Lewis, who generally prefers big canvases, oil paint, and vibrant colours, produced the cover art. She also reads my papers, and is more than patient with the strange world of academics.

This is my fourth book with my editor, Dominic Byatt, and his assistant, Amanda Watkins. I am grateful for their creativity, encouragement, and support.

Alec Stone Sweet
February 2002

Contents

List of Figures

List of Tables

Law, Courts, and Social Science

Over the past half-century, the domain of the litigator and the judge has radically expanded. In successive waves of democratization and state reform, a 'new constitutionalism' (Shapiro and Stone 1994) has swept across Europe and made inroads into Africa, Latin America, and Asia. In moves of enormous consequence, new constitutions typically repudiate legislative supremacy, establish fundamental human rights as substantive constraints on legislators and administrators, and provide for judicial protection of these rights against abuses by public authority. At the international level, events appear as dramatic and transformative. The European Court of Justice has fashioned a quasi-federal, legal system out of a treaty (Stein 1981; Weiler 1999); the judicialization of the GATT was consolidated and institutionalized as the legal system of the World Trade Organization (Hudec 1992; Stone Sweet 1998a); the scope and effectiveness of regional and global human rights regimes have steadily expanded (Helfer and Slaughter 1997); and transnational business has constructed a private, 'a-national' legal system that today competes with national law and state courts (Dezelay and Garth 1996; Mattli 2001). We could go on. Our point is that it will be increasingly difficult for scholars who do empirical research on government, or governance, to avoid encountering a great deal of law and courts.

During this same period, the relative status of legal scholarship in the field of political science has steadily declined (Shapiro 1993a). This is not the place to chronicle or critique that discipline's uneasy relationship with one of its sub-fields. What is clear is that social scientists now focus increasingly on a range of issues that implicate law and courts. Game theorists in political science, for example, have shown on how rules and veto points structure legislative processes and condition policy outcomes (for example, Tsebelis 1999), while 'institutionalists' of a more sociological or constructivist bent argue that rule systems themselves help to shape identities, roles, and tastes (for example, Giddens 1984; March and Olsen 1989). Often enough to matter a great deal, the relevant 'rules of the game' are in fact legal rules; legal doctrine shapes the strategies of those who pursue their interests through litigation; and courts constitute crucial veto points in policy processes (Stone Sweet 2000; Vanberg 1998a, b). Further, how judges interpret legal rights and duties can heavily condition the way the roles and identities of actors and groups are in fact defined (Hattam 1992). In international relations, two decades of research stamped with the 'international regime' label concerned law in some significant way (Kratochwil 1989; Stone 1994), and some regime theorists may finally be ready to take that fact seriously (for example, Goldstein *et al.* 2000). What is striking, however, is the great extent to which the (re)discovery of law and courts is proceeding without much engagement with the work of those who have specialized in their study.

At the same time, the legal academy has steadily incorporated, into research and the curriculum, perspectives that are external to the law, including those of the social sciences. It is no longer uncommon for academic lawyers to use concepts and methods developed by economists, sociologists, and political scientists, and to critically engage the latters' findings. Put differently, legal scholars are today far less committed to the proposition that law and adjudication are *sui generis* subjects that can be understood only through the specialized techniques of the lawyer.

These themes—the development and diffusion of judicial power, the challenge of building a social science of law and courts, and the ongoing relationship between legal and social science scholarship—have been omnipresent preoccupations in our own research.

Overview of the Book

This volume is a compilation of eleven papers—some old, some new—on the politics of law, courts, and judging. We embarked on this project, in part, because we see a theoretical cohesiveness to this work as a whole. We will try to demonstrate coherence as we proceed. Substantively, the papers tackle quite diverse topics, including the law-making dynamics of third-party dispute resolution, paradoxes of precedent, the discursive foundations of judicial power, the reciprocal impact of courts and legislatures, the successful diffusion of constitutional judicial review, the networking of legal elites, and the sources and consequences of the creeping 'judicialization of politics' around the world. Some chapters, including this one, elaborate concepts and theory meant to guide research. Where we can, we derive testable hypotheses or generate predictions about how legal systems emerge, develop, and mutate. In other chapters, we test our hypotheses. Our chosen empirical settings include the European Union, France, Germany, the United

States, and international trading regimes, public and private, and we discuss findings in still other legal systems, such as the Islamic and Imperial Chinese.

Chapters 1–5 each contain two pieces, one by each of us, addressing a common topic. These are preceded by co-authored introductions that are meant to serve three purposes. First, we explain how the materials presented relate to the more general purpose of developing a broad-gauge social science research agenda on law and courts. Second, we discuss the original motivations for writing these papers, given our intended audiences and our engagement with the relevant scholarship at that time. And third, we trace important, but perhaps not always obvious, connections between the two offerings. Chapter 6 consists of a co-authored piece.

Orientations

In this first chapter, we present two papers that were published, as journal articles, exactly 35 years apart. Each elaborated a relatively general approach to judicial politics, emphasizing underlying social logics not just of law and courts but of politics and government. In them, we sought to engage broader scholarly trends in the social sciences, which entailed ignoring or rejecting outright existing modes of legal scholarship. We both explicitly denied orthodox distinctions between law and politics, between the legislator and the judge, and between legal reasoning and other forms of decision making. Finally, we both drew linkages among diverse literatures, that is, between styles of scholarship that had developed without much reference to one another. These points deserve more discussion, not least because they presuppose a particular view of law and courts and of how the study of judicial politics has developed.

Political Jurisprudence and its Critics

In democratic states most government officials achieve legitimacy by acknowledging their political rule and claiming subordination to the people through elections or responsibility to those elected. Judges, however, claim legitimacy by asserting that they are non-political, independent, neutral servants of 'the law'. Alone among democratic organs of government, courts achieve legitimacy by claiming they are something they are not. Moreover the principal observers and commentators on courts are lawyers who have a vested interest in the legitimacy of courts and thus in furthering the pretences on which that legitimacy is grounded. In the US, especially, where the courts are one of the three co-equal branches of government and exercise a veto power over the actions of the other two, it has always been impossible to ignore their place in politics. So the study of courts in the US has involved a dialectic of denials and assertions of the obvious.

There have been a number of major intellectual episodes in this dialectic, among which was the sociological jurisprudence movement of the early twentieth century (Friedman 1967: 336–42) followed by the legal realist movement (Rumble 1968) of the 1930s. By the 1950s, the orthodoxy of an independent neutral, non-political judiciary had strongly reasserted itself. At this time, however, a number of political scientists had begun aggressively to assert the political nature of courts and to study them using the same theories and modes of empirical analysis applied by political scientists to other political phenomena.

In the early 1960s, Shapiro was asked to contribute to a law review symposium on jurisprudence. Borrowing terminology from the older sociological jurisprudence, and an orientation from the realists, he entitled his contribution 'Political Jurisprudence', which became a widely acknowledged label for most of the political science-oriented research on courts that occurred in the next several decades. The defining characteristic of the many kinds of work that fell under that label was an open, childlike acknowledgement of the obvious, or at least of what was obvious to all except those with a vested interest in denying it: that American courts were significant actors in American politics. A considerable liberation of intellectual energies occurs when this simple acknowledgement, unhampered by endlessly sophisticated reassertions of judicial independence, neutrality, and apoliticism, serves as the basis for research on courts. Scholars could begin, without apology, to ask the questions about judges asked about other political actors: how did they make policy decisions, how did they relate to other political actors, why did they sometimes succeed and sometimes fail in politics, how did their work styles and organization affect their political efficacy?

The term 'political jurisprudence', which served as the title to the 1964 article reproduced in this chapter, quite obviously echoed the name 'sociological jurisprudence'. As such it no doubt claimed more significance than it deserved. For it was only a portmanteau expression for whatever work on law and courts was being done at the time in political science that could be distinguished from lawyer-like, doctrinal analysis. There was, however, actually a certain common core to all this work: the unashamed acceptance of judges and courts as part of government, and thus amenable to the same modes of analysis as applied to other political actors and institutions. That is the central premise of this volume.

The key word was 'unashamed'. That courts were somehow, to some degree, political had been conceded by legal scholars for some time. Typically, however, the concession has been grudging. In the United States, where the federal courts comprise one of the three great constitutional branches of government, the other two are labelled the 'political branches'. Courts were—and, often enough, still are—defined as independent and neutral, with a little bit of political 'if' and 'but' mixed in.

Juridical scholarship of the 1950s and 1960s lived very much in the shadow of the New Deal conflict with the Supreme Court (Shapiro 1986a). Even after the great judicial leap forward of the School Desegregation Decision (USSC 1954), the legal orthodoxy of the day fell into two schools at least on the topic of the power of the Supreme Court to declare Congressional statutes unconstitutional. Proponents of 'judicial self-restraint' claimed that such a power ought not to be exercised by the Supreme Court because such an exercise would unavoidably infringe on the prerogatives of the political branches. The proclaimers of the 'preferred position' doctrine argued that the Court ought not to intervene against Congressional economic measures but should intervene against Congressional invasions of 'rights', other than property rights, because the Constitution gave a special preference to rights over the majoritarian democratic claims of the other branches. So one wing of orthodoxy conceded that all judicial review of legislation was political, the other that all review except the particular kind it favoured was political. Both the schools agreed that, no matter what evils it had done in the past, the Supreme Court ought now to stay out of politics. And the background claim was that, aside from the denounced forms of constitutional judicial review, the rest of what courts did was not political.[1]

It was natural that some political scientists would begin to deviate from that background claim and to accept ungrudgingly that judges and courts were in politics. American political science has always been excessively concerned with the Supreme Court and constitutional law to the exclusion of other courts and law. That court and that law were the most obviously political. The Supreme Court was part of American government. Political science was the study of government. There would be a natural tendency for political scientists to apply the same methods to the study of the Supreme Court as they did to the rest of government. The New Deal was one of the greatest

---

[1] Shapiro discusses these matters at length elsewhere, including Shapiro (1963; 1966a, b; 1986a, b; 1990a).

American political episodes; the struggle over the Supreme Court one of the most dramatic incidents of that episode. In that context political scientists were bound to look at the Court and bound to look at it as part of politics. Finally, for various odd reasons having to do with the historical development of political science and law as disciplines and of American universities, political science had confined itself to the study of 'public law'. If any law were to be political it would be public law, that is, the law about government and its relations with the citizenry.

Most fundamentally, however, the divergence between the orthodoxies of the legal academy and the researches of political scientists occurred because of the different relationships of academic lawyers and political scientists to what they study. The lawyer scholar is still a lawyer. Lawyers are, ought to be, and must be, defenders of courts. Courts rely for their institutional legitimacy on their reputations for independence and neutrality. If courts are political that fact needs to be hidden by the judges themselves and by those who are the dependants of courts. Even if the fact must ultimately be acknowledged, it must be glossed, excused, denatured, and palliated in every possible way. There is no doubt that American political science exhibits a strain of patriotism and citizen education in its study of American government. But it holds no particular brief for courts over other government institutions. And ultimately its self-proclaimed science compels it away from legitimacy building and towards accurate description and explanation. Political scientists do not have the duty to defend courts that lawyers have, and they do have an inclination to celebrate rather than disguise politics when they see it, in courts as well as elsewhere.

The study of law and courts is dominated by lawyers not political scientists. When the schools of judicial self-restraint and preferred position dominated constitutional law scholarship, most political scientists who devoted themselves to 'public law' simply sat at their desks in one or the other of those schools. Those schools themselves, however, even if only negatively, emphasized the political aspects of constitutional law and courts. And 'public law' political scientists, precisely because they concentrated on the US Supreme Court, always necessarily lived cheek by jowl with political scientists attempting to build general theories of American politics, theories that did not flow from a special professional obligation to proclaim the independence and neutrality of judges.

Neither sociological jurisprudence nor legal realism had challenged the independence and neutrality of courts. Sociological jurisprudence had really envisaged democratic legislatures as the primary social engineers, with judges faithfully following the statutory blueprints. The judges depicted by legal realism mixed a lot of themselves and their own preferences into their blueprint reading, but they made their own decisions without fear or favour.

The 'political jurisprudence' of the 1950s and 1960s went further because it depended not only on sociological jurisprudence and realism but also on the then-dominant political science approach to American politics, group theory or pluralism (for example, Peltason 1955; Truman 1958). That theory depicted American politics as a linked set of arenas through which interests sought access to government in their struggles with one another to achieve public policy outcomes that favoured themselves. For pluralists, a democratic or good government decision was one that successfully aggregated group preferences. Precisely because the pioneers in this way of thinking aspired to general theory, and because they accepted that courts were one part of the three-part constitutional government of the United States, they made at least nominal passes at incorporating courts into this group preference, group access, group struggle and aggregation model. Litigation was naturally viewed as one mode of activating government, and courts one set of arenas for achieving policy goals. However nominal, such a move took the courts out of the realm of independence and neutrality, and down into the day-to-day politics depicted by pluralist theory.

It did not seem to matter how much political jurisprudence insisted that groups gained access to different political actors in different ways, that different kinds of political actors might give different weights to the various interests and the values they were aggregating, or that some might arrive at different results than others. No matter how much we emphasized that all politicians were not alike, or that judges did their form of politics differently from legislators and executives, it was the assertion that judges were political actors, and could be studied in the same ways as other politicians, that gained attention and caused offence.

When Shapiro incorporated much of the original political jurisprudence article into the first chapter of a book, *Law and Politics in the Supreme Court: Studies in Political Jurisprudence* (1964), he added an introductory passage. Many years later one of his most distinguished colleagues at the University of California, Berkeley Law School told him that, when assigned to read the book as a first-year law student at Yale, this passage made him physically ill. Here it is:

The Supreme Court is an agency of American government. So are the Interstate Commerce Commission and the House Rules Committee. The taxpayer who descends on Washington to have his tax status altered may turn to the Internal Revenue Service, the House Ways and Means Committee, the Supreme Court, or his own congressman. The businessman who is worried about government regulation of his enterprise may deal with the Department of Commerce, the Supreme Court, one of a half-dozen regulatory agencies, the Justice Department, and the President himself. The labor union seeking freedom from government curbs on the strike weapon begins with the Supreme Court, the Secretary of Labor, the Justice Department, Senator Humphrey, or a Congressional investigating committee. The Chamber of Commerce president who wants a new yacht basin for his community may visit a Senate committee or the Corps of Engineers but probably not the Supreme Court.

These examples could be multiplied endlessly, but the point is simple enough. For those who want something from government—and the purpose of government is after all to satisfy people's wants—Washington is a place where specific agencies or individuals can do specific things for specific people. For some people, the Bureau of the Budget is more helpful and thus more important than the Secretary of the Treasury. For others, the Senate Foreign Relations Committee is more helpful than the Supreme Court.... The Supreme Court, like other agencies, has different powers and different functions depending upon who wants it to do what, when, and in conjunction with or opposition to what other agencies or political forces.

That Shapiro's queasy colleague was assigned the book at all bears witness to the Yale Law School's dedication to the avant-garde. The article excerpted here was intended to be, and remains, a slice-of-life report of a then new direction in political science studies of law and courts. Because the tag 'political jurisprudence' became a standard and convenient label for much of the work done by 'public law' political scientists from the 1950s onwards (see Stumph *et al.* 1983), perhaps it is worth briefly outlining what happened subsequent to the article's appearance. The first response by the doyens of legal scholarship to the whole political jurisprudence movement was to briefly acknowledge it but simultaneously to dismiss it as the naive misunderstanding of outsiders and claim that it said nothing that lawyers had not known all along anyway (for example, Cox 1976: 106; Mishkin 1965: 67–8; see Shapiro 1966*a*). Although in some sense contradictory, both stances had a certain validity. Like most attacks on orthodoxy, political jurisprudence had a tendency to claim too much, particularly to excessively discount the degree to which judicial discretion was influenced and constrained by the very professional orthodoxies that political jurisprudence was attacking.

It is true that judges do camouflage political actions in legal discourse, but—more than many political jurisprudence investigators have been willing to admit—the need for camouflage and the belief in camouflage to some degree determine the agendas and substance of judicial choices. It is also true that lawyers, both academic and otherwise, and journalists and politicians had noticed judicial politics long before political science came along. Most American States have some form of popular election for most judges. The great political power involved in judicial review—that is, the power of courts to veto statutes allegedly in conflict with the Constitution—had been a subject of endless debate and controversy since before the founding and given rise to frequently repeated calls for restraining the judiciary. What was new in political jurisprudence was not the acknowledgement of judicial politics but its treatment as normal, natural, matter-of-fact, and central rather than an exception to be attacked, specially justified, explained away, or fudged. It remains true, even now, that lawyers are more comfortable with 'constitutional interpretation' and 'statutory interpretation' by courts than with the bald 'judicial law-making'.

Political jurisprudence was initially more ignored than derided by the legal academy, precisely because it came from the outside. The critical legal studies movement (CLS) enjoyed quite a different reception, spreading alarm and consternation (Tushnet 1991). One cause of the alarm was the strong Marxist and/or utopian socialist strains in CLS, but CLS essentially was late-blooming political jurisprudence. Its fundamental position is that law equals politics. But, in contrast to the—at least nominal—neutrality of political jurisprudence, CLS is quite sure that law equals wicked—that is, capitalist—politics. Nevertheless it is the 'politics', not the 'wicked', term of the equation that led to serious questioning within the legal academy as to whether CLS people should be teaching in law schools at all, given that they 'didn't believe in law' or that one of their goals was 'trashing' it. Political scientists, already long inured to political jurisprudence, and also, unlike most academic lawyers, enjoying a nodding acquaintance with Hegel and his gang, mostly greeted CLS with 'So what's new?'

In the late twentieth century, economics crowned itself the king of the social sciences and, in fact, has had an enormous impact on law as the 'law and economics' movement. In political science, economics entered as 'rational choice' and 'positive political theory'. With its emphasis on utility-'rationality' and its concern for efficiency, it also carried, if anything, a pro-capitalist bias, so it was far more palatable to the law faculties than CLS. Yet in relation to political jurisprudence and political science more generally, there is a lot of déjà vu all over again here. When law and economics, rational choice, or positive political theory turns its attention to legislation, statutory interpretation, and constitutional and administrative law, it typically offers a colourized version of the pluralism or group theory that had become the central orthodoxy of political science not long after *Gone With the Wind* first appeared televised, in black and white. In the supposedly new 'economic theory of legislation', we are told, the key to understanding legislation itself, and the judicial reception of it, is that statutes are the products of the aggregation of group preferences and can be replaced or amended only by the same or alternative coalitions of legislative groups, given stable decision rules (for example, McCubbins, Noll, and Weingast 1992). As the political jurisprudence article presented here indicates, this group theory was a major element in the initial construction of political jurisprudence.

Positive political theory has adopted the mantle of 'the new institutionalism' but so do some of rational choice's most virulent critics. For the purposes of this discussion, these differences do not matter. What does matter is that the return to institutional analysis overlaps in obvious ways with parts of the political jurisprudence agenda. When after the Second World War 'behaviouralism' swept political science, the study of law and courts was demoted to a very minor place in the discipline. For behavioralism taught that we ought to pay attention to what actors really did rather than to what the formal rules, such as constitutions, said they ought to do. The new institutionalism, introduced in the 1980s by critics of rational choice (March and Olsen 1984), corrected behaviouralism by focusing on how formal and informal rules and procedures actually did influence, constrain, and sometimes even determine what organizations and actors do. If the rules really matter, then law and courts must really matter. Since the mid-1980s, the 'institutionalist' elements of political science, its concern for how legal rules defined political arenas, and for how law and judicial law-making interacted with other parts of politics, has meant that the rest of political science has come to notice law and courts. Indeed, as the next section indicates, Stone Sweet's contribution to this chapter makes broad claims about the centrality of rules and judicial modes of governance to the core concerns of institutionalist theory across the social sciences.

As Shapiro's article here indicates, the move to a more scientific, 'behavioural' social science played a major part in the development of political jurisprudence. Initially, its most prominent and pioneering aspects, and one of its important enduring features, is the systematic study of judicial voting behaviour on multi-judge courts, and judicial decision-making more generally (see Baum 1997; Segal and Spaeth 1993; 1999). One of the reasons for treating law as politics is the degree to which judges' political or policy preferences—or their 'attitudes'—determine their decisional behaviour. The new institutionalism, however, is teaching us again that judges as political actors themselves play in a game in which their own preferences are constrained by rules and by the rule-defined positions occupied by other players in the game. Further, as Stone Sweet's contribution here emphasizes, the social power of judges largely flows from their authority to announce rules and their propensity—or duty—to give reasons for their decisions (see also Shapiro's paper in Chapter 4). So, in some senses, the new institutionalism is another déjà vu story for political jurisprudence. It had been studying institutions all along. Institutionalist approaches, however, typically modify, or de-emphasize, the behavioural-attitudinal element of political jurisprudence by reasserting that the judges' political behaviour is constrained by rules and that normative deliberation and giving reasons also constitute political behaviour that can be modelled as strategic behaviour.

The pluralist political theory that had been the jumping-off point for much political jurisprudence also came under attack on both empirical and normative grounds.[2] Empirically, group approaches survived in law and courts studies by adding to pluralist insights a focus on the extent to which legal rules, opportunities for litigation, and judicial law-making are sometimes major factors in the construction of group identities, and that identities make a difference to broader political outcomes (for example, McCann 1986). At the normative level, pluralism has been attacked as a covert and sometimes overt defence of the status quo in American politics (for example, Mansbridge 1990; Fishkin 1990). Certainly, pluralist theory tends to define any government policy that is the product of the aggregation of group preferences as, by definition, a democratic or even a good policy: a point taken up by game-theoretic research proceeding from Arrow's impossibility theorem. The first line of attack has been that, given the unequal political resources of groups, pluralist decisions were not necessarily either democratic or good. The second line has been that, quite apart from problems of disparate group power, the aggregation of group preferences may not yield the true public good or sufficiently respect individual rights. Particularly in the realm of constitutional law, a strong reaction to what is viewed as the excessive positivism of political jurisprudence has developed (for example, Kahn 1994). Political jurisprudence had given a central place to 'values', but values treated as the attitudes of judges or the policy preferences of actors in the legal process. It has been positivist in this sense of being concerned with the 'is' rather than the 'ought', but including in the 'is' the values that political actors in fact hold, as well as a concern for questions of what difference those values in fact make to political action and policy outcomes. Political jurisprudence certainly embraced the empirical side of pluralism and in doing so was heir to its alleged normative deficiencies. But it did so relatively self-consciously, as the final section of the original article indicates,

---

[2] Throughout the development of political jurisprudence, some political scientists continued to engage in doctrinal analysis aimed at establishing the true or best 'interpretation' of constitutional language, or what the constitution ought to mean. One cogent criticism of legal realism, and then of political jurisprudence, was that telling judges that they were making law rather than simply applying it did not do the judges much good unless you told them what law to make.

and normative matters have been the subject of much further discussion (especially Shapiro 1989a, b).

One further point about normative questions and political jurisprudence deserves attention. Because of the initial connection of political jurisprudence to pluralist theory, it might reasonably be thought that political jurisprudence asserted that judges were moved only by the interests at play and not also by more general values. The paragraph quoted above from Shapiro's *Law and Politics* looks that way, but note that it is written not in terms of what judges think and do but what litigants want from them. His tendency (for example, Shapiro 1962; 1971a; 1986c) to link judges and constitutional doctrines to 'policy' and 'policy-making' also may appear to emphasize group interests over more general 'values'. Frankly, at the time it had not occurred to Shapiro that a statement to the effect that judges were policy makers would be taken as a claim that judges did not care about differences between good and bad law and policy. The word 'policy' always connoted a concern for doing good things, and that point is made explicitly at various points. The Preface to *The Supreme Court and Public Policy* (Shapiro 1969), for instance, notes that the 'Supreme Court is, first and foremost, a group of men seeking to make good decisions about public policy. . . .' In *Freedom of Speech: The Supreme Court and Judicial Review*, Shapiro (1966b) attempts, too awkwardly perhaps, to treat values, like free speech, as the interests of 'unorganized groups'. And, perhaps too belatedly, his contributions (1996a; 2001a) to two American politics and policy volumes argued that American politics were a politics of values and ideas as well as a politics of interests. It would be an excessively narrow pluralism, or a naive behaviouralism, that insisted that politicians, including judges, did not think about good and evil in making policy decisions. Political jurisprudence, however, does insist on treating these broader values not as eternal truths but as beliefs that motivate the relevant political actors.

The term 'political jurisprudence' may justifiably be attacked as involving more than a bit of self-importance or puffery. It was originally adopted as a shorthand description of what political scientists were doing to fit into a law review symposium on jurisprudence. 'Jurisprudence' is usually taken to suggest a full-scale legal philosophy, not just a cluster of empirical findings. A legal philosophy without a normative component would surely be woefully incomplete. It may well be argued that a political jurisprudence that is no more than a cluster of empirical investigations ought not to carry the awesome title of a 'jurisprudence'. Along with a host of academic lawyers, today a number of political scientists are engaged in the normative aspects of constitutional scholarship. In its initial formulation, political jurisprudence claimed to be no more than a school of inquiry, although its quantitative wing may have laid more ambitious claims to having the exclusive or true path of science for the study of law and courts. Yet even in the heyday of quantitative approaches, more conventional doctrinal studies continued to be pursued by many, if not most, political scientists. The current revival of normative legal philosophy, built around Rawls and Dworkin and a return to natural law concerns, coupled with the proclivity of political theorists to move from the history of political thought to actual normative theorizing, has deeply influenced the law and courts sub-field of political science. If political jurisprudence can ever be taken to have made exclusivist claims, such claims have now clearly been refuted by a flourishing normatively oriented scholarship. We prefer the more modest claims originally made, that courts and judges are part of government, and therefore must be studied empirically, as other parts of government are. The point no more denies the legitimacy of normative or prescriptive study of law and courts than that of the study of the rest of politics. In recent years efforts to develop post-consequentialist ethics have led to much talk of 'deliberative' democracy and of law and courts as arenas of deliberation rather than mere arenas of group struggle. Shapiro has taken up these matters in the first chapter of *Who Guards the Guardians* (1988).

Yet one last, perhaps discordant, note must be added. Political scientists working in the political jurisprudence mode are seeking to do empirical science, acknowledging of course some irreducible element of ideology in all scientific endeavour. Political scientists in the doctrinal, normative pursuit of constitutional and other legal truth tend to become submerged in the methods of the academic lawyers who dominate that pursuit. In looking at the scholarship of academic lawyers, and particularly those engaged in constitutional studies, it has always been and remains wise to ask 'Who's the client?' Even as contemporary legal scholarship strives toward a more scientific stance, the advocacy tradition remains deeply embedded. Most law review articles continue to be briefs for one side or another in the next anticipated important case. Political scientists who seek legal truth rather than describing how others seek legal truth are very, very likely to fall into this adversary tradition. It is a noble tradition, but those of us who approach it from the outside should keep our salt ever at the ready.

Judicialization and Governance

Pluralist theory began to decline in the 1970s, partly due to attacks on it from proponents of the 'back to the state' movement (Evans, Rueschemeyer, and

Skocpol 1985; Nordlinger, Lowi, and Fabbrini 1988), a trend that later congealed, as just mentioned, into the 'new institutionalism'. By the 1990s, institutionalist theory had infected all of the social sciences (March and Olsen 1989; North 1990; Powell and Dimaggio 1991), if in rather different and not always compatible forms (surveyed by Hall and Taylor 1996). 'Judicialization and the Construction of Governance' was partly a product of, and partly a response to, these trends. As important, it took for granted the basic lessons of the political jurisprudence movement.

Readers will notice that, compared with Shapiro's piece, Stone Sweet's paper seems hardly to be about law and courts at all, and says virtually nothing about public law-political science. The fact that he trained in comparative politics and international relations, and indeed never took a graduate political science course in law, might be relevant. In any event, his attraction to law and courts comes out of more general theoretical interests, especially in the nature and explanatory status of institutions—rules and procedures—the problem of explaining institutional change, and the complex relationships between rules, organization, argumentation and decision-making.

Underlying this orientation is the assertion that most of what we think of as specific to the world of law, courts, and judging is and should be studied as a subset of more generic social phenomena. Thus, law comprises one matrix within larger normative structures that human beings use to govern themselves. Judges are third-party dispute resolvers, who are to be distinguished from other such entities—for example, mediators, arbitrators, and even legislators and administrators—in relative, not absolute, terms. Legal reasoning, among other things, constitutes a highly formalized species of analogic reasoning, which is basic to how all people, everywhere, manage environmental complexity and solve coordination problems. And adjudication documents just how mutually constitutive instrumental rationality—for example, a decision to expend resources to litigate—and normativity—for example, the development of legal arguments—can be. In Chapters 2 and 4 we develop these themes further. Completed in 1996 and published three years later, 'Judicialization and the Construction of Governance' had four interrelated objectives. First, it sought to elaborate a theoretical model of *governance*, defined as the social mechanisms through which rules systems are adapted, over time, to the needs and purposes of those who live under them. Following from this definition, *government*—the activities of hierarchically ordered, organizationally differentiated structures one finds in the modern state—constitutes one form of governance, but not the only one (see Chapter 5). A focus on governance is, by definition, a focus on institutional change, that is, on the question of how rule structures emerge, change, and mutate over time. In the paper, Stone Sweet does so by demonstrating how the domain of action or agency—individual decision-making—could be linked, over time, to the domain of structure—institutions—through a meso-level, political form: the third-party dispute resolver, or judge. It is obvious that third-party dispute resolution (TDR) is not the only type of governance one finds in the world. Still, Stone Sweet's strong claim is that TDR constitutes a primal, archetypal mode of governance, whose dynamics capture many of the basic logics of government that social scientists usually study in much more specific guises.

As noted above, Shapiro's 'Political Jurisprudence' crystallized a move on the part of at least some public law-political scientists to be more self-consciously scientific. It did so by abandoning focus on the purely formal and legalistic aspects of law and courts, turning instead to the various ways in which courts were connected to other arenas of politics. Shapiro's exhortation was to widen the scope of sight: observe American government not just American courts; see the political system not just a legal system; examine policy-making behaviour, not just legal reasoning and justificatory rhetoric. He then added a call to work towards more general, empirical theory: use those tools and methods made to perform general tasks in the social sciences, not just the particular and arcane tools of the jurisprud. On the scope of sight point, at least, Stone Sweet goes a couple of steps further, pitching the theory at a level of abstraction that all but denies the *sui generis* nature of law and courts and draws into the purview of the theory phenomena typically considered to be extra-legal.

A second, overlapping purpose of the article was to elaborate a general model of judicial politics capable of guiding comparative and historical research on the development of new political systems broadly conceived. Although 'Political Jurisprudence' concerned the study of American judicial politics, Shapiro later distilled and refined some of the most important insights in later comparative research that culminated in *Courts* (Shapiro 1981a; see Chapter 4 of this volume). In the 'Judicialization and Construction of Governance' article, Stone Sweet combined Shapiro's reductive move to the triad, informed by a reading of relevant legal anthropology, with theoretical materials he had developed in his own comparative research on institutional change through TDR. *Courts*, after all, had a great deal to say about the role and function of TDR within a political regime, but said next to nothing about judicial law-making. Stone Sweet's research, on the other hand, has always emphasized the transformative capacities of judicial rule-making through feedback onto the greater political system. The resulting mix was then translated into the grammar and vocabulary of institutionalist theory, both to enhance the generic, if abstract, nature of the arguments and to address as many audiences as possible.

From the point of view of the study of law and courts, the task undertaken in this paper was to develop a theory of how a particular type of social system—a rule-of-law community—emerges and evolves, and with what political consequences. It focused on the development of specific causal relationships between three factors: social exchange, or contracting; third-party dispute resolution; and rules. Rather than observe how full-blown, fully articulated legal systems operate, with lots of litigators, judges in robes, and established courts, Stone Sweet chose to examine social spaces in which the rulers had explicitly rejected courts and judicially enforceable rules at the *ex ante* constitutional moment, because they wished neither to have their interactions with each other governed by binding law nor to share their own authority with judges. In theorizing how judicial power emerges and evolves in these kinds of communities, he assumed, one would be better positioned to uncover the fundamental social dynamics of judicial politics more generally. In his own work, the model proposed in the 'Judicialization' article led directly to the development and testing of a dynamic theory of European integration, that is, of the construction and institutionalization of supranational governance in the European Union, of which courts are only a part (see Chapter 4 and various papers in Sandholtz and Stone Sweet 1998; Stone Sweet, Sandholtz, and Fligstein 2001).

A third objective of the article was to synthesize 'utility-rational' and more 'normative-constructivist' approaches to institutions and change. Stone Sweet did so by dividing the overall process of normative development into discrete stages, deducing the separate logics that govern each stage, and then demonstrating how and why institutional change depends crucially on the co-constitutional and symbiotic properties of strategic behaviour and normative deliberation. Triadic dispute resolution, the argument goes, constitutes a privileged mechanism for forging links between institutions and decision-making, structure and agency. Although the paper speaks for itself on these points, some background discussion may be useful, particularly as these issues have been played out in scholarship on law and courts.

The political jurisprudence movement succeeded in breaking down distinctions between courts and other governmental organs, and between judges and other official policy-makers. Shapiro stressed that judges did a lot of politics. Not only could judges be expected to have their own policy interests, but the policy instruments they possessed would at times be irresistible to potential litigants, such as individuals and groups frustrated with existing legal arrangements or legislative inaction. Although he insisted that courts were essential parts of political regimes, and that judicial processes were embedded in larger political processes, Shapiro never denied that litigators and judges pursued politics in somewhat different ways from other government officials. Shapiro treated legal discourse as a medium of politics; legal doctrine is sometimes the policy outcome to be explained, and sometimes the cause whose consequences for politics are to be explored. Stone Sweet could not see how a comparative social science interested in law and courts could possibly progress without taking very seriously these basic points, as adapted appropriately to the study of any polity in which courts are minimally active and effective.

That said, some adherents of 'Political Jurisprudence' aggressively denied the independent force of the law, doctrine, or norm-based deliberation to shape outcomes. As we have already mentioned, a long line of research has claimed that judges seek to enact, through their decisions, their own policy preferences, and that judges do so relatively unconstrained by the law (for example, Schubert 1963; Segal and Spaeth 1993). In an ambitious article that sought to crystallize a growing dissatisfaction with this orientation, Rogers Smith (1988; see also Stumph *et al.* 1983) argued for an alternative to 'Political Jurisprudence': a 'normative jurisprudence' that took as its task exploring the 'relatively autonomous' impact of legal consciousness and normative reasoning on political outcomes (see also the very important piece by Gordon 1984). To put things too simply, in his dissertation *The Birth of Judicial Politics in France* (Stone 1992a), Stone Sweet sought to integrate—then emerging— 'historical institutionalist' approaches to comparative politics, ideas found in Shapiro's *Courts*, and Smith's call for a normative jurisprudence, in order to explain the evolution of the French constitution since the 1789 Revolution. The introductory chapter to that book surveys these literatures in ways that still seem relevant to current debates.

Finally, the article expresses a deep dissatisfaction with the static, functionalist accounts of institutions and governance that had been propagated by, among others, international regime theorists (for example, Keohane 1984), students of 'constitutional political economy' (for example, Brennan and Buchanan 1985), and proponents of law and economics approaches to courts, in political science particularly. In these approaches and in many of the relevant works that claim to be applying or developing 'positive political theory', scholars have obsessively focused on the design of institutions, and have denied, implicitly and sometimes openly, that they meaningfully evolve through use in ways that were unintended from any *ex ante* moment. For example, the so-called positive theory of delegation—principal-agent theories of agencies and courts—has only just begun to work to correct its own myopia on this score. Critiques have multiplied (for example, Moe 1987; Pierson 1998; Thatcher and Stone Sweet 2002), including on how the framework has been applied to courts (for example, Stone Sweet and Caporaso 1998a; Stone Sweet 2000; 2002); but delegation theorists have hardly begun to deal with the sources and consequences of judicial law-making.

In the paper, Stone Sweet partly adopts a functionalist mode, maintaining the assumption of utility-rationality throughout in order to provide a level playing field, as it were. But he goes on to show why, in certain social settings of which the judicial is a paradigmatic example, rational or strategic action, on the one hand, and normative deliberation and argumentation, on the other, will develop interdependently. And under certain conditions, the theory goes, the move to judicialized governance will provoke and manage institutional change, reconstituting the world in ways that were both unintended and impossible to predict beforehand by those who created the system.

Political Jurisprudence

Martin Shapiro

A school of jurisprudence rarely emerges full-blown at a single instant or immediately announces itself as something new and different in the world of legal scholarship. Bentham's *Principles of Morals and Legislation*, one of the most startlingly original and seminal contributions to modern legal thought, might have been greeted by one of today's omniscient and pinch-minded reviewers, transplanted back to 1789, as 'a rather interesting application of the thought of several minor continental writers to English conditions'. While we can now trace a whole Kantian school of legal theory, it still remains questionable whether Kant himself had a theory of law. Furthermore, the contemporary world does not often find itself blessed with such commanding figures as Bentham and Kant. New intellectual movements are more often the collective work of smaller minds and the products of synthesis, recombination, and shifting application of existing ideas. I believe that such a new movement is afoot in legal theory, and I propose to call it 'political jurisprudence'.

This new movement is essentially an extension of certain elements of sociological jurisprudence and judicial realism combined with the substantive knowledge and methodology of political science. Its foundation is the sociological jurist's premise that law must be understood not as an independent organism but an integral part of the social system. Political jurisprudence is, in one sense, an attempt to advance sociological jurisprudence by greater specialization. It seeks to overcome the rather nebulous and over-general propositions of the earlier movement by concentrating on the specifically political aspects of law's interaction with society and describing the concrete impact of legal arrangements on the distribution of power and rewards among the various elements in a given society.

From judicial realism, political jurisprudence derives a peculiar concern for the attitudes and behaviour of judges and the environment of judicial decisions. Indeed, many of the political jurists have devoted most of their efforts to devising a methodology that will allow them to refine and system-atize the impressionistic insights of the realists by isolating and measuring the strength and direction of judicial attitudes and relating them to the actual patterns of decision.

Moreover, the new jurisprudence shares with all modern American think-ing about law the premise that judges make rather than simply discover law. Without this premise there could be no political jurisprudence, for one of the central concerns of politics is power and power implies choice. If the judge had no choice between alternatives, if he simply applied the rule supplied him by the tablets and reached the conclusion commanded by an inexorable legal logic, he would be of no more interest politically than the IBM machine that we could soon design to replace him. 'Political' can only be linked with 'jurisprudence' when it is realized that choice inheres in those phases of human endeavour that have traditionally been the object of jurisprudential study.

Finally, political jurisprudence is fundamentally indebted to political sci-ence, and its development is intimately related to the growth of political science as an independent discipline. Political jurisprudence is, among other things, an extension of the findings of other areas of political science into the realm of law and courts, an attempt to rationalize the presence of public law as a field study within the discipline, and an effort to round out polit-ical science by somehow integrating legal and judicial facets into the total picture of political life.

Because political jurisprudence owes so many immediate intellectual debts and because it represents the extension and crossbreeding of several lines of continuous intellectual endeavour, it is impossible to say exactly when the movement achieved a distinct identity or, for that matter, even to argue that it is a movement totally distinct from other contemporaneous developments in law and the social sciences. Moreover, although the total number of polit-ical jurists is not very large and a certain amount of leadership and disciple-ship is present, political jurisprudence has not produced any commanding intellectual figure or even set of figures, nor an orthodoxy to which all the members can subscribe. Attempting to describe and delimit it is, therefore, something like trying to analyse a literary or artistic movement. We all gen-erally know what and whom we are talking about if the theatre of the absurd or post-abstractionist painting is mentioned. Yet it might be extremely dif-ficult to describe exactly what common characteristics held each of these schools together. Differences, indeed direct conflicts, between various works of the same school would be mentioned, and interminable arguments would develop over whether certain marginal figures were to be included or not.

In the end, artistic movements tend to be defined in terms of tone, approach, concern for the same or similar problems, and a shared reaction to past movements rather than by a stylistic and substantive checklist. More often than we are willing to admit, movements in the social sciences and philosophy must be described in the same way. Political jurisprudence is such a movement, and basically I shall attempt to describe it here not by a general analysis of a purportedly complete philosophical system but a survey that hopefully will suggest a general tone and approach as well as indicating some differences, conflicts and weaknesses.

Courts as Political Agencies

The core of political jurisprudence is a vision of courts as political agencies and judges as political actors. Any given court is thus seen as a part of the institutional structure of American government basically similar to such other agencies as the Interstate Commerce Commission, the House Rules Committee, the Bureau of the Budget, the city council of Omaha, the Forestry Service, and the Strategic Air Command. Judges take their places with the commissioners, congressmen, bureaucrats, city councilmen, and technicians who make the political decisions of government. In short, the attempt is to intellectually integrate the judicial system into the matrix of government and politics in which it actually operates and to examine courts and judges as participants in the political process rather than presenting law, with a capital L, as an independent area of substantive knowledge. Quite fundamentally, political jurisprudence subordinates the study of law, in the sense of a concrete and independent system of prescriptive statements, to the study of men, in this instance, those men who fulfil their political functions by the creation, application, and interpretation of law.

Political jurisprudence is, in a sense, the opposite of Coleridge's 'willing suspension of disbelief' as a tool of understanding. The political jurist instead suspends his belief in the whole web and myth of speciality, mystery, and tradition that surrounds and supports the judge. Adopting a wide-eyed, and, some will grumble, too open-mouthed stance, he sees not the successor of Ulpian and Coke but only one of many government employees, operating in a bureaucratic structure, performing certain governmental services, and generally engaging in the same political processes as his fellow public servants. The political jurist simply wishes to know what this fellow does in _____nment, how he does it, why he does it, and what his relations are with others in the same government structure and to the citizenry whom the government services. To be sure, in seeking to successfully answer these questions, he may have to reintroduce many of the concepts he has initially ignored if only in the form of objectively incorrect but politically relevant belief systems held by the actors he studies. Again the distinction is one of tone and approach. The political jurist begins with what any fool could plainly see if his eyes were not beclouded by centuries of legal learning: that judges and courts are an integral part of government and politics, would be meaningless and functionless outside of government and politics, and are, therefore, first and foremost political actors and agencies. If all this seems obvious, it is amazing how frequently one must touch base with the obvious in order to avoid being caught off guard by the masses of writing about law and courts which are based on different and often unconsciously held premises.

The new jurisprudence is in several ways a natural result of American experience. We are all told very early in life that the Constitution divides our national government into three great branches, and one of these is the Supreme Court. Thus the very Court that has always been pre-eminent in the American consciousness has always been considered pre-eminently an agency of government. Moreover, our mutually reinforcing preoccupations with the Supreme Court and the Constitution have made constitutional law a peculiarly important subdivision of American legal studies. And constitutional law is the most openly political of all the areas of law. The Supreme Court and its constitutional decisions have consistently played a significant and often highly controversial role in American political history. *Marbury v. Madison, Dred Scott*, the sick chicken, steel seizure, and school desegregation cases are the very stuff of politics. While the notion of an independent judiciary may have been carried further in this country than anywhere else, the central place of the Supreme Court in the American political scene has kept us from equating independence with apoliticism or defining independence in terms of an isolated sphere of competence only peripherally related to public affairs. At least since 1937, it has become an American commonplace that the Supreme Court is either rightly or wrongly a political power holder.

It is hardly surprising then that the Supreme Court has served as the focus for much of the new jurisprudence and indeed for much of the initial opposition to it. To begin with, the whole debate over judicial modesty versus judicial activism has been essentially an attempt to define the political role of the Court and its relations to other facets of American politics. The titles of some of the leading works—*Congress and the Court* (Murphy

1962a), *The People and the Court* (C. Black 1960), and *The Least Dangerous Branch, The Supreme Court at the Bar of Politics* (Bickel 1962)—suggest the nature of the debate, not that all the participants share the viewpoints of political jurisprudence. The most extreme judicial self-deniers, Justice Frankfurter, and Learned Hand (Hand 1958), seconded by academic commentators,[1] have argued that the Court should not, need not, and cannot engage in politics, that judicial review is essentially a political function, and that the Court should, therefore, cease exercising its power of review or exercise it only very rarely and under the most extreme provocation. Thus, the judicially modest are fundamentally apolitical in their jurisprudence, conceiving of courts as essentially non-political institutions and resenting Justice Marshall's ill-considered institutional foray into American politics. The most poetic tragedy of the Frankfurter-Hand-Mendelson style of judicial modesty is that, having convinced everyone that judicial review was an essentially political not legal function, they have been unable to convince either a majority of the Justices or the predominant body of professional and academic opinion that the Court ought to give up review. Thus the Court continues to exercise and the legal profession to approve a function that, thanks to the work of the modest themselves, is admittedly political. In this way, the judicially modest have, albeit unwilling, made a considerable contribution to political jurisprudence.

This old style of judicial modesty is generally on the wane today and has been replaced by a new style of modesty reflected in the works of such commentators as Robert McCloskey and Alexander Bickel. In the context of our discussion here, it need only be said that the new school of modesty accepts the legitimacy of judicial review and thus of a political role for the Supreme Court and concerns itself with precisely what the Court can and cannot do considering its rather limited power. It is modest in the sense of urging the Court not to embark on tasks that are beyond its political capacity to complete or may react negatively on the Court's overall political position. Thus today the debate over judicial modesty takes place almost entirely within the framework of political jurisprudence since nearly all the parties begin from the premise that the Court, at least in the sphere of judicial review, is a political agency and that the problem of when, where, and how it should exercise its review powers is essentially a political problem.

However, the above statement is necessarily a qualified one. Not every participant in the current debate over the Court is per se an active subscriber

---

[1] Wallace Mendelson has been the most prolific academic proponent of judicial modesty and has issued a very long succession of articles and reviews defending and rationalizing Justice Frankfurter's opinions. See Mendelson (1961) for a summary of his views.

⌐⌐ the tenets of political jurisprudence. Professor Black, for the activists, for instance tends to revert to the Hamiltonian and Marshallian argument that the Constitution is law and the Supreme Court is a court of law that must therefore enforce the Constitution when it is violated (C. Black 1960). Such an argument is, of course, fundamentally apolitical, equating review with the 'normal' or routinely legal functions of courts. Judicial review becomes nothing more than a technical exercise in conflict of law jurisdiction. Professor Hyneman, in an attempt to synthesize the whole debate from the standpoint of political science, which is, in effect, a rather rambling defence of modesty, concludes that the Court is political in the sense of participating in government policy-making, but that a sharp contrast should be drawn between the political and the judicial process (Hyneman 1963). On closer examination, however, this all boils down to the old saw that the Court is not democratic and, therefore, *ought not* to be political.

Nevertheless, the debate over modesty is essentially a debate over the political role of the Court. Moreover, again thanks to the efforts of the modest themselves, particularly Frankfurter, the issue of modesty has become entangled in every substantive area of constitutional law so that constitutional scholarship as a whole has become essentially a political discipline. When every constitutional question must be considered not only on its merits, that is, in terms of traditional legal analysis of the meanings of constitutional provision, statute, precedent, and so on, but also in terms of whether the Court is the proper governmental agency to provide the answer, then all the constitutional business of the Supreme Court involves political considerations. While much constitutional commentary is still written in the traditional mode, there has been an increasing tendency to introduce political analysis directly into the discussion of constitutional questions. This tendency is particularly marked in the area of the first amendment.

The principal opposition to political jurisprudence has also arisen in the area of the Supreme Court's constitutional business. The plea for neutral principles of constitutional law voiced by Professor Wechsler and his followers is, in reality, an attempt to substitute the traditional vision of an apolitical, non-policy making, law-discovering court for that of a court embedded in the political process and making political decisions. The Supreme Court by process of legal reasoning and communion with the Constitution and the body of Anglo-American law is to divine guiding *legal* principles and, like all mystics, is to do so by divorcing itself from the interests and immediate problems of this everyday world.

The concept of neutral principles has gained such great popularity precisely because it appeals to that still powerful segment of legal thought which resents the attempts of sociological jurisprudence and judicial realism to break law out of its independent sphere and place it in the context of society (see Levy 1960). The attempt to treat judges as essentially participants in politics, government, and policy-making, ineluctably linked to other such participants, represents the extreme of integration of law into real life. The argument that there are neutral principles in-dwelling in the law itself and discoverable by a specifically judicial or lawyer-like mode of thought is basically an attempt to return jurisprudence to the position of splendid isolation that it enjoyed in the heyday of analytical jurisprudence. This attempt has been largely inspired by and is a direct challenge to political jurisprudence.

Naturally enough then the rebuttal to the neutral principles concept has formed an important wing of the new jurisprudence by re-emphasizing the law and policy-making roles that are inevitably thrust on the Supreme Court. Since the Court generally deals with the 'trouble cases', it is typically called upon to decide precisely those questions for which neither the existing body of law nor the other agencies of government have been able to provide a solution. In short, it is asked to make social policy, and to do so it cannot depend on neutral principles but must look to its own assessment of the social and political interests involved and its own vision of the long-range goals of American society. In other words, it is asked to perform the same tasks that every other political decision-maker is asked to perform and to do so as a complementary and supplementary segment of the whole complex of American political institutions. Thus runs the message of the anti-neutralists, a message that puts them squarely in the centre of political jurisprudence.[2]

So far I have discussed only work that specifically revolves about the judicial review powers of the Supreme Court. If the political treatment of law and courts was confined to this area, it would constitute a special approach to an exceptional problem rather than a jurisprudence of relatively general applicability. But I have begun in this area largely because it serves as one of the channels through which political considerations historically flowed into the study of law, not because it is the only or leading area of political jurisprudence. The principal focus of the new jurisprudence has instead been an attempt to integrate courts into the general framework of governmental institutions and the political process quite apart from a rationalization of the power of one court to do one thing, that is, declare statutes unconstitutional.

Undoubtedly the leading attempt in this area has been David Truman's *The Governmental Process* (Truman 1958). This book presents a general theory

---

[2] I have attempted to make these points at greater length and with appropriate citations in Shapiro (1963).

of politics built around the notion that political activity is fundamentally interest group activity and that the process of government proceeds through the access of groups to governmental agencies and agency performance in response to group demands. Courts are treated as governmental institutions to which different groups have varying degrees of access that they employ to enlist the judges in support of their interests. For Truman, politics is group politics and courts are firmly embedded in the group struggle.

Probably because the first general theory of politics into which the courts were fully integrated was group theory, a considerable body of political jurisprudence using the group hypothesis has developed (see Peltason 1955). Particular attention has been paid by such authors as Jack Peltason (1955), Clement Vose (1959), and Samuel Krislov (1959) to groups which have been especially successful in gaining access to the courts and to their methods of access or lobbying. Since the bar, as a group, has a peculiarly intimate relation to the courts, there has been an increased interest in its political role.

However, other theories of politics may provide equally useful insights. For instance, in a critique of group theory, Elmer Schattschneider (1961) has argued that politics is not entirely group struggle. When one group sees itself outfought in the initial group arena, it is likely to extend the boundaries of the battlefield by broadening the issues. In other words, whichever group finds itself outnumbered in the initial alignment of groups appeals for outside reinforcements by recasting the issue in terms that will attract the attention of groups not at first concerned. This process is likely to snowball or escalate until issues have been so broadened that general public sentiment comes into play and the issue is finally settled, not by the interplay of special groups, but by mass popular opinion. In this context trial court litigation might be conceived as an initial or limited area and the appellate process as a mode of extending boundaries, or even initial litigation as an attempt to expand an issue beyond the legislative or bureaucratic sphere.[3] For instance, Negroes as a group, finding that the immediate alignment of groups in the South disfavoured their goals, used Supreme Court litigation to broaden the issues and attention-drawing power of the controversy and eventually overcame their local group disadvantage by enlisting national popular support.

Not necessarily dependent on group or non-group theories of politics has been a general inclination on the part of political scientists to view government in the context of decision- or policy-making processes rather

---

[3] Of course, even the initial trial is a broadening of arenas by introducing the government into a dispute that initially concerned only the two parties.

than formal structures. The emphasis on process is, in effect, an emphasis on the interaction and reciprocal influence of governmental agencies in terms of where, when, and how each actually participates in decisions. Jack Peltason's *Federal Courts in the Federal System* (Peltason 1955) and Victor Rosenblum's *Law as a Political Instrument* (1955) were pioneering efforts to fit courts into this policy-making process framework by showing how they interact with other governmental agencies at all levels. A recent and outstanding text designed to introduce beginning law students to their field suggests its approach in its title, *The Legal Process: An Introduction to Decision-Making by Judicial Legislative, Executive and Administrative Agencies* (Auerbach *et al.* 1961) and sets both courts and law firmly within the sphere of public policy-making. Robert Dahl's article 'Decision-Making in a Democracy: The Supreme Court as a National Policy-Maker' (1957) is an attempt to generally assess the relations of the Supreme Court to other members of 'the dominant national alliance', and there have been several attempts to describe the Court's policy-making role in relation to other agencies in specific areas of its jurisdiction.

The case study technique of examining court decisions popularized by Alan Westin (1958) is also part of the movement toward examining what courts do in the total political setting of their decisions. It is, to be sure, a bit confusing to talk about case studies of cases. But the case study technique in the social sciences refers to a research design that focuses on a given decision, or set of related decisions, and then develops in the greatest possible detail all the institutional and individual attitudes and behaviour that led up to and came out of the decision. Such depth studies are designed to validate or suggest the broader hypotheses which it is the goal of the social sciences to formulate. When applied to law, this technique can be used to focus on a given court decision and develop the political matrix in which it occurs showing that the decision is not an independent or isolated event but an integral part of a political process in which many agencies interact with one another.

While most of the efforts to fit courts into the general pattern of politics have, so far, occurred at the level of American national government, several recent studies by Herbert Jacob, Kenneth Vines, and others have dealt with the political role of state and foreign courts (Jacob and Vines 1963). Relations between the US Supreme Court, the lower federal courts and the state courts, which have traditionally been handled in the conventional legal categories of jurisdiction, have also begun to receive some attention in more realistic political terms. The most suggestive approach proposes a view of lower c(as essentially bureaucratic structures suggesting that the problems o highest appellate courts may be basically similar to those of other political leaders vis-à-vis their bureaucratic subordinates (Murphy 1962b; 1959).

The Attitudes of Judges and Courts as Small Groups

So far I have been describing what might be called the institutional wing of the new jurisprudence which attempts to integrate courts as political institutions and judges as political actors into the general pattern of American political institutions. In a fundamental sense it is this wing of the new jurisprudence that is the most radical, for it tends to extend the teachings of sociological jurisprudence to their logical extreme and break down any remaining barriers between law and politics. The term 'social engineer'—so appealingly dispassionate and scientific—replaced the black robe with the white laboratory coat. Political jurisprudence rends the euphemism and calls a policy-maker a politician.

Strangely enough, however, it is not this but another wing of political jurisprudence that raises the most hackles. The nature of this wing might be suggested by Gutman scales, bloc analysis, Shapeley-Shubik indices, game theory, and so on, in short by charts and graphs, X's, Y's, and symbolic equations. Yet in describing these intellectual phenomena it would be misleading to speak of a quantitative school of political jurists or to treat the quantifiers as a separate group. First of all, quantification or statistical analysis is not an independent approach to any body of subject matter. At its best it suggests neither what questions are significant, what data is relevant, nor what ought to be done with the answers. Quantification is simply a tool and in political jurisprudence it is usually a tool for expressing more clearly and systematically observations that have been or might be made by other methods. Quantification may be used without any particular intent to contribute to an essentially political analysis of courts as it is in the *Harvard Law Review*'s annual statistical description of the previous term's work of the Supreme Court. Or statistics may be used as one mode for carrying on the essentially institutional analysis we have already described. For instance, one might prepare statistical summaries of the incidence of Supreme Court reversals of acts of Congress or of State courts of appeal in order to partially determine how much power the Supreme Court has wielded over other agencies at what times on what issues (see Ulmer 1959). Thus several quantitative studies have already appeared in earlier citations supporting my description of the policy-making approach to courts. Or quantitative devices might be used, as we shall see shortly, in attempts to analyse sub-institutional problems such as the attitudes of individual judges.

Moreover, many of the treatments that at first glance seem somehow mathematical are really nothing more than logical propositions expressed in the language of equations or other symbolic systems and thus are not actually quantitative or only incidentally so. And, of course, such modes of expression too can be used in support of all sorts of approaches to the Court. For instance Schubert's (1962) 'Policy Without Law: An Extension of the Certiorari Game' uses the formal language of game theory to indicate, among other things, that the Supreme Court's certiorari practice may be determined not by formal rules of jurisdiction but by the policy preferences of the Justices. Since the thrust of Schubert's piece is that certiorari is one mode of Court participation in the policy-making process, it makes more sense to consider it in the context of the policy-making approach to the Court than to isolate it in a methodological ghetto called 'game theory approaches'.

Indeed, the attempt to lump all 'counters' together is really a function of the basic distaste to be found among many students of law for any other than their own traditional language. It is rather as if English and American lawyers accustomed to writing in English, and impatient with irregular verbs, lumped all the legal studies of French writers under the category French jurisprudence. Once the lumping is done, it is much easier to make blanket statements about the absurdity of writing about law in French than it is to analyse in detail whether any of the French writers have had anything useful to say in their peculiar language. I shall have more to say of this later. For the moment it is enough to avoid categories that shed more heat than light.

But for this heat and light problem I would be tempted to call this second wing of political jurisprudence the behavioural approach. Those of my readers who are political scientists will know what rocks and shoals lie along that course. Suffice it to say that political scientists have for some years been engaged in a great debate between behaviouralists and non- or anti-behaviouralists that is complicated by the fact that it is difficult to define 'behaviouralism' precisely. Much of the writing that I shall presently describe has been produced by self-acknowledged behaviouralists and so has become part of the debate. Due to a kind of cultural lag in the area of public law which I do not have the courage to try to explicate here, the struggle broke into a white heat in that field after a modus vivendi had been reached in most other areas of political science. Because I believe this verbal battle to be ephemeral, I do not use the label 'behaviouralist' here in order to avoid encumbering my description of a new jurisprudence with the categories of an obsolescent debate.

There is another reason as well. While it is undoubtedly true that in fact much of the new jurisprudence is a result of the somewhat delayed incursion of behaviouralism into the study of law, it is inconvenient to emphasize behaviouralism as such excessively. To do so would tend to obscure the fact that the phase of the new jurisprudence I am about to describe is a logical development of judicial realism and that the basic continuity between realism and political jurisprudence is very great. What others might choose to call the behavioural wing of the new jurisprudence is basically an attempt to systematize and confirm the insights of judicial realism through techniques borrowed from the social sciences. While it is perfectly proper to stress the methodological continuity of the psychological and sociological study of judges with the psychological and sociological study of other people and thus speak of 'judicial behaviour' as a branch of a broader behaviouralism, I choose instead to emphasize the jurisprudential continuity of new methods of assessing judicial attitudes with more traditional attempts to gain insight into the judge's mental processes.

After all, how a judge thinks—how he arrives at the conclusion he does— has always been a central concern of jurisprudence. The logical analysis of analytical jurisprudence was basically designed to show what mental processes a judge went through in order to reach his decision. For all the seeming anachronism of such phrases as *stare decisis* and *ratio decedandi*, they were and are great surgical tools designed to dissect the anatomy of judicial decision and show us just how each thought of the judge related to every other until the final system was complete and the judgement rendered. Analytical jurisprudence rested on the assumption and assertion that judges thought logically. When later jurisprudential movements destroyed this concept of independent legal rationality, they took upon themselves the task of discovering how judges did in fact think. Carodozo's *Nature of the Judicial Process* shows how difficult that task became once legal logic had lost its sovereign role and illustrates what inexact and impressionistic substitutes post-analytical jurisprudence provided. The rule scepticism of realism added the final touches. Hunch and sense of injustice theories (Frank 1949) were final confessions that, cut adrift from traditional legal logic, and confined to traditional tools of analysis—largely introspection—jurists could do little more than hang a tag on determinants of decisions which they knew were there somewhere but could not describe or analyse.

One of the tasks of political jurisprudence has been, through the use of new tools, to reopen the examination of judicial thought processes. Such an attempt follows directly from the premise that judges are political actors. For students of politics have long been widely concerned with the relation of socio-economic background and psychological make-up to political attitudes and the relation of attitudes to political action (see Key 1961; Lasswell

1930). Put another way, if judges are viewed as policy-makers, then it is natural to ask of them, as one asks of other policy-makers, how do their individual value preferences affect their policy decisions. The traditional concern with judicial thought processes meshes nicely with the modern interest in the motivational aspects of political action.

In order to determine the effects of individual attitudes on judicial decisions, one must first identify the attitudes, and so far the bulk of attitudinal research by Glendon Schubert (1958), S. Sidney Ulmer (1961a), and Harold Spaeth (1963a, b) has been aimed in this direction. Basically the effort has been to derive judicial attitudes from judges' voting behaviour by the mutually supporting techniques of scalogram and bloc analysis. Leaving aside the details of technique which are clearly and adequately described elsewhere, the logic of these studies is simple and straightforward. A scalogram collects a set of cases all of which invoke a common set of social, economic, or political problems—say the civil liberties cases. If Justice Douglas always votes for the individual asserting violation of his liberties, regardless of the legal and factual circumstances, he probably has very strong pro-civil liberties attitudes. If Justice Warren votes for the individual most of the time but not quite as often as Douglas then he probably has strong pro-civil rights attitudes but not so strong as Douglas.[4] In bloc analysis the voting patterns of multi-judge courts are analysed and if it is found that Black, Warren, Douglas, and Brennan for instance vote together most of the time on a certain variety of case, it seems probable that they share some common attitude toward the policy issues raised in that sort of case. By determining what blocs form on what kinds of issues, inferences can be made about the shape and distribution of attitudes among the various Justices. So far the description of attitudes has been rather rough, beginning with Herman Pritchett's pioneering efforts at group analysis which came down to little more than left and right categories (Pritchett 1948; 1954). More recently attitude clusters defined in terms of libertarianism and economic liberalism have been identified.

There are several other methods of defining the political attitudes of judges other than extrapolating them from their voting behaviour. Obviously biographical study is one of these, and one by the way that is not statistical or qualitative or behavioural in any peculiar sense but nevertheless is an integral part of the attitudinal approach. Judicial biography has a long and honoured tradition in the United States, but much of it results from the notion that some of the judges were great men and the lives of great men

---

[4] Of course, basic to scale analysis is the assumption that if a true scale can be constructed, then the scaled material is ordered along a single attitudinal dimension.

should be chronicled. Judicial biography enters the mainstream of political jurisprudence when it becomes a conscious attempt to discover what the values, philosophies, and ideologies of judges were in order to discover how those views affected the way each judge thought about and decided cases.

John Schmidhauser has suggested collective biography as a supplement to individual biography in this area (Schmidhauser 1959). Data on the socio-economic backgrounds, education, mode of recruitment into judgeships, previous occupation, party affiliation, and so forth, of judges can be gathered and, using this data, inference can be made about the content and distribution of judicial attitudes. Where correspondences can be found between background and decisional behaviour, it may be inferred that attitudes corresponding to that background have actually played a part in reaching the decisions. Here again, statistics rears its head, but as a facilitator of mass biography rather than a peculiar or mysterious form of discourse set apart from other streams of study.

Parallel to this attitudinal research, and using much of the same data and techniques, is a rather specialized wing of political jurisprudence that deals with the internal relations of multi-judge courts. Once judges are viewed as actors and decision-makers rather than law-finders, the mutual influence of members of a judicial panel on one another takes on considerable interests. One approach is to treat the nine Justices of the Supreme Court as a small group in the context of what we know of the sociology of small groups (Snyder 1958; Ulmer 1961b; Newland 1961). The extent of leadership exercised by the Chief Justice, which has always been of concern to students of the Court, can be studied in terms of political leadership (Murphy 1962a; Danelski 1962; Ulmer 1963). While most of the bloc analysis has been aimed at identifying attitudes, similar analysis can also be used to chart the group politics of a court itself or the influence over final outcome that 'swing' justice may have.

Finally there is at least potentially a wing of political jurisprudence that may be labelled 'crude behaviouralism'. It is also closely linked to judicial realism and ultimately to Holmes' overstated definition of law as a prediction of what courts will do. If, for instance, we can discover that Justice X has over a long period in the past consistently voted for labour and against management, we have learned something useful quite aside from whether we can speak meaningfully of pro-labour attitudes. While perhaps we cannot scientifically predict that Judge X will continue to vote for labour in all future cases unless we can explain why he has done so in the past, we can predict at the level of prudence. Past patterns of judicial decisions, even when we can find no explanation for them and therefore must treat them as below the level of theoretical significance, may provide us with a useful tool for rough and ready prediction. Whether a given group is more likely to get what it wants out of a given court or judge or had better try a different court, or some other agency of government entirely, is a significant political question to which an immediate imperfect answer is often more desirable than a long, deferred perfect one.

Attitudinal analysis will often yield the simple information that a given judge has in all past cases voted for a particular policy or group. When we find that Justice X has consistently voted pro-labour, that is a political fact with political impact regardless of his intentions. The analysis of the extent to which a court's decisions favour or disfavour certain interests and other agencies of government, wholly aside from inferences as to whether intention to do so motivated the decisions, aids in the assessment of that court's impact on the political process and its relation to other parts of government. Since one of the principal tasks of political jurisprudence is to discover the functions and powers of courts vis-à-vis other political agencies, gross calculations of the effects of decisions are relevant to political jurisprudence as a whole if not directly to the problem of judicial attitudes. Thus many of the calculations that leave us undecided as to the motivations of say Justice Frankfurter are quite helpful in assessing the sum of the political impact of his decisions. Surely the results of a political decision-makers choices, particularly when they favour a given policy or policy-maker, are just as important as, or more important than, his reasons for making them.

Criticisms and Proposals

There has already been and is yet likely to be a great deal of criticism of political jurisprudence. I shall attempt to sketch some of these criticisms and suggest replies. Because political jurisprudence is a relatively new movement, much of the criticism is directed to its incompleteness. Therefore, many of my replies will in fact be proposals for future research.

Probably the principal complaint about political jurisprudence is that it obscures the uniqueness of law and legal institutions. In constantly repeating that courts are political agencies and judges political actors, and dealing with courts and judges as an integral part of government, political jurisprudence does tend to emphasize the similarities between courts and judges and other political institutions and politicians. But if all this seems to add up to the statement that judges are just a bunch of politicians, then the mistake is in the eye of the beholder and in the unfavourable connotation frequently attached to the words 'politics' and 'politician'. The study of things political is, to be sure, partially aimed at exposing similarities between various political actors and institutions, but surely it is also aimed at discovering their differences. The State Department, the Cook County democratic machine, the Vatican, the ICC, and the Supreme Court are all political agencies and share certain common features. But, in saying this, I suppose no one believes that I am saying that the Secretary of State, Jake Arvey, the Pope, the chairman of the ICC, and Chief Justice Warren are or should be exactly the same kind of men, thinking the same kinds of thoughts, and doing exactly the same kinds of things. If I say that Al Capone and FDR were both politicians, I am not saying that the President was just a gangster.

It is true that initially political jurisprudence has probably overemphasized the commonality between courts and other agencies of government. But it is so difficult to eradicate the fundamentally apolitical outlook of both lawyers and laymen, who constantly and almost instinctively backslide into the clichés of the black robed myth, that it was inevitable and necessary that the point be made by overemphasis. Now that the essentially political role of courts is relatively firmly established, it should be possible for political jurisprudence to turn more of its attention to analyses of the differences in political role between courts and other agencies. The proliferation and complexity of modern government is largely based on the differentiation of function among agencies. If courts and judges were not performing a political function somewhat different from other political agencies and personnel and bringing relatively unique qualities into the political arena, they would not be nearly as politically successful as they are. Political jurisprudence in the future will seek to explore the special qualities of courts and in the light of those qualities determine what particular governmental chores suit the courts better than their fellow agencies.

Political jurisprudence is also open to the criticism that it has focused almost entirely on the Supreme Court and constitutional law. By picking the admittedly most political court and most political body of law as the basis for creating a model, it might be seriously distorting its description of the relation between politics and law. Again there may have been an initial sin of overemphasis to make the point. It is easier to get Americans to grasp a political or governmental context for the Supreme Court than for other courts. But that does not mean that in reality other courts are less political. Surely the lower courts collectively make a great deal more law than the Supreme Court and some individual courts make considerably more policy in particular areas than do the courts above them. The fifth circuit for instance is much more influential in the development of oil and gas policy than is the Supreme Court. Moreover, distinctions between constitutional, public, and private law are only matters of degree. The Supreme Court's anti-trust jurisdiction involves broader-ranging political considerations than does its fourth amendment business; and areas like labour law exhibit an inextricable tangle of constitutional principle and statutory interpretation. No elaborate argument is required to prove that such eminently private law areas as contract and tort are vehicles for public policy and for the regulation of individuals by government in the public interest (see Green 1959–60). The government is the third party to every private suit and is so in the very form of the law and the judge who administers it.

Nevertheless, there is no doubt that political jurisprudence has concentrated too heavily in the past on Court and Constitution. Political science as a discipline passed through a long period of excessive concentration on national government largely because the plethora of divergent State and local institutions presented an intimidating prospect for study. Eventually, however, there was a great explosion into the field of State and local government. We are, I hope, on the verge of a similar explosion in jurisprudence. Part of that explosion will be in the form of study of discrete State supreme and other courts with the same thoroughness as the US Supreme Court has been studied. As yet we have almost no descriptive data, for instance, on the operation of intermediate appellate courts (but see Peltason 1961).

Probably the most pressing of all the tasks of political jurisprudence is the development of a systematic description and analysis of the relation between lower and higher appellate courts in terms of power, influence, and differentiation of function. Let me give just one example to suggest the range of problems. Certain federal circuits build up special expertise in certain fields of public policy, for instance the fifth circuit's oil and gas jurisprudence just mentioned. The admiralty jurisdiction of the second circuit also comes to mind. We know that in other parts of government specialization and expertise can be powerful forces fostering independent policy views and excessive resistance to supervision and coordination on the part of subordinate agencies. The same specialization often provides the political tools for fulfilling those policy views and making good the resistance. To what extent does specialization and the resultant expertise of certain circuit courts cause them to adopt different views than their more generalized counterparts and resist or seize policy leadership from the Supreme Court in those areas that especially interest them? To what extent have litigants who have a choice of circuits taken advantage of these phenomena to achieve the ends they desire? What methods, if any, have the highest appellate courts used to achieve supervision over and coordination of such specialized lower-appellate courts?

In spite of the great prominence of appellate courts in the American judicial structure, generally speaking we as yet know very little about the fundamental problems of inter-agency relations and coordination posed by our appellate court structure. I have already said that the most promising approach seems to be that of Walter Murphy, who views the lower courts as a form of bureaucracy. However, up to this point little has been done to relate the tools that administrative, organizational, and communications theorists have developed for the study of other hierarchically organized bureaucracies to the study of courts. This kind of endeavour should become a core area of political jurisprudence in the future.

Finally, political jurisprudence in spite of its close relation to judicial realism has done very little with trial courts, largely, I think, because their role in the policy-making process is least evident and they are most difficult to study. However, in recent years political scientists have considerably developed the technique of direct observation and interrogation of local units of government. We should now begin to send scholars into our local courts to systematically observe their behaviour over fairly long periods of time, interview litigants, counsel, and subordinate court officers, and where possible interrogate the trial judges themselves. We could then begin to build up the body of empirical data necessary to proceed beyond the very vivid but quite haphazard and impressionistic studies of Judge Frank (Frank 1949).

Moreover, we know little of the relative power and function of local courts within the policy-making processes of local government. More effort must be made to exploit the current boom in urban studies in the United States to yield information on this point in addition to the routine statistics on case load and delay that are now available. In this respect a crucial series of questions about any governmental agency is: how well does it do the jobs assigned it, what services can it best perform, and is it acquiring or losing functions? These are key political questions because a governmental agency gains or loses power as it is able to provide more or fewer services, more or less efficiently to more or fewer individuals and interest groups. That is, a governmental agency recruits the political support essential to maintaining its position vis-à-vis other governmental agencies by performing services for some segment of the public or other governmental agencies. The less service it provides, the less support it is likely to recruit and the less influential in the general decision-making process of government it is likely to become. The transfer of many public services from general trial courts to labour arbitration panels, workmen's compensation commissions, domestic relations and juvenile tribunals, parole officers and boards, and a host of other special mediational and decisional bodies is, at least from the point of view of political jurisprudence, a major shift in the structure of government and a reduction of the political power of courts and judges. Moreover, much of the study of these matters has proceeded on the basis of rather naive discussion about the 'merits' of various bodies and the workload of the courts. It is an old truism of public administration that shifts in organization and jurisdiction are never simply technical. They are almost invariably vehicles for policy change. The transfer of a particular service from one governmental agency to another inevitably alters the nature and direction of the service. Organizational change thus implies a shift in who gets what, the basic question of politics. Obviously the shift of decisional services from courts to other agencies must have the consequence of favouring some social interests over others or, more precisely, favouring a different set of interests than the older arrangement did. This is obvious in the shift to labour arbitration boards, but just as true in the transfer of juveniles to special courts for special treatment. One of the tasks of political jurisprudence will be to analyse this essentially political problem in an essentially political way. While it has been presented here in the context of local government, the problem also exists at other levels and obviously is at the heart of such disputes as that over the scope of judicial review of administrative findings. Again this is basically a problem in intergovernmental relations and bureaucratic control. Just as we must assess the political relation between higher and lower appellate courts, we must fit the trial courts into the judicial policy-making process.

Aside from the general criticism that political jurisprudence overemphasizes the similarity between courts and other governmental agencies, it is likely to be argued that it considers courts and judges to the almost total exclusion of law. The central concern of jurisprudence is after all law, not simply judges. The import of this criticism will, of course, depend on whether you believe that there is something in law which can be discovered only outside of the men and institutions that make and apply it and to whom it is applied. In short, for the exponent of natural law, political jurisprudence is a very partial jurisprudence indeed but, as I hope to show presently, not an incompatible one. Accepting, *arguendo*, that political jurisprudence is a partial one, that is not enough to condemn it. Indeed, the absence of a single all-encompassing theory and philosophy of law is the leading phenomenon of twentieth-century jurisprudence and has been so much commented upon and so closely linked with the general fragmentation of contemporary political philosophy that nothing further need be said about it at this point. If political jurisprudence is not complete and all-encompassing, it is in good company.

I believe, however, that a somewhat less modest case can be made for political jurisprudence. Legislation, that is, the passage of statutes by legislatures, had by the early twentieth century become the principal mode of law-making. Today it is rivalled by administrative law-making. As long as Anglo-American law was largely common, that is, judge-enunciated, law and the judge was viewed as law discoverer or deducer, Anglo-American jurisprudence could concentrate on an abstract examination of legal principles and how the judge did and should relate those principles to specific fact situations. Once the emphasis shifts to law-making, and to law-making by legislators and bureaucrats, such a jurisprudence becomes increasingly narrow and divorced from the realities of law. The crucial problem of modern American jurisprudence is to frame a legal theory and philosophy that somehow integrates statutory and administrative law with its more traditional concerns (see Hurst 1950).

Most scholars would agree, I think, that a jurisprudence based entirely on general examinations of the nature of law, divorced from analysis of how the law is made and applied and what it actually does, runs the danger of excessive formalism and eventually complete divorce from real law in the real world. As a result, study of the judicial process has always played an important part in jurisprudential endeavour. But today, when the bulk of law is intimately connected with the legislative and administrative process, any jurisprudence which combines general discussion of law with examination of the judicial process alone is highly incomplete and distorting.

It is for these reasons that political jurisprudence provides an opening toward a more complete American jurisprudence. By emphasizing the inseparability of courts and judges from a political process that includes legislatures and bureaucracies, the new jurisprudence focuses attention on the need to incorporate the study of legislative and administrative law-making into legal theory. Political jurisprudence uses the tools of political science, tools originally designed for the analysis of legislatures and bureaucracies. Having incorporated the methodology of political science into jurisprudence for the purpose of studying courts, jurisprudence thus equipped will also be in a far better position to undertake the study of legislative and administrative law-making. For the student who sees that instances of law-making by the judiciary are inseparably tied to the politics of legislatures and administrative agencies will inevitably turn his sights to the entire political and governmental matrix of law. Political jurisprudence will naturally expand from a political analysis of the judiciary to an analysis of the entire law-making process and its relation to traditional jurisprudential concerns. Today the focus of law and law-making is in what we used to call the 'political branches'. What better way to bring those branches into the jurisprudential fold than through a political jurisprudence?

Having made the most sweeping claims for political jurisprudence, admittedly on the basis of projected tendencies rather than solid results, and largely for the purpose of showing that even a partial jurisprudence may be useful in contributing to a broader one, it might be well to also make the most modest possible claims. There are many areas of law in which courts must either openly or covertly, consciously or unconsciously, formulate a political theory or establish some vision of the behaviour of their fellow political actors. For instance, in dealing with contempt of Congress prosecutions, the federal courts must develop a whole theory of Congressional investigations. What are they and what should they be? What is the relation between the investigating committee and the House or Senate which authorized it? What procedures are appropriate to committee hearings in light of their functions and relation to their parent body? Examples could be multiplied endlessly. Quite obviously in the area of administrative law alone, there are hundreds of questions of law that depend upon notions of what agency behaviour is and ought to be.

Unfortunately, when one comes to look at these decisions, a great many of them seem to be based on incredibly naive or formalistic assumptions about the nature of American government and how it operates. At least in those areas where legal judgments must inevitably be based on political fact and evaluation, political jurisprudence could substitute some knowledge of what we actually know about politics and government for the clichés of the civics text that we so often find in or slumbering behind legal discussions (see Horn 1960; Shapiro 1962).

The need for a more intimate relation between what we really know about government and the legal rules it formulates is probably clearest in the field of statutory interpretation. One of the most fruitful applications of political jurisprudence would be a full scale re-examination of the canons of statutory interpretation and the uses of legislative history in the light of what we have learned in recent years about the actual workings of legislative bodies as opposed to their formal procedures. In this respect it must be admitted that many of the political superficialities to be found in legal discourse are actually consciously adopted legal fictions like the plain-meaning rule, which is an attempt to force the legislature to speak clearly, not an assumption that it does. Admitting the usefulness of legal fictions, political jurisprudence might still indicate just where truth leaves off and fiction begins and which fictions are not purposeful tools but half-conscious assumptions about the nature of American government that have no basis in fact. A fiction, particularly a fiction about government, is useful precisely to the extent that we know it is a fiction. Beyond that point it may be more dangerous than useful. In any event political jurisprudence will, I hope, put a stop to studies like one I recently read—and one by a political scientist at that—which managed to discuss the Supreme Court and federalism for 30 pages without any reference to the substantial body of knowledge about how American federalism actually works that has been gathered by political science in the last 30 years. No matter how telling the criticisms of the institutional wing of political jurisprudence, it does provide us with much knowledge that is plainly applicable to the analysis of many legal doctrines.

While the institutional wing has been the object of some attacks, largely I believe because of sins of omission that can be remedied, it is the wing of political jurisprudence that concentrates on the attitudes and actions of individual judges which has taken most of the broadsides.

We have already noted the general distaste for statistical examination of judicial attitudes and voting. But in fact we all count and make at least rough quantitative assessments. What practising lawyer has not on occasion advised a client—predicted?—that a suit would be unsuccessful, not on the basis of the legal question but because his past experience indicated that such suits are usually lost? The experience he calls upon is simply unconscious quantification. The gossip of every county court house and the little internal moans or cheers that go up when the practising lawyer finds out which of his cases are going to which judges, are simply unsystematic attitudinal conclusions based on quantitative observations over time. It would take a sternly disciplined student of constitutional law indeed not to mentally count up to at least five when he is asked nearly any question about the current meaning of the first amendment or the due process clause. We all count. Some of us use our fingers and some use statistics. As a matter of fact both simple counting and relatively sophisticated statistical analysis have been used by eminently respectable and lawyer-like figures. It is, therefore, probably not statistics alone but statistics used in conjunction with attitudinal and behavioural studies that are the main target.

There are to be sure some glaring weaknesses in the bulk of the attitudinal research that has been done so far, the most marked of which is its circularity. Observing that a certain judge always votes for the civil rights claimant, the attitudinal researcher says he has a 'pro-civil rights attitude' which is proposed as the cause of the pro-civil rights voting behaviour. Thus the behaviour under another name becomes its own explanation. At best this method is tautological.

There are also some difficulties with several of the principal methods employed in isolating attitudes. The general logic of Gutman scaling is not entirely clear. Its logic is further attenuated when scaling is transferred from the area for which it was intended into the analysis of judicial attitudes. The Gutman technique was designed for the examination of a random sample from a much larger universe. If the sample scaled, then the universe was presumed to be orderable along a single attitude dimension. But the scalograms of Supreme Court voting are not random samples. The cases used are preselected and are chosen precisely because the investigator hopes they reveal a single attitude dimension. The result is that it is never certain whether the Justices scale—that it can be arranged along a single attitudinal dimension like pro- to anti-business—or whether the cases scale, yielding the desired results because of the factors employed in their non-random selection.

Attempts to derive attitudes from observation of group voting behaviour or alliances encounter similar difficulties. In the larger world it may be possible to safely assume that a number of people who consistently act in the same way and in conjunction with one another share an attitude. But where only nine persons are present and confined by an elaborate set of decisional rules that rigidly delimit their possible choices of action, it is not safe to infer that, just because four or five Justices always vote together on certain issues, they have the same attitudes on those issues. Indeed bloc analysis has typically shown us a bloc of four and then five Justices who automatically become a bloc because they oppose those four although they seem to have nothing else in common.

All this is not to say, however, that the bulk of attitudinal research has also been valueless. Quite the contrary. In the first place the data in social science can rarely be made to 'prove' anything. Scalogram and group analysis are suggestive and provide important evidence even if they are not absolutely without scientific flaw. Few of us would be unwilling to accept the proposition that if a given judge always votes for the union, even when most of his colleagues find the law to point the other way, he probably is governed at least in part by pro-union sentiment. Second, the general problems of inference can be and have been reduced by careful extension and interpretation of the data. If a judge always votes pro-business in business regulation cases, he might do so for many reasons, legal or attitudinal. If he is also found to vote pro-business in business-labour disputes and tax cases, we surely make a fairly good case for pro-business attitudes. Third—and this applies particularly to scalogram analysis—there is no reason to impute lack of intellectual honesty to researchers simply because their methods cannot guarantee absolute impartiality and exactitude in the scientific sense. So long as we can examine their case selection for ourselves and replicate their work, their findings need not be treated with particular suspicion. Moreover, some of the problems of lack of randomness in the selection of cases to be scaled can be solved by selecting all of the cases within a given subject area so that in effect one proves that the universe scales by scaling the whole universe.[5]

Perhaps the best answer to the weakness of much of the attitudinal research, particularly to its basic problem of circularity, is more and different attitudinal research. We would obviously be in a much better position to show the kind and degree of relation between judicial attitudes and judicial decisions if we were to establish the attitudes independently and then compare them with the judges' decisions, rather than finding that the attitudes derived from the opinions match the opinions from which they were derived. A start has been made in this direction by using direct questionnaires to establish judicial attitudes (Nagel 1963). In the future both socio-economic analysis and survey research techniques, which are widely used in the social sciences, should be employed in the development of a body of independent data on the attitudes of judges. Moreover, the depth interviewing techniques recently used in the analysis of state legislatures and now of city councils could be used to gather such data and more especially data on the difference in attitude between judges and other politicians, particularly on the question of how each conceives his own political role.

However, since attitudinal research up to this point has been more suggestive than conclusive, there has been some outcry that the results have not been worth the effort, that statistical approaches have only tended to confirm what we knew already. This argument is really part of the general debate between behaviouralists and non-behaviouralists in which the behaviouralists are accused of employing fancy methodologies to prove the commonplace. But it can hardly be possible that all our truisms and clichés are correct since many tend to contradict one another. Systematic analysis designed to test traditional knowledge cannot, therefore, be wasted even when it tends only to confirm some of our previous impressionistic notions.

Nevertheless, the problem of lack of originality seems particularly acute in the attitudinal area of political jurisprudence. It has been further aggravated by the kind of overenthusiastic claims about returning the study of law from

[5] This technique has frequently been used in the literature cited earlier, although the problem remains as to whether the universe chosen—all the labour cases, for instance—is a universe within the logic of the Gutman method or simply a large but non-random sample. Often in statistical work, increasing the number of cases decreases the possibility of distortion. But since the number of Justices remains constant at nine, increasing the number of cases actually seems to increase the chances that the cases rather than the Justices happen to scale. I am indebted for this latter point to John Sprague.

its dark corner to the mainstream of intellectual endeavour, systematizing a previously anachronistic discipline and replacing a collection of clichés with a new science, that are to be expected in a new intellectual movement but nevertheless bring a pang of regret that adolescence must precede maturity. Novel methods are not to be confused with new results. And unfortunately most of the old clichés that the new attitudinalists have been able to puncture are clichés that no well-informed traditionalist currently believes or over which there had already been considerable disagreement based on conventional analysis, disagreement that statistical findings somewhat sharpened but did not end. After a thorough review of the new literature, I cannot honestly say that it has so far made any startling new contribution to our knowledge of courts and judges. Its value has largely been in presenting further evidence for certain already well-formulated hypotheses. Again, however, it must be insisted that this is not a negligible accomplishment.

An important factor in this concern over originality is that attitudinal and small group analysis has so far been largely concentrated on the Supreme Court. The level of traditional scholarship is so high in this area, the examination, re-examination, and comparison of data even by traditional and allegedly cumbersome means so thorough, that no new method, statistical or otherwise, is likely to bring more than a small increment to what we already know.[6] The claimed economies and capacities for original insight of statistical analysis in general and more particularly of attitudinal research will be given a better test as political jurisprudence shifts its major emphasis away from the Supreme Court about which in a sense we know too much. The new methods seem best suited to the study of lower courts which have been relatively neglected by traditional analysis and seem peculiarly suited for statistical and sociological treatment because of the huge amounts of data to be correlated and interpreted.

On the Inseparability of Traditional[7] and New Analytical Techniques

Skimming through the recent writings of Schubert, Ulmer, *et al.*, the casual reader, depending upon his prejudices, might conclude either that the

---

[6] It might be added in passing that before we accuse the attitudinalists of wasting time elaborately proving clichés, we might consider whether the hundreds of thousands of often routine or formalistic words written about the Supreme Court and its opinions every year really represent the best allocation of scholarly resources.

[7] By 'traditional' I mean the analysis in depth of the facts, law, and reasoning of judicial opinions according to the dialectical conventions that lawyers and judges normally employ.

new research represented a formalistic game totally divorced from the real substance of law or a simple and blessed release from the stylised and highly complex manoeuvrings of traditional case analysis. The result is likely to be a debate over whether the new techniques can independently do the job that traditional analysis had formerly done and do it better. Such a polemic should in general be avoided, for to my knowledge no political jurist has ever claimed that the new methods were either totally independent or sufficient means of examining the work of courts. It is true, however, that for the most part the users of new techniques have contented themselves with the academic courtesy of conceding the legitimacy of other scholarly work rather than systematically explicating the dependence of their own findings on traditional analysis. It might be well then to indicate something of the interdependence of new and traditional method both to disabuse the 'outsider' of the notion that an important wing of political jurisprudence is no more than wild-eyed scientism and to show the acolyte that he is not relieved of the duty of learning the traditional services.

The scalogram has surely been the most prominent of the new tools. Yet as we have seen the cases used in each scalogram have not been the result of random sampling. They are carefully selected and in most instances the inclusion or exclusion of a given case, particularly of ambiguous or multi-issue cases, has been supported by traditional analysis going to the substantive legal issues. On the whole the case groupings have been just those that any traditionalist would have chosen and have been openly dependent on traditional analysis. Whether or not to establish sub-scales or engage in multiple counting and what cases are to go into what sub-scale are questions that are also largely dependent on examination of the substantive content of the decisions.

Where a scale appears to meet statistical requirements of reliability but is imperfect in the sense that some of the votes of certain Justices are inconsistent with their general scale position, these inconsistencies may be explained by peculiar factors that become evident when the Justices' opinions are subjected to traditional analysis. Where cases that logically fit into the group of cases to be scaled are in fact inconsistent or disruptive of the scale patterns, these inconsistencies may be explicable by turning to the legal issues in the case and the opinions of the Justices. Again all this is not meant to imply that the scales have unconsciously or obscurely smuggled in outside conclusions based on other techniques. The employment of traditional techniques and conclusions has been open and purposeful.

Bloc, factor, and game theory analysis are also closely tied to traditional techniques. It is generally impossible to say that the discovery of a bloc of four or five appellate judges constitutes more than a purely formal statement of congruent behaviour unless the statistical presence of the bloc is supported by analysis of the members' opinions to discover whether they express or acknowledge attitudinal agreement. The necessity of forming judicial as well as legislative majorities may often make strange and antagonistic bedfellows. A pioneering attempt at applying factor analysis to Supreme Court behaviour was able to derive acceptable vectors and intensities but the initiators of the study concluded that only subject-matter specialists could give substantive labels to their formal descriptive statements (Thurstone and Egan 1951).[8] While some game theory analysis may proceed purely on the basis of voting behaviour, most will require fairly elaborate traditional analysis since the judicial game requires that the players govern their strategies in part by legalistic conventions. If for no other reason, this is true because certain of the players may place a high premium on legal reasoning and other traditional concerns.

Finally, attitudinal-statistical approaches can be used most independently in those situations in which differences in judicial behaviour are most clearly explicable in terms of differences in broad social attitudes like pro- or anti-business sentiment. If all the judges decided all the cases on the basis of a few fixed attitudes, we could all afford to sit back on our Gutmans. But even the analyses of the Supreme Court done up to this time show clearly that things are not so simple. Scale analyses for reasons sufficient unto the method have usually omitted unanimous decisions. Nevertheless, such decisions make up a significant part of the whole, are probably the least dependent on attitudinal differences and the most related to conventional legal thinking of all varieties of decision, and, therefore, are likely to remain heavily dependent on traditional and rather complex legal reasoning for explication.

More important, both bloc and scale analysis show a middle category of Justices. Assuming for the moment that a near-perfect scale does show that the Justices are ordered according to a single attitude, the scales also typically show a set of intermediate Justices falling between those who always vote for and those who always vote against a certain social issue or policy. Their position on the scale indicates that they hold the scaled attitude less strongly or less extremely than those of their colleagues at the two ends of the scale. Since these Justices vote 'no' in some of the categorized cases and 'yes' in others, while their colleagues with more strongly held attitudes tend to vote consistently 'yes' or 'no', it is precisely this intermediate category of

---

[8] Schubert (1962) has attempted to avoid traditional analysis by using scalogram analysis to formulate suitable labels. But this only transports the traditional analysis one stage backward to the construction of the scales.

Justice whose votes frequently decide the Court. Thus scale and bloc analysis paradoxically tend to show that the decisions of the Court as opposed to the decisions of individual Justices are made on the basis of relatively weak attitudinal differences and thus are least amenable to these techniques. It is precisely those Justices whose votes are most decisive in the disposition of cases whose behaviour can least readily and neatly be explained by proposing a direct, unadulterated relation between their social attitudes and their legal decisions. And because of the basic circularity of most attitudinal research, we cannot actually tell whether these intermediate Justices vote the way they do because of relatively weak social attitudes or in spite of relatively strong ones.

It is the unanimous cases and those decided by the votes of the intermediate Justices that are most likely to exhibit decisions based on something more complex than simple social attitudes. Since these constitute a major share of the Court's business, it is likely that traditional analysis will continue to play a larger part than the new techniques in the analysis of the Court's relations with other political agencies.[9]

Attitudinal-statistical techniques are also highly dependent on traditional analysis as a check on their conclusions. Their whole basis is that an observed uniformity of behaviour must indicate a single attitudinal factor at play, but, for any attitude other than the attitude of following the law, this would be true only if the data were random in the sense that the legalities of the cases randomly favoured for instance first the business and then the anti-business litigant. If a single decisional rule, that is, a 'legal' or 'technical' rule, or a series of decisional rules when applied to the selected cases would yield the observed uniformity, then the cases are not random and the uniformity is not conclusive for either the identification of attitudes or the supposition that the identified attitude was the cause of the observed uniformity. The more initially structured the cases, the less reliance for inferences about attitudes may be placed on observed uniformity of decision. More particularly, statistical standards of reliability established in areas where data is highly

---

[9] It should be added that the long presence of two such justices as Black and Douglas is something of an historical accident and encourages the kind of simple social attitude analysis that seems to suddenly take all the complexities out of public law. Ulmer (1960) struck at this oversimplification in group analysis some time ago. One of Schubert's most recent pieces (1963) stresses the complex and varying motivation of the Justices. These pieces indicate an increasing tendency towards subtle and complex analysis and, of course, the more complex attitudinal-statistical analysis becomes the less attractive it becomes as a substitute for traditional analysis since it loses its initially promised capability of quickly cutting through a mass of traditional obfuscations to the simple truth.

random or can be randomised are not necessarily applicable in areas where data is highly structured.

The work of courts tends to be highly structured for several reasons. First of all, a statute, either by design of the legislature or simply because it is a single set of words with a relatively clear meaning on its face, constantly applied to similar fact situations, may consistently favour one interest in the community over others—indeed statutes do and are designed to do just this. Therefore, in the area of litigation covered by a given statute, the legalities are not likely to randomly favour one interest and then another.

Admittedly appellate courts tend to get those cases where the legalities are not absolutely clear. It is this tendency toward randomness that makes attitudinal-statistical studies even passingly plausible. But most cases do clearly arise under a single statute. Typically cases under a given statute tend to keep coming to appellate courts because two alternative interpretations continue to be held by different judges or litigants. But once a single appellate judge has determined that interpretation X is correct, he is likely to consistently interpret the statute as meaning X even though other legal authorities believe it to mean Y. Furthermore it is not outside the realm of probabilities that he chooses interpretation X not because it suits his attitudes about what interest should be favoured but because he believes that the legislature really intended or the plain meaning of the statutory language really requires interpretation X, although some of his colleagues disagree. Indeed he may feel that the reason why the case comes up on appeal is that the legislators really intended X and those people—including judges—who wish they had intended Y keep trying to read Y into the statute. Thus a judge who decides cases under a statute that he feels favours business may issue consistently pro-business opinions because he desires to enforce the statute not because he has a pro-business attitude or allows his economic attitudes to dominate his legal views.

Attitudinal-statistical approaches may attempt to overcome this phenomenon by drawing their categories broadly so that cases arising under two or more statutes are thrown together. Any uniformity that is observed then cannot be ascribed entirely to the phenomenon described above. But admitting that legislatures are not entirely consistent in always choosing one interest over another and are not notorious for highly coordinated legislative programmes, it is probable that two or more statutes which are closely enough related to be lumped together for attitudinal research may very well have been inspired by similar legislative choices as to which interest should be favoured. It is not inconceivable that two statutes both of which will involve businessmen as litigants are both clearly intended by the legislature to favour business interests so that consistently pro-business decisions under both statutes may still establish only a judge's desire to follow Congressional intent, not a pro-business attitude. Of course, the more statutes are lumped in a given category the less likelihood there is of consistent legislative intent. Nevertheless, it is probable that many interlocking series of statutes are intended, either consciously or as a result of the long-dominant position of a given political coalition in the legislature, to consistently favour certain interests over others.

The materials of judicial decision are further structured by the phenomenon of litigation as a form of political activity. Interest groups frequently undertake campaigns of litigation aimed at getting the courts to change the existing state of the case law. Or they may resort to the courts precisely because they find that the current state of the law in the courts favours them more than the current state of other political arenas. Opinions consistently favouring a given group may not mean that the judge is shaping the law to favour the group, but that the group has found that the existing law favoured them and resorted to the courts precisely for this reason. Thus the cases that come before the courts may not be random on their legalities but pre-selected by litigating groups.

Administrative and regulatory agencies frequently find that, due to changes in economic or social conditions, a statute whose intent has long been acknowledged, or a line of decisions that is clear and consistent, is now yielding undesirable results, that is, results that favour social interests that the agency does not favour. Such agencies may persistently litigate cases with the hope of getting judicial amendments. For instance, the National Transportation Policy was framed in the 1930s when trucking was an infant industry and, therefore, it provided special aids to truckers vis-à-vis railroads. The ICC, applying the act in the 1960s, may repeatedly attempt to shift its thrust to end a favouritism that seems unwarranted in today's changed circumstances. The agency may try to accomplish this goal by petitioning Congress to amend the act or alternatively by issuing a set of pro-railroad, anti-truck rulings in marginal cases. In the subsequent litigation, the commission seeks to gradually nudge the Supreme Court into accepting its views and thus amend the statute without legislative action. Is a judge who consistently resists the prod of the ICC exhibiting an anti-regulatory agency or pro-railroad attitude, or is he simply attempting to obey Congressional commands however outdated and incorrect they may be?

Again this problem can be overcome by extending the range of cases considered to cover more than truck certification business of the ICC or more than one regulatory agency. But it is also likely that there are institutional pressures that cause all the regulatory agencies to push against outdated commands of Congress so that a consistent anti-regulatory agency position might evidence not a pro-business, anti-regulation attitude but a pro-Congress, anti-amendment-without-statute attitude. In other words, the cases may be read *Regulatory Agency v. Business* but be decided *Regulatory Agency v. Congress*.

The pool of litigation is thus not a random one but is often marked by litigational campaigns that may bring similar parties under similar legal rubrics to an appellate court over and over again. Uniformity of decision may, therefore, indicate either an attitude favouring a given variety of party or an attempt to maintain a consistent position toward the legal rubric.

Finally, correspondence of litigating party with legal rule litigated may lead to consistencies that seem ordered on the basis of social attitudes but in fact reflect some other structuring of the materials. This is perhaps only a variation of what I have just written. Even without conscious litigational campaigns, certain kinds of people will consistently invoke the protection of certain constitutional provisions, statutes, or previous court decisions. It is the poor who usually invoke the right to counsel clause, labour unions that invoke certain of the unfair labour practices provisions of the National Labor Relations Act, Negroes who invoke *Brown v. Board*. A judge who has no markedly pro-Negro attitude might nevertheless consistently vote for Negroes if all the cases that reached his court involving Negroes were educational desegregation cases. A judge who had no particular love of labour unions might compile a wonderfully pro-union record if all the labour cases involved prohibited employer anti-union practices. Of course all the cases involving Negroes are not desegregation cases and all the cases involving unions are not employer practices cases. But there is a sufficient level of correspondence between party and legal rule that a given line of decisions by a given judge may sometimes indicate commitment to a given interpretation of the rule rather than an attitude toward the parties. It is true that commitment to a given interpretation of the rule may itself be initially the result of an attitude toward the parties, but, unless one entirely rejects legal training and logic as operative forces in the judicial mind, such commitment might alternatively be the result of rational-legal calculation based on the perhaps incorrect notion that laws do have an objective meaning whether we like it or not.

I am not suggesting that all of these factors are always operating or even that any one of them is always operating sufficiently to render attitudinal-statistical analysis inoperative. However, in every instance where statistical methods are employed, traditional analysis will be necessary to isolate and assess these factors and determine to what extent they undercut the statistical propositions. In some instances such analysis may result in discarding the statistical propositions. In others, it will be used to indicate that no undermining factors can be discovered. In a great many instances, of course, the result will be something between full abandonment and acceptance of the initial attitudinal analysis.

A word further must be said about the statistical extension and manipulation of categories to avoid or at least mitigate the three problems of non-randomness sketched here. Broadening categories is not an automatic or complete solution. Let us say we are attempting to establish a pro-civil liberties attitude. We begin with freedom of speech and show that judge X consistently disfavours speech claims. When we are told that this may be because all the speech cases in question involve state action and thus issues of federalism, we add no-establishment of religion cases and show that he disfavours all such claims. In reply we are told that he may do so not because he is anti-civil rights but because he is convinced by historical research that the no-establishment clause was not intended by the framers to create a wall of separation. As we add areas, we may be greeted each time by a new decision rule based on legislative intend, *stare decisis*, judicial modesty, reasoning from neutral principles, and so on, which explains the judge's behaviour on grounds totally divorced from civil rights attitudes. When we find that the sum total of all these decisional rules just happens to be a consistently anti-civil rights position, we may be suspicious, but our respondent may be right. There will rarely be enough categories available for introduction to statistically prove that it is an anti-civil rights attitude that motivates the decisional pattern and not a series of interrelated or even independent decisional rules which coincidentally yield consistent anti-civil rights results. It is not beyond the realm of belief and certainly not beyond the realm of statistical possibility that four or five firmly held legal doctrines largely divorced from any single social attitude may in 30 or 40 cases yield a pattern that falsely suggests such an attitude.

The same kind of problem exists when analysis proceeds by reduction. Let us suppose that we suggest that Justice X is anti-business and our respondent replies that most of the decisions on which we base our conclusions are regulatory cases and in fact what they show is that the Justice defers to administrative expertise. We then reply that Justice X has upheld 70 per cent of the regulatory commission decisions unfavourable to the regulated firms but only 14 per cent of those favourable to them. Our respondent replies yes, but your 86 per cent of favourable agency findings rejected by Justice X are all cases in which the administrative agency went beyond its expertise and attempted to in effect amend the statute without Congressional consent. Again we may be suspicious, but we are unlikely to be dealing with numbers large enough or a universe sufficiently suitable to 'prove' our case statistically. Probably our best bet at this point would be to return to traditional legal analysis in order to discover whether the cases in which favourable agency findings were rejected are really distinguishable from the others and consistent with the position toward agencies taken by the Justice in the opinions initially labelled anti-business.

Finally, those committed to attitudinal approaches are attempting to avoid many of the problems I have suggested by including 'legalistic' attitudes among those to be studied. But this returns us directly to traditional legal analysis as an integral part of constructing categories for statistical use. The nice thing about pro- and anti-business or civil rights or economic liberalism labels was that attitude categories could be constructed without case analysis simply by looking to the nature of the parties who had won and lost in the best 'bad man's law' tradition. The work of Grossman and Spaeth suggests that when we begin dealing with judicial attitudes about law and the judicial process instead of about US Steel and the AFL-CIO, we can only frame categories of cases that will isolate such factors, save for a few areas that are purely jurisdictional, by traditional analysis of the cases. There is no other way to divine which cases struck which of the Justices as raising procedural, role of the Court, or interpretive problems just as or more important than the nature of the two parties.

Moreover, such attitudes are much more difficult to isolate and express in the yes–no or plus–minus language of statistics than hypothesized attitudes toward the parties, and tend to return the study of judicial motivation to the rather murky mixture of legal reasoning and social judgements from which the simple format and glorious white space of scalograms sometimes seem to be rescuing it.

In summary then, traditional analysis plays an important role in establishing the categories and format of the new forms of analysis, is required for support and interpretation of the findings of such analysis, and is frequently a convenient proof or check on both its methods and conclusions. In this connection it should be added that some of the political jurists have been guilty of a considerable number of errors or overstatements and their conclusions have been subject to a number of specific criticisms that could have been avoided or anticipated by more thorough traditional analysis and exposition. These errors are doubly unfortunate because they are often seized upon to discredit the new methods when in fact they are simply evidence that few of us are perfect in our scholarship, traditional or otherwise.

Traditional, statistical, and behavioural techniques are now inextricably mixed in political jurisprudence and will undoubtedly remain so. Not all political jurists need use all of them, nor need we waste time trying to determine an orthodox 'mix'. Either in the mind of a single scholar or in the complementary work of several, most problems in political jurisprudence will require a variety of approaches in order to build up a cumulative solution.

The Perennial Question: Is and Ought

Critical students of jurisprudence who have bothered to follow me this far are likely by now to have two dread words, 'naive' and 'positivism', ready at hand. It must be confessed that, either out of naivety or because many of its participants see themselves primarily as political scientists not students of law, political jurisprudence so far has failed to provide itself a theoretical rationale that grapples with the problems of twentieth-century legal philosophy. This is a serious flaw in a movement that is so heavily dependent on sociological jurisprudence and legal realism both because there have been serious theoretical differences between the two and because each has been challenged by a revived idealism. However, I do not think this flaw is a fatal one because neither the conflict between sociological jurisprudence and realism nor the debate between positivism and idealism has yet been resolved. For the moment at least political jurisprudence can attach itself to the realist and positivist causes and refer its attackers to a set of arguments hallowed by extended if not particularly fruitful development. Nevertheless, the strength of the revival of various forms of natural law jurisprudence requires some comment on the particular relation of political jurisprudence to the normative or valuational aspects of legal philosophy.

Political jurisprudence is basically positivistic in the sense of seeking to describe the political-legal process as it is rather than prescribing how it ought to be. But if political jurisprudence is positivism, it is a peculiarly value-laden kind of positivism. The whole attitudinal wing is, of course, attempting to discover what values the participants in law-making hold and how these values affect their law-making activity. The essentially political inquiry into what governmental tasks the courts do efficiently and what services they fail to perform satisfactorily includes a determination of how well the courts function as creators and appliers of moral standards (see Shapiro 1961). The general emphasis of political jurisprudence on judges as policy-makers has inevitably made the demand that judges articulate their values and social goals an integral part of political jurisprudence (see Miller and Howell 1960; Miller 1961). For policy-making is by its very nature purposive activity implying a choice between alternative means and ends based on some notion of the good. The judge as policy-maker must, therefore, make moral choices.

I am well aware that many scholars view the reduction of values to psychological data, which then become part of the 'is', as the final positivistic rape of moral philosophy. Similarly the emphasis on purposive elements in law-making may be viewed as a false reduction of law to will and appetite ignoring elements of reason and justice. Finally a jurisprudence which claims that the ought is an essential part of law, while at the same time devoting itself entirely to the is, may well be accused of either insincerity or misdirection. In the face of these arguments, it is not entirely satisfactory to say the political jurisprudence, by emphasizing the political and, therefore, valuational or purposive nature of law, provides a gateway for the passage from empirical to normative study. A gateway is not enough. Someone must go through it and tell us what is beyond.

But if political jurisprudence in the end shows itself incomplete, it at least points to the reasons for its own incompleteness and, indeed, for the unresolved quality of all modern jurisprudence. Since law and law-making are an integral part of the political, legal philosophy is an integral part of political philosophy. The problem of those who wish to create a value-oriented rather than descriptive jurisprudence is that, apart from the Neo-Scholastics, they have been unable to formulate a coherent and generally acceptable statement of the values around which a new jurisprudence could be built. Indeed, since the admittedly sub-philosophical jural postulates of Roscoe Pound, nearly all the talk has been of the need for and means of finding moral principles rather than the substance of those principles (for example, Northrop 1959). The reason for this failure is quite obviously the failure of post-Marxian political philosophy to provide any acceptable 'truths' about the nature and ends of the government (see Shklar 1957), and more particularly the failure of liberal-democratic philosophy, busy defending its threatened procedural axioms, to come to grips with the substantive issues that lie behind the phrase 'public interest'. The Neo-Scholastics in fact can appear so self-satisfied and complete only because they deal with law with a capital—or natural—L, or point out the contradictions of other political philosophers, rather than attempting the real and much more difficult task of integrating scholastic theories of law into modern catholic political philosophy, a philosophy that has yet to prove itself congruent with modern industrial society.

Until political philosophy revives sufficiently to provide us with a set of ultimate truths or a reasonable facsimile thereof, jurisprudence is likely to concern itself with more immediate questions. There is a whole range of intermediate ought problems that we must solve now even though our ultimates are shaky. Ought property owners be forced to sell to Negroes? Ought competitive sectors of the economy be allowed to become oligopolistic? Ought the jurisdiction of juvenile courts be extended? If political jurisprudence provides us with some information on the functions of law-makers in our society and in the process prods those law-makers into conscious political evaluation of their own governmental roles and the role of government in general, it will have contributed as much as, and perhaps more than, its contemporaries to the valuational aspects of jurisprudence.

Judicialization and the Construction of Governance

Alec Stone Sweet

The triad—two contracting parties and a dispute resolver—constitutes a primal social institution, a microcosm of governance. If this is so, in uncovering the institutional dynamics of the triad we uncover an essential logic of government itself. Broadly stated, my objectives are twofold: to defend the validity of these contentions and to demonstrate their centrality to the discipline.

The article proceeds as follows. After introducing key concepts, I present a model of a particular mode of governance. By 'mode of governance' I mean the social mechanism by which the rules in place in any given community are adapted to the experiences and exigencies of those who live under them. The theory integrates, as tightly interdependent factors, the evolution of strategic (utility-maximizing) behaviour and normative (cultural or rule-based) structure. It captures dynamics of change observable at both the micro level, by which I mean the behaviour of individual actors, and the macro level, by which I mean the institutional environment—or social structure—in which this behaviour takes place. In the discussion, the mechanisms of change that are endogenous to the model are specified, and the conditions under which we would expect to see these mechanisms operate, and fail to operate, are identified. I then employ the model to explain two hard cases of systemic change: the international trade regime, established by the 1947 General Agreement on Tariffs and Trade; and the French Fifth Republic, founded in 1958. In the conclusion, I draw out some of the implications of the analysis for our understanding of the complex relationship between strategic behaviour and social structure.

Originally published in *Comparative Political Studies*, 31 (1999), 147. Reproduced by kind permission.

Dyads, Triads, Normative Structure

The model is comprised of three core elements: the *dyad*, the *triad*, and *normative structure*.

The dyad, 'the simplest sociological formation' (Simmel 1950: 122), is any 'pattern of [direct] exchange' between two individuals or groups (see Foster 1977). The dyad alone defines, more or less comprehensively, a wide range of basic human relationships. Examples exist wherever we look for them. In marriage—the union of two people; in feudal polities—the tie between serf and vassal; in parliamentary democracies—the dichotomy of party of government and party of opposition; in industrial production—the interdependence of capital and labour; and in international relations— the network of allies and enemies: dyadic structures constitute core social identities of individual entities. Because dyads bind single units together, they are primordial *social* institutions. They are both building blocks to society—that is, they can be linked in chains and clusters to form larger social formations—and they develop quite naturally within such constructs.[1]

The normative basis of the dyadic form is reciprocity. Reciprocity is the glue holding the dyad—society—together, which accounts for why it exists in every human community about which we know anything (Gouldner 1977). Stripped to essentials, the norm holds that 'people should help those who help them' (Gouldner 1977: 37). Promises made are to be kept; debts incurred are to be repaid; kindnesses received are to be recognized and returned. Reciprocity, according to Simmel (1950: 123, 135) gives to the dyad 'a special consecration' by linking each party to 'a common fate'.

The notion that reciprocity is crucial to the maintenance of social systems has been a staple of social science (for example, Hobhouse 1906; Malinowski 1932; Parsons and Shils 1951). With the rise of neo-rationalism in contemporary political science, analytical priorities have shifted from the normative and social contexts of politics to strategic choice contexts within which individuals seek to maximize their utility. Although neo-rationalists also privilege the dyad, they problematize reciprocity in particular and norms in general (for example, Axelrod 1986). Indeed, the paradigmatic metaphors of game theory—Prisoner's Dilemma, chicken, the assurance games—focus our attentions on the fierce difficulties of establishing and maintaining dyadic cooperation. Dyadic forms are inherently unstable, neo-rationalists

---

[1] In noticing the ubiquity of relationships organized in twos, I do not mean to imply that dyadic forms are all that matter. I focus on them as a representation of 'the social' for theory-building purposes, namely, to obtain advantages that come with reduction.

tell us, because each party faces powerful incentives to ignore no obligations, thereby cheating on the other.

I will return to a discussion of neo-rationalism later. For now it is enough to recognize that dyadic forms can accommodate *cooperation*, which can be socially enabling, and *conflict*, which can be socially debilitating.

The triad—two disputants and a dispute resolver—is a universal, if under-theorized, phenomenon (but see D. Black 1998: Ch. 6). I understand the triad to be a primal technique of organizing social authority and, there-fore, of governing. The underlying reason for this is simple: the triadic entity is the guarantor of reciprocity. Quite literally rooted in the dyadic form, the triad brings an external presence to the dyad, a presence whose interest is in the fate of 'a common fate', that is, in the durability of social relationships across time. Viewed functionally, triadic dispute resolution (TDR) serves to perpetuate the dyad, given changes in the preferences or identities of the two parties or changes in the environment. As Simmel (1950: 145) puts it: 'the triad indicates transition.' The triadic entity responds to, and is a crucial agent of, social change.

Two ideal types of triadic dispute resolution are relevant to the analysis. The first is *consensual TDR*, triads constituted by the voluntary consent of both disputants, that is, by an ad hoc act of delegation. The act recognizes but also confers social authority, or legitimacy, on the third party. Siblings appeal to parents, classmates to one another or to a teacher, villagers to a shaman, a chief, or a sage. The second type is *compulsory TDR*, triads that are permanently constituted by jurisdiction: dispute resolution processes are triggered by one party to a dispute against the will of the other. In this type, office replaces delegation (Shapiro 1981*a*: Ch. 1), that is, an initial—constitutional—act of delegation is frozen in place for the life of the polity. Courts are the paradigmatic form of compulsory TDR—but legislative bodies perform similar social functions.

To move from the dyad to the triad is to construct a particular form of governance: the triadic. In dyads, conflict can be debilitating; but conflict is constitutive of the triad. Once activated, TDR performs governmental functions: to generate normative guidance about how one ought to behave, to stabilize one's expectations about the behaviour of others, and to impinge on *ex ante* distributions of values and resources. Stated simply, the social function of TDR—governance—is to regulate behaviour and to maintain social cohesion as circumstances change.

The final element of the model is normative structure: the system of rules—or socially constituted constraints on behaviour—in place in any community. A great deal of controversy surrounds the subject of norms and rules, their status and explanatory value. Although this paper is partly a response to this controversy, I do not attempt to resolve it here.

What I call normative structure is equivalent to what North (1990: 3–6) calls 'institutions', variously: 'the rules of the game', 'customs and traditions', 'conventions, codes of conduct, norms of behavior, statute law, common law, and contracts'. It is congruent with how Eckstein (1988: 790; see also Wildavsky 1987) conceptualizes 'culture': 'mediating orientations', those 'general dispositions of actors to act in certain ways in sets of situations'. It conforms to March and Olsen's (1989: 22) notion of 'rules': the 'beliefs, paradigms, codes, cultures, and knowledge' that permit us to 'identify the normatively appropriate behavior'. It equates norms, as Taylor (1989: 135) does, with 'ideologies' and 'culture', and it conceives of 'institutionalized rules', in Jepperson's (1991: 145) terms, as 'performance scripts'.[2]

Despite clear differences in how structure is understood, culturalists and at least a few neo-rationalists agree on far more than we might expect. For Eckstein (1988: 791–2), culture allows people to 'decode experience … to give it meaning', which 'saves virtually all decision costs'. For North (1990: 6, 17, 25), institutions, a subset of which is 'culture'—'a language-based conceptual framework for encoding and interpreting … information'—'exist to reduce the uncertainties involved in human interaction', thus saving 'transaction costs' (see also Johnson 1997; Kreps 1990). Normative structures enable human interaction by simplifying the range of choices available to individuals and by investing those choices with meaning.

Across the social sciences, change in normative structure has proved difficult to theorize (for example, Eckstein 1988; Powell and Dimaggio 1991: Ch. 1; Taylor 1989; Tsebelis 1990: Ch. 4). We better understand the logic of institutional inertia. Rules facilitate exchange between individuals, creating opportunities for collective action. Behaviour that responds to these opportunities, once locked in—for example, in dyadic forms—reinforces normative structure. In culturalist or constructivist terms, because normative structures constitute individual and collective identities, and therefore give meaning to action, they are difficult to change by way of action without

---

[2] I am aware that I have just assembled, in a very small tent, a disparate group of scholars who traditionally do not agree on many first principles, least of all how we ought to think about social structure. I have referenced them together for two reasons. First, I am seeking to build a theory that strips governance down to its constituent elements, structure being one such element. Although the scholars cited disagree for some very good reasons, we can easily identify what each of them means by structure; we can also see that, despite distinctly different approaches to research, structure fulfils more or less equivalent functions. Second, if, as I am claiming, my theory is relevant to the study of governance generally, my audience must be broad not narrow.

a concomitant change in identities. In either case, it is clear that the reproduction of particular ways of doing things inheres in the organization of human community.

In the next section, I model the transformation of the normative structure, focusing on the dynamics of change that are endogenous to the logic of dyads, triads, and rules.

Constructing Governance

Figure 1.1 depicts a simple model of the *process* by which systems of governance emerge and evolve. An adequate theory of this process must account for the following:

- strategic behaviour: how individual actors conceive and pursue their interests within any given community;
- policy-making: how values and resources are distributed within any given community; and
- systemic change: how the normative structure in place in any given community is constituted, maintained, and revised.

The model breaks down this process into four stages, each a chronological shift along a circular path, moving clockwise. Movement is generated by the relative intensity of two relationships: of the dyad and triad, and of

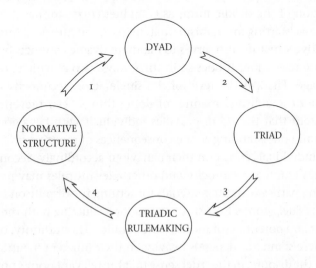

Fig. 1.1. The construction of governance

normative structure and strategic behaviour. Although each shift is conditioned by what has happened in prior stages, the discussion highlights distinct aspects of these relationships.

Shift 1: Normative Structure to Dyadic Contract

The theory holds that we can move, by virtue of a self-sustaining process, from a single dispute about the terms of a dyadic contract to an elaborate governmental system.

To get to a dyadic contract, we need two individuals and at least a rudimentary normative structure. By 'dyadic contract' I mean the rules of exchange—or those promises—voluntarily entered into between two persons. Contracts can be implicit or explicit. The promises made in an 'implicit dyadic contract' are uncodified and 'lack ritual or legal basis'; the 'explicit dyadic contract' codifies promises that are meant to be legally binding (Foster 1977: 16). Both forms establish reciprocal rights and duties among two contractants.

In contracting, two individuals coordinate their self-interest in terms of some shared view of the future. Such coordination is difficult, if not impossible, without at least a primitive cultural framework: in the form of language—communication—and in the form of the norm of reciprocity, which is embedded in notions of individual commitment, reputation, and responsibility. Reciprocity, a crucial building block of society, enables the construction of the dyadic form; as Gouldner (1977: 39) has it, the norm constitutes a 'starting mechanism' that 'helps to initiate social interaction'.

Normative structure also serves to maintain dyadic contracts by facilitating dispute resolution. It does so in three ways, two of which are relevant at this stage. First, at the level of the single actor, reciprocity—or a relevant rule or established manner of doing things—can prevent disputes to the extent that the norm provides individuals with behavioural guidance and an understanding of the consequences of reneging on a promise, and that individuals constrain their behaviour accordingly. Second, once a dispute has erupted, reciprocity and other relevant rules may provide the contracting parties with the materials for settling the dispute on their own, dyadically. Such norms furnish the bases for evaluating both the disputed behaviour and potential solutions to the conflict. The authority, or legitimacy, of these standards depends heavily on their inherent 'neutrality' with respect to the dispute, in the strict sense that the relevant norms pre-date the dispute.

Shift 2: Dyad to Triad

The legitimacy of dyadic relationships is rooted in the self-interest of the contracting parties; at this point, I exclude from the analysis dyads constituted by coercion.[3] For each party, the contract must be functional in the sense that its existence depends on the perception that the benefits of constructing and maintaining the dyad outweigh the costs, and that the benefits of a particular dyadic form outweigh the benefits of going it alone. The dyadic contract coordinates egoistic motives, in the form of rules—reciprocal rights and duties—for the duration of the contract.

Once formed, rules organize how conflict is identified and understood. As a dyadic relationship proceeds or as circumstances change, the meanings attached to the same set of rules by the contractants may diverge; or the relative value of the dyadic relationship may decline for one or both of the contracting parties; or, having calculated 'best strategies', one or both of the parties may succumb to incentives to renege on obligations—the Prisoner's Dilemma. In any case, the dyadic form generates a massive functional demand for dispute resolution in the form of rule-interpretation.

Dyads, aided by rules, often resolve disputes on their own. When they do so, the dyad comprises, in the parlance of legal anthropology, a 'legal level' (Collier 1973: Ch. 1). If disputants fail to resolve their dispute dyadically, they may choose to delegate the matter to a third party, thus constituting a new legal level: the triadic.

This act of delegation can be understood as a simple—and universal—act of 'common sense', as Shapiro (1981a: 1) does. It can also be understood in rationalist-utilitarian terms. Delegation is likely when, for each disputant, going to a third party is less costly, or more likely to yield a desired outcome, than either breaking the dyadic contract and going it alone, or attempting to impose a particular settlement against the wishes of the other disputant. For each disputant, the short-run risk of delegation is the prospect of a settlement in favour of the other. In the long run, however, the more two disputants interact with one other—the more a relationship is perceived as beneficial by each party—the less that risk matters. Other things being equal, each contracting party may expect to win some disputes and to lose others, over time, against a backdrop of absolute benefit. The social logic of delegation,

---

[3] In excluding coercion from consideration, the model does some violence to reality. Surely all dyadic relationships reflect or organize ongoing power relationships that contain elements of—at least implied—coercion. I nevertheless theorize a consensual rather than a coercive model of governance in order to focus attention on outcomes that result exclusively from the internal logic of rules, dyads, and triads. Put differently, mine is a theory of ideational and normativ physical or material, power (influence).

like that of the dyadic contract, is one of long-range utility: each party must believe that it is better off attempting to resolve a dispute than dissolving the relationship altogether.

Of course, the calculation of costs and benefits need not favour the move from dyad to triad. Both parties may possess a powerful commitment to maintaining, rather than resolving, their conflicts. When the core identities of the parties are constituted in opposition to one another, TDR will be ana-thema. Examples might include certain conflicts between the United States and the Soviet Union during the cold war, and between the Irish national-ists and the Ulster Unionists in Northern Ireland. Further, in the absence of minimal levels of trust, or lack of information about trustworthiness, the more likely it is that delegation itself will be viewed by one or both of the parties as potentially more costly than beneficial. At a minimum, agreement on a dispute resolver whose impartiality and wisdom is recognized may be a crucial first step, but agreement may elude the parties. Thus, although the move to triadic governance is a means of overcoming low levels of trust and weak behavioural norms, that move itself is not automatic.

These points accepted, dyadic conflict and the delegation of these conflicts to a third party is the fuel that drives the model. If disputants choose not to delegate, or are unable to agree on procedures, or if they are always able to resolve their disputes dyadically, or if one of the disputants is always able to impose a solution on the other, the theory implies, there would be neither TDR nor evolution in governmental forms.

Shift 3: The Crisis of Triadic Legitimacy

Once constituted, the triadic dispute resolver faces a potentially intractable dilemma. On the one hand, the third party's reputation for neutrality is cru-cial to the social legitimacy of the triad itself (see Shapiro 1981a). Disputants would be loath to delegate disputes if it were otherwise. Yet, in resolving disputes, the third party may compromise her reputation for neutrality by declaring one party the loser. That is, after all, what each of the disputants hopes. We can express the dispute resolver's dilemma as a fundamental interest: her interest is to resolve dyadic conflicts while maintaining the social legitimacy of TDR. In pursuit of this objective, she deploys two main tactics.

First, the dispute resolver seeks to secure legitimacy by defending her behaviour normatively, as meaningfully enabled and constrained by rules embedded in normative structure. Normative structure facilitates TDR, just as it facilitates dyadic dispute resolution, by providing ready-made standards

Fig. 1.2. The dispute resolver's calculus

of appropriate behaviour and solutions to conflicts. Reciprocity—'promises shall be kept'—animates the dyadic form; it also animates the exercise of TDR to the extent that the dispute resolver works to restore substantive fairness and a sense of trust among the parties.

Second, the dispute resolver anticipates the disputants'—or a community's—reactions to her behaviour, especially if she decides or is asked to take a decision. Compliance is a crucial test of the social legitimacy of consensual TDR. Figure 1.2 depicts this calculus. Position A.1 represents the substantive outcome desired by disputant A, and position B.1 represents the substantive outcome preferred by disputant B. Outcomes situated between positions A.1 and A.2—substitute B.1–B.2 for B—represent outcomes that the dispute resolver believes will not provoke A to refuse compliance. The space between B.2 and A.2 constitutes the dispute resolver's assessment of the range of decision-making outcomes that will lead to the resolution of the dispute, to compliance, and—much the same thing—to the re-establishment of a disputed rule. The calculus also helps her to fashion settlements that avoid the declaration of a clear winner or loser: in the area between B.2 and A.2, each disputant achieves a partial victory. For some disputes, the positions of A and B are more polarized, and no B.2–A.2 space exists; in such cases, the dispute resolver is unable to deploy the tactic: she has an interest in creating such a space by, for example, mediating between the parties. These are 'hard cases', ones in which the dispute resolver can expect that any decision taken is likely to result in public protests or even non-compliance. If she does attempt to resolve the dispute by rendering a decision, her legitimacy will rest all the more on the persuasiveness of normative justifications.

Shift 4: Triadic Dispute Resolution and Rule-making

Modes of TDR can be arrayed along a continuum constituted on one pole by mediation and on the other pole by adjudication. In mediation, the dispute resolver helps the disputants arrive at a mutually satisfactory settlement of the conflict. In adjudication, the dispute resolver authoritatively resolves the dispute on her own. In practice, nearly all TDR takes place on inter-mediate points between these two poles. Dispute resolvers move back and forth along the continuum—or threaten to do so—continuously in order to enhance their flexibility, limit their political exposure, and maximize their influence over the disputants. In any move along the continuum toward adjudication, the dispute resolver is led, with increasing precision and formality, to announce her decision and to provide a rule-based justification for it.

In adjudicating, the dispute resolver simultaneously resolves a dyadic dispute and enacts elements of the normative structure. Both are forms of rule-making. First, she makes rules that are concrete, particular, and retrospective: that is, she resolves an existing dispute between two specific parties about the terms of one dyadic contract. Second, in justifying her decision—in telling us why, normatively, a given act should or should not be permitted—she makes rules of an abstract, general, and prospective nature. This is so to the extent that her decision clarifies or alters rules comprising the normative structure.

This latter form of triadic rulemaking constitutes a predictable response to the crisis dispute resolvers face—tactic 1 above. Yet it raises a delicate, second-order legitimacy issue. From the point of view of the disputing parties, it makes evident that the exact content of the rules governing the dispute could not have been ascertained at the time the dispute erupted. The perception of the dispute resolver's neutrality erodes as her capacity to make rules is revealed. The dispute resolver can mitigate, but can *never* permanently resolve, this problem. Most important, she can work to cast TDR as deliberation about the precise relationship of abstract rules to a concrete dispute, portraying her decision as a record of these deliberations. In doing so, she portrays triadic rule-making as a by-product of TDR rather than an outcome that she desires in and of itself.

In this way, TDR generates a discourse about how people ought to behave. Because rules, reasoning about rules, and the adaptation of rules to specific social needs constitute the core of this discourse—and, I would argue, of the evolution of norms more generally[4]—precedent follows naturally. Precedent helps to legitimize TDR by simultaneously acknowledging rule-making behaviour, while constraining that same behaviour with a rule: that like

---

[4] My position is largely congruent with Robert Sugden's. Sugden (1989: 93-6) suggests that norms—he focuses on 'conventions'—develop in path dependent, self-reinforcing ways, one mechanism of which is the ubiquity and naturalness of normative reasoning itself. Normative structures are inherently expansionary to the extent that they enable people to reason from one situation to another by way of analogy. The move to precedent—and, therefore, to something akin to case law—is one result of analogical reasoning. If this is so, TDR is embedded within, and further reinforces, the path dependent nature of the greater process through which rule systems evolve.

cases shall be settled likewise. In encapsulating this sequence—*dyadic rules -> conflict -> deliberation -> triadic rulemaking -> precedent*—TDR organizes discourse about a community's normative structure. In doing so, TDR performs a profoundly governmental function to the extent that dyadic contractors are drawn into this discourse and help to perpetuate it.

Shift 1: (Re)Constructing the Dyad

In moving through shifts 1–4, we see how the dyad, the triad, and normative structure can be knotted together. And we see how a single dyadic conflict can generate a process of systemic change, the constitution or reconstitution of a mode of governance. Thus: a dyadic dispute erupts; the disputants delegate the matter to a dispute resolver; the dispute resolver resolves the conflict in a process involving normative reasoning, revising— at least subtly—normative structure. In returning to shift 1, the impact of structure on strategic behaviour, we come full circle to our initial starting point. But we find ourselves in a rather different world this time: the individuals comprising the dyad have learned something about the nature of their relationship—the rules governing their exchange—and about the environment—the normative structure—which sustains it.

Put simply, TDR has reconsecrated the contract and re-enacted the normative structure. The dispute resolver may have done so in a relatively conservative manner, fashioning a partial victory for each disputant and appealing to rules whose prior existence is relatively unquestioned. In so doing, she has reinforced the existing structure while clarifying its domain of relevance and application. The dispute resolver may have done so in a relatively progressive manner, declaring a clear winner and loser while revising an existing rule or crafting a new one. In so doing, she has reshaped normative structure, expanding its domain.

Given two conditions, such rule-making is likely to generate powerful pedagogical—or positive feedback—effects to be registered on subsequent exchange and dispute resolution. First, contractants must perceive that they are better off in a world with TDR than they are in a world without TDR. If they perceive as much, and if they are rational in the sense of being utility-maximizers, they will evaluate the rulefulness of any potential action and anticipate the probable outcome issuing from TDR. Second, the dispute resolver must understand that her decisions have some authoritative—that is, precedential—value.

If these conditions are met, TDR will inexorably become a powerful mechanism of political change, and dyadic exchange will inevitably be placed in the 'shadow' of triadic rule-making. As we move around the circle a second time, and then again and again, this shadow will deepen and expand, covering more and more forms of human interaction. A virtuous circle is thereby constructed: to the extent that TDR is effective, it lowers the costs of dyadic exchange; as dyadic exchanges increase in number and in scope, so does the demand for the authoritative interpretation of rules; as TDR is exercised, the body of rules that constitutes normative structure steadily expands, becoming more elaborate and differentiated; these rules then will feed back onto dyadic relationships, structuring future interactions, conflict, and dispute resolution.

This dynamic, self-reinforcing process can be understood variously. Conceived in economic terms, the process operates according to the logic of increasing returns and path dependence (Arthur 1994; North 1990; Pierson 1997). As it proceeds, dyadic exchange will be channelled down narrower and narrower paths, that is, individuals will continuously adapt their behaviour to increasingly differentiated sets of rules. It is also institutionalization: a process through which specific social contexts will be increasingly defined by specific rules of behaviour: those curated by the triadic entity. Individuals will absorb and act upon these rules, thus (re)making themselves and their community.

Dyadic and Triadic Governance

Dyads and triads organize human community, constituting modes of governance to the extent that they are *institutionalized*: constructed and maintained by rules. Dyadic forms flourish in hierarchy, often coexisting or symbiotic with triadic forms. Patron-client networks are an ubiquitous example (Landé 1977). When vertically stacked, as in Confucian and military systems, a chain of dyadic relationships links the rulers with the ruled and thus establishes hierarchy. New institutionalist political economy captures such hierarchies in 'principal-agent' models of organization (Moe 1987). Dyadic contracts also give order to anarchy, as they do in international relations (Stone 1994). Examples include the 'balance of terror' system of deterrence (Hoffmann 1991) and the elaborate world constructed by the bilateral treaty.

Triadic governance is institutionalized in one of two basic modes: consensual and compulsory. My model demonstrates how a purely consensual form of triadic governance can evolve. Movement around the circle is driven by the complex mix of harmony and tension that inheres in the relationship between rules and self-interest. Coercive sanctions and enforcement mechanisms are conspicuously absent from the account (see note 3). Instead, movement depends upon specific actors—the dyadic contractants and the triadic dispute resolver—identifying their respective interests in some, rather than in other, ways and behaving accordingly. To capture these requisite conditions, the model is expressed in terms of statements that begin with 'when', 'if', and 'to the extent that', statements that apply to specific contexts.

It follows that actors are always capable of blocking movement at crucial points around the circle. Two contractants may choose to dissolve their contract rather than delegate to a third party. The dispute resolver may render capricious decisions without normative justification. After a dispute has been adjudicated, and if a clear winner has been declared, the loser may refuse to comply with the decision. If such behaviour is, or becomes, the normal state of affairs, triadic governance will be stillborn, and social entropy will result. In such a state, reciprocity and other elements of normative structure do not, on their own, sustain social exchange; and triadic dispute resolvers do not function, on their own, to restore reciprocity given dyadic conflict and change in exogenous circumstances.

The function of sanctions is to buttress dyadic and triadic dispute resolution. By sanctions, I mean social provisions that penalize non-compliance with rules and triadic rule-making. To the extent that they operate effectively, sanctions counteract behaviour that blocks the restoration of reciprocity among disputants.

In consensual triadic governance, sanctions are informal but potentially fully effective. Individuals will be led to abandon existing contracts, or avoid entering into future contracts, with a chronic rule-violator, an individual who wilfully disregards obligations imposed by a dyadic contract or by a triadic dispute resolver. To the extent that this occurs, the violator forgoes the benefits associated with social exchange and suffers stigmatization—the loss of reputation. If the violator's behaviour has led all other actors to refuse contractual relations with the violator, social exclusion is the sanction. Banishment, virtual death, is the ultimate penalty associated with consensual governance.

In compulsory triadic governance, explicit rules govern this sequence: *dyadic contract -> triadic dispute resolution -> decision -> compliance*. Such rules commonly: enable the move from dyad to triad in the absence of the consent of one of the parties; require the triadic dispute resolver to consider the complaint;[5] oblige the parties to comply with the terms of an eventual decision; and organize enforcement measures in cases of non-compliance.

---

[5] If only to decide not to decide.

Like the move from dyadic to triadic governance, the transition from consensual to compulsory TDR is inherently the stuff of political development. The move is not automatic because the condition necessary for transition is not sufficient. The condition is that, for any community or pool of potential contractants, existing normative structure fails to provide an adequate framework for social exchange, while the social demand for coordinative rules and dispute resolution has increased. This may occur for a variety of reasons. The potential contractants may be strangers, that is, they do not share a common normative structure; or changes in normative structure may not have kept pace with changes in the nature of social exchange within a given community. A community of neighbours can become a group of strangers as a result of migration, increased social differentiation, or the division of labour. In any case, when existing rules cannot sustain social exchange at an optimal level, people have an interest in developing new ones. The condition is not sufficient because the construction of such rules is a potentially insoluble collective action problem. Thus, the model does not predict that TDR always produces systemic change. On the contrary, when people (1) share a relatively comprehensive normative structure and (2) interact on an ongoing, face-to-face, basis—that is, where information relevant to exchange is virtually perfect and transaction costs are virtually zero—TDR tends to re-enact, rather than to remake, social norms. In such contexts, the existing normative structure is sufficient; informal sanctions are highly effective;[6] and mediation is preferred to adjudication.[7]

As political development has proceeded in the world, so has the ubiquity of compulsory triadic governance. Generating and imposing new normative structures that replace or supplement previously existing structures is perhaps the only, or at least the most efficacious, means of providing a system of governance for individuals who are otherwise strangers to each other. At the

[6] Game theorists make this point in the guise of the Folk Theorem, developed in the literature on repeated games: for example, Fudenberg and Maskin (1986); Kandori (1992).

[7] Ellickson (1991) tells us that Shasta County ranchers refuse to use, or even educate themselves about, the laws meant to govern and resolve disputes concerning grazing rights, fencing, and stray cattle. Invoking 'good neighbourliness', they prefer to settle such disputes dyadically or by quiet mediation, according to well-established norms. But when a Texas rancher moves into the community and openly disregards these rules, litigation is the result. Collier (1973), in her study of how the various legal levels operate among Mayan Indians in Zinacantan, found a complex blending of dyadic dispute settlement and mediation, and a hostility towards formal Mexican law and courts mitigated only in dealings with outsiders. At the time these books were published, both communities shared relatively stable normative structures possessed of relatively high social legitimacy. If in both communities TDR was ubiquitous, third parties were not used to provoke, nor was dispute resolution expected to result in, normative change.

extreme, organized coercion reinforces TDR processes, guaranteeing, with force if necessary, social exchange, dispute resolution, and the enforcement of rules. The modern state is the institutionalization of coercive TDR.

The Law-maker and the Judge

With the development of the modern state, the authority to govern—the power to resolve disputes and to make rules—tends to be divided among two separate figures. Separation of powers doctrines notwithstanding, the law-maker and the judge are not easily detached from one another.

The point can be made in terms of the model. The model demonstrates how a full-blown system of governance can be constituted and maintained by TDR processes alone if shifts 1–4 are iterated ad infinitum. The dispute resolver governs by the pedagogical authority of her decisions. Triadic rule-making is legislative in nature: it adapts, over time, a given normative structure to the demands of dyadic exchange. But TDR is a relatively inefficient means of rule-making since it proceeds on a case-by-case basis. In delegating law-making powers to a legislator, a community establishes a far more efficient means of revising normative structure. Nonetheless, in legislating, the legislator performs a dispute resolution function. As part of normative structure, laws help to prevent conflict from arising in the first place and to facilitate the resolution of conflicts that do arise. Further, because the legislator fixes general rules for an entire community, it generates a crisis of legitimacy no less intractable than that which afflicts the dispute resolver. This crisis animates political life in the form—again—of a quest to construct rules to constrain rule-making.[8]

Even when judicial and legislative functions are separated, comparative institutional advantage produces legislative-judicial interdependence. The law-maker makes rules whose reach, among other things, is *immediately* general and prospective; the judge makes rules whose reach, among other things, is *immediately* particular and retrospective. If the judge is expected to enforce the law-maker's law, and if this law is meant to be binding, coercive TDR is required. If, for reasons elucidated, TDR results in rule-making, then compulsory TDR results in the authoritative reconstruction of the law-maker's law. The legislator therefore shares rule-making power with the judge.

---

[8] For example, the constant struggle to establish or to revise constitutions, electoral systems, and legislative and judicial process.

TDR and Systemic Change

Triadic governance facilitates social exchange and the adaptation of rule systems to the exigencies of those who exchange: hence its social utility.[9] Other things being equal, it must be that dyadic governance is inherently less flexible and more brittle than triadic governance. Whereas conflict can destroy dyadic contracts, conflict activates TDR and establishes the parameters of a politics that can recast the normative basis of social exchange.

My theory holds that TDR, if exercised on an ongoing and effective basis, is a crucial mechanism of social cohesion and change. To put it in constructivist terms, triadic governance coordinates the complex relationship between structures and agents (Giddens 1984), helping to constitute and reconstitute both over time. In culturalist terms, it serves to counteract forces favouring social 'anomie' or 'entropy' by adjusting general 'guides to action' to 'the relentless particularity of experience' (Eckstein 1988: 795–6) by, among other things, generating normative discourse. In rationalist terms, the move from the dyad to the triad replaces games like the Prisoner's Dilemma or chicken with an entirely different strategic context. Although game theorists have begun to notice the challenge (for example, Calvert 1995), they have had difficulty modeling the kinds of triadic games implied by this article— and by a good deal of judicial politics more generally—not least because, in these games, the evolution of rule structures is endogenized and normative reflection and argumentation are part of the 'game' (see Stone Sweet 1998*a*; Vanberg 1998*b*).

In the next section, I demonstrate the power of the model to explain systemic change, by which I mean a fundamental transformation in how normative structure is constituted and sustained in any given human community. The evolution from dyadic to triadic governance, and the transition from consensual to compulsory TDR, are unambiguous examples. To the extent that such evolution occurs, there will be a commensurate change in the social basis of exchange, that is, in how individual actors understand and

---

[9] I am not suggesting that the development of a stable mechanism of TDR is the only way to achieve the virtuous circle depicted by the model. Cases in point are Avner Greif's accounts (1989; 1993; 1994) of how other, quasi-triadic mechanisms have performed similar functions. In his analysis of trade relations in the Mediterranean region during the late medieval period, Greif shows that the expansion of overseas commerce depended heavily on the activities of middlemen, organized as the Maghribi Traders' Coalition, operating within a relatively fixed rule system: the Merchant's Law. In Greif's account, and in the theoretical and empirical materials I present here, outcomes depend on the extent to which three factors—(1) social exchange, (2) organizational capacity to manage potential conflict associated with exchange, and (3) rule structures— develop ____, thereby constituting a dynamic system of reciprocal influence. A related theoretical ____rk has been developed to explain the dynamics of European integration (Stone Sweet ____dholtz 1997; Stone Sweet and Caporaso 1998*a*).

pursue their interests in coordination with other actors. Systemic change, then, implies the transformation of collective and individual identity.

(Re)Constructing the Polity

It would be a relatively simple task to demonstrate the general relevance of the theoretical model to the field of judicial politics. One could, for example, review the now burgeoning political science scholarship on the political impact of judging around the world.[10] For reasons that inhere in the theory, we would learn that, in any given society, the judiciary's share of total governmental authority and influence varies with the degree to which it possesses and exercises the power to review the lawfulness of activity, public and private. The task is simplified by the fact that political scientists generally study courts, which are fully constituted mechanisms of coercive TDR.

I propose, instead, to examine the impact of TDR on two polities in which judicial power had been initially, and by design, excluded. By 'judicial power' I mean the capacity of a triadic dispute resolver to authoritatively determine the content of a community's normative structure. In my two cases—the international trade regime and the French Fifth Republic—new normative structures—an international treaty, a national constitution—established rules governing relations between specific political actors—states in the GATT, elected officials and state institutions in France. The regular use of TDR led to the mutation of these relations, and new polities were thereby constituted.

I will use the term 'judicialization' as shorthand for this mutation, for—the same thing—the construction of judicial power. Judicialization is a process sustained by the interdependence of dyads and triads, and of rules and strategic behaviour. It is observable, and therefore measurable, as modifications in the conduct of dispute resolution and social exchange. The 'judicialization of dispute resolution' is the process through which a TDR mechanism appears, stabilizes, and develops authority over the normative structure governing exchange in a given community. The 'judicialization of politics' is the process by which triadic law-making progressively shapes the strategic behaviour of political actors engaged in interactions with one another.

A full treatment of the cases is beyond the scope of a single paper.[11] Of necessity, my treatment is schematic and abbreviated, focusing on the

---

[10] After decades of neglect, the field of comparative judicial politics now thrives (for example, Shapiro 1981a; Shapiro and Stone 1994; Tate and Vallinder 1995; Volcansek 1992).

[11] I rely heavily on detailed studies of the judicialization of the GATT system (Hudec 1992; 1993; Stone Sweet 1997) and of the French Fifth Republic (Stone 1992a; 1996).

relationship between specific theoretical predictions and empirical outcomes. The theory asserts that TDR organizes political change so as to facilitate the survival of societies in which individuals interact with each other
on a continuous basis. The theory predicts that, as the scope and intensity of
these interactions increase, so will the demand for the adaptation of normative structure by way of dispute resolution. If and when dyadic dispute
resolution fails to satisfy this demand, there will be pressure to use TDR if a
triadic mechanism exists, or to invent such a mechanism if it does not exist.
Once individuals have moved to the triadic level, the internal dynamics of
TDR will drive processes of judicialization. The dispute resolver will seek to
balance the competing claims of disputants, but will also generate precedent to legitimize decisions. Triadic rule-making will gradually reconfigure
normative structure and, in so doing, reconstruct social relations.

The Judicialization of the International Trade Regime

When the General Agreement on Tariffs and Trade (GATT) entered into
force in 1948 and was institutionalized as an organization, 'anti-legalism'
reigned (Long 1985: 70–1; Hudec 1993: 137). Diplomats excluded lawyers
from GATT organs and opposed litigating violations of the treaty. In the
1950s, TDR emerged in the form of the Panel System. Panels, composed of
between three and five members, usually GATT diplomats, acquired authority through the consent of two disputing states. In the 1970s and 1980s, the
system underwent a process of judicialization. States began aggressively litigating disputes; panels began treating the treaty as enforceable law, and
their own interpretations of that law as authoritative; jurists and trade specialists replaced diplomats on panels. The process generated the conditions
necessary for the emergence of the compulsory system of adjudication now
in place in the World Trade Organization (WTO).

Normative Structure and Dispute Resolution

The GATT is the most comprehensive commercial treaty in history, today
governing more than five-sixths of world trade. In the 1955–74 period, membership jumped from 34 to 100 states; 124 states signed the Final Act of the
Uruguay Round, establishing the WTO, in 1993. The treaty's core provision
is a generalized equal treatment rule, the Most Favored Nation (MFN) principle, which rests on reciprocity: each party to the GATT must provide to
every other party all the advantages provided to other trading partners. The
treaty further prohibits, with some exceptions, import quotas. The organization also supports an inter-state forum for legislating trade law: eight

'rounds' have reduced most tariffs to the point of insignificance and, less successfully, restricted non-tariff barriers to trade.

The treaty exhorts members to settle their disputes dyadically, in accordance with GATT rules. The potential for a trade conflict to move to a triadic stage was implied: if state A could demonstrate that it had suffered damages due to violations of GATT law committed by state B, state A could be authorized by the GATT membership as a whole to withdraw advantages or concessions that it would normally be required to accord state B. Almost immediately, however, member states invented the Panel System to resolve disputes.

As institutionalized in the 1950s, the system blended mediation and consensual adjudication against a backdrop of ongoing dyadic dispute resolution. Defendants could not be compelled to participate in TDR. By denying consent, a state could block the construction of a panel, reject proposed panellists, and refuse to allow a ruling to be reported. Relative to compulsory forms of adjudication, the system appeared grossly inefficient. The original function of panels, however, was to facilitate dyadic conflict resolution, not to punish violators or to make trade law. Diplomats, trade generalists who saw expedience in flexible rules and detriment in rigid ones, sat on panels. When mediation failed, panels could, with the consent of the disputants, resolve conflicts according to relevant treaty provisions.

Before 1970, states did not exploit the connection between TDR and rule-making. But, being both imprecise and rigid, the regime's normative structure proved insufficient to sustain optimal levels of trade over time. The treaty mixes a few hard obligations—the MFN norm and tariff schedules—with a great many statements of principle and aspiration. Despite its flexibility, important GATT provisions could be revised only by unanimous consent. Although the success of the GATT was partly due to normative imprecision—the more vague a rule, the easier it was for states to sign on to it—textual imprecision was often locked in by the unanimity requirement. The tension is obvious. Achieving optimal levels of exchange partly depends on the continuous adaptation of abstract rules to concrete situations, but the GATT legislator was ill-suited to perform this adaptation for the trade regime.

Dyad to Triad

Beginning in 1970, the largest trading states turned to the Panel System not just to resolve their trade conflicts but to make trade policy. Statistics tell part of the story (Appendix). After falling into desuetude in the 1960s—only seven complaints were filed—TDR exploded into prominence afterwards. Of the 207 complaints filed through 1989, 72 per cent were filed after 1969, and 56 per cent after 1979. The four largest trading states—Canada, the European Community (EC), Japan, and the USA—dominated panel proceedings: in the 1980s, over 80 per cent of all disputes registered involved two of these four states.

The expansion of global exchange, and the domestic political consequences of that expansion, broadly explain the renaissance of TDR. Bilateral exchange among the big four—Canada, the EC, Japan, and the USA—rose from $US15 billion in 1959 to $44 billion in 1969, to $234 billion in 1979, to $592 billion in 1989. As trade redistributed resources and employment across productive sectors within national economies, domestic actors mobilized to protect their interests. And as these economies came to produce virtually the same products for export—for example, electronics, automobiles, food products—trade relations were easily interpreted in zero-sum terms.

By 1970, new forms of protectionism had proliferated, the Gold Standard currency regime was rapidly disintegrating, and the American trade deficit had become chronic. The need for clearer rules and better compliance was acute. At the same time, the GATT legislator had failed to liberalize certain crucial sectors—for example, agriculture—to dismantle the mosaic of non-tariff barriers that had emerged in response to tariff reduction—for example, restrictive licensing policies and production standards—and to regulate other practices that distorted trade—for example, subsidies. Led by the USA, which was also groping for ways to reduce its trade deficit, governments turned to the Panel System.[12]

Three general motivations animated the move to TDR. In the vast majority of instances, states initiated complaints in order to induce other states to modify their domestic trading rules. As we will see, GATT panels proved to be a relatively effective means of doing so. Second, states appealed to panels in order to alter, clarify, or make more effective existing GATT rules. This motivation overlaps the first, since virtually all trade disputes are translatable into a general argument about the meaning and application of specific treaty provisions. Disputants worked to persuade panels to adopt their versions of GATT rules, in order to encourage the spread of practices they considered lawful and to discourage practices they considered unlawful. Third, while difficult

---

[12] Disputants tend to litigate what diplomats failed to legislate. Conflicts over agriculture and subsidies paralysed trade negotiations, and they also dominated TDR processes after 1970. Of 115 complaints filed in the 1980s, 51, or 44%, concerned trade in agricultural goods. Of the 44 disputes filed citing one of the GATT codes, 21, or 48%, relied on rules found in the subsidies code.

to verify, governments sometimes participated in TDR to delegitimize—and thus facilitate the revision of—their own trade practices.[13]

To maximize their success, governments had a powerful interest in replacing diplomats and generalists with lawyers and trade specialists. The Americans understood this immediately; the Nixon administration turned GATT litigation over to trade lawyers in 1970. By that year, the enormous complexity of trade disputes—the resolution of which requires determining (1) the extent to which a specific domestic law or administrative practice conforms with treaty provisions, and (2) the extent to which, in cases of non-conformity, such a law or practice had caused, or might cause, trade distortions—was far beyond the capacity of anyone but the lawyer and the expert. Once introduced by the Americans, lawyerly discourse perpetuated itself. Lawyers filed detailed legal briefs attacking or defending particular national policies; faced with detailed questions, panels gave detailed answers; lawyers then understood the reasoning supporting such answers as guidelines for future litigation strategies. The EC and Japan initially resisted the move to legalism; but they became active participants after being bombarded with complaints by the USA and Canada. By the early 1980s, all of the major trading states had armed their Geneva staffs with permanent legal counsels.

Triadic Governance

In activating TDR, GATT members delegated to the Panel System an authority that is inherently governmental. As panels exercised this authority, they generated three sets of political outcomes; these outcomes can be explained only by attending to the dynamics of TDR.

First, panels altered the terms of global exchange by provoking, with their decisions, the modification of national trading rules. If complied with, every decision declaring a national rule or practice inconsistent with GATT rules concretely affects the lives of importers, exporters, consumers, and producers. Statistics (Appendix) show that activating TDR worked in favour of plaintiff states: plaintiffs enjoyed a success rate of 77 per cent in the 1948–89

---

[13] In 1988, the USA instituted proceedings against the EC's payment regime for oil-seed processing. A panel ruled that the programme both discriminated against foreign processors and functioned as an indirect subsidy for EC producers. France, invoking the consensus norm, sought to suppress the decision but the EC adopted the ruling over France's objection. The EC then replaced the payment system with a new one. In effect, the EC had used TDR to delegitimize an outmoded, costly programme of which France had blocked revision within internal EC lawmaking processes. Complaint #179, US v. EC (22 April 1988). Complaints have been assembled and numbered chronologically in Hudec (1993: Appendix). I use Hudec's reference system to refer to cases in this and subsequent notes.

period, rising to 85 per cent in the 1980s. The rate of compliance with adverse decisions was 74 per cent in the 1980–9 period.

To resolve many of the most complex disputes, panels had no choice but to reach far into national jurisdictions. Thus, a panel ruled that a US law providing a special administrative remedy for patent infringement claims involving imported goods violated the GATT since defendants stood a better chance of winning in district courts.[14] To arrive at this decision, panellists investigated US litigation rates and judicial outcomes, concluding that biases in the administrative procedure constituted a discriminatory bias affecting trade. In separate cases, panels required Canada to force provincial governments to remove taxes on foreign gold coins, and to force provincial liquor boards to change regulatory practices favouring domestic alcoholic beverages.[15]

Panels reinforced their influence over policy outcomes by elaborating guidelines for state compliance. In explaining why a given national practice was or was not inconsistent with GATT obligations, panels suggested GATT-consistent versions of the practices in question: such behaviour inheres in triadic rule-making. In 1986, to take just one instance, the EC attacked the Japanese system of taxation for alcoholic beverages.[16] The system, which classified products into dozens of categories corresponding to different tax rates, resulted in importers paying higher taxes than Japanese producers for similar products. The panel declared the system to be inconsistent with the treaty, and announced a general rule: national tax schemes must treat all 'directly competitive' products equally. It then elaborated a hypothetical system based on equal treatment, demonstrating precisely what a lawful system would look like. The Japanese subsequently adopted a system similar to the panel's.

Second, in response to the exploitation of TDR by states for their own political purposes, panels reinvented themselves as judges, the authoritative interpreters of the regime's normative structure. This process, predicted by the model, can be tracked and measured. As the number and complexity of complaints grew, panels produced longer decisions and increasingly precise interpretations of treaty provisions.[17] In complicity with GATT litigators, citations of past decisions became increasingly common and expected.

---

[14] Complaint #162, EC v. US (29 April 1987).

[15] Complaint #132, South Africa v. Canada (3 July 1984); complaint #139, EC v. Canada (12 February 1985).   [16] Complaint #154, EC v. Japan (6 Nov. 1986).

[17] In the 1948–69 period, the average length of reported rulings was 7 pages; in the 1970–9 period, the average length rose to 15 pages; after 1985, the average reached 48 pages (Hudec 1992:11).

Once constructed as a precedent-based discourse about the meaning of GATT rules, panel decisions became a fundamental source of those rules. Such rule-making took place despite the absence of a doctrine of *stare decisis* in international law, and despite the refusal of the member states to formally recognize the precedential value of decisions. Certain treaty provisions—for example, the MFN norm, rules governing taxation and quotas—emerged as sophisticated, relatively autonomous domains of legal discourse.[18] In these domains, rules can today be understood *only* in light of a dense and nuanced case law. Although the substance of this law is far beyond the scope of this article, panels ratcheted up national responsibility to justify any claimed exceptions to liberal trading rules which, among other things, served to expand the grounds for future complaints.

Panels also generated rules governing their own jurisdiction (Hudec 1993: 258–65). By the end of the 1980s a stable case law asserted that, among other things, panels could:

- not only review the consistency of national acts with the treaty but could also detail what kinds of similar, if hypothetical, acts might violate GATT rules;
- announce answers to questions not raised by plaintiffs but which were nevertheless relevant to other trade disputes; and
- report a ruling even if the dispute on which it was based had become moot—for example, as a result of prior dyadic settlement—in order to clarify GATT rules and thus facilitate future dyadic and triadic dispute resolution.

Third, judicialization processes reconstructed how states understood the nature of their own regime. States reacted to the development of a rule-oriented mode of governance not by suppressing it but by adjusting to it. Their lawyers filed more and increasingly legalistic complaints, and their diplomats ratified judicialization in official agreements. Thus, the 1979 'Understanding' on dispute settlement placed the GATT's system on legal footing for the first time, codified dispute settlement procedures, and gave legal force to panel reports. In 1981, citing the overwhelming complexity of litigation facing panellists, states permitted the establishment of a Legal

---

[18] Breaking down GATT complaints filed in the 1980s with reference to the article of the Agreement in dispute provides some indication of the relative density of these areas. In 115 filings, disputants invoked specific parts of the Agreement 212 times. Four areas of the law account for 71% of total claims: the MFN norm (Arts 1 and 2, 21%); non-discrimination in taxation and regulation (Art. 3, 10%); elimination of quotas (arts. 11, 13, 34%); and nullification or impairment of benefits (Art. 23, 6%). Of the 66 instances in which the special codes were invoked, the codes on subsidies were involved 41 times (62%). See Stone Sweet (1997).

Office charged with rationalizing procedures and providing support for panel members. And in the Uruguay Round of 1986–92, states asked an autonomous group of experts to study how TDR could be strengthened. The fruit of their efforts was the legal system of the WTO.

The Final Act of the Uruguay Round transformed the GATT into the WTO. The treaty, which is—implicitly—treated as a form of a constitutional law, provides for a system of compulsory adjudication of disputes. The new rules: automatically confer jurisdiction on panels upon the reception of a complaint; no longer permit unilateral vetoes of any stage by either party; and provide for a broad range of measures to punish non-compliance. An independent appellate body is charged with handling appeals from panels. The body is to be composed of seven members who possess 'demonstrated expertise in law'.

Undeniably, the move from consensual to compulsory TDR could not have taken place without a convergence in the preferences of the most powerful trading states. The US had advocated more efficient dispute settlement since the 1970s. The Americans had even taken measures in domestic law to unilaterally punish those who blocked or refused to comply with GATT decisions; and the move provoked the EU to adopt similar measures. Facing a trading world in which GATT rules might be enforced unilaterally by the most powerful states, the rest of the world joined the USA and Europe in working to strengthen multilateralism.

But, if converging state interests were crucial to the enhancement of TDR in the GATT, judicialization generated the context necessary for that convergence. Judicialization is socialization. As states gained experience with dispute settlement, as panels performed their dispute resolution functions, as a stable case law enhanced legal certainty, GATT members could afford to view triadic rulemaking as a useful, cost-effective guarantor of regime reciprocity. In the 1980s, states did not consider abolishing the Panel System but debated how best to enhance it. By the end of the decade, a collective future without effective TDR was no longer a serious option.

The Judicialization of the Fifth Republic

The 1958 Constitution is France's fifteenth since the Great Revolution. Like its predecessors, the constitution enshrined an official state ideology, the 'general will', the twin corollaries of which are statutory sovereignty and the prohibition of judicial review. In the 1970s, a process of judicialization began. Legislators turned to the Constitutional Council to resolve their disputes about the constitutionality of pending legislation; the Council responded by developing the constitution as a system of substantive governing policy-making. As these interactions intensified, the Council became an active participant in the legislative process; legislators became active participants in the construction of constitutional law; and a new ideology, that of constitutionalism, replaced the ideology of the general will.

Normative Structure and Dispute Resolution

Until the 1970s, the history of French constitutional law was barely more than a chronicle of how state structures were successively remade by the alternation in power of republicans, restored monarchs, emperors, and generals. As normative structures, French constitutions were brittle. They legitimized the authority of those—temporarily—in control of the state, but were incapable of organizing enduring relationships between those who competed for that control. The Fifth Republic, imposed in the midst of virtual civil war, initially appeared just as brittle. A blueprint for Gaullist rule, the constitution was not broadly welcomed or shared by the country's political elites. The political parties of the left voted to reject the document in a parliamentary ballot they lost.

As ratified by popular referendum, the constitution departed from republican traditions in two ways. First, it redistributed law-making power away from parliament—the National Assembly and the Senate—and to the executive—the President of the Republic and the Government, that is, the Prime Minister and ministers of state collectively. Statutes proposed by the government were meant to be ratified by the legislature. Second, it established a new state organ, the Constitutional Council, to police this redistribution. The founders did not conceive of the Council as a judicial body. In contrast to all other European constitutional courts, the Council does not hear appeals from the judiciary or from individuals, and prior legal training or judicial experience is not a requirement for membership.[19] The founders rejected proposals to include in the constitution a bill of rights over which the Council would exercise jurisdiction, for fear of subverting statutory sovereignty.

In its original form, the constitution enabled but narrowly circumscribed TDR. According to these rules, any of four officials—the President, the Prime Minister, the President of the Assembly, or the President of the Senate—may ask the Council to review the constitutionality of a statute but only *after* that statute has been definitively adopted by Parliament and *before* its entry

---

[19] The Council is composed of nine members; the President of the Republic, the President of the Assembly, and the President of the Senate each appoints three members who serve nine-year terms.

into force. If the Council determines that a statute's provisions have been adopted according to procedures that are inconsistent with constitutional rules governing the legislative process, it annuls those provisions, blocking their entry into force. Once a referral has been received, the Council decides within a maximum delay of 30 days. In striking contrast to North American constitutional judicial review, only statutes that have not yet been promulgated are open to review in France; once in force, statutes are immune from judicial scrutiny.

Two constitutional revisions modified the Council's jurisdiction. In a 1971 decision, the Council, prompted by a referral of the President of the Senate and publicly encouraged by law professors and the media, annulled a piece of government-sponsored legislation for the first time. In relying on a rights text, it effectively incorporated a bill of rights, partly unwritten and ill-defined, into the constitution. In 1974, a Constitutional Congress voted to extend to parliamentary oppositions—formally, to any 60 deputies or senators—the power to refer statutes to the Council for review. Combined, these changes radically expanded the rule-making capacities of TDR. Henceforth, any partisan dispute about legislation, once translated into a dispute about constitutional rights, could be used to activate TDR.

Dyad to Triad

In the 1958–70 period, the Council rendered only six decisions, siding each time with the Prime Minister in disputes between the government and parliament over their respective legislative powers.[20] Since 1974, the Council's caseload has been constituted, almost exclusively, by opposition referrals alleging the unconstitutionality of legislation proposed by the government and the parliamentary majority.[21] When in power, parties of the left and the right have decried the Council's growing authority over the law-making processes; and both have threatened to abolish the organ in order to restore 'the sovereignty of the general will'. In opposition, left and right have exploited, without apology, the capacity of TDR to obstruct majority rule.

Oppositions are attracted to TDR for a simple reason: the Council is the only state institution capable of altering legislative outcomes that is not controlled by the government and the parliamentary majority. Referrals extend the legislative process to include another stage: triadic rule-making. The

---

[20] In 1962, the body also refused to rule on a complaint made by the President of the Senate.

[21] By 'parliamentary majority' I mean those parties that support the government in parliamentary votes.

move to TDR alters the strategic context of French policy-making, redistrib-
uting political initiative in the opposition's favour and reducing the influence of the government and the majority over legislative outcomes. When
the opposition activates TDR, the government and the majority are placed
on the defensive, forced to participate in processes they do not control.

After 1974 referrals quickly became quasi-systematic (Appendix). Since
that year, opposition parties have referred every annual budget and, since
1981, virtually every major piece of legislation. In the 1974–80 period, the
Giscard presidency, 46 laws were referred to the Council, or 6.6 a year; in
the 1981–7 period, the first Mitterrand presidency, 92 laws, 13.1 a year, were
referred. The average number of references has remained above 10 per year
ever since. Expressed in different terms, since 1981 about 30 per cent of all
legislation adopted has been referred,[22] a huge ratio since most legislation
is politically non-controversial and does not lead to a formal roll-call vote at
the time of adoption. Substantively, the vast majority of referrals allege that
the referred law violates one or more constitutional rights capable of being
recognized by the Council. Virtually costless, referrals work: since 1981, more
than half—57 per cent—-of all referrals resulted in a Council annulment.

As predicted by the model, the regular use of TDR produced a self-
sustaining process of judicialization. Referrals provoked the Council to
construct the constitution, that is, to justify annulments in terms of an
authoritative interpretation of constitutional rules; and the construction of
constitutional law provoked more referrals. Also predicted—see the discussion of shift 1, above—triadic rule-making exercised a powerful pedagogical
influence on the strategic behaviour of law-makers.

Most important, triadic rule-making generated a stable politics of
deterrence and anticipatory reaction. As the web of constitutional constraints on law-making expanded and grew more intricate, the government
became susceptible to a kind of constitutional blackmail. The opposition
learned that it could enhance its legislative influence by threatening to refer
a bill under discussion to the Council unless the government and majority
agreed to amend the legislation as the opposition saw fit. In the 1980s, parliament has adopted hundreds of amendments, rewriting dozens of important
bills, pursuant to constitutional debates triggered by such threats (Stone
1992*a*; 1996; formal model in Vanberg 1998*a*).

As constitutional referrals, threats to refer, annulments, and
constitutional blackmail became commonplace elements of legislative
process, law-makers had every reason to upgrade their legal expertise.

---

[22] Excluding the statutory ratification of international agreements.

The government, aided by its legal adviser, the Council of State, began to review the constitutionality of all draft bills before submitting them to parliament.[23] And the major political parties turned to young law professors—specialists in 'the new constitutional law'—to help them draft referrals, respond to referrals, and to attack or defend bills on the floor of parliament.

Triadic Governance

The move to triadic governance generated three sets of outcomes that deserve our attention.

First, the Council evolved into a powerful policy-maker, a kind of adjunct legislative body with the capacity to veto, amend, and even propose legislative provisions. Annulments have blocked or radically altered a score of major legislative initiatives. In 1982, the Council vetoed the left's nationalization bill, ruling that the legislation would not have provided sufficient compensation to expropriated stockholders. In 1984, it vetoed key provisions of the press law, thwarting the left's bid to counter the rapid concentration of the newspaper industry. In 1986, it blocked the right's attempts to deregulate the press and broadcast media. And in 1993, it gutted the right's attempts to restrict immigration and to expand administrative authority to expel asylum seekers.[24]

Further, the Council, in clarifying exactly why a given legislative provision is unconstitutional, provoked new legislative processes designed to 'correct' unconstitutional bills. These processes serve to implement the Council's rule-making. Thus, in its decision on nationalizations, the Council told the government exactly how stockholders must be compensated. The government complained that its legislative authority had been pre-empted, but dutifully incorporated the Council's preferred compensation formula into a new bill. The changes raised the cost of nationalizations by 25 per cent but secured promulgation. In more than 20 decisions on the penal codes—statutes specifying crimes, penalties for committing crimes, and judicial procedures—the Council has vetoed dozens of proposed legislative modifications while laying down precise rules governing how these codes must or must not be revised. The opposition has given agency to these rules by systematically threatening to refer new reforms that do not sufficiently respect the dictates of the Council's case law.

Second, the Council reinvented itself as a court. Systematically implicated in the legislature's policy disputes, the Council worked to portray its

[23] See Stone (1996) for details.
[24] Respectively, Conseil (1982a; 1984b; 1986a, b; 1993).

decision-making as inherently judicial: a formal exercise in reasoning about rules. Council decisions initially took the form of a series of terse syllogisms, containing virtually no argumentation. In the late 1970s the Council began producing longer, more carefully crafted decisions, responding point by point to arguments made in referrals.[25] Predictably, referrals lengthened and became more sophisticated. As decisions accumulated in areas of intensive legislative activity, technical domains of case law inevitably emerged. The Council developed an array of linguistic formulas—one of several functional equivalents of precedent in civil law systems—which it repeated again and again to clarify its positions; and it began to reference, at first subtly, then more overtly, the commentaries of leading legal scholars. In the late 1970s a new autonomous field of legal scholarship emerged, devoted to the doctrinal analysis of the Council's case law. Constitutional law now flourishes in the academy.

Third, triadic rule-making reconstructed the very nature of the French polity. Since the Revolution, the constitution has been understood to be a law that enabled state officials to govern, while unenforceable. Republican constitutions proclaimed statutory supremacy and prohibited judicial review of statute: perhaps a moot point since constitutions did not contain rights provisions, and public liberties that were recognized in statute could be rescinded by majority vote. In the absence of TDR, French constitutional law was static; it developed no dynamic life of its own. Today, the constitution is a living law that binds all public authorities in their interactions with each other and with private individuals.

For the first time in history, French constitutional law is case law: the law is what the Council interprets it to be, despite the formal absence of a doctrine of *stare decisis* in the civil law tradition. In consequence, French legislative politics, which operated on the basis of majority rule, has been reconstituted as a constitutional politics, which operates as a continuously evolving, rule-based discourse governing the exercise of legislative authority. In this politics, legislators continuously incorporate into the language and practice of policy-making a vocabulary and grammar of constitutional law. Law-makers do so in order to maximize their own political effectiveness. In their interactions with each other, they debate and take authoritative decisions about the constitutionality of statutes before them. This inherently

[25] Council decisions consist of numbered paragraphs. In the 1974–9 period, the average length of decisions, calculated annually, was 7 paragraphs, with a high of 8 in 1975. In the 1980–6 period, the average length of decisions, calculated annually, was 23, never falling below 13, with a high of 42 paragraphs in 1983 (Stone 1992*a*: 101).

'judicial' behaviour, institutionalized in the 1980s, is now a ubiquitous feature of the legislative process.[26] Referrals transfer these constitutional debates to the Council. In this way, legislators participate in the construction of the constitution, providing the legal materials for constitutional adjudication, and legitimizing the Council's political authority.

Last but not least, judicialization also transformed the nature and function of the French judiciary (Cour de Cassation 1995). As constitutional review steadily undermined legislative sovereignty, judges asserted their own authority to interpret statutes and enforce the constitution. In the early 1980s, the supreme court—the Cour de Cassation—developed a rule that requires civil judges to do what traditional constitutional orthodoxy forbids, namely, to rewrite by interpretation statutory provisions so that they conform to constitutional law.[27] Litigants now not only invoke constitutional rights in their arguments, they sometimes win. Recently, France's high administrative court, the Council of State, has begun converting its own 'general principles of law'—a body of judge-made restrictions on administrative action that includes 'individual liberty', 'equality before the law', and 'freedom of conscience'—into equivalent rights developed by the Council.

After two centuries, the French constitution is judicially enforceable law.

Conclusion

One virtue of the model is its inherent capacity to translate between micro-level effects or outcomes and macro-level effects or outcomes, simultaneously. The theory generates testable propositions about behaviour and outcomes at both levels. These propositions can be evaluated by focusing empirical attention—at one point in time, at one level of analysis—on the strategic interaction of individuals, the micro level, or the development of normative structure, the macro level, while holding the other level constant. The theory implies, however, that we will not be able to explain systemic

---

[26] In parliament, formalized rituals, in the form of parliamentary 'motions of unconstitutionality', organize deliberations. The motions require the chamber to debate and rule on the bill's constitutionality. The opposition, the government, and the majority support their respective positions by citing constitutional texts, legal scholarship, and the Council's existing case law. If the motion passes, the bill is declared unconstitutional and it is killed. Because votes are governed by party discipline, motions never pass. In the 1981-7 period, the National Assembly debated and voted on 94 motions of unconstitutionality; the Council rendered 93 decisions over the same period (Stone 1996).

[27] In the presence of a law deemed unconstitutional, all that judges can do is correct the law by rewriting it, since a law once promulgated is immune to review.

change adequately if we privilege, systematically and a priori, the ca͟u͟ͅ importance of one level vis-à-vis the other. The point deserves elaboration.

I have argued that how systems of governance emerge and evolve has everything to do with the interdependence of rules and strategic behaviour. If I am right, shift 2 is partly the province of neo-rationalism and game theory. Rational individuals maximize utility by adjusting behaviour, including how they reason through and talk about norms, to changes in rules of the game. In clarifying the scope and content of existing constraints, triadic rule-making shapes how players calculate the pay-offs of available strategies. Stage 3—the triadic dispute resolver's response to the dilemma posed by the delegation of political authority—can also be understood in neo-rationalist terms. Her interest in her own survival leads the triadic figure to behave in predictable ways.

The analysis also suggests that neo-rationalism alone is inadequate to the task of explaining systemic change. Game theorists rely heavily on structure, conceived as fixed rules, to provide the conditions necessary for predicting outcomes from strategic interaction. Although the macro level is an integral part of any game-theoretic analysis, all the action that matters actually occurs at the micro level. Game theorists openly admit that they have barely begun to theorize the dynamics of institutional change (see Tsebelis 1990: Ch. 4). This article suggest that to the extent that neo-rationalism does not account for crucial mechanisms of social change, including the relatively autonomous, independent impact of normative discourse, its explanatory scope is limited. Put in terms of my theory, the value of neo-rationalism declines as we move from the right to the left hemisphere of the circle (Fig. 1.1).

The social world produces, consolidates, and stabilizes structure in various ways. I have focused here only on the capacity of TDR to generate an iterated, organized, and therefore *social* process of reasoning about rules. The theory predicts that, once constituted, triadic governance will organize the future by constructing and then managing the causal relationships between social exchange, conflict, and normative development. Once these relationships are established, TDR perpetuates a discourse about the pertinence of rules to behaviour, and this discourse gradually penetrates and is absorbed into those repertoires of reasoning and action that constitute political agency. Read this way, stages 4 and 1 are partly the dominion of students of institutionalization and structuration. Organizational theorists (Powell and Dimaggio 1991), social psychologists (Rosenberg 1995), constructivists (Giddens 1984; Onuf 1989; 1994; Wendt 1992), culturalists (Eckstein 1988), and public law, 'new institutionalists' (Smith 1988), reject the neo-rationalist assumption that the essential properties of individual actors, or of rationality itself, are exogenously fixed or inherent. Instead, individual identity—how actors form, comprehend, express, and pursue their preferences—is understood to be socially constituted and therefore capable of being socially reconstituted.

My theory, in effect, incorporates the constructivist point, without denying that self-conscious, strategic behaviour at the individual level is a permanent fixture of social life. Self-interested behaviour, in fact, animates the model. But the efficacy—or rationality—of this behaviour is heavily conditioned by macro-level structure; and components of this structure are significantly independent of micro-level phenomena.

If I have correctly identified the causal linkages connecting dyadic exchange, TDR, and normative structure, then those who initiate TDR cannot meaningfully control the outcomes produced by triadic rule-making. Viewed over time, from the *ex ante* perspective of those who contract and delegate, outcomes will not mechanically reflect the distribution of preferences and capabilities among the actors within a given community. Rather, because triadic rule-making secures and enhances the relative autonomy of normative structure—and of normative discourse—vis-à-vis actors, the world it builds is only partly predictable by them, and can therefore be only partly intended. Put differently, the world of triadic governance evolves according to the logic of *path dependence*, manifested by the increasing dominance of triadic rule-making—for example, case law and precedent—over the content of normative structure, and *lock-in*, manifested by the institutionalization of those forms of social exchange that best respond to the evolution of this rulemaking (for applications to political analysis, see Pierson 1996a; 1997).

To return to my cases: the theory predicts that, given certain specified conditions, a sustained move to TDR will reconstruct, gradually but inevitably, the nature of governance. In the two polities examined here, and in more formal tests of the theory,[28] this prediction was borne out. States and French politicians began as jealous guardians of their own sovereignty, deeply hostile to judges and to legalism; in pursuit of their own political objectives, they delegated meaningful political authority to triadic dispute resolvers; and triadic rule-making reconfigured the Fifth Republic and the trade regime. The evidence further suggests that the move to triadic governance stabilized and made both polities more resilient in the face of potentially debilitating

---

[28] Stone Sweet and Brunell (1998a) and Stone Sweet and Caporaso (1998a, b) test a series of specific hypotheses derived from the theory in their explanation of European legal integration, the process through which a trans-national legal system for the European Community has been constructed.

conflict. Propositions about the future are also suggested. There will be no French Sixth Republic; rather, the French are already living in the new, more supple republic institutionalized by triadic governance. And in the WTO a powerful supranational governmental authority will emerge: litigation will steadily rise; and judges will generate an expansive legal discourse that will gradually reshape the inter-state discourse on trade.

To conclude, it bears repeating that systemic change is explained, but not preordained, by the theory.[29] Judicialization processes could have been blocked or reversed; states and parliamentarians could have stopped activating TDR; they could have renegotiated new normative structures to govern their relations; they could have abolished judicial power. But, unwilling to forgo the benefits of TDR and unable to agree on alternative arrangements, they did not.

Instead, they constructed triadic governance and triadic governance reconstructed them.

---

[29] See note 7 and corresponding text. Further, I have left under-theorized, or ignored altogether, certain patterns of behaviour that are of obvious importance. First, I had little to say about why and how actors negotiate the terms of their exchange in the first place, although the more commitment-based are the rule-structures they build, the more push for judicialization we can expect; I thank Nicholas Onuf for reminding me of this point. Second, the kind of perpetual motion machine theorized, one that produces ever higher levels of legal discourse and triadic authority, has not functioned in most polities in the world, past or present. Two families of negative cases were nonetheless identified. Actors may be willing to tolerate, or even cultivate, dyadic conflict without moving to TDR. In some cases, as when their respective identities are constituted in opposition, disputants may have a higher interest in maintaining the conflict. In other cases like zero-sum situations, for example, no joint gains issuing from dispute resolution are possible; and in still others, neither party may be willing to budge from original, fixed, and radically opposed positions—there is no negotiating space for the triadic entity to exploit. A second class of negative cases concerns instances in which the move to TDR does not tend towards rule-making but to rule-reinforcement and social control. Finally, I provide no theory of judicial rule-making, that is, how the dispute resolver interprets and makes rules. Nonetheless, core elements of such a theory are implied in the 'Constructing Governance' section (Shift 3, and note and corresponding text), and in my treatment of the two case studies.

Appendix

Table 1.1. Dispute settlement activity in the GATT, 1948–1989

	1948–59	1960–69	1970–79	1980–89	Totals
Complaints					
Complaints filed	53	7	32	115	207
Settled: conceded by defendant	22	2	12	28	64
Settled: withdrawn by plaintiff	10	0	5	40	55
Settled: panel rulings	21	5	15	47	88
Panel activity					
Panels convened	25	5	22	59	111
Rulings rendered	21	5	15	47	88
Published opinions	9	4	14	19	46
Rulings					
No violation by defendant	6	0	7	7	20
Violation by defendant	15	5	8	40	68

Source: Adapted from data presented in Hudec (1993: Ch. 11).

Table 1.2. Dispute settlement 1980–1988: Compliance among selected states

State	Complaints against	Adverse ruling	Compliance*	Non-compliance**
US	36	9	6	4
EC	30	9	5	3
Canada	9	6	4	2
Japan	14	4	4	0
All other states	14	7	7	0
TOTALS	103	35	26	9

* Includes promises to comply made by defendant state. ** Includes three instances of non-compliance on part of the EC; the disputes were settled to the plaintiff's state's satisfaction after subsequent trade negotiations.

Source: Adapted from data presented in Hudec (1992: 34–5).

Table 1.3. The review activities of the French Constitutional Council, 1958–1993

	1959–73	1974–80	1981–7	1988–93
Referrals	9	66	136	98
President	0	0	0	0
Prime Minister	6	2	0	4
President of the Assembly	0	2	0	1
President of the Senate	3	0	2	3
60 deputies, or 60 senators	0	62	134	90
*Decisions**	9	46	92	70
Censuring text	7	14	49	38
Favourable to text	2	32	43	32

* Due to multiple referrals, the number of referrals since 1974 is larger than the number of decisions.

Source: Stone (1996).

2

Judicial Law-making and Precedent

The relationship between judicial activity and law-making is a crucial question for any social science of courts because law-making, or the ongoing adaptation of rules, is the most salient activity of all organs of government. In Western legal systems, it can hardly be denied that courts make rules all of the time, since these activities are minutely recorded in case law, and thus it is impossible to deny that judges are political actors. Nonetheless, the assertion that judges engage in a mode of law-making that is exclusive to adjudication, which sets them apart from other law-makers or the 'political' branches and strictly limits their law-making discretion, typically follows. This is the method of law-making associated with the rule of precedent and the common law doctrine *stare decisis*. In this chapter, we examine some of the problems posed by this formulation. As important, both pieces address, in different but complementary ways, a great paradox: how can it be that judicial decision-making constantly succeeds in changing law while being governed by pre-existing law?

Towards a Theory of *Stare Decisis*

Those who wish to assert that judges are political actors engaged in policy-making must confront the claim that judges employ modes of decision-making peculiar to themselves, setting them apart from politics and compelling them to follow the law rather than make it (see Levy 1988). In one particular legal realm, it has been impossible for the legal academy to camouflage judicial law-making by calling it 'interpretation'. Even in the most conventional view, the Anglo-American common law is case law not statutory law, that is, law made by judges not legislators. One of the most noble accomplishments of legal doublethink is its ability to refer to the common law as judge-made law while at the same time asserting as a general and universal proposition that judges apply rather than make law, and thereby are to be distinguished from politicians. The principal mode of screening this obvious contradiction has been to assert that common-law judges follow a special set of rules of decision, called *stare decisis*, which puts them outside of politics and prevents them from making personal policy choices. If it can be shown that *stare decisis* is not a mode of decision-making peculiar to common law or all judges but rather a set of procedures and techniques common to all policy-makers, then judicial law-making is more clearly revealed.

Stare decisis treats, in any given area of law, each judicial decision as a potential precedent for the next round of litigation or, rather, treats the body of rules and reasoning announced in previous cases as binding upon the judge deciding the current case. Like cases shall be decided alike. Where a new case is not exactly like the old ones, legal reasoning—that is, reason by analogy—will yield results most consonant with the previous cases. In this way, judges may not simply decide each case as they choose but must decide it according to the established case law. Yet it is acknowledged that the substantive rules of common law do change over time. This change is attributed not to judicial policy discretion but to the application, in a succession of cases, of stable common law principles to changing circumstances. The law changes. The law is judge-made. *Stare decisis*, however, magically separates the judges from the politics of policy choice that characterizes other law-makers.

Shapiro (1965), in a piece titled 'Stability and Change in Judicial Decision-Making: Incrementalism or *Stare Decisis*',[1] sought to show that *stare decisis*, far from being a unique set of rules for judicial decision-making, was in reality only a peculiar terminology for expressing a decision-making strategy followed by all policy-makers. In work that was eventually to win him the Nobel Prize in Economics, Herbert Simon set out a theory of incremental decision-making elaborated most notably in a famous book by March and Simon (1958), later paralleled in slightly different language in work by Braybrooke and Lindblom (1963). Borrowing from Cyert and March (1963), Shapiro's article summed up the techniques of incrementalism in the following way:

1. Multiple, changing, acceptable-level goals. The criterion of choice is that the alternative selected meet all of the demands—goals—of the coalition.
2. An approximate sequential consideration of alternatives. The first satisfactory alternative evoked is accepted. Where an existing policy satisfies

---

[1] The piece was published in *Law in Transition Quarterly*, a short-lived journal that is unobtainable in most libraries. It was substantially reproduced as a section of the first chapter of the book *Supreme Court and Administrative Agencies* (Shapiro 1968).

the goals, there is little search for alternatives. When failure occurs, search is intensified.

3. The organization seeks to avoid uncertainty by following regular procedures and a policy of reacting to feedback rather than forecasting the environment.

4. The organization uses standard operating procedures and rules of thumb to make and implement choices. In the short run these procedures dominate the decisions made.

Point 4 was modified by adding a notion of themes borrowed from Lindblom. Instead of citing any rule at all, the decision-maker may offer a number of factors to be taken into account in reaching a decision without specifying weights or priorities among them. Rules of thumb are rules stated as short-term, tentative, and approximate guides subject to frequent modification on the basis of feedback rather than as eternal verities. Decision-makers will mix themes and rules of thumb to give themselves decisional freedom at crisis points, while handling myriad routine decisions more routinely.

Incrementalism was contrasted to 'synoptic' decision-making, that is, processes of decision in which all information about the facts bearing on the matter has been gathered, all values or preferences of the decision-maker have been identified and prioritized, all policy alternatives that might achieve those values under those factual conditions have been considered, and the single best policy is finally chosen. Incrementalism is claimed to be a more rational strategy than synopticism for a number of reasons. It takes account of the ascending marginal costs of acquiring more and more complete facts, more and more exactly stated and prioritized values, and a longer and longer list of less and less plausible policy alternatives. These are costs that synopticism leaves out of account. Incrementalism also takes into account the fact that public policy decisions typically take place under conditions of considerable uncertainty both about existing facts and about what causes will lead to what effects. Taking small steps and waiting for feedback before taking more steps reduces the risks generated by such uncertainties. And incrementalism eases the path of collective decision-making, where it is unlikely that the prioritized lists of values of each participating decision-maker will exactly coincide with that of every other, even if each individual were prepared to make such a list. Instead, incrementalism specifies stopping the decision-making process as soon as a solution is discovered that each of the decision-makers is willing to accept. Such a process 'satisfices' everyone, in Simon's terms, and saves on the rising marginal costs or impossibility of reaching a decision that would fully satisfies each individual's value sets.

The task was to show that the rules or practices of *stare decisis* were simply those of incrementalism stated in other terms. Judges are to keep doing what they had done in the past, that is, to follow precedent, unless a new case reveals trouble or incompleteness in past policy. In such cases the advocates and the judges are not to bring forward every fact, value, and policy alternative that might bear on curing the trouble. Strict rules of evidence and pleading limit what is to be considered to those matters nearest to what has been considered in the past. All common lawyers know that the best way to get judges to do something new is to show them that it is so close to what they have been doing all along that they could claim that it was what they have been doing all along. It is precisely this emphasis on small-step changes that allows scholars and judges to insist that the common law changes to meet changing circumstances, but that judges, unlike legislators, are not engaged in policy-making choices. The famous reasoning by analogy so celebrated by the high priests of the legal academy is precisely this emphasis on small step change—if not the same as before at least as much like what came before as possible. Similarly, we have the famous common law virtue of reaching new rules not at one fell swoop but by 'the case-by-case process of inclusion and exclusion', that is, judicial small steps with further litigation as feedback. Finally, new common law rules are commonly the product not of one decision but of a string of decisions, and often by multi-judge courts with personnel changing over time. Thus, they typically are collective decisions that 'satisficed', that is, were good enough to garner a necessary number of judicial votes but not necessarily anyone's perfect result.

Shapiro's initial article was designed only to bolster the political jurisprudence claim that judges were engaged in politics: common law judges, far from employing a peculiarly legal decision-making procedure, were engaged in precisely the same incremental decision-making strategy that one would expect of any set of collective policy-makers pushed by efficiency considerations.

The second piece in this series was 'Decentralized Decision-Making in the Law of Torts' (Shapiro 1970). Initially incremental decision theory had been introduced as an aspect of the study of organizations. At that time the study of political organizations and/or bureaucratic polities was flourishing. If judges and courts were to be studied as a part and parcel of politics, it would follow that courts, too, should be approached as organizations. As we argue in Chapter 4, one organizational way of looking at courts is in terms of a hierarchy running from a base of multiple trial courts to an apex of highest, or final, appellate court. One form of *stare decisis* is vertical: 'lower' courts following the decisions of 'higher' courts. But another form of *stare decisis* involves a court following its own previous decisions, or even the decisions of other courts to which it is not hierarchically subordinated. If we combine a concern for organizational behaviour with an interest in this 'horizontal' *stare decisis*, an interesting line of inquiry or research arena is suggested.

Most students of organizations assume in one way or another that the activities of organizational units at the same level in a hierarchy are coordinated vertically, through monitoring and commands from above and through resource dependencies. Our fascination with Weberian hierarchies tends to direct our attention away from possible horizontal coordinating devices in which units at the same level communicate directly with one another. Those who begin not with organizations but with *stare decisis*, in its horizontal as well as vertical forms, will immediately see that if courts are organizations, then horizontal *stare decisis* is a means of coordinating communication among units at the same level in hierarchical court organizations. Now let us add a standard American political science concern with federalism. We can easily see the national courts of a unitary state as a hierarchical organization. How are we to conceive of all of the member State courts collectively in a federal polity such as the USA? The State courts of each State, considered separately, are hierarchical organizations. The State courts of all the States together might not be considered parts of a single organization at all, although the very concept of federalism tells us that they are somehow or other parts of a larger whole.

What American lawyers knew all along, however, was that State courts frequently cited decisions of courts of other States as a routine part of the practice of *stare decisis*. They also knew that while the various bodies of common law, such as tort, contract, and property law, of some American States differed somewhat from that of other States, they were far more alike than different.

One of the great advantages of the law and courts field within political science is that it lies at the intersection of social science and law scholarship. A lot of serendipitous collisions occur at that intersection. If you combine a social scientist's concerns for organizations and federalism with the lawyer's knowledge of horizontal *stare decisis* among courts of different States, you may come up with *stare decisis* as a coordinating mechanism among units in a non-hierarchical organizational space. There are huge bodies of American law in the hands of the States, not the central government. They are generally the same, but not quite the same, across all or most of the States. That sameness is often the product not of parallel state legislation but of parallel court decisions. Why and how? It is the task of the tort article to explain the why and how. There is not a single obvious right answer. But horizontal *stare decisis* is one of the possible answers.

One of the great disadvantages of the law and courts field within political science is that it is often called 'public law' (see also Chapter 5). In a short piece in *PS*, a more or less informal journal of internal political science communication, Shapiro (1972*b*) argued that such a designation was an arbitrary result of higher education politics in the USA, that the public law-private law distinction was less and less tenable even in Continental Europe where it had been invented, and that it barred political scientists from studying vast areas of law centrally implicated in the discipline's defining interest in 'who gets what' or 'the authoritative allocation of values.' If we leave aside criminal law, which is not quite but almost public, political scientists even today are concerned almost exclusively with so-called public law.

If, however, one were concerned with organization theory, *stare decisis*, and federalism, and thus with the phenomenon of the more or less sameness of important bodies of State law, one is inevitably led not to public law but to private law, torts, contract, and the like. It is in these areas that common law—judge-made, precedent-oriented law—is most prevalent, and where statutes—law made by legislatures—play a subordinate role. It is precisely these private law areas in which parallel, unhierarchically coordinated judge-made law is most evident. It is precisely in these areas that coordination through horizontal interstate *stare decisis* is most plausible and worth looking for. Thus, the particular task set in this piece could serve as a vehicle for Shapiro's, admittedly not very successful, attempt to move law and courts political scientists beyond the public law barrier.

The piece itself argued for a multi-causal explanation of the high level of uniformity in the tort laws of the various States. One of the causes proposed was the success of horizontal *stare decisis* as a mode of non-authoritative legal communication, a form of what today would be called 'soft law'. Even under the strictest view of *stare decisis*, courts in one State are not bound to follow precedents from another. Lawyers and judges may cite them, however, as more or less persuasive, in terms of either reasoning or what seems to be working elsewhere under not very different conditions. By tracking the spread of various changes in tort doctrine, the article seeks to show that this *stare decisis* practice is not empty formalism or mere disguise, but a mode of coordination where the players feel the need for such coordination. Or, to put the matter differently, we get changes in national tort law through non-hierarchical, incremental changes in State tort law coordinated by *stare decisis* communication.

This piece also provided an opportunity for a further extension of the initial incrementalism article. The law and economics movement was in its early days and the bulk of the writing on whether the common law is efficient had not yet appeared (for example, Rubin 1977; Priest 1977). This piece employed the notion of a national litigation market. Lawyers monitored the decisions of courts. On the basis of that monitoring they made thousands of individual decisions about when and under what circumstances to sue. Judicial *stare decisis* practices provided the lawyers with probabilistic but relatively reliable information about what cases they were likely to win. If a given set of facts and arguments had yielded victory in one jurisdiction, they were likely to win in another. Interstate horizontal *stare decisis* was both a cause and an effect. Lawyers urged the courts of one State to follow decisions favourable to their client's position that had been handed down in another, and the resulting interstate citation by courts further motivated lawyers to bring forward similar urgings. This approach also sought to move the attention of political scientists beyond judges to lawyers as crucial players in the law-making process, a point to which we shall return in a later chapter. If this piece were written today no doubt it would express the same ideas in the language of networks, organization fields, institutional isomorphism, epistemic communities, and governance.

The examination of a large body of case law, such as torts, also allowed for a certain corrective to the enthusiasms of incrementalism. Almost inevitably what started as an attempt at empirical theory, seeking to describe how organizations actually reached decisions, began to take on normative overtones. If incrementalism was more rational than synopticism because it properly took into account the excessive costs of making perfect decisions, then incrementalism must be the correct mode of decision-making. There was a considerable implication that incremental decision-making was necessarily successful decision-making. The tort piece sought to discern a number of different patterns or sequences of incremental judicial decision-making. One pattern is the ideal one of relatively frequent and steady small incidents of judicial law-making, keeping the law in step with changing social and economic conditions. But the body of tort case law indicates a number of other patterns, including ones in which insistence on *stare decisis* leads to stasis or failure. The torts piece was designed for a book that sought to examine both legislatures and courts as decision-makers. Ultimately it argues that legislatures will intervene with major, that is non-incremental, statutory 'reforms' of bodies of law when *stare decisis*, that is, judicial incremental policy-making, fails through either stasis or proceeding step by step into a dead end. Incrementalism does not guarantee success. Yet its advantages cannot be denied, and we shall return to its advantages in our subsequent consideration of successful judicial review.

Those who pursue quantitative studies of judicial decision behaviour have piled up what is to them, and to us, conclusive evidence that the votes of Supreme Court justices, in particular cases, reflect their attitudes or policy preferences, not just the precedents. Yet somewhat to their surprise, we suspect, the debate about precedent versus free judicial discretion goes on. Is that simply because the legal establishment is so invested in hiding the truth of judicial law-making that it cannot face up to evidence to the contrary? When the actors in any political process spend an enormous amount of time and effort in a given activity, or insist on employing a certain discourse, it is likely that it serves some purpose beyond sheer dissimulation. Lawyers and judges expend enormous resources collecting, communicating, and purporting to govern their decisions by precedent. The incrementalism and tort pieces, as well as the article reprinted in this chapter, argue that *stare decisis* serves purposes beyond camouflage. It serves as a declared commitment to, and set of rules for, judicial incremental policy-making, which is a vehicle for the coordination of the various units of court organizations and a means of improving communication throughout the legal communications network.

Shapiro (1968), in the course of introducing incrementalism at the beginning of the book *The Supreme Court and Administrative Agencies*, offered a further explanation as to why the precedent versus free judicial discretion debate never goes away, no matter what the weight of quantitative evidence on the side of discretion. As the 'Judicialization' model presented in Chapter 1 shows, the opposition between precedent-based deliberation and the successful building of legal norms through the exercise of judicial policy discretion is a false one. In some respects, all of Shapiro's and Stone Sweet's research argues that the two processes are symbiotic on one another. We are not really dealing with an either/or matter. In reality, *stare decisis* constrains the range and direction of judicial discretion rather than forbidding it or simply camouflaging it. It is a form of what today we call 'path dependence'.

Stone Sweet's paper in this chapter asserts that how legal argumentation and the judicial process proceed all but guarantee a certain important degree of path dependence. The current state of legal discourse on any particular point of law establishes what legal arguments are plausible, that is, claims on the law that may be offered by lawyers and judges within the canons of that discourse. The legal rule, or doctrine stated in the precedents, determines which range of alternative steps away from the status quo will be considered small and which will be considered large. If the courts constantly declare their allegiance to *stare decisis*, that is, their preference for small step changes, it would be foolish for lawyers to offer them large step changes except as a last desperate measure. *Stare decisis* does not compel the courts to abjure legal change or to make single correct legal changes. It does announce that judges would prefer to make small but reasonably consistent legal changes. *Stare decisis* does not dictate which of several offered small changes judges should choose. Discretion and choice remain. It does imply that (1) judges may accept none of the changes unless the current law gives trouble, that (2) they are likely to prefer one of the available small changes rather than a big one, and that (3) a new small change will be announced as compatible with the last small change they made.

In *Supreme Court and Administrative Agencies*, Shapiro (1968) sought to show, through a number of diagrams that look rather like the currently fashionable decision trees of the game theorist, that *stare decisis* tends to establish vectors, or paths. Judges are free to make successive choices of any single policy point that lies in an arc or locus of policy points close to that path, or central tendency, or line of precedent, but are constrained not to choose a particular policy or rule or doctrine that lies distant from that path. Indeed judges do vote their policy preferences, but they are constrained to choose the policy they prefer among those that can plausibly be argued to fall close to the existing line of precedents. Lawyers and judges expend an enormous amount of words on precedent because those words signal which particular legal changes are close enough and which are too far away from the existing state of the law to be worthy of judicial consideration. That is why, ultimately, what judges say is even more important than how they vote. For what they say today constrains the range of what they will vote on tomorrow, and sends signals to lawyers as to what proposed policy changes judges are willing to consider. And, as we argue further in Chapter 3, what judges say today often dictates not just what lawyers, but also what legislators, will say tomorrow.

The incrementalism article had treated *stare decisis* as a mode of decision-making by individual judges and courts collectively. Research on appeals showed *stare decisis* to be a mode of hierarchical control of court organizations and of political regimes more generally (Shapiro 1980; 1981a: 49–56). The tort article added that precedent-oriented legal practice provided coordination for non-hierarchical court organizations. The article reprinted here adds a further dimension: *stare decisis* is a communications rule that ensures high levels of redundancy in legal communications, providing mutual support and reassurance to widely scattered policy-making units operating in a very noisy environment.

Towards a Theory of the Path Dependence of Judicial Institutions

Stone Sweet's contribution to this chapter follows directly from 'Judicialization and the Construction of Governance'. Since these connections are made explicitly in the paper, they require only brief discussion here.

The dynamic model of judicial politics proposed in Judicialization is animated by an underlying causal mechanism, that of positive feedback, or increasing returns to the institutions generated through triadic rule-making. In all of Stone Sweet's work, the notions of path dependence and precedent have been invoked in one way or another, but neither was adequately theorized. 'Path Dependence, Precedent, and Judicial Authority' takes some preliminary steps toward doing so, and raises some outstanding problems that are not resolved, even in a preliminary way. Although the call to notice and examine path dependence in the study of politics is now increasingly heard (see Pierson 2000), a literature establishing the theoretical foundations of the path dependent development of specific types of political institutions remains, at most, embryonic. The object of this paper is to specify the micro and meso conditions necessary for the path dependence of judicial institutions—doctrine, or what the paper calls 'argumentation frameworks'—and to develop a set of propositions capable of being tested in any legal system.

As in 'Judicialization', Stone Sweet grounds the argument in terms of a generic institutionalism, integrating rational choice and sociological notions of institutions in crucial respects. The tension between rational choice and sociological-constructivist models of institutions (Hall and Taylor 1996; Stone Sweet, Sandholtz, and Fligstein 2001) is viewed as an expression, if at a higher level of abstraction, of the debate between those who see judges as following precedent—a logic of appropriateness and duty—and those who see judges as pursuing their own policy preferences through their decisions—a logic of consequence and choice. The dynamics of precedent-based law-making are theorized partly around the findings of cognitive scientists working on analogical reasoning and decision-making, and partly around the pioneering work of Brian Arthur (1994) and Paul David (for example, 1994) on the nature of path dependent systems.

If these priorities were to inform a general social science of courts, one would naturally read Shapiro's paper as an essay in organizational sociology, and do so alongside the first four chapters of James March and Johan Olsen's influential *Rediscovering Institutions* (1989), as well as those works already discussed. Shapiro on *stare decisis* can also be read as an early bridge between political jurisprudence and what later became the law and economics movement, a topic Stone Sweet briefly considers in his paper. There are further, obvious connections between the Shapiro pieces and 'Path Dependence, Precedent, and Judicial Power'. Both see the incremental development of legal institutions as a consequence of the various ways that lawyers and judges rely on one another to do their jobs effectively, given the indeterminacy of legal rules and the fact that governance through case-by-case dispute resolution is perforce decentralized governance. And both assess the rationality and efficiency of pre-existing rule structures to what judges do, not in absolute terms, but as heavily conditioned by a mix of constraints by uncertain environments, the random sequencing of inputs, and cognitive limitations.

As usual, Stone Sweet largely ignores many relevant and important debates in public law political science. In this case, however, he engages classic ideas developed in more-or-less mainstream, or orthodox, legal theory. These are arguments that heirs to political jurisprudence would typically dismiss as part of the problem, a source of obfuscation, rather than one of the keys to understanding the development of legal systems. Put crudely, the claim goes as follows. To the extent that the idealizations of precedent and judicial discretion propagated in positivist legal theory—for example, that of H. L. A. Hart and Neil MacCormick—actually model what judges really do, if only in part, then judicial institutions will develop along *strong* path dependent lines for the reasons identified by Stone Sweet. Stated inside out, if Stone Sweet has correctly identified why and how judicial institutions become path dependent, then it must be, if only in part, because positivist dogmas actually hold some minimal purchase on judicial behaviour. We suspect, however, that our various arguments to the effect that legal reasoning and justificatory rhetorics actually serve a social purpose are unlikely to quell either the 'legal doublethink' or the precedent versus discretion debates mentioned above.

Last, Stone Sweet developed the paper with comparative purposes in mind.[2] It is commonplace in comparative law scholarship to note, first, the

---

[2] An earlier version of this paper (Stone Sweet and McCown 2000), co-authored by Margaret McCown, also contained analysis of comprehensive data on the development a precedent-based case-law system in the European Community. This part of the research will appear in Stone Sweet's book *The Judicial Construction of Europe* (forthcoming), in future papers to be co-authored by McCown, and in McCown's own research.

formal absence of the doctrine of *stare decisis* in Continental legal systems and, then, to assert that this absence constitutes a crucial difference between legal systems. However, the best systematic research has shown, as one would readily predict from the papers presented in this chapter, 'that there are no great differences in the use [of precedent] between the so-called common law and civil law systems' (Summers and Taruffo 1991: 487). For its part, 'Path Dependence, Precedent, and Judicial Power' was written to guide Stone Sweet's ongoing research on triadic governance and on new legal systems— such as the *Lex Mercatoria* of Chapter 5—where the doctrine of *stare decisis* is explicitly precluded or otherwise denied.

Our overarching claim, of course, is that precedent underpins judicial authority, and is therefore a basic element in the social logic of courts, everywhere.

Towards a Theory of *Stare Decisis*

Martin Shapiro

I shall propose in this article [1] a new theory of *stare decisis*—a term I use loosely to mean the practice of courts in deciding new cases in accordance with precedents—that draws upon the insights of communications theory as well as upon some previous work of my own on the decision-making process in tort law. The attempt to apply communications theory to the law is not new or—given that judicial decision-making is a species of verbal behaviour—unexpected. Previous efforts to apply communications theory to problems of judicial decision-making have foundered, however, on a lack of clear conception as to what that theory means and can tell us about the judicial process, and it is with an attempt at clarification of the relevant concepts that I begin.

Communications theory is not a unified body of thought. It has three quite distinct branches. The first, 'syntactics', is concerned with the logical arrangement, transmission, and receipt of signals or signs. It is the domain of the electrical engineer; its concern is with the transmission of signals, whatever their meaning. The second is 'semantics', which is concerned with the meaning of the signals to people. The third is 'pragmatics', which is the study of the impact of signal transmission on human behaviour (Cherry 1957). This tripartite division is not wholly satisfactory; we shall return to that point.

The key concepts of syntactics, for our purposes, are 'information', 'redundancy', and 'feedback', of which the first two are best discussed together. For the telegraphic engineer, information is the content of a signal that could not have been predicted by the receiver; it is a probability concept. The more probable the transmission of a given sign, the less information its

Originally published in *The Journal of Legal Studies*, 1 (1972), 125. Copyright © by the University of chicago. Reproduced by kind permission.

[1] For some suggestions from the standpoint of semantics and related approaches, see Probert (1968). Feedback loops are sometimes added to the standard Eastonian Model as applied to legal systems (see Murphy 1964). Sigler (1968*b*) presents a more highly elaborated cybernetics model.

actual transmission conveys. 'Redundancy' is the opposite of information. It is the introduction of repetition or pattern into the message. If the telegrapher sends each message twice, his second sending is redundant and contains less information than his first. If we establish the convention, rule, or pattern that two dashes will always be followed by a dot, then the actual transmission of the dot after the two dashes will be redundant and contain no information because the dot placement in the sequence could always be predicted without actual transmission.

The ideal transmission, then, in terms of pure 'information' would contain absolutely no repetition and no pattern. The engineer finds it wise, however, to introduce redundancy at the cost of reducing the information content of a message because otherwise any loss of information due to malfunctions in the transmission system would be undetectable and irremediable. It is only when we can predict, at least partially, what message we are going to receive that we can spot an erroneous omission or substitution in the message and call for its correction. The ideal message, then, will contain the highest proportion of information and the lowest proportion of redundancy necessary to identify and correct errors in transmission.

Thus it will be seen that redundancy and information, in syntactic terms, are reciprocals of each other, but the situation is more complex when we consider the semantic dimension of communication, for both information and redundancy convey meaning. And the line is even more blurred when we consider the pragmatics of communication. Writing on the 'New Communication', Weakland (1967) has said '. . . there is no "redundancy". . .', his point being, of course, that repetition and patterns in messages do have behavioural significance to the participants in the communications process. Such redundancies carry a freight of meaning, knowledge, and/or stimuli to the receiver and in this important sense are not redundant.

Redundancy may be introduced into messages to facilitate the diagnosis of information-transmission errors and the transmission back to the sender of messages enabling him to correct his errors. This identification and transmission back is feedback. It is important to distinguish syntactic from cybernetic feedback. The former involves transmission back concerning error in the sense of incorrect transmission or receipt of information between sender and receiver within the system; the latter involves transmission concerning error in the sense of incorrect adjustment by the system to the outside world. Thus, high levels of syntactic feedback indicate trouble in the transmission facilities of the system rather than the sensitivity and learning that are typically imputed where high levels of cybernetic feedback are present. Simply to speak of feedback in general is quite misleading.

As I said at the outset, most attempts to apply communications theory to legal processes have foundered on a failure to keep clear these important distinctions among the relevant concepts of communications theory. It would appear a worthwhile undertaking to attempt an application of such concepts as information, redundancy, and feedback that paid due regard to their origins in syntactics and clearly labelled all shifts from syntactic to cybernetic or semantic or pragmatic levels of analysis. The remainder of this article is devoted to that endeavour, beginning with some general remarks on legal communication.

So long as it can be argued—and in view of the long tradition of Anglo-American legal thought it can be argued fairly persuasively—that the opinions of American and British courts embody an original and peculiar mode of thought that can be analysed and understood only within the very scheme of analysis presented within the opinions themselves, the only scientific mode of legal analysis is ethnographic. I have tried elsewhere to indicate that judicial logic can be viewed as a species of the incremental mode of decision-making that is common to many political organizations (Shapiro 1965). The concept of redundancy seems to me promising as a further tool in integrating legal discourse into more general discourse.

At the most superficial level, it is obvious that legal discourse organized by the rules of *stare decisis* emphasizes, and itself insists that its success rests upon, high levels of redundancy and, therefore—remembering our original theoretical formulation—low levels of information. The strongest legal argument is that the current case, on 'its facts', is 'on all fours' with a previous case and that the decision in that case is deeply embedded in a long line of decisions enunciating—repeating—a single legal principle. In other words, the strongest argument is that the current case, treated as an input, is totally redundant and under the rules of *stare decisis* the duty of the judge is to transmit a message that is equally redundant. Of course the facts of a new case are never exactly on all fours with an old, and no line of precedents is ever totally clear and consistent. The point is that the rules of legal discourse seem to require each attorney to suppress as much information and transmit as much redundancy as possible.

At the semantic level, legal discourse is conducted in terms of highly redundant symbols. The string citation comes to mind in which authorities are piled up endlessly in support of a statement of the law in the opinion, brief, or text. The normal mode of criticizing such citations is to show that they actually contain information: either that (1) the cases in the citation do not say the same thing as the statement in the text or that (2) some of the cases cited do not say the same thing as the other cases cited. If the statement and the cases do not all say exactly the same thing—if the message is not totally redundant after the first bit of information—then a technical error or a violation of the rules of legal craftsmanship has been committed. The rules of the craft are obeyed only to the extent that, having received any portion of the craft message, a second craftsman could have predicted all the remaining portions.

Legal communication is also replete with highly redundant synonym use. In what has come to be referred to as the 'noisy marble' experiment (Macy 1953), subjects isolated from one another had to communicate to each other, by written message, the colour of marbles. At first, plain, solid colour marbles were used. Then cloudy, mottled, and indistinct marbles, still quite different from one another, were supplied. Those subjects who succeeded with the more difficult—noisy—marbles did so by markedly increasing the number of synonyms they used in describing their marble rather than by seeking the single 'best' descriptive word. When they finally had induced the receiver to understand which of the array of noisy marbles their synonyms were aimed at designating, they could in future communications use any single one of the synonymous words to designate that marble accurately. As the experimenters pointed out: 'Once the redundant coding has been used, and the errors reduced thereby, we may assume that the receiver remembers the synonyms used for a given symbol in the redundant code, and that in future messages these synonyms or alternate codes are understood even though not physically present' (Macy 1953: 403).

In the 'craftsmanlike' appellate opinion or brief, the argument is built sentence by sentence, with each sentence—often many of the phrases within each sentence—supported by a citation. A skilled lawyer, seeing the sequence of citations alone, could predict the argument or, seeing the argument alone, could predict the citations. Thus, either the argument or the citations are—and are supposed to be—redundant. Furthermore, the optimum situation for authoritative appellate decision-making is one where each citation is to a 'leading' case that is 'leading' precisely because its reasoning has been repeated, and it itself cited, in many other cases. The citation of a leading case name incorporates, in effect, other synonymous cases so that, as in the noisy-marble experiment, we may assume that the receiver remembers the synonyms used for a given symbol in the redundant code, and that in future messages these synonyms or alternate codes are understood even though not physically present. Furthermore, recognition of a case as leading assures the lawyer and judge that the issues involved were worked through not once but many times before the system settled on this particular case name as the symbol for its many synonymous treatments of the question.

It is significant, too, that a well-constructed legal opinion is likely to make the same point many different ways, in canvassing the issues, in meeting the counter-arguments, and so forth. When a later judicial craftsman cites the previous opinion, he imports the previous internal redundancy of that case into his own well-constructed—that is to say, internally redundant—opinion. Finally, the very practice of citation is the assertion that 'I am not saying anything new; I am only repeating what has already been said.'

Legal discourse in the style of *stare decisis*, then, is not a unique phenomenon but an instance of communication with extremely high levels of redundancy. Indeed, what we think of as the 'taught tradition', and thus the peculiar tradition, of the law is largely a set of coding rules for introducing redundancy into legal messages. It remains to consider why the legal system tolerates or requires such high levels of redundancy.

'Redundancy may be said to be due to an additional set of rules, whereby it becomes increasingly difficult to make an undetectable mistake' (Cherry 1957: 185). When we speak of *stare decisis*, we are speaking of such a set of rules. The importance of redundancy in error correction has been overshadowed by the somewhat imprecise adoption in political science of cybernetic models, with their emphasis on feedback. As noted earlier, cybernetic feedback involves messages to the organism correcting errors in its adjustment to the environment. It thus draws attention away from the problem whether the receiver within the organism has received correctly the message from the sender within the organism. Here I wish to stick to the sender-receiver problem and thus view redundancy and feedback as two sides of the coin of correcting message errors. The question why there are high levels of redundancy in the legal system thus inescapably entails the questions: are there—and if so why—high levels of communication error?

It seems a reasonable hypothesis that complex organizations are necessarily involved in high levels of signalling. High levels of signalling will lead to high levels of syntactic noise—the larger the number of signals, the more likely they are to interfere with one another—and even higher levels of semantic noise will occur since the subjects of the messages of our complex organization will themselves be complex and ambiguous—noisy in the sense the mottled marbles were. High levels of noise should invite the deliberate introduction of high levels of redundancy to counteract the noise, but the high levels of redundancy, by reducing the information content of the organization's messages, will handicap the organization's ability to meet changing circumstances unless some strong countervailing mechanism is present (Cadwallader 1959).[2] This reasoning seems plausible; but does it

---

[2] For a slightly different formulation in terms of polycentric organizations and multiplexing, see Dror (1968) and his note to Von Neumann (Dror 1950). The most significant statement by Dror

apply to the legal system? The answer, I believe, is that it does. I have been engaged recently in studying the evolution of policy formulation in tort law as if the 50 State supreme courts, the United States Supreme Court, and the British courts constituted a single organization marked by decentralized, non-hierarchical and yet coordinated decision-making (Shapiro 1970). I stress the 'as if' because I am working by analogy and assuming what is to be proved: that there are sufficient interconnections between my 52 decision-makers to justify treating them as an organization. On the side of my assumption is a massive and visible flow of messages among them and a policy product sufficiently unified to suggest something more than totally independent action and sufficiently diversified to suggest more than multiple, independent, but highly determined responses to a single overriding cause. Against my assumption is the suspicion that tort policy is so socially determined that 52 totally independent decision-makers would arrive at almost the same policy outputs, given the similarities between the communities in which they operate, even if there were no links between them. At the very least I think it is possible to ask how these courts managed to arrive at relatively unified forms of legal doctrine even if the general social environment independently, and without the aid of coordinating mechanisms, dictated the unified substance of policy.

Viewed in organizational terms, a central problem quickly emerges in the tort area. How do a large number of decision-makers manage to arrive at well-coordinated policy decisions—policy decisions are the output of this organization—when the organization is bereft of all the mechanisms of hierarchical control that we associate with classical organizational structures? None of the State supreme courts is legally subordinated to any of the others, nor, in the tort field, are they collectively subordinated to the Supreme Court, which, due to the sparseness of its tort docket, is far from being even *primus inter pares*.

Once the problem is stated in this way, our attention is immediately drawn to communications phenomena. A logical first guess would be that the organization has developed some set of special communications techniques that allow its decision-makers to cooperate: to substitute, somehow, mutual influence for command from above. Because of the large number of

is, '[a]s elaborated in modern cybernetics, the basic idea of redundancy is one of "multiplexing," that is, of having many units perform the same operation and passing their outputs through a threshold level that ignores mistakes made by some of the parallel units' (Dror 1950: 211). In law the 'threshold level' may be provided by the litigation market, that is, by the lawyers who, on the basis of professional skill, seize upon the 'thrust' or 'principle' or 'true doctrine' and cast off the 'aberrant' cases. See Dror's (1950: 182) description of the Rand Delphi projects in which panels of experts are asked to predict the future and then to predict again after seeing one another's first predictions. See also Landau (1969).

decision-makers and the very large volume of decisions necessary to keep tort policy attuned to a changing society, we would expect these communications techniques to absorb a disproportionately large share of the organization's resources.

In fact we discover that most of the participants in the organization have spent much of their educational and subsequent professional lives learning coding rules. More important, we find a vast body of communications personnel. The litigational market assures that thousands of lawyers will devote their energies to carrying messages from one court to the next, keeping each informed of what the others are doing. This flow of communications is not controlled by conscious plan or carefully structured communications networks, but rather by hundreds of thousands of individual decisions guided by the desire for personal profit. I use the term 'litigational market' precisely because I wish to suggest an 'invisible hand'.

For this market, like Adam Smith's, has many rules and conventions that harness individual greed to a higher cause. Under the rules of the game, the lawyer-communicator has the highest chance of winning if he can show a court that his client must prevail if the court keeps doing exactly what it has been doing; the next highest chance if he can persuade the court that it should do exactly what some other court has been doing; the next highest chance if he can convince it to do something slightly different from what it or some other court has been doing; and the worst prospect if he must argue that the court should do something markedly different from what it and other courts have done in the past.

It will be seen that the litigation market encourages the flow of a very large number of confirmation messages between independent decision-makers, reassuring each that the others have been agreeing with it. From the standpoint of syntactics, these messages are redundant, and they are not feedback since they are neither occasioned by, nor do they report, error.[3] When messages indicating differences between decision-makers are introduced, they are added in small numbers to the stream of reassurances, they emphasize the smallness of the differences, and they tend to suppress or conceal larger ones. Often they are syntactic feedback in the sense of exposing minor errors in understanding or phrasing rather than real policy differences.

---

[3] To the outside observer, using a cybernetic approach, they might appear to be positive feedback if he or she had made the quite independent determination that what the organization had been doing was an 'error' vis-à-vis its environment. Then such supportive messages would have the effect of making the organization persist in its past behaviour and thus make more and more errors. It is necessary to keep 'error' in the syntactic sense clearly separated from error in the broader cybernetic sense of failure to adjust to the environment.

In an earlier analysis of this material, basing myself on incremental theories of decision-making, I argued that this form of communication was the substitute for the rational-hierarchical control structures that play a major role in coordinating policy in other organizations. In other words, the tort organization goes to an extreme form of incremental decision-making in which there is a very strong bias against any change at all, only very small changes are ever considered, and differences between organizational units are de-emphasized, suppressed, or quickly mediated by requesting each unit to make small step changes in the direction of the other. Faced with a conflict between the authoritative cases in State A and State B, the lawyer is not likely to state the conflict clearly and ask the judge in State C to take his choice. Instead the lawyer will seek to 'harmonize' the authorities by bending each a little. If the judge in State C will accept the harmonization, then the new mediate position of State C will be used in future litigation to lever States A and B off their initial positions. The potential for conflict among 52 decision-makers is high and the style of decision-making I have described seems designed to create an atmosphere of mutual reassurance, support, and compromise and to avoid the emergence of rationally stated major policy differences, particularly differences stated as matters of principle.

But I now see that this analysis is incomplete. An important activity of the tort organization and its litigational market operating under the rules of *stare decisis* is to ensure extremely high levels of redundancy in the communications linking the decision-making units. A system that inevitably generates a great deal of noise, and one in which high levels of random error would jeopardize coordination, fully employs the standard techniques for the reduction of noise-caused transmission error. What appears in one light as an incremental, and thus non-rational, technique of decision-making appears in another as the most orthodox and rational solution to the noise problem.

It is well to recall at this point the argument that redundancies at the syntactic level are not redundant at the semantic level because they transmit the knowledge that the sender is repeating or patterning his message. The rules of legal discourse create redundancy in the first sense in that they make it easier for the receiver to spot unintentional errors in transmission and, more important, to spot intentional ones: for remember that the transmission channels here are lawyers with their own interests. In the same sense, redundancy in tort discourse reduces noise-caused errors in a net with many overlapping signals, and reduces receiving errors by decreasing the workload of each receiver—the amount of information he must process—to manageable proportions.

In the broader semantic sense the redundancy of tort communication, precisely because it conveys the additional knowledge that senders are repeating their messages, provides supportive reassurance to each of the communicator decision-makers that his fellows are with him. The adding of new information—requests for changes—only in very small quantities not only ensures the ability of the receiver to process the information but his willingness to accept and retransmit that information. Redundancy in this sense is a major solution to the problem of coordinating output in non-hierarchical organizations.

In this light we can begin to explain the survival of *stare decisis*, particularly in 'common law' areas of law, as the dominant mode of legal discourse. Its strength lies in its dual and mutually supporting contents of syntactic and semantic redundancy. *Stare decisis* viewed as redundancy is a fully rational, probably indispensable, method of solving the problem of syntactic noise in a system with very high message loads—which any system that proceeds case by case inevitably is. At the same time, the redundancy introduced for this syntactic purpose automatically and simultaneously becomes, at the semantic level, a heavy stream of the kind of information necessary to operate an incremental system of decision-making: information about mutual support and agreement in the form of constant repetition of previous agreement.

Of course the danger to an organization that relies very heavily on redundancy is that it may process so little information that it cannot learn. It is routinely argued, in the broader cybernetic context, that such organizations, if they are to survive, must have high levels of feedback to counterbalance redundancy. Such an argument illustrates the danger of failing to differentiate clearly between syntactic and cybernetic feedback. Cybernetic feedback is itself information. If the system employs high levels of syntactic redundancy, it does not have the 'space' to transmit much cybernetic feedback information to its receiving parts. To say high redundancy with high feedback is to say low information with high information.

The tort organization does have a partial solution to this paradox. The content of the litigational market's communications is highly redundant, although some level of cybernetic feedback is maintained in the form of requests for small changes. Here the virtue of *stare decisis* lies in the peculiar nexus it provides for syntactic and cybernetic phenomena. Following the rules of *stare decisis*, requests for legal changes, which are actually inspired by the failure of law to adjust correctly to the environment, and are thus cybernetic feedback, are put in the form of syntactic feedback, statements that some judge or lawyer has not correctly received the real message that was transmitted by the previous cases—their 'true principles'. In this way much cybernetic feedback information can be squeezed into a communications system that demands very high levels of redundancy, and it can be squeezed in without interfering with that sense of mutual support necessary to the coordination of non-hierarchical organizations.

In recent years political science has focused not on judicial opinions but on judicial decisions—who won and lost—as keys to understanding judicial attitudes. In legal theory and legal commentary more generally, there has been much attention to judicial opinions as justifications or explanations, and to what modes of justification and explanation are appropriate to legal discourse. But nearly all the commentators concerned with these problems treat the opinion *in vacuo*, asking whether it meets certain general standards and thus turning the problem into one of logic or philosophy.

Somehow we ignored the fact that appellate courts and the lawyers that serve them spend an overwhelming proportion of their energies in communicating with one another, and that the judicial opinion, itself conforming to the style of *stare decisis* and then manipulated along with others according to the rules of *stare decisis*, is the principal mode of communication. This massive pattern of communicative behaviour has persisted in the face of our insistence that it is what judges do, not what they say, that counts, in spite of repeated demonstrations that *stare decisis* does not yield single correct solutions and despite the failure of theorists to provide clear-cut descriptions of what a correct judicial opinion would look like.

It would seem appropriate, therefore, to examine the opinion-writing activity of courts in the context of communication, and once we do a striking finding emerges. The style of legal discourse that we summarize in the expression *stare decisis* is not a unique phenomenon peculiar to the Anglo-American legal system, not a unique method or form of reasoning or logic, but an instance of redundancy, the standard solution predicted by communications theory for any acute noise problem. And there is a further finding: the characteristic style of Anglo-American legal discourse persists because its rather standard and routine solution to the noise problem of a non-hierarchical organization like the courts yields at the very same time a pattern of redundant communication that is extremely useful, perhaps essential, to the incremental mode of decision-making that organizations of this sort typically adopt. If this suggestion has any merit, it should be possible for social scientists to treat the phenomenon of *stare decisis* as a problem in human communications rather than as exclusively one of logic and/or obfuscation.

Path Dependence, Precedent, and Judicial Power

Alec Stone Sweet

Given certain conditions, legal institutions will evolve in path dependent ways: that is, the social processes that link litigation and judicial law-making will exhibit increasing returns. Once under way, these processes will build the discursive techniques and modes of decision-making specific to the exercise of judicial power; they will enhance the centrality of judicial rule-making vis-à-vis other processes; and they will, periodically but routinely, reconfigure those sites of governance constituted by rules subject to intensive litigation.

The paper follows in a line of research on how new legal systems emerge, mutate, and mature, and with what political consequences (for example, Stone 1992*a*; Stone Sweet 1997; 2000). The concepts of path dependence and increasing returns have at times been deployed and given empirical content (especially Stone Sweet , Chapters 1 and 4, this volume; Stone Sweet and Caporaso 1998*a*); nonetheless, they were used to complement other theoretical materials and priorities, and were left under-theorized. Here I provide explicit theoretical foundations for the path dependence of legal institutions, and an argument as to why this should matter to social scientists and to lawyers.

A much longer version of this paper, co-authored by Margaret McCown, was presented at the Colloquium on Law, Economics, and Politics, the Law School, New York University, October 2000. The first part, presented here, provided a blueprint for collecting and analysing data on the use of precedent in the European legal system, analysis that comprised the second part of the original paper (Stone Sweet and McCown 2000). Margaret McCown, a graduate student in politics at Oxford, and Stone Sweet continue their collaboration on the second stage of the project. Ms McCown's contributions to this chapter were invaluable, but Stone Sweet is alone responsible for what is written here. He also benefited from discussions with James Caporaso, Paul David, John Ferejohn, Ronald Jepperson, Louis Kornhauser, Paul Pierson, Martin Shapiro, and Mark Thatcher.

Legal institutions are path dependent to the extent that how litigation and judicial rule-making proceeds, in any given area of the law at any given point in time, is fundamentally conditioned by how earlier legal disputes in that area of the law have been sequenced and resolved. The paper elaborates a model of adjudication in which institutional development and decision-making are linked through highly organized discursive choice-contexts, meso structures called 'argumentation frameworks'. Argumentation frameworks are curated by judges as legal precedents. Litigants and judges are assumed to be rational utility-maximizers; but they are also actors who pursue their self-interest in discursive ways, through argumentation and analogic reasoning. Sustained, precedent-based adjudication leads to outcomes that are both indeterminate *and* incremental: that is, they are path dependent. I conclude by addressing various implications of the argument which taken together define an agenda for research.

Theoretical Issues

To invoke the metaphor of path dependence as a shorthand summary of why a particular state of affairs emerges, changes, or persists may be a useful rhetorical device, but it can also be an empty one. Both proponents and critics of path dependence approaches to social institutions are right to insist on the need for clearer theoretical exposition and rigour (Goldstone 1998; Pierson 2000). Path dependent explanations are compelling only to the extent that they elucidate how effects and outcomes that operate and are observable at a systemic—macro—level, are linked, across time, to effects and outcomes that operate and are observable at the domain of the individual decision-maker: the micro level. Such linkages develop through a positive feedback mechanism: a nascent, or maturing, standard of behaviour induces increasingly larger, and better networked, individuals to behave similarly, that is, in ways that adapt to, and thus reinforce, that standard. In the sections that follow, I introduce basic concepts, and then discuss the conditions under which I expect legal institutions, especially judicially-constructed argumentation frameworks—what Americans call 'doctrine'—to develop in path dependent ways. And I specify the kinds of outcomes that mechanisms of positive feedback are likely to generate at both macro and micro levels.

Path Dependence and Feedback

The idea that certain kinds of processes and outcomes are better explained by a logic of path dependence and increasing returns rather than a logic of path independence and decreasing returns has gained more adherents across the social sciences, while remaining controversial. Long a staple of evolutionary economics (for example, Ayres 1962), the work of Brian Arthur (1994), Paul David (1985; 1994; 1997), and Douglass North (1990) has brought the idea to the forefront, provoking important discussions about its nature, scope, and applicability (for example, Goldstone 1998; Liebowitz and Margolis 1995). The idea is controversial because it is 'fundamentally hostile to a predictable, equilibrium economics' (Goodstein 1995: 1029), wherein the interplay of dichotomous forces—for example, supply and demand—will push systems—for example, markets—to stability through mechanisms triggered by decreasing returns. And, unlike a 'natural selection' approach to, say, the choice of technological standards, the path dependence approach does not assume the superiority of the choice ultimately made relative to other options. Indeed, economic historians have produced a long series of compelling empirical studies to bolster the claim that it is often 'only the sequence of choices—driven by chance and trivial circumstances—that will eventually give one technology the attributes of the fittest' (David and Greenstein 1990; Foray 1997: 735).

Increasing returns approaches are at least presumptively applicable to research on the evolution of political institutions, that is, to the study of how bodies of law—policy—are chosen through the activities of governmental organizations. I understand Pierson's (2000) arguments on this point to be more or less definitive, and will not rehearse them here. Instead, I take up two standard reference points for any general discussion of the topic: Arthur's (1994: Chs 2, 4) and David's (1994; 1997) summaries of their own ideas and findings.

Arthur identified the basic characteristics of social processes driven by increasing returns dynamics. First, initial conditions do not determine outcomes. Second, precisely because, at the *ex ante* moment, end points are unpredictable, the analyst will be able to explain any subsequently constituted state of affairs only in relation to a particular sequence of 'choices or outcomes of intermediate events [that have taken place] between initial conditions and the endpoint' (Goldstone 1998: 834). Third, to the extent that any intermediate choice determines the sequence and content of subsequent choices, the observed process will exhibit *non-ergodic*[1] properties. 'Small historical events can become durable effects' (Baumann *et al.* 1996: 160) through positive feedback: 'The micro behaviour of the system'—for example, the

---

[1] 'A path dependent process is "non-ergodic": systems possessing this property cannot shake off the effects of past events, and do not have a limiting, invariable probability distribution that is continuous over the entire state space' (David 1993: 29).

relevant decisions taken by individuals in the second instance—will amplify the 'distribution of choices produced during the first period' (Foray 1997: 741). Fourth, in so far as outcomes are embedded as aggregate social choices, or investments, the cost of transition away from the new standard will be high, even pre-emptively so. Last, these processes possess a common structure. At a beginning point, a range of choices, formats, or templates for a particular form of behaviour are available; at one or several 'critical junctures'[2] one of these choices gains an advantage, however slight, and this advantage is continuously reinforced through positive feedback. Ultimately, the choice becomes dominant, or 'locked in', as a relatively taken-for-granted state of affairs.

Systems become path dependent through positive feedback, essentially adaptation and network effects that are gradually institutionalized as stable practices. David[3] and Arthur showed that some kinds of situations would be more conducive to producing feedback than would others, especially those featuring positive network externalities. Because the adoption of a technical standard or certain kinds of social norms reduces uncertainty and enables large numbers of individuals to construct productive relationships with one another, the marginal benefits of adoption will rise with each decision by other actors to adopt. Snowballing ensues, which institutionalizes, or 'locks in', the choice. David (for example, David 1992) and Arthur also argued that increasing returns dynamics would be particularly prevalent in knowledge-based industries: localized learning mixes with network effects to produce path dependent dynamics and systemic inflexibility. Where certain fixed costs are associated with adoption, such as investments in infrastructure or training, the costs of reversing course or adjusting to a different or presumptively better standard is commensurably higher.

Some elements of David's work (see especially David 1994) connect to more sociological views of institutions. Institutions—from conventions to formal rules—structure social settings, 'by aligning individual's expectations' and priorities in ways that enable coordination, given cognitive limitations and the existence of multiple solutions to any given cooperation game (David 1994: 209–10), a standard formulation. Pushing further, David

---

[2] Critical junctures are not necessarily events that actors understood as 'big' or 'important' when they took place. Their importance may become clear only further downstream. Consider *Marbury v. Madison* (USSC 1803) or the European Court of Justice's decisions on direct effect and supremacy (see Chapters 4, 6).

[3] David contributed to the development of, and largely accepts, Arthur's account of path dependent dynamical systems. Nonetheless, he rarely invokes the concept of increasing returns, focusing instead on the consequences of non-ergodicity.

suggests that it is the dynamic, and path dependent, interplay between institutions, organizations, and agency that generates complex institutional
arrangements (see also North 1990). For our purposes, the critical issues
are how such arrangements are selected and how domains, once organized
through rule structures, reproduce themselves. As sociologists have long
understood, organizations not only become possible on the basis of rule
structures but also serve to reinforce and to evolve new institutions, allowing actors to respond incrementally and more or less predictably to changes
in the environment.

Simplifying, David argues that the more any organization—or linked
clusters of institutions and organizations, an *organizational field*—possesses
effective procedures for processing information, adapting rules to situations,
and monitoring the activities and performance of individuals, the more
likely it is that the domain of action governed by that organization will
evolve in path dependent ways. Organizations develop and instil 'codes'
that socialize actors into relatively coherent, 'ideal-type' roles (following
Arrow 1974; cited in David 1994: 212–13). Socialization, of course, is a ubiquitous form of positive feedback, and therefore is easily understood in
terms familiar to students of path dependence more generally. The codes—
heuristics, ideal-type roles, or 'performance scripts' (Jepperson 1992)—that
guide action in any field typically exhibit some measure of non-ergodicity
and irreversibility. Whether borrowed and adapted wholesale or gradually
developed through trial and error, such codes:

...are not instantly created and learned, and so constitute a form of 'durable capital' whose costs are 'sunk'; they become more refined and ... ingrained through
repeated use, rather than eventually wearing out, [in contrast to] most tangible forms
of productive capital. (David 1994: 212–13)

With use, institutions supporting the domain typically become more differentiated and the codes more increasingly articulated. In so far as they
do, actors will, in order to access and exploit the organization's resources,
specialize 'in the information capable of being transmitted by the codes'.
Although specialization enables productive activity, it also imposes costs,
to the extent that actors, over time, 'become less efficient in acquiring and
transmitting information not easily fitted into the code' (Arrow 1974: 57).
Specialization provokes branching within the codes and vice versa; branching is a prototypically path dependent mode of institutionalization; and
institutionalization proceeds through feedback mechanisms (see also Stone
Sweet, Chapter 1, this volume).

The similarity between these ideas and those of the 'new instituti ists' in sociology (for example, Powell and Dimaggio 1992), and particularly the John Meyer group at Stanford (research surveyed in Jepperson 2001) should be obvious.[4] In myriad ways, organizations function as gatekeepers to discrete domains or fields. They recruit, instruct, and credential actors; and they authorize certain kinds of political activities while discouraging others.

The Path Dependence of Legal Institutions

Theoretical interest in the process through which judicial authority emerges and evolves over time seems never to have been widespread or sustained in the social sciences.[5] Law is commonly presumed to be relatively stable feature of the social environment; and the sources and consequences of judicial rule-making are often ignored or explained away. Game theorists assume fixed rules in order, among other things, to assess the likely impact of different legal regimes (for example, Baird, Gertner, and Picker 1994), and they have not resolved problems associated with modelling the dynamics of judicial rule-making (see the exchange between Vanberg 1998*b* and Stone Sweet 1998*a*). Constitutional political economy focuses almost exclusively on institutional design, as if constitutions do not evolve meaningfully once they enter into force and as if constitutional adjudication and rule-making did not exist (for example, Brennan and Buchanan 1985; Voigt 1999). The field of law and economics generally seeks 'to explain and to evaluate the content of legal rules rather than the process by which they are created' (Kornhauser 1992*a*: 169). And in much of the world where a formalist legal positivism still reigns as orthodoxy, scholars typically depict the law as a self-contained system that predetermines outcomes (Merryman 1985; Schlink 1993).

There are some obvious reasons why the processes through which legal institutions evolve ought to be subject to the dynamics that typify the evolution of non-ergodic dynamical systems more generally. Legal rules are, after all, standards of behaviour that judges select, enforce, and revise. Judicial rule-making, being more or less authoritative, should function to reduce uncertainty about the nature and scope of the standard, and also to provoke and reinforce feedback effects: there is rarely an analog to judicial authority

---

[4] David himself does not make these connections explicitly.
[5] Interest has grown substantially in recent years, for example: Dezelay and Garth (1996); Greif (1989); Milgrom, North, and Weingast (1990); Stone Sweet (1999*b*); Shapiro (1988).

in accounts of how technological standards are selected or discarded in a decentralized market. If judges begin to construe contracts in ways that impose one type of risk allocation on parties rather than another, then future contractants will have an interest in adapting to this rule-making to the extent that risk allocation is basic to commercial exchange and given that the parties know that a legal dispute between them is always possible. Judges help actors resolve basic assurance dilemmas: their activities increase the confidence, among those contemplating adoption, that a sufficient number of others will make the same choice (see Gillette 1998: 819–20). Further, if the judicially curated standard becomes the actual standard, then it is all the more likely that disputes that arise under it will be resolved through subsequent adjudication.

Some institutionalists, concerned more with identifying basic mechanisms of institutional change rather than with the work of law and courts per se, give judicial rule-making pride of place. North (1990), for example, argues that courts, by enforcing property rights and adapting the law to changing circumstances, reduce the transaction costs associated with impersonal exchange, helping societies expand markets and wealth (see also Stone Sweet and Brunell 1998a). For March and Olson (1989), the incremental techniques of common law adjudication comprise a paradigmatic mechanism for generating, and then continuously revising, the norms and 'logics of appropriateness' that organize human community. In the legal literature, a handful of important articles explicitly take, or argue for, a path dependence perspective on the development of legal institutions (for example, Gillette 1998; Kornhauser 1992a, b; Roe 1996; Stearns 1995), if for varied purposes.

In the rest of the paper, I seek to push this agenda forward by specifying the theoretical foundations of a path dependent model of adjudication.

Organizational Factors

Legal institutions—for example, substantive law, rules of standing and jurisdiction, doctrinal principles, cannons of construction, and so on— partly evolve through adjudication. I argue here that certain common features of adjudication favour the path dependence of these institutions *if some minimally robust conception of precedent exists*. I do not claim that these features are essential characteristics of all legal systems, or that they exert the same effect everywhere. Indeed, where these features are not present, or where the effects of the factors discussed are mitigated by other unspecified factors, I expect the path dependence of legal institutions to be commensurably weaker.

First, courts typically do not control the temporal order of cases that come before them. In any legal domain, judicial rulings on cases that come first will exert influence on subsequent litigation and judicial decision-making. This will be so to the extent that courts frame their decisions in light of past decisions and litigants adapt their claims to the courts' rule-making (see below). Where a judicial decision itself provokes a stream of cases, such as when a ruling expands the opportunities for, or enhances the benefits of litigating for some class of individuals, increasing returns properties are most obvious. In any event, in the overall process of selecting a legal rule, or in clarifying its meaning over time, there are likely to be significant 'first mover advantages' not unlike those identified by economists (see Mueller 1997). In negative terms, the claim is that, if one could run a sequence of cases differently, one would find that judicial outcomes too would be different, and they would trace a different path.

Second, adjudication constitutes a dichotomous discursive field in which specific legal questions are typically asked in a 'yes-no' format (Kornhauser 1992a: 171). Each party seeks different answers from the judge, and each makes counter-arguments in light of the other's claims. In the next section, I draw out some of the consequences of this structure for how legal actors are likely to behave. For now, it is enough to note that judges not only answer at least some of the questions posed to them but also give reasons for why they have chosen one result over another.[6] Dispositive answers given to yes-no questions possess the inherent capacity to block one path of development while encouraging another. Further, when judges justify their rulings with reasons, they at least implicitly announce prospective rules which subsequent litigants will understand and use as templates for future argumentation in cases that are similar in some salient way. If this is so, the *path independence* of legal institutions will be unlikely or exceptional.

Third, adaptation and network effects, to be registered on the behaviour of judges, lawyers, and professors, are facilitated by the fact that records of judicial activity are heavily documented. Published decisions typically include a description of the relevant or settled fact context of the case, a survey of the main arguments and counter-arguments, the dispositive decision, and the justification. The lawyers' briefs and other summaries of the parties' arguments are also usually available. Lawyers, who through training and practice

---

[6] In some polities, some courts are legally required to provide written legal justifications for rulings made.

learn to take their cues from these materials, are commonly organized into relatively autonomous groups that roughly map onto relatively autonomous domains of the law. If domains of law develop along separate path dependent lines, then the processes that serve to construct various networks of legal professionals will also be path dependent.

Fourth, judicial rule-making is typically embedded in dense matrices of legal rules, some of the properties of which will favour, again, increasing returns logics. As noted, the pre-existing records of relevant judicial activity will heavily condition the work of lawyers and judges, given almost any conception of precedent. Further, at any given point in time, the existing law relevant to any specific dispute may itself be relatively inflexible and path dependent in the sense of *being more or less immune to change except through adjudication*. This point applies to bodies of substantive law—particular distributions of rights and obligations governing interactions in a specific social context—but also to procedure and to principles of standing and jurisdiction. Last, but not least, modern legal systems typically organize legal acts hierarchically, and this fact has consequences for system inflexibility, that is, for the capacity of other political actors to alter or reverse judicial outcomes.

To take a concrete example, the German Basic Law confers upon the Federal Constitutional Court the authority to defend constitutional rights, and declares the primacy of those rights over any other conflicting legal provision. Any German statute can be attacked for violating rights provisions by almost any actor in society, public or private; if the German Court agrees with the petitioner and strikes downs a statute, reversal is virtually impossible, except through a subsequent decision of the Court. This is because the Basic Law protects basic rights from substantial change through constitutional amendment. More generally, wherever constitutional judicial review operates in a routine and minimally effective manner, the path dependence of constitutional law, because of its normative supremacy vis-à-vis other legal norms, will be assured. Given network effects, the relative inflexibility of any body of law will be largely determined by two factors: (1) the density of judicial rule-making in that area, and (2) the relative ease or difficulty of overturning the law-making effects of judicial decisions through non-judicial means (see Stone Sweet 2000: Chs 2, 3).

In summary, how courts typically operate and how legal actors typically behave are likely to provoke and then sustain the path dependent development of litigation and judicial rule-making. Given some underlying notion of precedent, these processes can be expected to exhibit some significant degree of randomness—through the vagaries of sequencing—and non-ergodicity—through the survival of rules announced in past rulings;

and judicial rule-making can be expected to provoke positive feedback effects—more litigation and the construction of litigation networks—and to move the law along paths that are relatively inflexible—that is, costly or impossible to reverse.

Judging and Precedent

Precedent is basic to the path dependence of the legal system. It is at the heart of the organizational code that judges curate and lawyers learn. If courts did not justify their decisions with reasons, or if legal communities did not consider the records of these justifications to be relevant to the conduct of future litigation, then there would be no increasing returns to this code. In this section, I stipulate the micro-foundations of precedent, and thus elaborate a very specific view of the phenomenon. As with any such stipulation, I will surely leave out elements that others consider to be crucial.

I note beforehand the existence of a dense, if disjointed, literature on precedent and the doctrine of *stare decisis*. The orthodox view, continuously reiterated in traditional academic discourse, has it that precedent and *stare decisis* perform a set of linked functions. They help judges discover and to apply rules of law presumed to be discoverable; they enhance legal certainty for the law's subjects; and they help judicial law-making—an intrinsically decentralized mode of governance—achieve a semblance of centralization and systemic coherence. Others take perspectives external to the law per se. For Stone Sweet (1999b) and Chapman (1994), precedent follows naturally from giving reasons for decisions, which is one of the basic techniques judges have to counter the permanent 'crisis of legitimacy' in which they find themselves (see also Shapiro 1980 and Chapter 4). Shapiro (this Chapter) argues that it enables courts to receive and to emit clearer signals in the face of an 'acute noise problem', the sheer quantity and richness of litigation that confront judges.[7] Rasmussen (1994) argues that the doctrine that precedents are binding serves to enhance each judge's power with respect to future judges, thus accounting for its popularity. For Stearns (1995: 1357), *stare decisis* allows courts to escape 'cycling' problems—majority voting situations in which there is no Nash equilibrium—being the 'social choice equivalent of the proscription on reconsideration of a rejected motion' that one finds in legislatures (see also Kornhauser 1992a). Each of these logics has merit, and I draw connections with some of them in the discussion that follows.

---

[7] Heiner (1986) re-specifies the problem as one of uncertainty and imperfect information.

Further, since the advent of legal realism there has been a long-running debate on the question of whether, why, and how precedents are binding (recent expressions include: Caldeira 1994; Knight and Epstein 1996; Segal and Spaeth 1996). Empirically, we know that legal actors routinely behave as if the legal materials contained in past court decisions were directly relevant to their purposes in the present; but we also know that judicial outcomes regularly escape parameters that pre-existing law would fix. Although by no means my central objective, this paper responds to this controversy. Most important, I reconceptualize the relationship between precedent and judicial rule-making as one in which the former enables the latter.

Precedent: Analogic Reasoning and Argumentation

Two basic claims about law and judges underlie my conception of precedent. First, judicial outcomes are fundamentally indeterminate. The generic source of the law's indeterminacy lies in the essential tension between the abstract nature of the social norm on the one hand, and the concrete nature of human experience on the other. Any particular social situation is in some meaningful sense unique, whereas norms are specified in light of an existing or evolving typology of fact contexts, an abstraction that deprives situations of some of their richness. One could imagine a world in which this tension did not exist. In a community governed by what Neil MacCormick (1989: 1) has called the 'special providence model of law', for example, a perfect normative system clearly specifies, for every individual in every possible situation, the rights and duties necessary for the community to achieve optimal collective good. In such a community, the law would constitute a 'complete' social contract (see Milgrom and Roberts 1992: 127–32). In the world we know, all bodies of law are imperfect and incomplete, hence one of the basic social functions of courts: to adapt norms of behaviour to the needs of those who live under them, over time, given changing circumstances.[8]

Second, judging, far from being a *sui generis* activity, is instead a manifestation of a deeply rooted human penchant for using analogic reasoning to make sense of, and to manage, the complexity of the environment. For cognitive psychologists, analogical reasoning is the process through which people 'reason and learn about a new situation (the target analog) by relating it to a more familiar situation (the source analog) that can be viewed as structurally parallel' (Holyoak and Thagard 1997). The ability to construct analogies is widely considered to be an innate part of thinking (Keane 1988;

[8] If judges are expected to resolve legal disputes in light of the dictates of the law, then they will have little choice but to 'complete' the law on an incremental basis. That is, judges will become law-makers.

Vosniadou and Ortony 1989; Holyoak and Thagard 1995; Mayer 1992). Unfamiliar situations, those that individuals cannot understand through their generalized knowledge, stimulate the formation of analogies which are used to conceptualize *and* to find solutions to problems (Keane 1988: 103). The set of potential source analogues is defined jointly by (1) the specific, immediate problem to be resolved, or situation to be conceptualized, and (2) the past experiences of the individuals constructing the analogy. Legal argumentation constitutes a species of analogical reasoning: actors reason through past decisions of the court—the equivalents of source analogues—to characterize the interplay of new fact contexts and legal interests raised by a dispute—the target analogue—and to find an appropriate solution to it.[9]

Psychologists have also engaged the question of what constitutes an appropriate or effective analogy. Research has shown that the most successful analogies—those that best enable people to conceptualize situations and solve problems—maximize certain values, what the literature refers to as 'constraints' (Spellman and Holyoak 1992). The greater the conceptual similarity between source and target, the more the internal relationships between their core elements are structurally parallel, and the better able to offer solutions to the problems posed, the more effective is the analogy. Holyoak and Thagard (1997) have shown that problem solvers generally do seek to maximize each of these values, and in doing so they enhance the overall coherence of analogic thinking. Moreover, even when the choice of source analogue is guided by the conscious, goal-oriented purposes of the individual, the constraints guiding analogy formation nonetheless impose a degree of consistency on the sorts of mappings that will be considered effective and legitimate.

It is an obvious, but not a trivial, thing to note that analogy formation is a perfectly path dependent process, in that each transfer or adaptation of a source analog to a target analog is possible only by virtue of a prior outcome of analogic reasoning which, in turn, depends upon the sequence of situations and problems that individuals have *already* confronted and resolved.

---

[9] I have quite consciously not referenced the scholarly literature in law and philosophy on the uses and abuses of analogy in reasoning. My point is that analogical reasoning is part of the deep structure of legal reasoning, regardless of how legal actors actually use it. In legal scholarship, analogical reasoning is more or less taken for granted as one of the mechanisms through which case law develops. Murray (1982: 833) calls it 'a vital tool in legal reasoning' and Sunstein (1993: 741) states that 'reasoning by analogy is the most familiar form of legal reasoning', but both lament the lack of serious attention given to its actual role in producing legal outcomes. I am aware of only two studies that relate the cognitive psychology of analogical reasoning to precedent-based legal reasoning (Marchant *et al.* 1991; 1993); both report experiments using subjects untrained in the law, and neither examines litigation or judicial outcomes.

Research has shown that, at any given moment in time, people have some discretion, or exercise some degree of conscious choice, over which analogue gets mapped onto unfamiliar situations and how; but the set of available analogues is finite, having been determined by prior events and choices. In adjudication, analogic reasoning has been institutionalized as a set of relatively stable practices. Lawyers and judges use it self-consciously, and the results of their deliberations are, I repeat, heavily documented, which facilitates the identification and mapping of appropriate analogies. Of course, in crafting their arguments and decisions, litigators and judges also work to achieve logical or systemic coherence through other methods, such as deduction and abduction.

Although analogic reasoning infuses the organizational codes that structures the domain of law and adjudication, it is also a functional instrument of decision-making. Litigation raises questions concerning which and how legal norms are to be applied to concrete situations, and with what social consequences. Judges will answer these questions in light of how they have answered questions raised with respect to prior, analogous situations rather than willy-nilly, because skilled analogic reasoning is basic not only to skilled action per se but to the judges' own social legitimacy. By formalizing the results of analogic reasoning into precedents, say through abduction, judges give the legal system a measure of 'relative determinacy' (see Sartor 1994: 200–2). In providing analogues to other actors, they enhance the coherence of the litigation environment, thus reducing randomness and noise. And by grounding judicial rule-making in discourses present in existing case law, the judges mitigate the problem that the precise content of the law governing a particular social situation could not have been known to the parties at the time their dispute erupted (see Stone Sweet, Chapter 1, this volume). None of these points is incompatible with the view that those who litigate and those who judge are goal-oriented. Indeed, the argument is that legal actors will sharpen their analogic reasoning skills through training and use, precisely because they are rational, strategic actors operating within an organizational code that requires such skills of them.

I now turn to precedent or, more precisely, to *argumentation frameworks*. Prior legal decisions constitute the materials that enable the construction of such frameworks. Legal systems are webs or clusters of relatively autonomous argumentation frameworks.

Argumentation frameworks are discursive structures that organize (1) how parties to a legal dispute ask questions of judges and engage one another's respective arguments, and (2) how courts frame their decisions.[10] Following

---

[10] Due to space limitations, only the main features of such frameworks are discussed here.

Sartor (1994), these can be analysed as a series of inference steps represented by a statement justified by reasons or inference rules that lead to a conclusion. Such frameworks typically embody inconsistency to the extent that they offer, for each inference step, both a defensible argument and a counter-argument from which contradictory—but defensible—conclusions can be reached. In resolving disputes within these structures, judges choose from a menu of those conclusions.

In practice, legal argumentation, unlike purer forms of logical deduction, tends to be 'non-monotonic'. In monotonic reasoning, 'no logical consequence gets lost by extending the premises from which it has been deducted' (Sartor 1994: 191). The primary source of non-monotonicity in legal discourse is the dialectic relationship between new facts or information about the context of the dispute, and the existing premises that underlie normative conclusions. Particularly susceptible to this dialectic are those argumentation frameworks that contain normative statements that (1) announce general rules and then justified exceptions to those rules, and (2) govern how conflicting legal interests ought to be balanced, or how the conflict between two otherwise applicable norms is to be resolved (for example, when two rights provisions conflict). In balancing situations, which are ubiquitous in constitutional and administrative law, 'only the particular circumstances of a case allow a choice to be made', while any new situation 'may render new arguments possible, which may defeat previously valid ones' (Sartor 1994: 191, 197).

We have returned to the point made earlier : that legal systems and judicial outcomes are indeterminate. Nonetheless, argumentation frameworks provide a measure of at least short-term systemic stability to the extent that they condition how litigants and judges pursue their self interest, social justice, or other values through adjudication. To be effective, legal actors have to be able to identify the type of dispute in which they are involved, reason through the range of legal norms that are potentially applicable, and assess available remedies and their consequences. Such frameworks, being formalized analogues, help actors do all of these things and more. They require actors to engage not only in analogic reasoning but in argumentation. Considered in more sociological terms, they are highly developed, meso-level structures that connect institutions—the law—to the domain of individual agency by sustaining deliberation about the nature, scope, and application of norms. In culturalist terms, they enable specifically placed social actors to adjust existing if abstract 'guides to action' to 'the relentless particularity of experience' (Eckstein 1988: 795-6) on a continuous basis. Precedent is basic to judicial governance, allowing it to proceed incrementally from pre-existing institutional materials.

An Example

One can expect to find argumentation frameworks wherever one finds sustained litigation, irrespective of standard distinctions made in comparative law.[11] The basic elements of argumentation frameworks are legal norms—normative statements[12]—as these norms have been interpreted and applied by judges in past disputes. Such structures amalgamate normative materials for the purposes of solving particular legal problems. In tort litigation, for example, judges resolve the problem 'is the defendant responsible for damages allegedly suffered by the plaintiff?' on the basis of how a set of lower-level questions has been argued and answered. These include questions concerning the definition and measurement of negligence, risk assumption, and so on, as well as how chains of causality are to be constructed from the facts. Clusters of rules assembled from different streams of case law typically organize how these different questions are posed and answered. The precise mix of questions and the amalgamated clusters of normative statements that enable legal actors to respond to any given set of questions constitute the relevant argumentation framework.

It may be useful at this point to provide an example of the development of one such argumentation framework, that governing the question 'is flag burning a form of symbolic speech that is protected by the first amendment?' Simplifying, the framework is designed to handle two kinds of lower-order questions. First, what constitutes symbolic speech? Second, to what extent does government have a legitimate, constitutionally recognized interest in limiting rights to symbolic speech?

The answer to the second question came first. In *O'Brien*, the US Supreme Court (USSC 1968*a*) recognized that certain communicative acts, although wordless, might constitute forms of speech protected by the Constitution. Nonetheless, the Court ruled that the government could regulate such acts if certain criteria had been met. *O'Brien* had burned his draft card, in violation of a federal statute, in protest against the Vietnam War and military conscription. The Court let stand his conviction on the grounds that the statute's purposes went substantially beyond the mere stifling of speech; the

---

[11] The best systematic, comparative research has shown that 'there are no great differences in the use [of precedent] between the so-called common law and civil law systems' (Summers and Tartuffo 1991: 481). Sartor (1994) gives two detailed examples of argumentation frameworks, the first drawn from Italian torts, the second from German constitutional law.

[12] 'All statements (obligations, permissions, authorizations, applicability rules, interpretation canons, preference evaluations, definitions, etc.) susceptible to being used in justifying legal conclusions are fully entitled legal norms', not least because they 'interact reciprocally in the game of arguments and counter arguments' (Sartor 1994: 200).

draft card fulfilled a variety of administrative functions, such as communicating the rights and duties of the bearer. In deciding the case, the Court was
led to formulate the following 'test':

a government regulation is justified if it is within the constitutional power of the
government; if it furthers an important or substantial government interest; if the
government's interest is unrelated to the suppression of free expression; and if
the incidental restriction on alleged First Amendment freedoms in no greater than
is essential to the furtherance of that interest.

Announced in this general and prospective way, this rule could be expected to induce argumentation and deliberation of a specific kind, in light of
specific fact contexts.

In subsequent cases, the Court gave the concept of 'symbolic speech'
a name and conferred on it the protection of the first amendment (for
example, USSC 1969). In *Spence* (USSC 1974*a*), the Court defined symbolic
speech as those wordless acts in which 'an intent to convey a particularized message [is] present' and that 'in the surrounding circumstances the
likelihood [is] great that the message would be understood' by those who
witness it. Henceforth, those who would claim first amendment protections
for symbolic speech will have to convince the Court that their acts 'pass' the
Spence test. They do so in full knowledge that the government will argue the
contrary.

By the time of the Texas flag burning case (USSC 1989), the argumentation
framework governing symbolic speech was sufficiently developed to structure, more or less completely, the proceedings. The Court, working through
the Spence test, agreed with Mr Johnson that his act of burning the flag, on
public grounds during the 1984 National Republican Convention, constituted symbolic speech. Proceeding to balancing, the Court rejected Texas'
assertion that the State's interest in protecting the flag—because Texans 'ven-
erate' it—outweighed Johnson's speech rights. After all, to the extent that
the flag actually did function as a symbolic repository of collective meaning,
Johnson's act could not but be collectively understood (Spence). Given its
declared interest, the State's prohibition of flag burning could not be disso-
ciated from the direct suppression of speech, and it therefore failed the third
prong of the *O'Brien* test.

In *Texas v. Johnson*, the law governing symbolic speech was extended
to flag burning, with spectacular political effects. But the decision, from
the point of view of the argumentation framework, broke no new ground.
Instead it reinforced the centrality of a specific cluster of normative statements, found in *O'Brien* and *Spence*, to these types of situations. Further,

the outcome in Texas is a path dependent one, proceeding from a particular sequence of accumulated judicial refinements of answers to questions that serve to specify the legal interests of those who would litigate symbolic speech cases. It bears mention in this regard that the law of symbolic speech is relatively inflexible, as defined above,[13] and will likely remain so as long as the framework remains stable. At the same time, like any balancing framework, this structure provides courts with a great deal of flexibility in that it allows them to justify a ruling for either the speaker or the government: the fact context, not the law, will vary.

Precedent: Rationality and Adaptation

I assume that all legal actors are rational in the sense of being utility-maximizers. I assume that judges seek to maximize, in addition to private interests, at least two corporate values (see also Stone Sweet 2000: 139–50). First, they work to enhance their legitimacy vis-à-vis all potential disputants by portraying their own rule-making as meaningfully constrained by, and reflecting the current state of, the law. Second, they work to enhance the salience of judicial modes of reasoning vis-à-vis disputes that may arise in the future. Propagating argumentation frameworks allows them to pursue both interests simultaneously. Judges may also seek to enact their own policy preferences through their decisions. Yet the more they do so, or the more that other actors understand them to be doing so, the more likely judges will be to attempt to hide their policy behaviour in legal doctrine. Once policy is packaged as doctrine, it will operate as a constraint on future judicial law-making to the extent that doctrine narrows the range of arguments and justifications that are available to litigators and judges, and to the extent that the law is path dependent.

I assume that litigators are seeking to shape the law in ways that will most benefit their clients, at the moment and in the future. Given the costs of litigation, non-judicial actors will pursue their interests through adjudication only so long as expected returns exceed those costs. In public law litigation, this calculation will be partly conditioned by perceptions of the relative cost and likelihood of achieving the same policy change through other means, such as lobbying for legislative reform. They will do so in full knowledge that there will be others who will work to block legal change. In any given domain of law, rationality means deploying those litigation strategies best adapted to achieving desired legal outcomes, given the current state of the law, as

---

[13] In response to the decision, the US Congress adopted a statute to protect the flag, a law later annulled by the federal courts. A constitutional amendment designed for the same purpose was proposed but never adopted.

that law is constituted by argumentation frameworks. Those who litigate more frequently in any given domain will invest more heavily in mastering the intricacies of relevant frameworks, the organizational field's codes, and in charting their evolution over time. This is another way of saying that the more the law is path dependent the more we can expect it to branch, and the more incentives legal elites will have to specialize, not least in order to participate in the development of the law.

Implications

If the law is path dependent for the reasons identified, then a range of complex issues are raised. It may also be that, at some times and in some areas, legal institutions are relatively *path independent*. This possibility, too, raises a set of important and unanswered questions.

The Indeterminate Norm and Judicial Discretion

Figure 2.1 helps to simplify and summarize the argument made thus far, namely, that adjudication functions to reduce the indeterminacy of legal norms through (1) use, that is, argumentation, interpretation, application, and (2) the propagation of argumentation frameworks. The line between

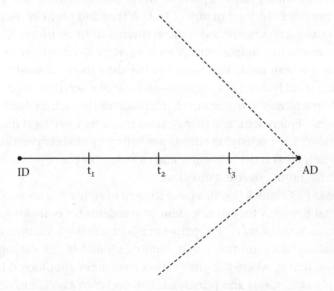

Fig. 2.1. The indeterminate norm and judicial discretion

point ID—absolute indeterminacy—and point AD—absolute determinacy—defines the extent to which any given rule can vary along one dimension, that of determinacy. Point ID represents a theoretical pole at which there exist no stable, collective understandings of the meaning and scope of application of the rule. Point AD represents the opposite theoretical pole, at which the collective understandings of the meaning and scope of application of the norm are perfect; neither ID nor AD is realistic. For any given norm, indeterminacy is a relative condition: it will vary in context and over time. If the law is path dependent, for the reasons given, the position of the norm on this continuum will move from left to right over time, as the rule is adjudicated. The broken lines spreading from point AD define the range of defensible arguments available for how a rule must be applied to resolve disputes arising within that rule's purview. The space constitutes the judge's *zone of discretion* within which the judge chooses among available options and justifications. If the law is path dependent, this zone will narrow over time, as the rule is adjudicated. That is, argumentation frameworks that appear will move from left to right: choice narrows; and frameworks become more articulated. As this space narrows, so does the discretion of the judge.

The argument made here bears directly on certain debates within contemporary legal theory. In so far as legal institutions are in fact path dependent, certain strains of positive legal theory must be considered at least presumptively right or supportive of the theory presented here, and other strains of legal theory must be presumptively wrong. In the former category we find the positivist legal theory of H. L. A Hart and his heirs. Hart (1994: especially 124–41), understood judicial discretion to be inversely proportional to normative indeterminacy so long as judges did their jobs in an 'adequate' or 'reasonably defensible' rather than in an 'arbitrary' or 'irrational' manner. Judicial law-making—the use of discretion—is defensible rather than arbitrary to the extent that it proceeds through analogic reasoning, in light of precedent, and to the extent that it 'renders' legal rules 'more determinate'. The underlying criteria governing a justified extension of the law into new areas is the 'relevance and closeness' of the new situation to a pre-existing, norm-governed situation.

For Neil MacCormick (1978), a close student of Hart's, the primary objective of legal theory is the development of standards for evaluating judicial decisions as 'good or bad', 'acceptable or not acceptable', 'rational or arbitrary'. Bad decisions are those that cannot, ultimately, be packaged as a deduction, that is, where the justification given does not proceed logically from explicated norms and principles. Bad decisions also fail to adhere to the 'principle of formal justice' defined as *like cases shall be decided in like fashion.* For MacCormick, judges can produce good decisions only through a combination of *good* analogical reasoning and *good* justification:[14] precisely the mix of ingredients that generates argumentation frameworks and makes them path dependent. Further, good decisions definitively structure lawyers' strategies (positive feedback): *good* strategies will reinforce existing frameworks and will plead for incremental adjustments to the law from judges (see the related comments in the Introduction and Shapiro's contribution to this chapter).[15] Last, even where consequentialist—policy—arguments trump purely legal ones, judges are likely to choose from a menu comprised of defensible rulings, not all rulings that are imaginable. These points, because they link the production of doctrine to the dynamics of prospective judicial law-making,[16] are generally consistent with arguments made in this chapter and elsewhere in this book.

But they also contrast with what the law and economics movement typically asserts. Law and economics imagines a market for legal institutions. Stable institutions that do emerge are assumed to be Pareto-efficient since if they were not they would be abandoned and replaced. In the world imagined, institutions are plastic—both malleable and disposable—and new ones can be generated with little or no cost. In such a world, the analyst needs to know a great deal about the needs of the economy and about how to calculate transaction costs and efficiencies, but little or nothing about how the law has developed through use. We agree that there is a market for legal rules that litigation and adjudication help to construct. But we see

---

[14] 'In short, rules can be ambiguous in given contexts, and can be applied in one way or the other only after the ambiguity is resolved. But resolving the ambiguity in effect involves choosing between rival versions of the rule ... once that choice is made, a simple deductive justification of a particular decision follows. But a complete justification of that decision must hinge then on how the choice between the competing versions of the rule is justified ... ' (MacCormick 1978: 67–8).

[15] '[T]he requirement upon a litigant's lawyers to frame his case as a legal claim or defense imposes ... two limits on the formulation of the case: first, it must be so formulated as to avoid conflict with existing rules—here the possibility of 'explaining' and 'distinguishing' unfavourable precedents ... must be borne in mind; and secondly, it must be formulated in such a way that it can be shown to be supported by analogies from existing ... law ... preferably authoritatively stated by judges ... or by ... respectable legal writers ... or *faute de mieux* newly minted by counsel as explaining and rationalizing some relevant group of acknowledged rules' (MacCormick 1978: 121).

[16] '[I]t seems that appreciation of the necessary universality of justifying reasons for the decision of particular cases can enable us clearly to explain otherwise puzzling features of the doctrine of precedent. It does so by focusing on the way in which, quite apart from any doctrine of [*stare decisis*] in any official or binding sense, the constraints of formal justice obligate a court to attend to the need for generic rulings on points of law, and their acceptability as generic rulings, as essential to the justification of particular decisions' (MacCormick 1978: 86).

no reason to assume, a priori, that the world constructed is an optimally efficient one.

Efficiency and Rigidity

The allocational efficiency of any institution is not determined by the degree to which that institution was the outcome of a path dependent process. As David (1997: 21) puts it, 'Path dependence is not a sufficient condition for market failure'; the two questions are analytically distinct. The account of legal institutions offered here does not need the assumption that the law is at least as 'efficient' as all other possible institutional arrangements, only that such institutions are relatively functional for actors and make them better off than they would be in a world without such arrangements. Put differently, between some theorized optimality point or curve and a situation in which there is no rule structure at all, there exists a huge range of possible outcomes that may become institutionalized through sequencing and feedback of judicial rulings.

The issue of institutional rigidity or inflexibility is potentially more embarrassing. The concepts of path dependence, positive feedback, and increasing returns are all variables, yet this variance is rarely operationalized, let alone explained. Economic historians have produced persuasive, perhaps definitive, explanations of specific episodes of the path dependent development of technology, production standards, and networked systems. Taken as a whole, these explanations add up to something suggestive of a common framework of analysis. But little attention has been paid to path dependence as a dependent variable. If the argument of this paper is right, than ongoing, intensive adjudication will produce relatively discrete, path dependent lines of case law. There would seem to be no good reason to think that all argumentation frameworks, let alone the legal rules supported by case law, should be equally path dependent in the sense of being inflexible or 'locked in'. After all, courts may abandon precedent and start over; they may borrow doctrinal materials from other lines of case law considered more successful in some way; and the rule of incrementalism may be violated by dramatic new rulings. Likewise, there would also seem to be no good reason to assumed that legal elites should be networked similarly across time and domain. These are empirical issues that deserve sustained empirical attention.

Increasing Returns: To What, for Whom?

In this paper, the phrase 'increasing returns to legal institutions' is suggestive shorthand for the ways in which positive feedback, as managed by judges, generates network effects , helps to spread and entrench organizational codes, and produces path dependent legal outcomes. Yet increasing returns is technically a function, a measurable relation among variables: for example, the relationship of costs, or investments, to profits. It may turn out to be quite difficult for political scientists to produce compelling increasing returns explanations of political institutions if problems associated with operationalization and measurement or variables are not overcome. Where the law directly imposes transaction costs and conditions the exercise of property rights—for example, economic regulation, product liability—calculating the marginal benefits of adjustment to a nascent standard may be relatively straightforward.[17] Yet, in many salient areas of law and politics, calculating marginal costs and benefits is not straightforward, including in the example given above on symbolic speech.

I notice the problem but do not pretend to have resolved it. It is worth emphasizing that the argument developed here is that *argumentation frameworks are subject to increasing returns.* I do not deny that specific, dispositive legal outcomes can be produced through increasing returns dynamics, and may even become 'locked in' as any norm or standard of behaviour might be locked in. But my focus is on the development of argumentation frameworks, *not on the specific rule governing the situation*; the orientation flows in part from the assumption that legal rules are indeterminate. The production of argumentation frameworks is best modelled as a coordination game in so far as all legal elites—litigators, law professors, and judges—need such codes and are better off with than they would be without such frameworks. Such codes may have distributive consequences in and of themselves, but they also help to define and network the field of adjudication. They are thus basic to the social power of legal elites. The struggle, through litigation, to resolve specific disputes and to make rules to govern specific situations falls outside of cooperative game theory. Argumentation frameworks are the meta-rules that govern this struggle, and meta-rules are probably more easily produced and sustained than are outcomes pursuant to litigation, which is 'play within the meta-rules'. That said, the stability of judicially curated rules heavily depends upon the stability of doctrinal structures.

---

[17] Yet even here there are problems, which I thank James Caporaso for pointing out. In invoking increasing returns, do we mean to say that 'the marginal cost of making the nth decision is less than the average cost of all decisions?' Is there 'a supply curve for judicial decisions, in which the costs decrease and benefits increase at the margins?'

Conclusion

I have argued that certain characteristics of judging and of courts will favour the path dependent development of argumentation frameworks, which are the basic codes that define adjudication as an organizational field. At any given point in time, existing argumentation frameworks, and the substantive legal outcomes they help to sustain, will constitute the necessary causal conditions for the emergence of new frameworks, and thus for new extensions of the law.

In principle, the analyst should be able to chart the development of frameworks which should, in principle, chart the evolution of the legal system more broadly. The development of legal institutions will provoke the development of networks of legal actors specializing in that area of the law. For these actors, existing argumentation frameworks establish the basic parameters for action.

The basic unit of observation is the doctrinal or argumentation framework. If a legal system exhibits path dependent qualities, then the following expectations will be met *and* will be causally related to one another.

First, argumentation frameworks will link, through feedback loops, the activities of litigators and judges over time. Litigation will provide opportunities for judges to construct such frameworks, and subsequent litigants will take their cues from judicial rule-making. If such frameworks are path dependent, the sequence *litigation –> judicial rule-making –> subsequent litigation –> subsequent rule-making* will tend to reproduce itself as a self-reinforcing process sustained by a mix of analogic reasoning and the self-interest of legal actors, that is, potential litigants and judges.

Second, legal outcomes will be both indeterminate and incremental. By 'indeterminate' I mean that, the further downstream we are from any given prior point in the process of selecting or refining legal institutions through adjudication, the more unpredictable will be the content of the rule selected. By 'incremental' I mean that the substantive law and argumentation frameworks produced through this process will be predicated on outcomes and frameworks that had emerged upstream. Stated differently, how cases are sequenced and decided will organize the future.

Third, legal institutions will produce network effects that embed them in wider social practices and interests. Substantive legal outcomes and argumentation frameworks will become parameters for, focal points of, social action. They will be referenced and used by an increasing numbers of individuals and groups operating in an increasing numbers of arenas, including those not otherwise directly associated with adjudication.

Fourth, legal institutions will be relatively resistant to reversal or de-institutionalization. This outcome will be governed partly by the decision-making rules that govern reversal of the judicial law-making and partly by the relative embeddedness, through positive feedback, of outcomes over time.

3

Constitutional Judicial Review

In this chapter, three papers explore the politics of constitutional review, the power of a court or other organ of government to review the constitutionality of public acts, including legislation, and to void those acts as unlawful when they are found to be in conflict with the constitutional law. At the close of the Second World War, four federal states—Australia, Canada, Switzerland, and the United States—could be counted as polities in which review operated with at least minimal effectiveness, but there was very little review operating elsewhere.[1] Since 1949, dozens of states have adopted new constitutions providing for constitutional review. Given the high priority placed on protecting human rights in the regimes that followed the demise of fascism in Germany and Italy, military-authoritarianism in southern Europe and Latin America, and communism in eastern Europe, there was little choice in the matter. Today, the rights and review tandem is an essential, even obligatory, component of any move toward constitutional democracy.

There exists a multiplicity of approaches available for comparative research on constitutional review, of course, which we make no attempt to survey here. Instead, we begin by noting that social science research on comparative law and courts has never been sustained, even in the two sub-fields of the discipline that one might have hoped to see such an agenda develop: public law political science[2] and comparative politics. In most American political science departments, public law means American law and courts or, where jurisprudence is taught, it can also mean normative political theory. Courses on comparative law are rarely offered, so appropriate textbooks are nearly non-existent. Comparative politics people, following the lead of their public law colleagues, commonly ignore foreign legal systems in their

---

[1] The Scandinavian countries and Communist regimes had it but did not use it, if for different reasons. Irish review received little attention before the Second World War.

[2] Unlike the United States, where political science has always counted 'public law' as one of its sub-fields, European social science has noticed law and courts, if at all, as discrete parts of larger projects: for example, the sociology of lawyers as part of a sociology of the professions. We limit our remarks to American political science here.

studies of foreign countries. There have been important, if isolated, exceptions to these statements, but it is indisputable that social science scholarship
has fallen far behind the very obvious 'global expansion of judicial power'
(Tate and Vallinder 1995) now being witnessed.

The fact that the American Supreme Court is the only court with which
most American political scientists can be assumed to be familiar also has
consequences for how comparative materials might be engaged. Shapiro
(for example, 1993a) has long exhorted public law political science to move
beyond its fetish of constitutional law and the Supreme Court, perhaps with
occasional, and sometimes extreme, overstatement. However, to say that
we should do other than constitutional law is not to say that we should not
do constitutional law at all. And to say that we should do more than the
United States is not to say that we should not do the United States at all.
Indeed comparative research using the US legal system as one of the cases to
be compared can be a useful endeavour. At a minimum, the start-up costs
are usually lower. Indeed, Shapiro has compared the United States and the
European Union extensively (for example, Shapiro 1996; 1997; 1998b; 2002a;
and Chapter 4, this volume; see also Goldstein 2001).

One dimension of the work Shapiro presents here (see also Chapter 4)
is a very weak comparative technique, perhaps excused by its prophylactic
motives. Stone Sweet's (for example, Stone 1990; Stone Sweet 2000) research
proceeds from the fact that Austrian and German traditions of constitutional review, rather than the American model of checks and balances and
judicial review, has been the inspiration for the wide diffusion of constitutional courts in Europe.[3] Nevertheless, the long American experience of
more or less successful judicial review has long conditioned Continental
debates on the question of whether and how to develop a system of constitutional justice (Stone 1992a: Chs 1, 9). Further, the overwhelming American
presence and power in the immediate post-Second World War period mandated establishing rights and review in new constitutions for Germany
and Italy. Much of Shapiro's comparing of the US and European legal systems therefore boils down to telling non-Americans: 'if you are thinking,
"What worked in America might work here too", you had better understand
what really happened in America.' Hypotheses drawn from earlier American
experience, properly understood, could be tested against later non-American
experience. We emphasize that what Shapiro usually presents is time staged
analysis, not an assertion that the United States is more constitutionally

---

[3] See also Chapter 6.

advanced than other places or has served or should serve as a model for others.

A chapter on comparative constitutional law is a good place to add a further warning about its dangers. A current generation of scholars trained in American constitutional law, and engaged in the study of the Supreme Court, may have finally discovered constitutional judicial review in Europe. It seems, at least, that Americans now propose to go hunting there. That they have done so now, after years of ignoring the frantic signals of Donald Kommers (1976; 1989), Walter Murphy (Murphy and Tanenhaus 1977), and others, is largely due to the rampant development of European review itself, which public law political science probably could not have ignored forever.

Yet moving to Europe wearing American constitutional law blinders is likely to lead to singular misunderstanding and distortion of European experience. American constitutional law scholars have tended to neglect an intermediate realm of law lying between constitutional law and regular statutory law, exemplified by the Civil Rights Acts and the Administrative Procedures Act. Technically only statutes, they are constitution-like in being entangled with constitutions, treated as overarching norms applied in judicial review of a wide range of government—and often private—actions, and vesting wide discretion in reviewing judges. Anyone seeking to teach the US constitutional law of discrimination quickly finds how difficult and ultimately futile it is to do so without considering the Civil Rights Acts in relation to the Fourteenth Amendment. Nevertheless, there remains an almost automatic association of individual or human rights with constitutional law. As a result, those wearing constitutional law blinders are likely to focus exclusively on constitutional law when they move from American rights to European rights. To do so is to miss the boat, or rather to take it to a secondary port. For some of the most significant rights developments in Europe lie not just in constitutional law but in the realm between constitutional law and statutes, that is, in higher law that is not constitutional law.

To be sure, a substantial amount of European judicial review in the defence of individual rights is grounded either in specific constitutional charters comprised of rights-like provisions or in judicial discoveries, often exceptionally imaginative discoveries, of rights implications in constitutions. But another incredibly fruitful source of rights is the European Convention on Human Rights. The Convention is not a constitution but a treaty under international law. As such it creates an obligation for its signatory member states to respect the long list of rights enumerated in the treaty, but it does not vest any of those rights in individuals. Should the European Court of Human Rights find a signatory in violation of a rights provision of the treaty, it will seek to move the member state to bring its offending statute or administrative action into compliance, but it cannot do anything directly to remedy the injury to the individual the invasion of whose rights brought the case to the Court in the first place. Because European Convention rights are international law treaty rights, those rights typically do not attach to individuals directly, by virtue of the Convention itself. Instead, these rights enter into the national legal order by virtue of national statutes—or, in a few 'monist' states, through national constitutional provisions—that, in effect, 'domesticate' the Convention by incorporating it into national law. Rights domesticated by statute occupy a statutory, not a constitutional, rung in the hierarchy of legal norms.

In the conventional orthodoxy of European parliamentary systems, any new statute automatically supersedes preceding contradictory statutes. No earlier statute may bar contradictory statutory provisions subsequently enacted by the legislature. To claim otherwise would be to assert that the legislature lacked the power to amend or repeal its own statutes by subsequent statutes. Yet the various national statutes domesticating the Convention often do provide that they are to prevail even over subsequently enacted national statutes. In this sense, they are higher-law statutes, but not constitutional law. Thus constitutional law blinders will keep those domesticated Convention rights and their widespread judicial enforcement in Europe out of the picture.

Constitutional blinders also distort any attempt to deal with the new case law on rights in the United Kingdom. Until recently, the closest thing to constitutional individual rights in a country without a written constitution were some old statutes, like Fox's Libel Act, and certain judge-made restraints on administrative action. The vehicle for those restraints, however, has been the administrative law doctrines of *ultra vires* and natural justice. Of course, if American scholars actually did public law, which includes administrative law, this would not have mattered so much. But most of them do only constitutional law, and so are quite unprepared to deal with English administrative law. Recently the UK Parliament has enacted a human rights statute, which technically creates only English statutory rights, but is roughly comparable to continental statutes domesticating the European Convention. Even before the new statute, UK courts had adopted the position that they could not imagine that Parliament would enact statutes that violated the European Convention, which the UK had signed. It followed that it was the duty of judges to interpret statutes in such a way as to bring them into accord with the Convention. Many Continental courts follow the same practice, which is sometimes called 'principled construction'. All this, of course, is statutory interpretation, not constitutional law, but nonetheless it creates a regime of rights that are enforced as trumps against run-of-the-mill statutory provisions.

Thus, one of the newly flourishing judicially enforced rights regimes in Europe lies in international law and 'higher' statutory law, but not in constitutional law. And this matters much more in Europe than in the United States. As a pleading matter, American lawyers do have to know whether they are claiming under provisions of the Civil Rights Acts or directly under the 14th Amendment. But whether their claim is statutory or constitutional, federal courts are courts of general jurisdiction. The same American court will hear both claims, so lawyers will make both to them. In Continental Europe, however, a constitutional court is typically established as a special court which can hear only constitutional claims, and is the only court that can hear such claims. Thus, rights claims that technically are statutory, that is, arising under 'higher law' statutes or proposed as interpretations of regular statutes, go not to constitutional courts but to the—quite separate—regular and administrative courts. If the American habits of noticing only constitutional law and the Supreme Court are taken to Europe, then only European constitutional courts will be seen and much of the rights review—and a great deal of judicial empowerment—in Europe will be neglected.

France provides the most dramatic example of the problem. The French constitution provides for a separate constitutional court with exclusive jurisdiction over constitutional claims, but is open only to certain specified officials such as members of parliament, not to other courts or to individuals. The Constitutional Council discovered and then incorporated a bill of rights into the French constitution (Stone 1992a: Chs 1, 3). Its only jurisdiction, however, is the constitutional review of proposed French statutes—*after* their enactment by the legislature, but *before* their promulgation. Once promulgated, statutes, and administrative action taken under them, are forever protected from constitutional review through the Council. Meanwhile, separation of powers doctrines establishing the juridical supremacy of statute and prohibiting the regular judiciary from reviewing the constitutionality legality of statutes remain formally in place. So, if we use American constitutional law blinders, it would appear that a French individual may never go to any court seeking vindication of rights, and that by the time the rights-invading potential of any statute became evident, that is, during its enforcement subsequent to promulgation, no judge could do anything about it anyway.

Not so, and for two reasons. First, the French have enacted a national statute domesticating the European Convention on Human Rights and providing that it shall take precedence over even subsequently enacted French legislation. Thus today any French citizen can go, not to a constitutional court before a law is promulgated, but to a regular or administrative court after it is promulgated, for vindication not of constitutional rights but of higher statutory rights originating in international law. Second (see Stone Sweet 2000: Ch. 4), French judges on the civil courts now routinely engage in principled construction of statutes, in effect rewriting them so that they will agree with both the Convention and with the rights texts incorporated into the French Constitution, despite the absence of jurisdiction over the latter texts. And the French Council of State, the supreme court of appeal for the administrative law courts, is busily converting its general principles of law, which it had constructed and catalogued over the last century, into constitutional principles. It is doing so on the basis of its own readings of French constitutional rights, although these interpretations do not always accord with those of the constitutional court. Are we to miss all of this? Are the constitutional-Supreme Court sins of the American scholar fathers to be visited on the American scholar daughters?

Quite apart from carpet-bagging Americanists, there exists a small but growing group of political scientists, trained and located in the comparative and international relations sub-fields, that produce research on non-American legal systems.[4] This work rarely takes as its point of reference the American experience; it is published in mainstream comparative and international relations journals, and largely ignores the lessons of American public law scholarship—sometimes to its detriment, of course. This is the case of Stone Sweet, as well as the mostly younger political scientists who do research on the European Court of Justice (ECJ). In the 1990s, for example,

---

[4] Stone Sweet's paper 'Constitutional Politics in France and Germany,' presented here, was first published as a contribution to a Comparative Political Studies symposium on the political impact of European constitutional courts (Shapiro and Stone 1994). At the time we conceived this project, neither of the leading journals in the comparative field, *Comparative Politics* and *Comparative Political Studies*, had ever published, in their history, an article on the topics of constitutions, law, judges, or courts. Unfortunately, outside of EU studies, comparativists still barely notice law and courts, even when judges would appear to be central to their concerns. To take a recent and striking example, George Tsebelis, in his *American Political Science Review* article 'Veto Players and Law Production in Parliamentary Democracies' (1999), ignores courts entirely, even though constitutional—and other—judges fit his or any definition of veto players, and even though political parties and other individuals and groups regularly activate constitutional review mechanisms in order to block proposed legislative changes. Tsebelis is not alone. Adrian Hull (1999), who has recently examined the substantive focus of every article published in *Comparative Politics, Comparative Political Studies*, and *World Politics* since 1981, found that courts ranked near the bottom, with 0.9% of topics found, and constitutions ranked dead last with 0% of topics found, results that restate the findings of a similar study published in the 1980s (Sigelman and Gadbois 1983).

the European Court became the most studied court by social scientists after the US Supreme Court. American political scientists have produced a wealth of new books and dissertations on the ECJ (Alter 2001; Cichowski 2002; Conant 2002; Goldstein 2001; Mattli 1999; Nyikos 2000), along with an important stream of articles (Alter 1998; Alter and Meunier-Aitshalia 1994; Burley and Mattli 1993; Cichowski 1998; 2001; Golub 1996; Kenney 1999; Stone Sweet and Brunell 1998*a*, *b*; Stone Sweet and Caporaso 1998*b*; literature reviewed in Mattli and Slaughter 1998). Further, research on policy-making in the EU routinely incorporates the ECJ as a powerful policy-maker that interacts with other EU organs and with national politics in the making of EU law (Mazey 1998; Pierson 1996*a*; Pollack 1997; O'Reilly and Stone Sweet 1998; Sandholtz 1998; Sbragia 1998). Such work is regularly published in journals such as the *Journal of Common Market Studies* and the *Journal of European Public Policy*.

These are positive signs. Still, it may be worth stating clearly that, if the move to comparative law and courts leads only to some of us studying some European law, and then only European constitutional courts and the ECJ, then we will have little reason to celebrate.

The Success of Constitutional Judicial Review

Constitutional judicial review has always been viewed as the most politically controversial power held by judges, precisely because its exercise obliterates boundaries that allegedly separate things 'political' from things 'judicial'. Unsurprisingly, scholars have felt compelled to expend more energy defending the democratic legitimacy of constitutional review than they have any other activity of the courts. Given its anti-majoritarian nature, review needs defending. Just as important, however, are fundamental questions that are more effectively addressed if we set aside the endless, normative arguments about democracy and legitimacy, and focus instead on why constitutional review has proved to be functional, or useful, to those whom it operates to constrain. Why would political rulers freely choose to give the judiciary, or a particular court, the authority to control their activities? Why would the designers of the world's new constitutions, future legislators all, renounce parliamentary sovereignty and share their powers with judges?

Our approach to these questions may appear an almost naively straightforward one. We see review mechanisms as, first, governance structures designed to lock in commitments over indefinite time periods. Rulers establish review mechanisms to help themselves resolve the various collective action problems associated with making constitutional bargains stick, given changing circumstances and interpretations. Constitutional contracting itself produces a massive demand for the establishment of constitutional review. Generally, contracts can be said to be *incomplete* to the extent that there exists meaningful uncertainty as to the precise nature of the commitments made.[5] Due to the insurmountable difficulties associated with negotiating rules for all possible contingencies, and given that, as time passes, conditions will change and the interests of the parties to the agreement will evolve, all contracts are incomplete in some significant way. Constitutions are paradigmatic examples of what organizational economists refer to as 'relational contracts', agreements in which the parties seek to broadly 'frame' their relationship by agreeing on a set of basic 'goals and objectives', fixing outer limits on acceptable behaviour, and establishing procedures for 'completing' the contract over time (Milgrom and Roberts 1992: 127–33).

The logic of pre-commitment, or self-binding, has always lurked behind arguments for review within federal arrangements, a point stressed in the first of the two Shapiro papers presented in this chapter. Shapiro's second paper restates the idea, with judges working as junkyard dogs patrolling the contractual fences. It is also clear that the move to constitutional review in Europe partly proceeded from the nature of the conflict-laden bargains on constitutional rights provisions negotiated by the various political parties (Stone Sweet 2000: Ch. 2). More generally, if constitutional rights are desirable, and if the legislative majorities are not to be trusted to protect them, or the political parties do not trust each other, then review provides the obvious solution.

Nonetheless, when it comes to how modern systems of constitutional justice actually operate, purely functional perspectives—for example, seeing courts as general institutional solutions to the general problem of credible commitments—are woefully inadequate as explanatory theory. The dynamics of judicial lawmaking subvert efforts to derive predictions of what will happen from the preferences of those who delegated to judges in the first place, or from the details of institutional design. Constitutional review helps to define the paths along which the polity develops through clarifying, supplementing, or amending outright the constitutional law. Because the constitutional law fixes the rules of the political game, constitutional

---

[5] A *complete contract* would specify precisely what each party is to do in every possible circumstance and arrange the distribution of realized costs and benefits in each contingency so that each party individually finds it optimal to abide by the contract's terms (Milgrom and Roberts 1992: 127).

litigation-as-policy-making will attract opposition parties, individuals, and groups who have interests in moving policy away from the status quo, and those who seek to insulate policies that favour them from reform-minded legislators. To the extent that, in any polity, rules of jurisdiction are relatively extensive, rules of standing are relatively permissive, and rights provisions are relatively comprehensive, there is no a priori reason to think that constitutional adjudication will not incrementally extend its influence to all important arenas of policy-making in that polity. And where there is a steady case load, where judges justify their decisions with constitutional reasons, and where the constitutional text can be amended only with great difficulty or, in practice, hardly at all, we expect to find judicial lawmaking— constitutional case law—dominating the overall process of constitutional development. Simply put, those who construct such systems are unlikely to control how they will develop.

For these and other reasons, the 'principal-agent' literature of the so-called 'positive theorist', which also focuses on how courts help rulers monitor and enforce rules and commitments, typically miss what is most important when it comes to judicial review. We can push further. In the language of Majone (2001), the agency metaphor that animates standard principal-agent research on the politics of delegation, with its emphasis on the goals and resources of the principal(s), is not the appropriate metaphor. Far more applicable is the notion of *trusteeship*, whenever those who have delegated review powers—the principals—have transferred, for all practical purposes, the relevant 'political property rights' to other governmental actors, such as constitutional courts or central banks (Stone Sweet 2002). Where the principals' instruments of control are weak or non-existent, such actors' discretion is greater. This point may be put more generally, not only for constitutional review but for judicial review of the lawfulness of administrative regulations made pursuant to statutes. Where the principals, whether constitution makers or statute makers, delegate to judicial agents the power to police the contract, that is, to monitor the obedience of legislative and administrative agents, they necessarily are handing over some degree of relatively independent lawmaking authority (Shapiro 1988; 2002a). The extent to which the principals are able to rein back in, or otherwise shape the use of, such authority should not be assumed, but rather constitutes the crucial empirical question of the social scientist (Moe 1987; Pierson 1996a; Stone Sweet and Caporaso 1998a).

All of this is to say that judges with review powers possess certain institutional advantages, or resources, that can be exploited to help them survive the inevitable charges of usurpation that will be raised whenever they actually perform the tasks to which they have been assigned. The fact that judicial review has not only managed to survive but to spread to more and more systems is important evidence of its functionality, which we see as growing in the contemporary world. We nonetheless wish to define the success of a judicial review court in another way, namely, as the extent to which that court has succeeded in influencing the policy processes and outcomes in its polity. The crucial issues, then, are if and how the court has got the law it has made accepted by other actors, including political officials. We ignore entirely the question of whether the law it made was substantively good or bad.

Shapiro takes up this question in the first of his two contributions to this chapter. Basing the paper largely on American experience, he argues that constitutional judicial review is most likely to be successful (1) in the sense just explained, that is, as a solution to an acute commitment problem, (2) when a constitutional court is serving politically and economically powerful interests, or (3) when it has served such interests in the past and uses the legitimacy accumulated earlier to move on to the service of the less powerful. He argues that there are both historical and a priori reasons to believe that federalism review has the best chance of success while the success of human rights review would appear to be more problematic, at least when it is not a follow-on to long established judicial service to the politically advantaged. It is precisely at this point that Stone Sweet's contribution turns to the evidence for successful non-federalism review provided by recent European experience with rights. Indeed, what Stone Sweet has called the 'judicialization of legislative politics' is a relatively pure indicator of the success of a constitutional court, a point he argued in more general terms in Chapter 1.

Stone Sweet's paper 'Judging Socialism in France and Germany' grew from research begun as a graduate student (Keeler and Stone 1987; Stone 1989a, b; 1990), a project that culminated in the book *Governing with Judges* (Stone Sweet 2000). The overarching purpose of this work was to explain variation in the impact of constitutional courts and rights adjudication on other policy-makers, both legislative and judicial.

From 1985 through 1988, Stone Sweet lived mostly in Paris, working from an office located in the French National Assembly. During the early 1980s, the Constitutional Council had dramatically emerged as an important actor in the French legislative process. In his doctoral dissertation 'The Birth of Judicial Politics in France' (Stone 1992a), Stone Sweet traced the historical development of review since the Revolution and sought to explain the evolution of the Council's authority over parliamentary decision-making during the Fifth Republic. The methods employed were largely archival. He examined every piece of legislation adopted in the 1974–86 period, for example, in order to assess the impact of constitutional review at each stage of the lawmaking process: from the drafting of proposals, to amendment in parliament, to decisions to go to the constitutional courts for a final, constitutional, 'reading' of the bill, to effects of decisions on subsequent legislative processes. He called that impact 'judicialization'. Judicialization was found to vary across time and policy domain as a function, among other factors, of the intensity of the interaction between the government, the Parliament, and the Council, and of the internal development of the Council's case law. Stone Sweet also worked closely with the people who did constitutional politics in France: the deputies and senators who attacked bills for being unconstitutional, the law professors whom the political parties paid to write their referrals, and staff members at the Council who processed these briefs.

In subsequent research, Stone Sweet sought to elaborate a more general understanding of judicialization, first focusing on constitutional politics in Western Europe. The first of these attempts, originally published in 1994, is presented here. Designed as a 'structured-focused comparison' (George 1979), the paper uses a set of detailed case studies of judicial-political interaction during periods of government-led reform in France and Germany to say something more general about parliamentary legislating in the shadow of constitutional adjudication. The paper argues, for example, that, in heavily judicialized settings, legislators are induced to engage in constitutional deliberations: that is, they regularly behave as judges of the constitution. At the same time, constitutional courts function as specialized 'third chambers of parliament', intervening in, and often determining, legislative outcomes.

The final stage of this project, published as *Governing with Judges*, expanded the scope of inquiry in two ways. Italy, Spain, and the European Union were added as cases, and Stone Sweet undertook analysis of the relationships not only between legislators and constitutional judges but also between constitutional courts and the regular, or 'ordinary'—non-constitutional—courts. A more complete explanation of legislative impact is developed (Stone Sweet 2000: Chs 2, 3), focusing on three main variables: (1) jurisdiction, or modes of constitutional review; (2) the degree of centralized control over the legislative process—which is inverse to the number of veto points in the process—and (3) the relative state of development, by the court in its case law, of the constitutional rules that impinge on any given policy sector. Although the interactions between constitutional and ordinary judges have at times been full of conflict and controversy, and although the impact of the latter on the former varies significantly across cases, constitutional courts have gradually consolidated their authority over judiciaries, thereby enhancing their capacity to influence legislators and to control policy outcomes in other ways (Stone Sweet 2000: Ch. 4).

Rights and the Positive Legislator

Those unfamiliar with European systems of constitutional justice might be struck by the complex blend of 'legislative' and 'judicial' powers possessed by European constitutional judges. The modern European constitutional court is the invention of the Austrian legal theorist, Hans Kelsen. Kelsen developed the European model of constitutional review, first, in his role as the drafter of the constitution of the Austrian Second Republic (1920–34), and then as a legal theorist. His followers and close collaborators were present at the founding of the Federal Republic of Germany, and they proposed a variant of the Austrian system as an alternative to American judicial review. Kelsen's legacy was secured when constitutional reformers in Spain, Portugal, and most of central and eastern Europe rejected the American, but adopted the European, 'model' of constitutional review.

Kelsen (1928) understood that any jurisdiction that exercised the constitutional review of statute would inevitably participate in the legislative function: hence the insistence on concentrating review in a specialized court, rather than diffusing powers of review throughout the judiciary, as in the United States. He nonetheless distinguished what parliaments and constitutional courts do when they legislate. Parliaments, he argued, are *positive legislators*, since they make law freely, subject only to the constraints of the constitution (rules of procedure, rules governing federalism). Constitutional judges, on the other hand, are *negative legislators*, whose legislative authority is restricted to annulling statutes when the parliament's law conflicts with the law of the constitution.

Kelsen's distinction between the positive legislator and the negative legislator relies almost entirely on the absence, within the constitutional law, of enforceable human rights. Although this fact is ignored by his modern-day followers, Kelsen explicitly warned of the 'dangers' of bestowing constitutional status to human rights, which he equated with natural law, because a rights jurisprudence would inevitably lead to the obliteration of the distinction between the negative legislator and the positive legislator. Through their quest to discover the content and scope of the natural law, constitutional judges would, in effect, become super-legislators. Kelsen was right. As constitutional judges have consolidated their authority over the development of constitutional law, and especially of rights, traditional separation-of-powers dogmas have been shattered. Like Humpty Dumpty, they cannot be put back together again, at least not without abolishing jurisdiction over rights (see Stone Sweet 2000: Chs 2, 5).

In Chapter 6, we examine rights adjudication more closely. We argue there that the American and European models of constitutional judicial review have meaningfully converged, despite huge differences in separation-of-powers doctrines and forms of constitutional review.

The Success[1] of Judicial Review and Democracy

Martin Shapiro

Until after the Second World War, constitutional judicial review, that is, the power of a court to invalidate a statute or other action of government because it is in conflict with the constitution, really flourished in only three countries: the United States, Canada, and Australia. This obvious finding of comparative law led to a number of causal hypotheses.

Constitutional Judicial Review: The Federalism-English Hypothesis

First, successful constitutional judicial review is caused by and may be requisite to successful federalism. At the time these three countries were, with one more, the only really working federalisms among the nations of the world. And the one extra, Switzerland, also had a form of judicial review, although a much weaker one. This hypothesis was supported by the argument that a federalism required some institution to police its complex constitutional boundary arrangements. In more contemporary, public choice terms, the member States of a federalism have entered into a joint contract, each because it sees more benefit from entering than not entering. Even though each will wish to violate specific terms of the contract from time to time,

This paper is a composite of portions of two articles: 'The Success of Judicial Review', originally published in Sally Kenny, William Reisinger, and John Reitz (eds), *Constitutional Dialogues in Comparative Perspective* (Macmillan, 1999). Reproduced with the kind permission of Palgrave, and 'The European Court of Justice: Of Institutions and Democracy', originally published in *Israel Law Review*, 32 (1998), 3, reproduced with kind permission.

[1] The paper speaks of 'successful' or 'flourishing' judicial review. Such terms are both inexact and relative. 'Successful judicial review' means roughly that judges manage to make a relatively large number of relatively important policy decisions that are relatively fully implemented.

each will see that it is to its benefit that all others always obey the rules of the contract. Thus each, in spite of its own urges to deviate, will continuously support the creation and maintenance of some institution designed to spot and deter non-compliance by the others.

Against the federalism hypothesis runs the argument that an arrangement that places the third party conflict resolver between the member States and the central government within the central government itself can hardly make sense to the member States. Why should a State involved in a dispute with the central government support the creation and maintenance of an arm of the central government itself to resolve the dispute? For such an arrangement makes the central government the judge in its own case.

This apparent flaw in member State self-interest as an explanation of constitutional judicial review leads to a second hypothesis. Judicial review is caused by a peculiarly English allegiance to the rule of law plus the peculiar evolution of the British Empire in the eighteenth and nineteenth centuries. Because of the firmly held beliefs in judicial independence, neutrality, and fidelity to law prevalent in English-speaking cultures, citizens were prepared to vest the enormous power of constitutional review in courts, and/or member States were willing to allow a court nominally a part of the central government with which it was disputing to resolve the dispute. England itself did not have constitutional judicial review because it was not federal and/or because its seventeenth century revolutions had not sufficiently disrupted the English political traditions working against judicial review, traditions that had been disrupted by the movement of Englishmen abroad. New Zealand was not federal and South Africa was not English.

The post-Second World War period provides a good but flawed opportunity for substituting comparison for experiment to test the federalism-English hypothesis. A flawed opportunity, of course, because three of the four large nations that moved toward judicial review after the war—Germany, Italy, and Japan—did so more or less at the point of a gun. While some will dispute my evaluation, constitutional judicial review has not really worked in India or Japan. It has in Italy and Germany. Neither is English-speaking. One is federal and the other isn't. The pre-war dual hypothesis appears to be disconfirmed. As usual in comparative work, however, the n is so small that the two disconfirming cases may be special exceptions. Germany's long *Rechtsstaat* tradition may have substituted for English rule-of-law ideology so as to give member States confidence in a federal constitutional court. An even more special explanation may apply to Italy. Because of its formal switch of sides in 1943, Italy was not a conquered nation at the end of the war. It was not required to dismantle its old law and start over. It avoided that massive task by keeping its existing body of statutory law but writing a new constitution providing for judicial review. Instead of the massive, concentrated in time, task of rewriting all the accumulated Fascist laws, the Italian constitutional court could and did winnow them case-by-case over time. The success of judicial review in Italy may be attributed to this peculiar Italian situation and so does not necessarily undermine the federalism-English hypothesis.

The Division of Powers Hypothesis

The next comparative test was France, neither federal nor English and indeed with a very vivid anti-judicial tradition. It is here, of course, that Alec Stone Sweet's contributions are crucial (Stone 1992a). Stone depicts the French Constitutional Council as an enormous success that has become a very powerful participant in the French legislative process. If Stone is correct, then either we must denote France a special case like Italy or modify our federalism-English hypothesis. With France piled on Germany and Italy, and Spain and Hungary to come, it is probably time to entirely abandon the English portion of the hypothesis. Clearly judicial review can flourish in non-English speaking environments. It is also time to modify the federalism portion of the hypothesis. Although the US constitution involved both federalism and a division of powers at the capital—what Americans call 'separation of powers'—Canada and Australia, following the mother country, espoused unified government at the capital, 'parliamentary sovereignty'. Put the United States, England, Australia, and Canada together and you appear to get the irrelevancy of the organization of power at the capital to the flourishing of judicial review. The pattern of concentration versus division of capital power does not correlate to the pattern of judicial review. Germany and Italy are parliamentary sovereignty states where review came to prevail. Nevertheless, as Stone has shown, France clearly adopted review in the face of a somewhat hostile political culture precisely because in the Constitution of the Fifth Republic it had chosen to move from parliamentary sovereignty to a system of dividing power between parliament and presidency. The Constitutional Council is invented for no other purpose than to patrol the boundary between the two. Thus, still content to leave Italy an anomaly, we move to the modified hypothesis that judicial review is caused by a division of powers either federal or at the capital. Because not only division at the capital but also federalism is associated with judicial review, our modified hypothesis is saved from too tight a tautology. For if the hypothesis simply read 'division of powers at the capital causes review', it would not only be disconfirmed by Australia and Canada but would be the proposition 'judicial review causes itself', because judicial review is itself an element of capital division of powers.

There remains the alternative of treating France as a second anomaly along with Italy. There might be two reasons for doing so. The first involves turning Stone Sweet's own findings (Stone 1992a; Stone Sweet 1999a). In stressing the phenomenon of dialogue between the French legislative chambers and the Constitutional Council, Stone Sweet depicts not a constitutional court but a specialized third legislative chamber. If what the French have actually concocted is an innovative institutional arrangement that strengthens the capacity of the legislative body to make bona fide constitutional decisions about its own legislative initiatives, then France has constitutional review but not judicial review and does not arise to trouble our federalism hypothesis for judicial review. Serious thought must be given to this possibility (Stone 1992a; 1996; Stone Sweet Ch. 3, this volume).

The other route to French exceptionalism lies along the distinction between abstract and concrete review—a distinction pursued in the final chapter of this volume. A distinction long familiar to Continental analysts it is quite strange to those raised in the common law. Perhaps abstract review is so peculiar that it cannot be thrown in with other judicial reviews. Thus, as the extreme instance of pure abstract review, France might be entirely excluded from the data used to construct and test hypotheses concerning the causes of successful judicial constitutional review. Indeed, to combine the two routes to French exceptionalism, one might argue that pure abstract constitutional review is what makes the Constitutional Council a third branch of the French legislature rather than a court.

In France the exclusivity of abstract review was deliberately employed as a means of limiting review. In Germany the addition of abstract review to concrete review was deliberately employed to expand judicial review. Hungary also uses the combination to expand review. A court, conceding for the moment that the Constitutional Council is a court, that is for ever debarred from considering the constitutionality of a statute once it is enacted, and entirely debarred from ever considering the constitutionality of government action implementing statutes, is severely handicapped. Indeed the fierceness of the Assembly-Council dialogue that Stone depicts may result largely from the Council's knowledge that it gets only one time at bat. The German Constitutional Court, on the other hand, is secure in the knowledge that it gets as many turns at bat as it wants and gets to review the whole range of government actions from statutes through rules and down to individual government decisions implementing rules. I am inclined to submerge the distinction between abstract and concrete review in Germany, treating Germany as simply having very strong review. Abstract review in France may be treated as either strengthening the third legislative chamber argument or as a purely strategic move to limit the judicial review introduced by the Fifth Republic sufficiently to persuade a hostile French political culture to accept it.

All things considered, I would opt for claiming that the French indeed have achieved a flourishing judicial constitutional review peculiarly limited by its exclusively abstract character but still roughly comparable to constitutional judicial review elsewhere. If this is so, then I would also opt for modifying the federalism hypothesis for review to a more general division of power hypothesis.

Spain is the next test of the hypothesis. The peculiar regional autonomies of Spain do not sit easily in a federalism formula. And it may well be that the ethnic character of those autonomies undermines the confidence in judicial autonomy and independence that allows the members of most federal systems to have their disputes with central government resolved by a judicial arm of that government itself. Spain has more or less conventional parliamentary sovereignty. The consideration of Spain also makes it imperative for the first time to consider the dreaded topic of rights.

The Rights Hypothesis

From a purely contemporary perspective, it would appear more than a little odd to shape hypotheses concerning the flourishing of constitutional judicial review with no consideration of individual rights or civil rights and liberties or human rights. Nevertheless, the original English-speaking judicial reviews concerned themselves little with individual rights until long after they had achieved institutional legitimacy. The German court obviously was founded in part to protect individual rights and has done a flourishing rights business from the beginning. Yet Germany's highly complex federalism would have necessitated constitutional judicial review even if there had been no concern for constitutionalizing individual rights. The French Constitutional Council and the European Court of Justice have miraculously found bills of rights in constitutions that clearly do not contain them, but both did so in the context of an already firmly established division-of-powers jurisprudence. Only in Israel might it be fairly said that constitutional rights have generated judicial review. Indeed, in Israel the Supreme Court has generated a constitutional law of rights and judicial review to enforce those rights in the face of a dramatic failure to even promulgate a constitution. Israel can join Italy in our anomalies bag.

Spain then becomes crucial. The Spanish Constitution clearly grew at least as much from a concern for post-Fascist individual rights as from division of powers concerns. As already noted, constitutional judicial review is not especially promising as a tool for containing the centrifugal forces of regional, ethnically based, autonomy. The Spanish Constitutional Tribunal has done a flourishing rights business from the beginning. Unfortunately, not enough is known about Spanish judicial review, at least by me, to say whether Spain is the straw which along with Italy and Israel, and the European Court of Human Rights (ECHR) which I shall take up shortly, breaks the back of the division of powers hypothesis. It may well be that we must now entertain two, not necessarily mutually exclusive, hypotheses. Division of powers systems generate judicial review. Ideological commitments to individual rights generate judicial review. We might even time-stage these hypotheses. Those polities which first adopted judicial review did so because of division of powers. Rights concerns engendered recent judicial review. More probably, rights-generated judicial review now takes its place beside division of powers-generated judicial review with the expectation that both kinds will be found in the future. Most probably, a conjunction of division of powers and rights concerns is most likely to generate successful review.

It must be noted that while the ECHR is chock-full of rights and morals, it is also chock-full of division of powers. The ECHR is not part of any conventional state. It is an organ of the 'Council of Europe', which itself is a loose association of a number of European states, some kind of international organization, but even in that amorphous realm one with little concrete existence or day-to-day operation besides the Convention system itself. Technically speaking the Convention lies in the realm of international, not constitutional, law so that the Court does not do constitutional judicial review. It is not quite right totally to ignore this technicality. The basic question when we ask what causes successful constitutional judicial review is 'Why do politically powerful entities obey the orders of constitutional courts?' The ECHR is successful precisely because the obligation to obey of the member states is reduced to the level prevalent in international law from that prevalent in constitutional law. Essentially the Court must negotiate with an aberrant member state with the aim of persuading it to change its practice or its legislation. While to some degree member states feel some compulsion to defer to the Court's judgments, those judgments are directed to admittedly sovereign states. Yet the Court has rendered enough judgments that have caused enough changes in state practices so that it can be counted to a rather high degree as a constitutional judicial review court in the light of the realities as opposed to the technicalities.

The ECHR does not follow the pattern of a court established to police division of powers which later takes on rights jurisdiction. It was indeed established to do rights business and only rights business. On the other hand it is entirely a creature of a division of powers system with extremely weak powers given to the centre and most powers reserved to the periphery. If the question being tested is whether division of powers or rights ideology generates judicial review or do older judicial reviews depend on division of powers and recently established ones on rights, the ECHR is simply a bad test. It too thoroughly conflates division of powers and rights, in too peculiar a context, to help us much in constructing a theory of successful constitutional judicial review.

For a number of obvious reasons it is convenient to turn next to the European Court of Justice (see Kenney 1999; Shapiro 1992; 1999a; 2001b). It is a remarkably successful constitutional judicial review court. Indeed, it picked itself up by its own bootstraps having, by self-proclamation, converted itself from an international law to a constitutional law court. It has created a large body of constitutional jurisprudence that has become largely, if not entirely, a part of routinely enforced law of the forum of the 15 member states of the European Union. Established in the 1950s and reaching full bloom by the late 1960s, this Court certainly tends to confirm the division of powers hypothesis. Although it has also self-proclaimed an individual rights jurisdiction, clearly the overwhelming bulk of its business has been division of powers. And while, like the United States and Germany, from its origins it has done both areal[2] and capital division of powers cases, like both of them too areal division of powers cases far, far outnumber capital cases. Although it is frequently and correctly claimed that the EU is not a conventional federal state but *sui_generis*, it is also frequently and correctly claimed that, unlike the European Convention on Human Rights, the EU treaties are constitutional not international law and the ECJ unlike the ECHR a constitutional not an international court. There is no question that the ECJ fits the model of a constitutional court that is

---

[2] By an 'areal' division of power I mean one between the constituent units and the central regime of a confederal, federal, or similar system. See Maass (1959).

successful because it assures each member state that the others will obey the rules.

Next we may turn to the United Kingdom. Professor Susan Sterett's work (Sterett 1997; 1999) shows the degree to which administrative judicial review and statutory interpretation are a kind of quasi-constitutional review in the UK. Indeed, basing ourselves in Sterett's work, and following the vogue of speaking of 'soft law', we might begin to speak of a 'soft constitutional judicial review' whose vehicle is purported statutory interpretation. The American rule that a statute must be interpreted if possible so as to save its constitutionality is familiar to most constitutional scholars. Various pronouncements of the House of Lords that English law is to be interpreted in light of the assumption that Parliament intended to conform itself to the European Convention on Human Rights may be less familiar. Such judicial practices, boldly employed, can sometimes veto a statute, so that it is as dead as an outright finding of unconstitutionality.

No matter how strong a face may be put on soft constitutional judicial review in the UK, however, that polity can hardly be counted as an instance of successful constitutional judicial review. Admittedly the matter is one of degree, but in neither form nor substance nor quantity nor quality of policy influence do British courts yet come up to legitimate and effective constitutional judicial review powers. No matter what the past and future arrangement for the various Celtic lands, the UK is a land of parliamentary, not divided, government. And it is a land in which self-satisfaction about the rights of Englishmen under common law has dampened ideological concerns for independent constitutional guarantees of private rights.

In so far as the UK has been feeling external pressures toward soft constitutional judicial review, they have come from the rights-based, but anomalous, European Convention on Human Rights and from the division of powers-based EU. Perhaps the most important UK phenomenon for our purposes has been the organized and vocal sentiment there in favour of a written constitution. Clearly central to the movement for a written constitution has been the urge for a written, judicially enforceable bill of rights. In this sense the UK might be taken as evidence for the rights hypothesis, that is, that contemporary constitutional judicial review is based in rights rather than division of powers concerns. On the other hand, the movement in the UK has not succeeded, which may be taken either as evidence that rights concerns there are not strong enough to generate review or that, contra the rights hypothesis, rights concerns are not enough to trigger successful review.[3]

---

[3] The recent passage of a UK human rights statute authorizing limited judicial review tends, rather weakly, to strengthen the independent rights hypothesis.

Post-Leninist[4] Review

It is this proposition—that rights concerns are not enough to trigger successful constitutional judicial review—that allows us to get some comparative handle on the newest developments in constitutional construction. In relation to hypothesis testing we face the following situation at the point where the post-Leninist states appear to allow us our next round of comparisons. The federalism hypothesis, modified after France into the division of powers hypothesis, remains our best hypothesis. Italy, Israel, the ECHR, and perhaps Spain lead to an alternative, individual rights hypothesis. It is also possible to state the two hypotheses not as mutually exclusive alternatives but as a time-staged, branching pair: all older, and some newer, successful constitutional judicial reviews are caused by division of powers but tend to add individual rights-based legitimacy over time, and some more recently established successful, constitutional judicial reviews are wholly rights-based. The post-Leninist states present us with an interesting mix of division of powers and rights concerns.

It might be tentatively offered as a general proposition that constitution drafters will divide what they fear most in the central government. In earlier times legislatures were feared most and, where new constitutions were to be federal, a legislative house for the member States was also used. So in the United States and Germany we get the dual-purpose two-house division. The post-Leninist states come out of an experience of an excessively concentrated executive but one in which the excessive concentration usually existed behind constitutional forms involving both 'prime minister' and 'president' titles. When they write their new constitutions, such states naturally but paradoxically adopt the French model and divide their executive authority between president and prime minister. I say 'paradoxically' because the French division between president and prime minister was intended to strengthen, not weaken, executive authority. Nevertheless, when the post-Leninist states opted for a division of executive authority, in my view at least, they virtually were constrained to also adopt constitutional judicial review, just as the French were. The constitutional judicial review being adopted by the post-Leninist states seems to me a major confirmation of the division of powers hypothesis.

Quite a different story can be told about Hungary (Seitzer 1999). It is clear, of course, that fear of concentrated power and concern for individual rights

---

[4] I use the term 'post-Leninist' to describe states seeking to move from a one-party to a competitive party system. The term includes all states of the former Soviet bloc and Taiwan, which had single parties directly inspired by Lenin's teachings, and by analogy South Korea, Mexico, some other Latin American and African countries, and perhaps Japan.

are an indivisible package in the post-Leninist states. Thus they will not easily allow us to separate division of powers from rights as bases for judicial success. Moreover, we do not yet know whether constitutional judicial review will flourish in most of these states. The Russian Constitutional Court self-destructed in circumstances that make *Dred Scot* look like a self-inflicted scratch. Perhaps sometime or other it will reconstruct. Only in Hungary do we have what appears to be a clear-cut post-Leninist judicial success story. No doubt that's why Seitzer chose to write about it. You can't write much about things that haven't happened. But, from all accounts I have read, the Hungarian case breathes peculiarity. The political relationship between the legislature and the executive in Hungary remains highly tense and uncertain. There is an understandably chaotic quality to partisan politics which for the moment makes the Constitutional Court appear to be an attractive alternative. The Court's most significant decisions really have been about neither division of powers or rights but about a populist resistance to World Bank pressures to end the fiscal insanity almost inevitable in the radical economic shifts taking place. This move may well be a strategically wise one for the Court in terms of establishing long-term legitimacy, certainly wiser than the early political moves of the Russian Court. But its very wisdom lies in avoiding any test of whether a committed legislative or popular majority will yield to judicially imposed rights constraints. Ordering the Hungarian government not to obey the World Bank is equivalent to Marshall's great *Marbury* move of ordering his own court not to exercise some of the powers given it.

It may take comparativists a long time to discover whether the post-Leninist states as a whole will tend to confirm the hypothesis that rights ideology can generate successful constitutional judicial review. The situation in Hungary is very peculiar and complex. The Hungarian Court's apparently successful protection of rights involves such peculiar circumstances that it may not help us very much in the construction of a theory of successful judicial review.

Theorizing about review, however, may help us a good deal in dealing with the situation in the post-Leninist states more generally. The rivalry between the division of powers and rights hypotheses alerts us to the problematic nature of ideological commitment to rights as a basis for a flourishing judicial review. The three most successful and extensive judicial reviews are those of the United States, Germany, and the European Union. All three are division of powers-based. Two of the three also do have major rights components which may indeed well have outstripped their division of powers concerns. And there is a special reason why the third, that of the EU, does not; the parallel existence of the ECHR. For the US and Germany, however, the basic story may well be not one of review standing equally on the two legs of division of powers and rights but of economic and political elites and institutions being compelled to accept judicial protection of rights in order to get the judicial review needed to make a division of powers system work. Certainly that is what has happened in France. Judicial review courts in those countries have the security of constantly saying tacitly that, no matter how much you dislike our rights decisions, you can't do without us if you want to keep the basic institutional processes running.

There are two underlying assumptions here. One is that ideological rights commitments tend to be diffuse and relatively disinterested and thus to yield to the more focused and self-interested policy needs of the moment. The other is that division of powers commitments are powerfully institutionalized and may be heavily freighted with economic interest. Germany truly may have a two-legged review or even one in which rights have been the stronger leg from the very beginning. A number of very special factors, however, complicate the German situation. Obviously the immediate prehistory of German review is one. A second is the continuous presence of the armies of foreign states interested in imposing a rights regime on the Germans: a factor that tends to be ignored by admirers of German political development. A third is the cold war division of Germany that rendered West German individual rights and liberties a display piece against the rival East German regime. And, most importantly, German judicial review flourishes against the background of the German economic miracle. People who are getting rich find it easy to love rights.

If, then, of the three greatest judicial review success stories we stick to the US and the EU, the story is fairly persuasively one of economic and political elites accepting judicial review for the protection of rights as a minor cost of the benefit of review in the maintenance of the division of powers. Both the US and the EU begin largely over the benefits of a large free trade area that, for political reasons, can be achieved only by creating a federal or transnational political regime. In both, the judicial review court spends almost all of its energies in the institutional formative years of that regime in backing the very interests in free trade that were sufficiently dominant to create the regime in the first place. Both do so by review that quells sporadic member-State resistance and generally strengthens the hands of the new central institutions. Neither does any substantial individual rights business during the period in which its judicial review powers are being firmly established and legitimized. The European Court of Justice is dragged into the rights business only as a kind of compelled addendum to keeping its essentially economic division of powers business going successfully.[5] The US Supreme Court takes itself out of most rights business in a Marshall Court decision (*Barron v. Baltimore*, USSC 1833). After the Civil War, when the Court, along with all the other institutions of American government, has to rebuild its legitimacy, it does so by a vigorous defence of corporate power against populist government regulation; the European Court of Justice has exhibited similar tendencies. The New Deal and the Warren Courts, which turned review into a rights ratchet machine, did so on the basis of a stored legitimacy for review that had been built up through over a century of service to free trade and corporate growth.

The point for the post-Leninist states is obvious. The rights successes of the Warren Court that have so coloured international thinking about human rights, and the major successes of review in Europe, should not make us overly sanguine about the capacity of new courts armed with new judicial review to act as a primary force in the initiation of new rights. Hungary is an interesting testing ground, but it may be a very special place.

What for many years has been a commonplace of the more advanced political science teaching on constitutional law, and is now enshrined in a striking volume on the subject (Hoffman 1997), is that constitution writers and readers normally skip the two most crucial institutions of modern industrial democracies: parties and bureaucracies. Academic lawyers are so enamoured of judicial independence that typically they avoid seeing any connection between courts and political parties and denounce any connections they do see. The fact that all successful, domestic, constitutional judicial review systems—but not the ECJ and the ECHR—are associated with more or less democratic competitive party systems may help to remind us that the political parties-court connection is not always and necessarily a negative one. Russia, the other former Soviet pieces, the eastern European states, Mongolia, Taiwan, South Korea, Mexico, Chile, and other states are currently possibly on the move from non-competitive to competitive party systems. It may well be that competitive party systems are a necessary condition to constitutional judicial review; the curiously muted nature of judicial review in Japan may be partially a result of the curiously muted nature of electoral competition there (Ramseyer 1994). In spite of our distaste for party bosses calling judges on the phone, we ought now to undertake the direct

---

[5] The ECJ discovered that the Treaties contained individual rights provisions by implication in response to opposition to its assertions of supremacy from the German and Italian constitutional courts, which raised the spectre of ECJ economic decisions abridging individual rights guaranteed by the German and Italian constitutions. The ECJ was in effect saying, 'we will not abridge individual rights in the process of integrating the European economies'.

investigation of the relation between parties and judicial review that has been missing from most American constitutional scholarship, and this need is particularly pressing in studies of judicial review in post-Leninist states.

Constitutional Courts

The problem of democracy and judicial review is engendered by successful constitutional courts. For where courts are not successful in establishing veto powers over legislation, no problem, or only a very limited problem, arises. Of course, any court interpreting statutes in the process of applying them does some lawmaking. How much such lawmaking interferes with democracy depends on how easy it is for the legislature to legislate. Where legislatures can amend statutes easily, they can easily correct 'errors' of judicial statutory interpretation. Judicial review of the lawfulness of administrative action essentially involves the same power of statutory interpretation with the same potential for legislative correction.

Most of the nations of the world that do not have successful constitutional courts are not democracies. Indeed no state without considerable claims to democracy does have successful judicial review. These facts are clues to the obvious. Constitutional government is limited government. In the real world we do not encounter non-democratic limited governments although we encounter many shades of more or less democratic, more or less constitutional governments. So there is some affinity between democracy and constitutionalism. Unlike the one or the few, the people must believe either that they cannot or ought not engage in unlimited government of themselves. Whether it is 'cannot' or 'ought not' seems, to me at least, a crucial question.

Successful constitutional courts essentially engage in two rather different sorts of jobs. One is to referee boundary disputes between parts of government in constitutional systems that divide power among parts of government. The other is to sustain 'rights' against invasion by government action and/or—perhaps—inaction. There appears to be a general consensus that courts ought not to use their powers of constitutional judicial review to enact simply desirable new government programmes or to disestablish undesirable ones or to divide up resources among contending interests. Those who believe that constitutional courts can do no more or less than that are generally opposed to judicial review. For nearly every teacher of constitutional law there is the division of powers part and the rights part and maybe a few other miscellaneous bits and pieces.

Courts as Institutions[6]

If for the moment, and for the sake of argument, we assume that the essential or organic connection is between division of powers and review, then we may pursue the theme that the people believed that they *could* not govern themselves rather than that they *ought* not. This view of constitutions as a contract between principals and agents is an old and now again fashionable one. In effect, the argument runs that the people as principals contract with agents to run the government for them. The problem becomes how to enforce such a contract given the absence of any superior enforcing authority. There was the appeal to God or the right of revolution, but these were both uncertain and extreme remedies. It is a commonplace that where enforcement is uncertain contracts should be written so as to be as self-enforcing as possible. Constitutional division of powers is a very clever self-enforcement provision. It divides the agent into parts and sets each agent part to enforce the contract on the other agent parts. Each part's self-interest in defending its own agent capacities works to enforce the contract in behalf of the principal.

To this commonplace argument about constitutionalism, let us add an argument about the nature of courts. When two persons fall into a conflict they cannot resolve for themselves, it is natural for them to turn to a third person. Courts are instituted as third-party conflict resolvers. In order to successfully resolve conflicts, the third party must appear neutral and independent vis-à-vis the two parties in conflict. Courts acquire the virtues of neutrality and independence by announcing that their decisions are based on a legal rule that pre-existed the conflict. In reality, because a legal rule that would yield a clear choice of winner and looser in a particular conflict does not always pre-exist, courts will necessarily make legal rules from time to time and pretend they pre-existed the conflict which they are actually invented to resolve. Judicial review, that is, the power of a court to veto statutes and/or administrative actions, is one form of this covert lawmaking. A court exercising review finds a higher law rule under which a dispute about the validity of a lower law or decision may be resolved. Where no such rule exists the court makes it up while claiming otherwise.

Judicial review is a particularly precarious arena for this judicial pretence because the proportion of conflicts not actually falling under pre-existing legal rules is considerably higher in this arena than most others.

---

[6] The institutional theory of constitutional judicial review courts presented here is derived from Martin Shapiro (1981*a*; 1994), Paul Pierson (1996*a*), Wayne Sandholz and Alec Stone Sweet (1998*a*), Alec Stone Sweet (1999*b*).

Constitutions are likely to contain fewer specific, detailed, clear, pre-existing rules than are statutes. And new constitutional rules are usually less easily formally enacted than statutory rules. The entities at risk of falling into conflicts subject to constitutional resolution are likely to be very constitution-conscious and to work hard to frame their lower laws or decisions in ways that avoid overt or obvious violations of the higher law. Thus constitutional courts are likely to find themselves frequently in the position of having to make new rules because no pre-existing legal rule will resolve the conflict before them.

Put division of powers and judicial review together and we get the following. The people write a division of powers contract with the government so that it will be self-enforcing through the checking of each part of the agent by the others. One facet of this self-enforcing contractual mechanism is judicial review. Judicial review, however, is only one form of the general behaviour of courts: the resolution of conflict through the announcement, and thus inevitably the creation, of legal rules. Thus, in choosing judicial review as one of the self-enforcing mechanisms of the contract of government, the principals have chosen to give higher lawmaking power to one of their agents.

The constitutional theory sketched here is not only one of principal and agent but also an institutional theory of the constitution. It asserts that although any set of constitution makers may to some degree invent new, *sui generis* institutional arrangements, for the most part they can and must choose among a menu or catalogue of culturally defined pre-existing institutions, that is, well understood paradigmatic clusters of rules and regularities that define relatively fixed repertoires of behaviour among actors pursuing relatively fixed roles. In simple English, those creating constitutions for the most part are forced to choose among such pre-defined political institutions as legislatures, elections, bureaucracies, and so on. While they may 'customize' each of these in various ways, and choose to structure their interactions in various ways, constitution makers cannot avoid choosing institutions that, once chosen, will act in ways characteristic of those institutions, ways that had been institutionalized before the particular set of constitution makers chose that particular institution.

The 'junkyard dog' is a fierce dog kept confined during business hours and set loose to roam the junkyard all night attacking all and any interlopers. As to the owner of the junkyard who, for some reason, enters at midnight and comes to canine grief, there is a saying: 'If you buy a junkyard dog...' An institutional theory of constitutions argues that institutions like legislatures and courts have certain embedded behaviour patterns that will come out no matter the constitution matrix in which they are inserted, although, of course, they will be constrained by whatever constitutional matrix contains them. Thus if the people choose judicial review courts those courts will make constitutional law just as inevitably as dogs will bite. And courts unchained against interlopers may well bite the wrong person from time to time.

We have here Plato's classic problem of 'who guards the guardians?' or 'who watches the watchers?' (Shapiro 1988; Cappelletti 1980). If the people as principal choose judicial review as a mode of enforcing the contract of government, they also choose to take the bitter with the sweet of the institution they have chosen. The paradox faced by the people is that, in order to employ judges to police those to whom the people have assigned the power to govern, the people must surrender some power to govern to the judges. Some degree of lawmaking or policy-making discretion is inherent in the institution of judicial review because some quantum of rule-making is inherent in third-party conflict resolution.

With more or less postmodern posturing and citation of the appropriate European gurus, the same point can be made in terms of 'interpretation'. Constitutional judicial review requires that the behaviour of government be set against rules stated in a constitutional text. In order to do this job, reviewing courts must interpret the text. Whoever interprets text to some degree makes the text. The paradox faced by the people is that, in order to employ judges to interpret the contract through which they have assigned the power to govern, the people must surrender some power to govern to the judges. Some degree of lawmaking or policy-making discretion is inherent in the institution of judicial review because some quantum of rule-making is inherent in the interpretation of rules.

Even if setting judges to enforce a division of powers contract necessarily entails some popular consignment of lawmaking discretion to the judiciary, the assignment is contingent both as a whole and as to quantity. That is, subsequent to the initial consignment, the people may withdraw it or limit it. Indeed, in the initial consignment they typically will seek to limit it. If the people have chosen review as a device for limiting the power of others to govern, they will usually be interested in limiting the power of the judges as well. Either initially or subsequently part of this limitation may be provided by the language of the constitutional text. Such limitation is obviously subject to the problem that the judges become judges in their own case when they are called upon to enforce the text on themselves. Some of the limitation will usually be through various constitutional checks and balances in which other governors limit judicial governors in various ways. Courts come with built-in institutional weaknesses as well as strengths. Lack of enforce-ment powers is a notorious weakness of courts. Thus, just as a certain transfer of power is inherent in judicial review, so is a certain limitation on power. Courts cannot do much governing without the assistance of others, and in more-or-less democratic states they are unlikely to be able to govern without popular support even as much as other parts of government could.

The question of the inherent limitations on judicial review can be put in a somewhat different way. How must a reviewing court in a division of powers constitutional system act in order to achieve success?[7] I believe there are three keys to success.

Courts of Law

The first is the judicial myth itself. Whatever authority courts have is piggybacked on their appeal as third-party conflict resolvers. That appeal depends on their institutional reputation for neutrality and independence vis-à-vis the two conflicting parties. It is widely understood that such neut-rality and independence are not free-standing. Courts are courts of law. They are not supposed to be neutral and independent vis-à-vis the law. Quite the contrary. They must be in favour of it and dependent on it. They must maintain the stance that it is not the judges but the law that determines which litigant wins and which loses, even when that is not entirely true. The invocation of law, however, will not always and forever persuade out-siders or litigants of the neutrality and independence of the courts if the substantive judgments of the courts too frequently or egregiously appear to favour certain parties or classes of parties or if the courts in some other way offend popular expectations of neutrality and independence. Courts typic-ally invest enormous rhetorical effort in maintaining their reputations for neutrality and independence. The whole apparatus of judicial opinions is constructed to persuade the parties, the lawyers, and ultimately the pub-lic that there are good legal reasons for the decisions reached that are valid quite apart from the fear or favour of the judges. The endless debate over judicial self-restraint is largely a debate about what actions by courts risk undermining the myth of neutrality and independence.

---

[7] This is not the same question as 'What are the conditions under which review can succeed?' For instance, it may well be that, no matter what its own behaviour, a reviewing court cannot succeed in a regime without a competitive party system. The question here is what need a review-ing court do to succeed when the exterior conditions necessary for successful review are present and/or can be brought into existence by the court itself.

Courts get much of their political clout from a confusion that is endemic to legal thinking and is often signalled by the expression 'rule of law'. In its most primitive form that expression, and its not identical Continental equivalent *Rechtsstaat*, refers to the norm that the government must govern by actions in accord with existing law until it chooses to change that law. There is not even a hint in this concept that the law is neutral as between the citizens or independent of the will of the state. Quite the contrary: the suggestion is that the state is quite free to pursue its purposes, including fostering some social and economic interests and discouraging others, so long as it does so by promulgating general rules rather than engaging in piecemeal, discretionary, perhaps secret, actions each aimed at a particular individual. The rule of law in this sense is supposed to be neutral and independent only at retail, not at wholesale. The law is not independent of the state. The state makes what law it pleases. The law is not neutral as between interests or powers, preferences or categories of citizens but instead favours whomever the lawmakers wish to favour. The rule of law requires only that the state's preferences be achieved by general rules rather than by discretionary—arbitrary—treatment of individuals. The pre-Civil War courts of South Carolina and the pre-Mandela courts of South Africa were guardians of the rule of law in this sense. Nevertheless, they hardly could be seen by the black persons who appeared before them as neutral and independent in relation to black-white conflicts of interest. The courts might—or might not—succeed in protecting blacks from arbitrary injury, but they certainly were part of a regime of repression of blacks which the courts would treat as valid so long as it proceeded by repressive general rules.

We have come, however, to load a second, higher-law, human-rights meaning into the expression 'rule of law'. 'Rule of law' comes to mean not the rule of any law but the rule of good law and 'good' in some sense beyond and above the immediate and particular purposes of those in political authority. The rule of law becomes the rule of norms that are just and true in some universal sense and thus of laws that are neutral and independent in relation to the particular immediate preference of the government. Then the rule of law comes to forbid not only arbitrary state behaviour directed against particular individuals but bad state behaviour even when the behaviour is in the form of rules. This rule of law forbids both retail and wholesale bad state action (I. Shapiro 1994).

Courts are beneficiaries of this confusion of our thinking about the rule of law. Mostly courts only engage in retail rule of law, insuring that government obeys its own laws until it changes them but quite unconcerned that the government's laws are far from neutral as between the owner and the burglar, the debtor and the creditor, the destitute and those capable of caring for themselves. And, of course, most of the time it is quite out of the question that a court should be independent of the preferences expressed in such laws. On the contrary, a court is to be their faithful servant. Nevertheless, we somehow believe that courts are not only courts of law but courts of justice, not only servants of government but its supervisors. As guardians of the rule of law, courts are somehow implicated in preserving the higher law and natural rights against even those inequities achieved through general rules promulgated and obeyed by government itself.

Constitutional courts obviously are special beneficiaries of this binary notion of the rule of law. They are both courts of law neutral and independent at retail and courts of law with a certain neutrality and independence toward the law itself.

Rhetoric, myth, and a certain confusion may assist constitutional courts in exploiting their 'courtness' in support of their policy-making. It is not likely, however, that simply repeating loud and long that it is neutral and independent will be a successful strategy for a court that in its substantive judgments in division of powers cases consistently favours some of the power holders over others. In areal divisions, the central constitutional court must not appear constantly to favour the central government over the constituent parts or vice versa, and this is a particularly touchy point given that the central constitutional court is itself part of the central government. But even a constitutional court that consistently found in favour of the local governments and against its own would eventually lose its reputation for courtness. Not simply a rhetorical but some degree of real neutrality and independence in federal conflicts is one of the prerequisites of judicial success. If one tracks the 'federalism' decisions of the US, Canadian, and Australian constitutional courts and the European Court of Justice, very few periods will be found in which the central government or the States always win. The usual, simple-minded story of the Marshall Court as centralizing and the Taney Court as 'States' rights' is wrong. Both courts consciously strike a balance between national and State authority.[8]

In areal division of powers systems the central constitutional court must also take some care not to appear to favour certain member States or groups of States over others. If it does maintain this general reputation for neutrality it can survive particular periods in which some of its decisions antagonize a particular State or States. The relationship of the ECJ to Germany is a current example.

---

[8] USSC (1824; 1829; 1852).

Where constitutional courts operate in systems of central-government division of powers, they are rarely going to need much by way of reminder of the need for even-handedness, for they are pretty much the pygmy between two giants quite capable of taking care of themselves. The US Supreme Court in reality has played a very small role in the adjustments of constitutional power between Congress and the Presidency, those two institutions constantly making those adjustments by dealing directly with one another (Fisher 1978). The Court's relatively short list of 'separation of powers' decisions do not consistently favour either side. Nor do they show much clarity or consistency of doctrine. The French Constitutional Council has not been remarkably pro-presidential in spite of its Gaullist origins (Stone 1992a, b). The ECJ is in a more complex situation because of the marked inequality of the other central organs with a very strong Council, a very weak Parliament, and an uncertain relationship between the Council and the Commission. As in the United States, however, the Court has played a very secondary role, the Commission and the Council largely working out their own relationships (Tsoukalis 1993). The Court has adopted a compromise position in its one major treatment of the powers of Parliament (Weiler 1989). The early history of the Russian Constitutional Court illustrates how quickly and easily a court may lose its judicial legitimacy in the struggle of executive and legislative titans.

Case-by-Case Decision-making

A second institutional strength of courts in general that protects constitutional courts in particular is the low-visibility, technical, incremental, case-by-case mode of judicial decision making (Shapiro 1968: 73–91). There is, of course, a certain amount of 'abstract' constitutional review in many systems of constitutional law. Statutes are challenged on their face in a suit between one government organ and another (see Chapter 6.) By and large, however, it is the American style of judicial review in which new constitutional doctrines are announced in the course of deciding particular legal cases which themselves are viewed in the context of previous constitutional pronouncements in previous cases that is central to most constitutional courts' experience. Even in civil law cultures where *stare decisis* is not formally acknowledged, constitutional law almost invariably becomes case law employing precedential reasoning even when the court's opinions do not formally announce such reasoning (Landfried 1992; Stone Sweet 1999b).

Case-by-case decision-making generates a complex of institutional advantages for constitutional courts particularly in regard to potential clashes with other political institutions such as other government organs, political parties, and interest groups. Constitutional cases embed grand issues of politics and policy in particular disputes typically involving very small immediate stakes. Because the immediate stakes are low and the language and processes of litigation arcane, any particular constitutional case enjoys relatively low public visibility. Even when the doctrinal pronouncement of the court is strong, there is little by way of dramatic challenge to any power holder. The real impact of a particular decision will lie mostly in its future precedential operation rather than its immediate outcome. Those challenged may be—almost certainly are—aware of the real significance of the immediate decision, but they may have great difficulty in arousing their supporters over such a small event. Often they choose not to treat such a decision as a challenge and avoid a crisis. In electoral democracies political leaders usually operate with short time frames. A constitutional decision whose major real-world impact will come after the next election can be ignored and may well better be ignored or downplayed rather than allowed to become an issue in the next election (Orrin 1996). Case-by-case decision-making will usually allow courts some leeway in the timing of those decisions likely to cause controversy. Judges become skilled at turning cases aside on lesser issues. What is crucial here is the degree to which case materials as they are thrown up by the process of litigation allow the judges some capacity to combine particular fact situations involving particular parties and particular immediate outcomes with doctrinal pronouncements that have more, larger, longer-term political impact. The matter is one of degree. All politicians have some control of timing. All resort to various 'buy now, pay later' schemes. Case-by-case judicial decision-making is, however, a particularly good ground for easing into major policy change both by announcing big new law in small cases and by moving small doctrinal step by small doctrinal step into big changes.

This step by step into big changes is not only a means of finessing political crisis and avoiding confrontation. There is a second important dimension. Case-by-case decision-making contributes more to the institutional strength of courts than the strategic capacity to mix small immediate impacts with large, long-term policy initiation. Although incremental decision-making does not guarantee success, it is a mode of decision-making widely adopted by organizations operating in complex environments because of its capacity for risk reduction. All policy-making, and particularly that of government, is fraught with unanticipated consequences. Large initial moves entail the risk of large losses. Consequently a strategy of proceeding one small step at a time, preserving the option of slightly changing direction as responses come in to each step taken, the famous error correction through feedback, is very likely to yield better results than double or nothing All political actors have the option of more-or-less incremental policy-making most of the time. For courts too the matter is one of more or less. On occasion at least courts can take pretty big policy steps if they want to. Generally, however, they have the option of taking quite small steps. Their case-by-case mode of decision tends to keep them well within incremental bounds while legislatures are pushed in a non-incremental direction by the general and prospective nature of statutes. Courts are likely to be relatively sensitive, flexible, and generally successful policy-makers because their inherent decision-making style is incremental (see Chapter 2).

Legal Epistemic Communities and the Strength of Constitutional Courts

The policy-making of courts is not only typically low-visibility and incremental but is 'technical' in both language and substance. Students of contemporary government have discovered epistemic communities growing like weeds everywhere. Because much of modern government involves the fostering and regulation of complex technologies, much of it has become technocratic. The British belief that empires should be run by profoundly ignorant people with second-class honours degrees in classics has crumbled. Today government is increasingly government by expert. That means government by specialist. Specialists form separate communities, separated from the rest of us not only because they hold knowledge the rest of us don't have but because their members have in common the special perspectives that arise in the course of acquisition of that knowledge. Particularly since the atomic triumphs of one such community in the Second World War, we have become increasingly aware of, and suspicious of, our dependence on such communities.

Technocratic government by multiple communities of experts who represent their own peculiar preferences rather than those of people in general has come to be perceived as a threat to democracy (Weiler 1986; Shapiro 1979). The relation of expert policy-making communities to political parties has not been so frequently noted. Epistemic communities have been more analogized to interest groups and associated with interest-group 'capture' of government regulatory organs. Such communities are treated as yet another set of actors in the complex dance of interest groups that constitutes the policy-making mechanism of pluralist democracy. In the accounts of the relations between legislatures, political executives, bureaucracies, courts, and interest groups that are commonplace in the study of contemporary regulatory politics, epistemic communities typically appear as yet another disintegrative force, yet another player challenging the discipline of responsible and accountable government in the public interest. The engineers want to build the strongest, the economists the most efficient, the architects the most beautiful, the bankers the most profitable bridge just as the bicyclists want one with a bicycle lane and the concrete industry one made of reinforced concrete rather than steel beams.

Although we may well have been losing faith in all of modern government, we particularly have been losing faith in political parties. Recent concerns with party corruption are only the final and rather superficial cause of dissatisfaction. In either majoritarian or pluralistic visions of democracy, political parties are the essential mechanisms for aggregating the multiple interests and preferences which left to their own devices would otherwise render representative government unworkable. Representative legislatures have generally been thought of as the centrepieces of democratic government. Only party discipline could generate policy product from such large, diverse assemblies.

Party democracy worked fairly well for distributive politics and even for many public interest issues. Parties did not appear to be very good mechanisms for regulatory politics. Regulatory politics has been a response to rapid technological development. Stable technologies to which society has had a long time to adjust do not appear to require government intervention. Where new technologies have a major impact which disrupts standing social arrangements, government intervention is a more-or-less natural response. It may well be true that a great deal of subtle government regulation lies below the surface of traditional agricultural societies, in part in the tax law and the operation of various government monopolies and in part in ostensibly private law of property, inheritance, and trespass. But such regulation changes as slowly as pre-industrial agriculture changes, and concerns matters that the common gentleman understands or at least thinks he does. New and rapidly changing technologies bring regulation to the front-burner of politics, the steam engine and mechanical loom in England, railroads in the United States. These matters require more than common knowledge. Regulation of high technology constantly dramatizes the view that people who know are superior governors to people who don't know. And knowing, at least scientific and technological knowing, does not fit well into party politics, for party politics are about advantage and preference and sheer numbers, not about knowledge. In the United States it was said 'there is no Democratic or Republican way to pave a street' or to run a railroad for that matter. Parties that seemed so good at aggregating interests seemed quite inappropriate for aggregating knowledge.

This point was quite clear by the end of the nineteenth century. Even democratic polities began to build up expert governmental enclaves at least ostensibly reserved against party politics: the independent regulatory commissions in the United States, the grand corps in France, and various ad hoc commissions and bodies of inquiry in England. Yet such devices were necessarily troublesome for party democracy. At first the solution was to constantly reassert the ultimate subordination of experts to democratic politicians as in parliamentary sovereignty and presidential control of the executive branch. As this subordination came to appear increasingly illusory, both the United States and Europe became increasingly insistent on transparency and broad outside participation in technocratic policy-making. Indeed, those goals of transparency and participation have long replaced fairness as the central goals of the proliferating administrative law on both sides of the Atlantic (Schwarze 1992; Shapiro, this volume, Chapter 4).

That very growth in administrative law, however, signals our despair over political parties. Party government is no longer seen as capable of controlling and, more importantly, orchestrating regulatory policy-making necessarily dominated by experts. Instead the demos must be provided with both direct observation of and participation in the regulatory palaver of the experts. If the demos cannot beat the experts, it can at least join them.

Regulatory as opposed to distributive politics brings the problem of parties to the fore in another way as well. Both majoritarians and pluralists essentially deal in process rather than substantive norms. The question is not whether some government policy is substantively good or bad, whether the fish live or die under the purported protection of the clean water statute, but whether the statute was the product of majority will or the fair bargaining of the interested groups. Since mid-twentieth century there has been increasing concern with whether the fish live or die. It is not enough that, although they inadvertently die, the protective policy was made by majority vote or pluralist compromise. While political parties do fairly well at distributing farm subsidies and welfare state entitlements, they do not inspire much confidence that, unaided, they will come up with the correct cures for environmental degradation. Where correctness rather than tit for tat is at issue, there again raises its head the proposition that those who know something ought to be in control. Even more fundamentally, the suspicion arises that, when in pursuit of the good, something more than counting heads is involved. As the Western world perceives itself as moving from an agnostic politics of interests to a politics of values, particularly in environmental, health, and safety matters, parties appear less useful. Good at aggregating interests, they don't look good at aggregating values. Or, rather, values are not to be aggregated but pursued. The world 'deliberate' is liberally scattered about current political and legal theory as a flag signalling that we don't want party politics as usual but don't know what we do want, except that we do know we want to talk about 'the good' rather than the election returns (Shapiro 1995).

Epistemic communities take on some of the integrative tasks that parties are losing. They aggregate persons of somewhat differing interests around a core of common knowledge. The whole point of epistemic communities is, of course, that they combine knowledge, interests, and values in curious ways. Commonality of knowledge in and of itself leads to a certain convergence of interests and values. Those who share a body of knowledge and the discipline of learning it will have to some degree come to share common perspectives. Two economists are more likely to see the world in the same way than an economist and a poet. Two economists also have a common interest in the flourishing of economists and the discipline of economics not shared by an economist and a poet. And a poet is likely to be less concerned with efficiency than an economist. On the other hand, one economist may be a liberal democrat working for a labour union and the other a conservative investment banker.

We have tended to emphasize the commonalities in epistemic communities as we try to persuade people of their existence. It is, however, their combination of commonalities and divergences that makes them most interesting. For they can use their commonalities to achieve aggregation of their divergences. The economics community may do far better than the parties at arriving at an agreed international trade policy.

Those interested in law and courts have become alert to epistemic communities as impinging on the work of courts and legislatures. They have tended to neglect, however, the fact that courts themselves enjoy many of their institutional strengths by virtue of being embedded in one of the oldest and most flourishing of the epistemic communities: lawyers. Perhaps this link between lawyers and judges would be self-evident were it not for the fact that judges have typically been appointed by and become members of the government and thus apparently are separated from 'the bar'. The link probably is most obvious for the English-speaking world. In England itself judges were indeed appointed by and served at the pleasure of the Crown until 1700. Nevertheless, the judges very clearly were a senior committee of the barristers' guild. The common-law practice of drawing judges from among senior esteemed practitioners creates a union of bench and bar. In a very real sense both the law and the courts belong to the lawyers. The world of Islam is the same, where the political authorities must appoint the *khadis* from among the community of the learned. Among the major legal systems of the world, the Confucian is unique in preferring judges without legal training and prohibiting law practice.

The civil law tradition presents the intermediate case. Judges are law graduates but typically enter the judicial service immediately after their schooling and stay in it for life. Unlike in the common-law world, the practising bar is not the very centre of the profession from which a few members are sent off into judicial or government service. Instead, in civil law states the bar tends to be the least prestigious of a professional triumvirate of government service, judicial service, and private practice. Moreover, on the Continent law as a body of learning grew up as one of the three basic university subjects along with medicine and theology and so was less an esoteric, specialized body of knowledge than a common educational base for lay society, at least after university education became commonplace for the political class.

Yet for all this lawyers constituted a quite distinct social element even if law graduates did not. And in spite of early career divergence judges were lawyers. Even if the judges did not perceive the existence of courts and their jobs as totally dependent on the existence of law practice, the Continental bar certainly thought of its existence as totally dependent on the existence of courts. And no one, least of all the government, questioned the fact that judges were members of, and must satisfy the norms of, the legal profession.

Law is a community not only in its shared body of knowledge and its particular mode of thinking perceived by its members as both unique and superior. It is also an economic community in which the material self-interest of every member is dependent on the proper functioning if not of every other at least of many others. And it is a social community in which the prestige of each one and each part is dependent on the prestige of the other individuals and parts. If courts are in low repute, practitioners obviously suffer both financially and socially, but even government lawyers see their importance vis-à-vis other government officials eroded. To this picture must be added academic lawyers. For all its claims to free-standing academic prestige, the law professoriate's position has been greatly dependent on both the prominence of courts and the health of the profession as a whole, a point easily illustrated by the pitiable state reached by the legal academy under communism.

This interdependence and mutual support of lawyers and judges is so deeply embedded in the routine legal system that it is hardly noticeable. The relationship is more salient when we move to constitutional courts. The legal profession in the United States has enjoyed an enormous boost in prestige from American constitution worship and has, in turn, rallied to the support of the Supreme Court when it has come under attack. On the Continent academic constitutional lawyers in nations without constitutional judicial review were hardly at the top of the academic pecking order. In France those academics carefully nurtured and cultivated the new Constitutional Council and today seek to proclaim its constitutional law as fully worthy to stand beside the codes (Renoux and de Villiers 1994), which, of course, really means above them. And in a very real sense what they are claiming is that they have moved from being anomalous to being the leading law professors in France. Joseph Weiler (1993) has emphasized the central importance of legal Academe, the judges of the national courts, and a specialized bar in the legitimization of the European Court of Justice.

Constitutional courts are courts. They speak the lawyer's language. They provide the stream of cases that drive the lawyer's mill. They are a source of lawyer income and lawyer prestige. Lawyers are their gatekeepers and their conduit to the lay world. They are staffed by lawyers. Judicial 'craftsmanship' ultimately is judged by the norms of the lawyer's craft. No one can really understand or even keep track of the judges' incremental decision-making except lawyers. Lawyers are the opinion leaders of their public constituency. The epistemic community of law has an enormous self-interest in defending constitutional courts, most basically in proclaiming their courtness (Stein 1981). When constitutional courts enjoy great success, their success rubs off on all lawyers and all courts. When they are under attack, all courts and lawyers are under attack. Here again institutional choices tend to become self-enforcing. If judges and lawyers persistently and consistently proclaim that a constitutional court is not really a court at all, they may succeed in separating the constitutional court's fate from their own. Once they begin to acknowledge a constitutional court as a court, they will have little choice but to come to its defence, which becomes a defence of themselves.

From the outsiders' perspective the embeddedness of constitutional courts in lawyer communities generates the same paradox as other epistemic communities. To the extent that we wish to exploit the expertise of those communities so as to govern complex matters wisely and efficiently, we must yield some priority to their particular preferences and projects. To the extent that we go beyond granting such communities government access and actually incorporate them directly into the apparatus of government, we yield them even greater priority. Courts as government institutions directly incorporate lawyers into government. Courts as incremental, decision-makers declaring policy in the course of litigation incorporate themselves into the practise of law. Constitutional courts elevate this entanglement to the highest levels of government policy-making. If we choose constitutional courts we choose not only the government of judges but the government of lawyers. And the lawyers will praise and defend this government.

Division of Powers and Rights

My argument so far has been that, if the demos chooses to partially solve its principal-agent contracting problem by choosing a division-of-powers government contract that engenders boundary conflicts between parts of government and chooses the conflict-resolving mechanism of courts, it must take courts as they are with their inherent tendency to make rules and their impressive institutional capacity for self-defence. Today constitutional courts are more often engaged in rights than in division of powers business. There are two ways of approaching this rights business. One is to treat it as an inevitable concomitant of division of powers, that, if you buy the junkyard dog to protect the separation of powers junk, you can't keep it from roaming into the rights part of the yard as well. This may be true for one of two reasons. Either the dog has an inherent tendency to roam or someone wants to lure him into the rights piles.

The histories of constitutional courts support one or both of these versions of the division of powers story of rights. The US Constitution begins as a division of powers document. The Bill of Rights is added to supplement the division of power constraints that have been proposed for the new, feared, central government. The Supreme Court confines itself almost exclusively to division of powers business until well after the Civil War. It becomes involved in rights only after long and vigorous pressure from a powerful property rights lobby (Gillman 1993). Created explicitly to deal with newly constituted division of powers, the French Constitutional Council eventually discovers, quite miraculously, that there is a judicially enforceable bill of rights in the French Constitution (Stone 1992a: Chs 2, 3). Exactly the same thing can be said about the European Court of Justice. Miraculously the Court discovers a bill of rights somehow lurking in that document (Craig and de Burca 1995).

It may be that constitutional courts are so much courts of law and, at least in contemporary times, law is so much involved with rights that constitutional courts, by their very nature, will necessarily become involved with rights even if they have been established to deal with separation of powers. Or alternatively it may be that constitutional courts are not inherently attracted to rights but are inevitably pushed into rights by strong elite and popular pressures. Either way, if you buy a separation of powers court, you get a rights court.

The second approach to the current rights business of constitutional courts is direct rather than through the division of powers. The demos may choose to establish constitutional judicial review precisely because it wishes to use judicially enforced rights as an independent means of constitutional limitation on government.[9] Constitutional regimes of rights pursue quite a different logic from those of division of powers. Division of powers regimes are attempts to create self-enforcing contracts. Each part of government will block breaches by the others, with the constitutional court resolving conflicts that arise over these blocking moves. Constitutional-rights judicial review regimes do not aim at self-enforcing contracts. Quite the contrary. They anticipate that the government will from time to time seek to breach the contract and that the contract will be enforced against the government through litigation in the constitutional court. Division of powers cases do not occur when there is a clear and persistent majority because such a majority will eventually control all the divisions. Division of powers may pit national majorities against local majorities or momentary legislative majorities against a president elected by a different momentary majority. As the New Deal story in the United States suggests, however, clear majorities will soon end division of power conflicts by dominating all the divisions. Thus division of powers courts are not likely to confront persistent majorities.

Judicial review constitutional rights regimes, on the other hand, specifically contemplate judicial confrontations of majority preferences. The contract does not enforce itself. The court must enforce it against powerful, united, majority forces. Of course such a confrontation does not always occur. A thin majority of the moment may form as a product of complex and fragile logrolling in which various interests have been intricately compromised and balanced. A constitutional court may pull one card out of this house of cards and see the whole thing collapse, rendering successful counter-attack on the court impossible. Or the house may have collapsed

---

[9] Italy is a centralized country with parliamentary sovereignty. Its constitutional court is involved almost exclusively in rights cases. The European Court of Human Rights is exclusively a rights court.

under its own weight before the court intervenes. Nevertheless, rights enforcing courts are likely to confront firm anti-rights majorities from time to time. Indeed, that's what they are there for.

Moreover, for all the romantic international human rights talk, no one has forgotten that rights are emphatically stated interests, that when majority will face minority rights one of the things that is going on is a confrontation between two sets of interests and the deciding court is not only protecting rights but choosing among interests. Rights are about substance as well as procedure. The majority is not always told that it can have what it wants if it can put all the procedural pieces together. It is told instead that, sometimes at least, it can't have what it wants.

As we all know perfectly well, the standard response that once upon a time a constitutional majority wanted to limit the possible substantive preferences of all subsequent legislative majorities, and the constitutional court acts only in favour of that majority against the current one, has not proven entirely satisfactory. It is precisely this unending and unendable majoritarian debate that I wish to avoid recapitulating here (Ely 1980; Bickel 1960; Kahn 1994). What is clear is that, no matter how many prescriptions for a delicate balance between judicial activism and judicial self-restraint are offered, constitutional courts cannot resist going down the rights path.

Indeed, in spite of the endless and subtle writing seeking to reconcile rights and majoritarianism, the real issue that troubles us lies elsewhere. It may be that late in the nineteenth century and early in the twentieth century there was a clear choice of pure majoritarianism, under the name parliamentary sovereignty, in many Western nations. It is gone now even in England and France where it was most prominent. There is virtual agreement on rights throughout the West, some would argue throughout the world. The issue is not majority versus rights but judicial policy-making discretion. If constitutional rights are to be judicially protected, judges must make some policy decisions. Will judges exploit their rights jurisdiction to make policy decisions more appropriate to government organs subject to electoral mechanisms of popular accountability?

As with all judicial review, some degree of policy discretion is inescapable in constitutional rights cases because of the interpretation trap: that whoever is assigned to interpret text to some degree makes the text. Rights provisions of constitutions must be interpreted by courts if they are to be enforced by courts. And it is difficult and perhaps even undesirable to word such provisions very narrowly. So constitutional rights interpreters receive more than the minimum elbow-room.

The standard interpretative elbow-room is not really the main problem. The high degree of judicial discretion found in constitutional rights cases stems instead from our attitudes toward rights themselves. None of us believes in absolute rights. There are instances in which two constitutional rights conflict. The conflict cannot be resolved without treating at least one of them as less than absolute. That situation is, however, a mere anomaly. The basic problem is that no one believes that an individual right should be protected no matter how much damages to the rest of us the vindication of that right requires. Because US rights jurisprudence has been so long and vigorous, it provides endless examples of this phenomenon, particularly in relation to the right that Americans treat as the most absolute: freedom of speech. At the rhetorical level there is shouting 'fire' in a crowded theatre or publishing the sailing times of troop ships in time of war. At the practical level we get the exceptions of obscenity and libel and commercial speech from full First Amendment protection, as well as the exception for advocacy of the overthrow of the government as speedily as circumstances will permit, the clear and present danger rule for street corner oratory, and various limitations on the exercise of speech rights on private property and public property devoted to special uses with which free speech would interfere (Post 1995). Indeed, American constitutional law of speech is far more about the permissible limits on speech on than about freedom of speech.

The non-absolute nature of constitutional individual rights is vividly painted in the American case law, but it is obviously also emblazoned in the texts of most constitutions as well. The US Constitution protects against *unreasonable* search and seizure. The German Basic Law provides that many of its rights may be limited by 'general legislation'. The European Convention on Human Rights typically provides the right in the first paragraph and the qualifications on that right in the second paragraph of each provision. Ultimately the rights provisions of all constitutions come down to the proposition that government may not limit a right unless it has a very, very good reason to do so. All rights provisions come down to reasonableness provisions. If we then empower courts to enforce rights provisions, what we do is authorize them to decide the reasonableness of the acts of other parts of government.

Such reasonableness judgments are hardly foreign to courts. They make them in contract, commercial law, and tort cases all the time. But in most areas of law judicial findings of reasonableness can be rested on prevalent community practice and limited by standing lines of precedents involving hundreds of past decisions in closely comparable cases. Constitutional rights reasonableness decisions, particularly where statutes are involved, are usually more *sui generis* and more abstract and global in character. What is or is not reasonable rests far more on predictions of future choices and events than on well understood patterns of past behaviour. Ultimately a reviewing court must go through exactly the same calculations the legislator did. The point is not that constitutional courts sometimes blatantly serve particular interests and causes but that policy-making is an inevitable and inescapable part of reasonableness judicial review and rights review is necessarily reasonableness review. This was, of course, the well-known position of Hans Kelsen (1928) and Learned Hand (1958), who opposed rights review for precisely this reason.

Here again we are back to the junkyard dog. The demos or the majority is free to buy or not buy the dog, but it cannot escape institutional realities. Once bought, the dog will bite. And it must be said if ones looks at the contemporary world that 'once bitten, twice shy' does not apply. The more the rights dogs bite, the more of them seem to get purchased. The eagerness for rights manifests itself not only in the constitutional field but the statutory field, with a proliferation of statutory entitlements. The rhetoric of rights becomes so appealing that it becomes attached to public policy preferences like environmental protection that would appear to be so pressing that they would not need rights talk to further dramatize them. Trees have rights.

Lawrence Friedman (1985) fairly persuasively traces the growth in concern for rights to the growth in the pervasiveness of modern government. Rights provide individual protections against a growing governmental threat. The powers of democratic governments grow about as fast as those of authoritarian governments. Our first instinct is to grant new government discretion to deal with new problems. What principally distinguishes democratic states is the long-term tendency to bring each of those new discretions under the rule of law. One of the means of accomplishing that subordination of discretion to law is the creation of individual rights given priority over that discretion. Such rights are most effective against discretion if provision is made for their judicial enforcement. In this sense the demos chooses rights not as a reservation to the authority of its own majority against its own minorities but as yet another solution to the principal-agent problems generated by the contract of government. It is not majority rule versus minority rights but government discretion held within the terms of the contract by judicially enforced rights. Two additional phenomena must be noted. The first is the well-known shift from negative to positive rights. The second is the growing propensity to employ rights as weapons in interest-group struggles.

The move to positive rights is an attempt to assign relatively fixed, long-term priority to certain categories of public expenditure (Leibfried and Pierson 1995). It is precisely in the realms of taxing and spending that the people tend to vest the greatest discretion in government and to control that discretion not by law but by elections. To move taxing and spending under a judicially enforced regime of rights is a very fundamental alteration of the nature of democratic government. In Europe it has been socialists who have most vigorously counter-posed positive social rights to bourgeois negative rights, but socialists have never been particularly fond of judges. More generally, judges do not seem very attractive candidates for the making of taxing and spending decisions. Such decisions seem to demand a degree of general coordination beyond the case-by-case decision capacities of judges. They also involve so strong an element of sheer political distribution that substantial judicial involvement would be fatal to claims of judicial neutrality. And even if we confine ourselves to welfare state minima rather than substantial equality of material benefits, judicial enforcement of positive rights promises to entangle judges in endless quarrels over how much and what quality food, clothing, housing, and so on is even minimally enough. So, in spite of all the current talk about dismantling the welfare state, it is not positive social rights as such that are really at issue but the judicial enforcement of those rights. Rights judicial review is certainly beginning to move into the area of positive rights in many constitutional regimes. It remains to be seen whether much deeper judicial involvement in the 'who gets what' questions of the 'new property' will entail the extreme judicial crisis that the US Supreme Court's involvement with the old property once did. For the moment, however, judicially protected negative rights retain centre stage.

The second attendant phenomenon worthy of attention is what my colleague, Robert Kagan (1995), calls 'adversary legalism'. While along one dimension constitutional rights are universal or democratic reservations against the discretion vested in a government agent, along another they become devices for furthering particular interests against others. Litigation and the threat of litigation grounded in constitutional and statutory rights has become a commonplace of contemporary interest-group politics. Such adversary legalism may certainly pose a threat to the efficiency of democratic government by increasing transaction costs. If one subscribes to pluralistic theories of democracy, however, adversary legalism poses no particular threat to democracy as such. It is true that some decision-making power is shifted to non-elected judges, but pluralist democracy is full of non-elected decision-makers and/or decision-makers elected by some people who make decisions about the fates of other people. The mechanisms for much adversary legalism were put in place by legislative majorities who have authorized and facilitated judicial review as a check on the administrative discretion they have been granting. We are back to the junkyard dog again. Legislative majorities could sharply limit judicial review if they chose some other mode of limiting executive discretion. If you are a post-pluralist, 'deliberation' sort of democrat, then a case can be made that litigation fosters deliberation. And, with some notable exceptions, constitution makers appear to have believed in a sort of Adam Smith approach. Leaving the way open to constitutional rights enforcement through individually motivated litigation creates a litigation market in which the competitive selfish interests of individuals are harnessed to achieve the general good. The more adversarial legalism, the more the general interest in curing agency problems through rights creation will be enhanced by individual lawsuits seeking to vindicate constitutional rights.

On the whole I find the arguments I have been making in this paper more convincing on the divided powers front than on the rights front. And I believe that constitutional courts that must claim legitimacy purely on the basis of rights jurisdiction are on shakier ground than division of powers courts. Nevertheless, I think the same basic argument applies. The constitutional law of rights is not so much a matter of majority will versus minority rights as of the people as principal versus their agent government. In this context as in others, if the principals choose a particular institution, they must take the institutional bitter with the institutional sweet. If the principal has chosen judicially enforceable rights as a device for curing agency problems, there is no reason that judges should feel guilty about what courts institutionally do and must do to make such a device work: create a good deal of constitutional law of their own in the course of litigation. The real question is, as always, not 'yes' or 'no' but 'how much?'.

Democracy and Judicial Institutions

In summary, then, my general argument runs as follows. Let us assume that the constitutions of democratic states are themselves democratic, that is, enacted by the will of the demos. The constitution is a contract between the demos and government. The demos as constitution-maker faces the classic principal-agent problem when it establishes government by contract. How is the contract to be enforced on the agent? One option is a degree of self-enforcement through division of powers. If that option is chosen each of the agents of the demos will, it is hoped, use its portion of the divided powers of government to block violations of the constitution by the other agents.

Conflicts between parts of government are anticipated, indeed invited, but such conflicts if unresolved result in the destruction of the whole contractual arrangement. Thus the constitution makers may resort to a standard institution of conflict resolution: a court. If they do, to some degree, they must accept the inherent characteristics, practices, strengths, and weaknesses of the institution. If they elect courts for conflict resolution, they must accept some lawmaking by courts and a certain capacity for judicial self-defence of its lawmaking activity. The issue of whether such lawmaking and self-defence are somehow anti-democratic or anti-majoritarian is uninteresting. If the demos chooses the institution, it chooses the judicial lawmaking and judicial self-defence. Reciprocally courts that owe their existence to democratic institutional choice must act prudently or the choice may be withdrawn.

Not exactly the same argument applies to rights-enforcing constitutional courts. Here constitution makers have not engineered a situation of conflict between parts of government and then set up a court as resolver of those conflicts. Instead they have deliberately created a conflict between courts and the rest of government or chosen courts as a direct enforcement instrument of the principal on its agent. Again, as an institution the court is saying, 'if you choose us you must accept our lawmaking'. But here the court is acting not as a conflict resolver but as a direct protagonist against the rest of government and thus loses its ties to the most basic legitimacy or appeal of courts, that is, their usefulness as conflict resolvers. In division of powers cases, the division and thus the conflicts would exist whether the court existed or not. If the court is abolished, the conflicts continue and the need for resolution continues, now without a resolution mechanism. So in division of powers matters there is a big reason not to abolish constitutional courts. The elimination of judicial review would necessitate a total restructuring of the constitution. A rights court is far more dispensable than a division of powers court. Without a rights enforcer a democratic government can go on. A rights court must be even more prudent than a separation of powers court. A constitutional court that is both a rights and a division of powers court is in the best position because, even if its decisions along one of these two dimensions engenders majority opposition, its institutional integrity may be defended by those who want it to act along the other.

Constitutional Politics in France and Germany

Alec Stone Sweet

'Coordinate construction' refers to a condition in which both public policy and constitutional law are the products of sustained and intimate judicial-political interaction.[1] Such interaction is an increasingly important fact of government in Europe. Where this condition exists, the constitutional environment constitutes, in large part, the policy-making environment, and legislative processes structure the creative development of constitutional law. Where it pertains, parliamentarians behave judicially—debating and determining constitutionality—not unlike the way constitutional judges behave. Constitutional courts, for their part, behave legislatively—amending, vetoing, and even drafting legislation—not unlike the way legislators do.

This article examines the politics of coordinate construction in France and Germany. I begin with a general discussion of the role and impact of the French and German constitutional courts within policy-making processes. Case studies drawn from the legislative programmes of the first two Social-Liberal coalitions in Germany (1969–76) and the first Socialist government in France (1981–5) are then employed to ground a discussion of the coordinate construction of legislation and of constitutional law. These periods have attracted the special attention of students of policy-making as singular experiences of governments pledged to non-incremental reform agenda (Hoffmann, Malzacher, and Ross 1987;

Originally published as 'Judging Socialist Reform: The Politics of Coordinate Construction in France and Germany' in *Comparative Political Studies*, 26 (1994), 443. Reproduced by kind permission.

[1] A more narrowly conceived notion of coordinate construction, familiar to students of American constitutional law, captures the extent to which the legislature and executive engage in meaningful constitutional interpretation (see Fisher 1988).

Schmidt 1978). For the first time in the Federal and Fifth Republics, the left governed. Both governments promised democratization, redistribution schemes, and to alter the balance of power between labour and capital in favour of the former. These programmes not only polarized opposition but also strained the confines of existing legal regimes, administration, and jurisprudence. In consequence, constitutional courts, which remained dominated by appointments of the former majority, were enabled or required to develop previously unexplored areas of law.

Constitutional Courts and the Policy Process

Table 3.1 compares structural aspects of the French Constitutional Council (Council) and the German Federal Constitutional Court (FCC). Recruitment processes in both countries are highly partisan, with party affiliation generally well known. In Germany, the FCC is staffed primarily by professional judges or law professors; the number of members recruited from the ranks of professional politicians has gradually dwindled to between two and three (Landfried, 1989: 148–9). In France, former ministers and parliamentarians have constituted a majority of the Council members at all times, though legal expertise appears to be increasingly prized (Stone 1992a: Ch. 2). Research strategies and methods used by political scientists in the study of the internal dynamics of American courts are not easily exported to Europe. Secrecy and a powerful tendency toward public unanimity makes evaluation difficult or impossible: in France, the disclosure of votes and dissents is legally prohibited; in Germany, dissents have been permitted only since 1971, but are rare.

As the rest of this article seeks to demonstrate, an empirical political science of the behaviour of these courts can be constructed on the basis of policy-making impact. As Table 3.1 shows, constitutional judges are enabled or required by jurisdiction to intervene in policy-making processes. Politicians have the power to refer legislation to the constitutional court for a ruling on its constitutionality immediately on its adoption by Parliament. This process is called 'political review' or 'abstract review' because it is not dependent on concrete litigation or a judicial case or controversy. As will be shown in greater detail below, abstract review authority can be crucial to legislative politics. First, referrals serve to lengthen the legislative process to include what is in effect a final, definitive 'reading' of the bill by the constitutional court. Second, even in the absence of an eventual court

Table 3.1. Structure and mandate of the French and German Constitutional Courts

	France (1958)	W. Germany (1951)
Composition and recruitment		
Number of members	9	16
Appointing authorities	President (3)	Bundestag (8) by 2/3 vote
	President of the National Assembly (3)	Bundesrat (8) by 2/3 vote
	President of the Senate (3)	
Length of terms	9 years	12 years
Requisite qualifications	None	40–68 years of age; 6/16 must be federal judges; all must be qualified to be judges
Constitutional review authority		
Abstract review	Yes	Yes
Concrete review	No	Yes
Power to refer constitutional controversies to the court possessed by		
Politicians (abstract review)	President	Federal government
	President of the National Assembly	*Land* governments
	President of the senate	1/3 of Bundestag
	60 Deputies	
	60 Senators	
Judiciary (concrete review)	No	Yes
Individuals (concrete review)	No	Yes

decision, the very threat of referral by opposition politicians can alter the content and quality of legislative debate. Although the Council exercises only abstract review, the German court also hears cases referred by the judiciary as well as complaints submitted directly by individuals.

The Judicialization of Policy-making

The 'judicialization of politics' refers to the general process by which legal discourse—norms of behaviour and language—penetrate and are absorbed by political discourse. I mean to distinguish legal discourse from political discourse, which have always been interdependent, only minimally. Legal discourse, that of judges and lawyers, tends to be rule-laden, and is structured by doctrinal norms and the demands of exegesis. Political discourse, that of politicians and political scientists, tends to be interest-laden and is conducted in the language of power or ideology. 'Judicialized politics' are politics pursued at least in part through the medium of legal discourse. Although some may quibble with aspects of these definitions, there is probably broad agreement on fundamentals, at least at this level of abstraction.

At lower levels, consensus ends. One important macro-political effect of evolving judicialization in France and Germany has been to close off reform routes that would otherwise be open to reform-minded governments. As levels of judicialization rise, the web of constitutional obligation and constraint facing legislators becomes increasingly close-meshed. Some see the phenomenon negatively. Because judicialization pre-empts policy-making space while removing accountability from representative institutions, Landfried (1985), a German political scientist, has argued that it is 'dangerous for democracy'. Others see only virtues. Favoreu (1986; 1988), a French law professor, claims that judicialization moderates radical tendencies, encourages 'centrism', and ultimately succeeds in 'pacifying' politics. In the pacified parliament, political quarrels which, in the absence of judicialization would have been fought in ideologico-partisan terms, are 'appeased' and worked out more reasonably—in constitutional terms. For Favoreu, judicialized politics are pacified politics. The argument significantly underestimates the provocative nature of constitutional lawmaking and cannot account for those instances when the intervention of the court itself leads to an escalation of ideologico-partisan conflict (see Stone 1992a: Ch. 7). Normative debates like these are important and useful, but their settlement need not preclude research on and the evaluation of judicialization.

Policy processes can be described as judicialized to the extent that constitutional jurisprudence, the threat of future constitutional censure, and the pedagogical authority of past jurisprudence alter legislative outcomes. This definition is sensitive both to direct impact—a ruling of unconstitutionality is a veto—and indirect impact—policy outcomes may be altered by anticipatory reactions. We now know a great deal about the origins, development, and effects of judicialization, at least in France and Germany (Landfried 1984; 1985; 1989; Stone 1989a, b; 1990; 1992a). Focus on the judicialization phenomenon can contribute to theories of judicial impact. American Supreme Court studies of impact have been frustrated by difficulties in controlling for spurious correlations (Becker and Feeley 1973). Many judicialized processes in France and Germany, however, provide the analyst with a relatively closed, state-bounded arena for the study of judicial political interaction, anticipatory reactions, and compliance. Four general points deserve emphasis.

First, judicialization is an empirically verifiable phenomenon. Although a court's direct impact is obvious, indirect influence can be observed and to some degree measured by tracing legislation through the policy process to determine how and why it is altered as a result of constitutional argument. With the spectre of court intervention hovering over deliberations, governments may choose to compromise with the opposition rather than suffer constitutional censure. This effect is called 'auto-limitation': the exercise of self-restraint on the part of the majority in anticipation of an eventual negative decision of the constitutional court. Governments might also use constitutional arguments as convenient pretexts, and constitutional courts as convenient scapegoats, to deflect blame for abandoning measures once promised to party activists.

Second, judicialization is neither permanent nor uniform. Disaggregating constitutional court impact along sectoral lines shows that each policy area manifests its own dynamic of constitutional possibility and constraint, conforming to the intensity of judicial-political interaction and the development of constitutional control. Legislative processes are more or less judicialized as a function of this variation. In France, nationalization, privatization, media policy, criminal law, and electoral law are examples of highly judicialized policy areas; the same can be said for the criminal justice, campaign finance, education, and broadcasting sectors in Germany. Moreover, the perceived political legitimacy of constitutional review also appears to vary across issue area.

Third, constitutional courts and political oppositions are connected to one another by a kind of jurisprudential transmission belt. Oppositions judicialize legislative processes to win what they would otherwise lose in normal political processes. Abstract review processes provide courts with crucial opportunities to construct constitutional law, to extend jurisprudential techniques of control, and—the same thing—to make policy. As constitutional jurisprudence grows more dense and technical, so do grounds for judicial debate and the potential for higher levels of judicialization.

Fourth, creative techniques of control, which constitutional courts have developed in part to cushion their impact, have strengthened their dominance over policy outcomes. Courts have asserted the power to attach strict guidelines of interpretation (SGIs) to otherwise constitutional legislation. SGIs are statements that a law is constitutional only if it is interpreted as the court does. Enabling control while avoiding—potentially dangerous—outright annulment, the pronouncement of SGIs often results in unambiguous constitutional lawmaking. Courts might also accept the principle of a reform but not the means; courts then might be led to tell legislators how they ought to have written the law in the first place. A second legislative process is generated, which I call a 'corrective revision process': the re-elaboration of a censured text in conformity with constitutional jurisprudence to secure promulgation. Corrective revision processes lead to court-written legislation, with governments copying the terms of decisions directly into beleaguered legislation.

Accepting these commonalities, there is also variance in the conduct of constitutional politics in the two countries.[2] Originally created to guarantee executive supremacy over the legislative process, the Council today functions as an important constraint on the government and its parliamentary majority. Table 3.2 summarizes the Council's constitutional review activity. Most striking is the dramatic increase in the number of referrals, decisions, and rulings of unconstitutionality beginning in 1974. This increase is related to two general factors. First, a 1974 constitutional amendment granting the right of referral to parliamentarians radically expanded the system's capacity to generate review. Given the executive's mastery over Parliament, constitutional threats and referrals to the Council are by far the most efficacious weapons possessed by the opposition. Since the late 1970s, virtually every major bill, and every budget since 1974, has been referred by parliamentary minorities. Their efforts have been rewarded: since 1981 more than half of all referrals have resulted in annulments.

A second factor has been the Council's own activism. As originally conceived, the Council was denied control over the content of legislation, beyond confirming that Parliament had not pre-empted executive prerogatives. In the 1970s, the Council incorporated three texts contained in the preamble of the 1946 Constitution, opening up an unexplored area of substantive constraints on policy-making. These tests—the 1789 declaration

[2] Because my focus here is the impact of the French and German constitutional courts on legislative processes, important differences between these institutions are ignored or obscured. For treatments of the history and the operations of the courts themselves, see Kommers (1976; 1989); Stone (1992a).

Table 3.2. Constitutional review and the French Constitutional Council, 1958–1990

	1959–73	1974–80	1981–7	1988–90
Referrals	9	66	136	47
President	0	0	0	0
Prime Minister	6	2	0	2
President of the National Assembly	0	2	0	0
President of the Senate	3	0	2	0
60 deputies, or 60 senators	—	62	134	45
Decisions	9	46	92	31
Censuring text	7	14	49	17
Favourable to text	2	32	43	14

Note: Due to multiple referrals, the number of referrals since 1974 is larger than the number of decisions.

of the rights of man, the fundamental principles recognized by the laws of the republic (FPRLR), and the list of political, economic, and social principles particularly necessary for our times, that is, 'the 1946 principles'—today constitute higher law binding on the legislature.

The 1946 preamble has a history too complex and convoluted to address adequately here (see Stone 1992*a*: Ch. 1). What is clear is that: (1) the 1789 declaration, an expression of classical liberalism, generally embodied the right wing's version of rights; (2) the left, which enjoyed the strongest voice in the constitutional assemblies of 1946, accepted the 1789 rights of due process and legal equality but opposed, along with centrists and Gaullists, the 'sacred' right to property, not least because all three political tendencies were committed to nationalization policies; (3) the 1946 principles, an expression of social collectivism, constituted the left wing's version of rights; and (4) the mention of the FPRLR, left totally unenumerated, was included on the initiative of the right, which sought to guarantee rights to private—that is, Catholic—schools. Had the constitutional assemblies of 1946 foreseen the preamble's incorporation by the Council in 1971, only the 1946 principles would have stood a chance of being granted such status. The preamble now dominates French constitutional politics. In the 1970s, the left sought to enshrine elements of the 1946 principles, particularly the rights to strike and workers' participation, by going to the Council, but with little success (Stone

Table 3.3. The constitutional review activity of the German Federal Constitutional Court, 1951–1991

	Referrals	Decisions
Abstract review	112	62*
Referrals leading to a decision by		
Federal government		5
Deputies		14
Land governments		59
Concrete review	2,619	897
Constitutional complaints	82,253	3,689

* Due to multiple referrals and the consolidation of cases, the number of abstract review decisions rendered does not equal the number of referrals.

Source: Data compiled from FCC decisions and FCC statistical office.

1992*a*: Ch. 3). After 1981, the Socialists sought to give concrete expression to these principles in legislation, while the right systematically sought to block these initiatives, notably with reference to the declaration and the FPRLR. Preamble politics are thus legislative politics.

In Germany, the bargains struck by political elites in establishing constitutional review have held firm. The FCC was granted wide-ranging jurisdiction—perhaps the most wide-ranging of any court anywhere—and clear status as the guardian of constitutional rights and order (Kommers, 1989, Chs 1, 2). Table 3.3 summarizes the Court's review activities. In contrast to the Council, the great bulk of the FCC's case load involves review of legal disputes brought before it by either courts or individual litigants. The Court's activities are thus anchored in what are undeniably judicial processes, even if the legal order it is asked to defend, that of higher law, is inherently a political order. The Council, detached from the judiciary and exercising only abstract review,[3] arguably performs less a judicial than a legislative function (Stone 1992*b*). In Germany, a few scholars and even an FCC judge have argued for the abolition of abstract review on the grounds

[3] In 1990, President Mitterrand proposed a constitutional amendment to enable the Council to receive referrals from individuals through the court system. The opposition-controlled Senate killed the initiative, declaring that a new codification of rights would have to come first.

that it is needlessly provocative because unconstitutional laws will come before the Court eventually anyway (for example, Landfried 1984; *Der Spiegel* 1978).

The comparatively small number of instances of German abstract review is noteworthy. Several factors account for the difference. First, in contrast to the French practice, opposition parties have traditionally worked not to obstruct but to cooperate in lawmaking (Kirchheimer 1966; Lepsius 1982). Controversial laws that are adopted are most often sent to the FCC by governments controlled by *Länder* wings of the national opposition party. Second, the German policy-making process is heavily veto-laden, that is, multiple structural impediments serve to filter out audacious or non-incremental legislation (Scharpf 1977). The requirements of coalition government have allowed the small Free Democratic Party (FDP) to reorient policy toward the centre (Pulzer 1978); and the absolute veto of the Bundesrat—the upper chamber whose consent is required for about 55 per cent of all legislation—structures bargaining in the service of cooperative federalism (Lehmbruch 1978). The FCC is only the third filter of legislative ambition and thus receives few radical reforms if any at all. Virtually all commentators agree, however, that the FCC has exhibited increasingly high degrees of 'judicial activism' beginning at least in the 1970s (Johnson 1982; Landfried 1989). In France, where the Senate's veto is merely suspensive, the Council is the only policy-making institution that can impose its will on the government and its majority.

The Coordinate Construction of Legislation

The case studies of policy-making that follow examine the constitutional fate of some of the most high-profile reforms pursued by the German Social-Liberal coalition (1969–76) and the first French Socialist government (1981–5). Dozens of other examples from these and other periods could be used to illustrate the same general points about judicialization and coordinate construction. Focus on these periods, however, yields important advantages. The cases share structurally similar macro-political contexts, enabling an analytically tighter and politically more compelling comparative treatment. Within each polity, each set of policies (1) provides a multidimensional range of constitutional issues and lawmaking behaviour and impact, and (2) occupies relatively narrow time frames, eliminating problems associated with institutional development. Each of the legislative initiatives examined was a product of a highly judicialized legislative process capped by a constitutional court decision. In several instances, corrective revision processes were necessary to secure promulgation; and, in all cases, the impact of the Constitutional Court on final outcomes was extensive.

Social-Liberal Reform in Germany: 1969–1976

The change of power in Germany in 1969 transformed institutional inter-action at the heart of the German state. Conflictual opposition emerged for the first time in decades (Pridham 1982) and the Bundesrat, controlled by the Christian Democratic Union (CDU) was politicized to unprecedented levels (Lehmbruch 1978). The FCC, where the CDU made up a majority in each Senate of the Court, was also implicated in these partisan struggles. Commentators have noted that the Court exhibited far greater 'judicial act-ivism' engendered greater political controversy than it had previously, and had even served 'as a brake on [SPD, Social Democratic Party] reforms' (Von Beyme 1983: 186; see also Johnson 1982; Landfried 1984).

The centrepiece of the government's first programme was a series of for-eign policy initiatives, collectively known as *Ostpolitik*, aimed at normalizing the Federal Republic's relations with the Communist bloc. While the motiv-ations behind *Ostpolitik* were multi-faceted, its link to the coalition's reform programme was explicit: the SPD believed that building a more cooperat-ive relationship with the East would expand the coalition's latitude to push for fundamental domestic changes by, in essence, removing or mitigating the stigma of the party's 'socialist' and Marxist heritage (Tilford 1975). In 1972, following the conclusion of similar treaties with Warsaw Pact states, the Basic Treaty was signed by the two Germanies. The treaty pledged the parties to principles of non-interference, respect of existing borders, peace-ful settlement of disputes, and the exchange of diplomatic delegations. In short, the government of Chancellor Willy Brandt had all but accepted a Germany of two sovereign states.

The CDU and its coalition partner the Christian Social Union (CSU) (virulently opposed *Ostpolitik*, claiming that the policy represented a victory for the Eastern bloc in the cold war (Pridham 1975). Its position was easily constitutionalized. The preamble of the Basic Law makes clear that the divi-sion of Germany is repugnant and exhorts 'the entire German people' to work to achieve 'unity'; moreover, in a 1956 decision, the FCC ruled that the preamble imposed a 'constitutional obligation' to pursue reunification. On these grounds, Bavaria (CSU) asked the FCC to invalidate the treaty. Seeking to resist judicialization of the matter, Brandt allowed the treaty to enter into force after the Bavarian referral and during the oral-argument

stage before the FCC. The Court, after scolding the government for presenting it with a fait accompli, upheld the treaty, but pronounced SGIs, which
undermined its purpose (FCC 1973*b*). Ruling that no public authority could
accept divided German sovereignty, it declared that East Germany could not
be 'regarded as a foreign state'. Several of the guidelines laid down repudi-
ated the treaty in all but name; under one of them the East-West border was
judged to possess the same constitutional status as borders between *Länder*;
and the obligation to refrain from interference in internal affairs could not
include denial, within *East* Germany, of certain rights guaranteed by the
West German constitution.

The decision has perplexed and disturbed students of the Court (Johnson
1982; Leicht 1974: Ch. 4). In the service of jurisprudential coherence—
and perhaps partisanship—the FCC wilfully ignored geopolitical reality.
Comparison of the Court's decisions on foreign policy—rearmament, entry
into NATO—in the 1950s with the *Ostpolitik* decision reveals abandonment
of restraint in the area. As Von Beyme summarizes the view, the earlier
decisions represented an 'unrestricted vote of confidence in the foreign
policy of the Adenauer Government' whereas the 1973 decision constituted
a 'hardly concealed vote of no-confidence' (1983: 187).

The government had far less control over domestic legislation than
over foreign policy. The complex series of initiatives ultimately leading to
the University Framework Law of 1976 is a well-documented illustration
(Katzenstein 1987: Ch. 7). The law was promulgated after five years of tor-
tuous debate, punctuated by several crucial FCC decisions and successive
vetoes by the Bundesrat. The most controversial aspect of the original bill
was the provision to expand participation in university governance by giving
to three groups—teachers, both non-tenured and full professors, staff, and
students—voting parity on university councils. The reform was designed to
break up the monopoly of power possessed by full professors, a monopoly
that had led to inflexible university structures and the obstruction of other
democratization reforms (Tilford 1981). The CDU-CSU opposition laboured
to block any change in the status of professors and to retain, as much as
possible, *Länder* control over the domain of education.

While final touches were being made on the bill in cabinet, the FCC
ruled on a similar 1971 law adopted in Lower Saxony (SPD), which had
been referred by 398 professors (FCC 1973*a*; Kommers 1989: 437–43). The
Court ruled that the law violated Article 5 of the Basic Law: 'Art and science, research and teaching shall be free.' Ruling that the 'special position'
of university professors in research and teaching must always be maintained,
the FCC declared that professors must possess a majority share of votes in

decisions on teaching, and be able 'to assert themselves against the combined opposition of other groups' in decisions pertaining to research. The dissent of two SPD judges accused the FCC of 'exceeding its function and placing itself in the position of the legislature'.

The decision, by arming the opposition with detailed constitutional arguments, fundamentally altered the debate on the federal bill. The government, although claiming that its revised bill conformed to the FCC's ruling, was unable to maintain control over how that ruling would be translated into law. In the original bill, for example, a majority of council seats were allocated to teachers, a group which included assistant professors (Bundestag Drucksache 7/1328 1972: 64–5). The opposition, strengthened by the Bundesrat's veto, were able to delete mention of non-tenured professors, and then require a majority vote *within* the group of tenured professors to ratify certain decisions (Bundesrat Debates, 21 February 1975, 12 December 1975; Bundestag Drucksache 7/4462 1975). The law not only enshrined the FCC's preferred policy but, as a federal law, forced the policy on several *Länder* which had delayed compliance with the FCC's Lower Saxony decision (Blair 1978: 362).

The attempt to decriminalize abortion provides another example of an intensely judicialized debate leading first to an FCC veto and then to a corrective revision process implementing the Court's policy. The rank and file of both coalition parties supported the total decriminalization of abortion in the first trimester of pregnancy, and afterwards on medical and other grounds. At the November 1971 SPD conference, delegates supported such a solution by a vote of 638 to 59, and polls showed public support hovering at about 75 per cent (Braunthal 1983: 250–2). After intense two-year negotiations with critics, especially the Catholic church, the minister of justice decided to relax penalties for abortion only in cases of medical necessity, rape, and other social emergencies. In Parliament, however, the government lost control of the legislative process to SPD and FDP deputies, who rewrote the bill in conformity with party resolutions. The law was referred by 193 deputies and five *Länder*.

The FCC annulled the bill on the grounds that the legislature had violated 'right to life' protections contained in Article 2 of the constitution (FCC 1975; Kommers 1989: 348–59). With the two SPD appointees again strongly dissenting, the Court ruled that, because post-Nazi Germany had a special obligation to protect human life, including the embryonic, abortion could not be decriminalized; it would nonetheless not be punished when justified by certain health and social considerations. The FCC then went on to propose what was in effect draft legislation, which a corrective revision process ratified. In what appears to be the only high-level public expression of opposition to any FCC decision, the vice-president of the Bundestag protested that women 'would not accept or abide by the decision'; but she was overridden by the minister of justice, who stated that the government would, with regret, respect the FCC's ruling (Bundestag Debates, 7 November 1975: 13, 880).

The principal socio-economic structural reform in the SPD's programme was the strengthening of industrial co-determination. Backed by the unions, the party hoped to extend 'parity codetermination'—equal representation with management on supervisory boards—which existed in the coal and steel sectors to the rest of industry (Katzenstein 1987: Ch. 3). Debates focused principally on two conceptions of property: the Constitution (Article 14) guarantees the right to property, but it also states that property must serve the public good. Existing jurisprudence could not easily settle the matter, but seemed to favour the government's position: in a landmark case in 1954, the judges had declared that the Basic Law was 'neutral' with respect to the economic system, and that political authority enjoyed broad powers to shape and reshape the system (FCC 1954; Kommers 1989: 249–52).

The debate within Parliament, which lasted nearly two years, was fully judicialized. A special committee heard testimony from eleven constitutional lawyers called in to predict the FCC's future ruling on parity. This group split between those five jurists who argued that property rights were absolute and thus could not bear parity and those six jurists who argued that property rights in the context of large corporations must be balanced by the interests of society and workers. In the end, the committee recommended that Parliament err on the safe side and renounce parity. Politicians agreed, removing parity and adopting the bill all but unanimously. According to Landfried (1984: 47–63) this auto-limitation process was a disturbing case of excessive 'obedience in advance' of an FCC ruling. It is also true, however, that the pro-business FDP, lobbied fiercely by business organizations, opposed parity, so much that it is at least possible that parity would not have been supported by a majority of the Bundestag. In any case, the judicialized process allowed the government an excuse for reneging on a promise while keeping peace within the coalition.

The law was referred to the FCC by employers and business associations who, although not expecting annulment, hoped to pre-empt future legislation (Markovits 1986: 140). The FCC rejected the complaint, ruling that share ownership differs from 'tangible property' because 'its use requires the cooperation of employees', whose rights are also involved (FCC 1979; Kommers 1989: 278–82). The Court refused to speculate on the constitutionality of parity but it pointedly praised legislators for their debates on constitutionality, leaving the impression that the absence of parity may have been crucial to the ruling. This aspect of the decision, at least, is what business celebrated and the SPD and the unions feared (Markovits 1986: 141).

Although centred on parity co-determination, the SPD's industrial reform package included two other pieces of legislation: a profit-sharing plan to benefit workers and a vocational training bill (Webber 1983). Both were opposed first by business and then openly by the FDP. Profit sharing was never introduced, Chancellor Schmidt citing 'insoluble legal and technical obstacles' (Swenson 1989: 197). The second, a 1976 law originally designed to modernize and strengthen technical training by, among other things, making it less dependent on the short-term needs of capital, was watered down during nearly three years of deliberations. In its final form, the proposed structural changes were dropped in favour of expansion of the existing programme, to be financed by a business tax, as a means of alleviating youth unemployment. The government promulgated the law in spite of the Bundesrat's claim that the law required its consent. Six *Länder* referred the matter to the FCC, which annulled it on the grounds that the changes in administration indeed required the Bundesrat's consent (FCC 1980).

Although a detailed discussion of its jurisprudence on cooperative federalism is far beyond the scope of this article, the FCC's most important decisions on the subject of the Bundesrat's veto powers occurred under Social-Liberal government. During the 1969–76 period, the Bundesrat systematically opposed federal legislation, decisively vetoing 20 bills—to be compared with only 14 during 1953–69—and extensively rewriting or rejecting, with its suspensive veto, more than 130 others (Schindler 1991). Seeking to bypass the upper house, the government at times managed to exploit certain 'grey areas' in the constitutional division of federal and *Länder* competence, manoeuvres that were then attacked by CDU- and CSU-controlled *Länder* before the FCC (see Kommers 1989: 102–13).

Socialist Reform in France: 1981–1985

As in Germany, the new majority in France faced an upper house and constitutional court that remained in the hands of the right. During this period, the Senate systematically opposed every major initiative, but was just as systematically overridden (Tardan 1988). The Council, however, was a far more formidable obstacle. The right, which provocatively promised to use the Council as a kind of 'anonymous government', had appointed all nine members sitting in 1981; the left would appoint its first two members to the Council only in 1983. The 1981–5 period, in fact, produced an unprecedented series of annulments of major pieces of legislation and a noisy, prolonged judicial-political confrontation (Keeler and Stone 1987).

As expected, the fate of much Socialist legislation depended on how the Council resolved conflicts dwelling in the preamble. The first and most important of Socialist reforms, the nationalization of France's largest banks and industrial conglomerates, raised these conflicts directly (see case study in Stone 1992a: Ch. 6). The discussion, dominated by constitutional debate, focused on the respective status of three contradictory texts: Article 34, which grants to Parliament the sovereign authority to nationalize; the 1789 declaration—the constitutional incorporation of which was rejected by 429 votes to 119 in 1946— which proclaims (Article 17) property rights to be 'inviolable and sacred'; and the 1946 principles, which declare an *obligation* to nationalize in certain circumstances (line 9). In the absence of an enforceable preamble, Article 34 would have won without a fight.

The Council, while accepting Parliament's power to nationalize, vetoed the bill on the grounds that the compensation formula did not meet the constitutional requirements of Article 17 (1789); it then went on to elaborate its own detailed compensation formula (Conseil 1982a). Amid shrill protests of the decision by party militants, the government rejected calls for a referendum but warned that 'the institutional question'—that is, the Council's abolition—might be raised. It then copied the Council's compensation policy directly into new legislation, raising the costs of nationalizing by a full 25 per cent.

In policy-making terms, the Council's decision served to hold the reform hostage until stockholders had received sufficient ransom; indeed, no stockholder who has ever been bought out in any major nationalization has received terms as good as those in France in 1982. In jurisprudential terms, the decision harmonized the discordant terms of the preamble, settling the central controversy of French constitutional law. The Council ruled that the property rights proclaimed in 1789 had been neither eroded nor superseded, and then went on to declare that the 1946 principles could *never* weaken but only supplement the rights contained in the 1789 text. The decision, as one commentator put it, 'is a condemnation of the whole of socialist doctrine'; in another's, '[the French] republic . . . can never be a socialist republic' (Favoreu 1982b: 41). This result contrasts sharply with the FCC's jurisprudence of neutrality.

Although the majority refused compromise on the nationalization bill in Parliament, the 1982 decentralization bill underwent a wholesale auto-limitation effort. During its run through the legislative gauntlet, over 500 amendments—a record—were accepted by the government, and many of its most important elements were removed. By the time the bill was promulgated, 'the state of the new law [was] not very different from the situation...which existed previously' (Favoreu 1982a: 1265). The opposition, generally satisfied with the outcome, suppressed what had been expected to be an all-out attack on the bill in favour of a more modest referral, and, in consequence, the Council's decision was limited in scope (Conseil 1982b).

In addition to decentralization, the government's efforts to 'democratize' and widen participation rested on three other promises: reforms of the industrial relations regime—the Auroux laws—the electoral code, and structures of university governance. Although the debates on the Auroux laws were subsumed by the politics of nationalizations, the latter two reforms were judicialized and suffered decisive Council vetoes.

In the case of electoral reform, the Socialists had promised to establish proportional representation systems for local and national elections and to set aside a minimum number of slots for women on party lists. In its first attempt to make good on the pledge, the government targeted certain subnational elections. Although the bill did not originally include the sex quota, it was amended to stipulate that certain communal lists could not include 'more than 75 per cent candidates of the same sex'. This awkward language had a history, dating to the previous Parliament. In 1980, following the counsel of the law professor, Georges Vedel, the Assembly had unanimously approved a similar quota (National Assembly Debates, 20 November 1980: 4206-7); the bill died when Parliament was dissolved for elections.

The right attacked the 1982 version as an 'unconstitutional, demagogic, and dangerous' discrimination against men, and threatened referral. Over catcalls of 'dictatorship!' and 'what about hermaphrodites?', proponents of the bill, relying on Vedel—now a Council member—argued that constitutionality had been secured by the fact that the restriction applied to both sexes equally. With an eye to their standing among women, the opposition voted with the majority, and the bill again passed with unanimous support (National Assembly Debates, 26 July 1982: 4841-3; and 27 July 1982: 4899-918). Nevertheless, the right referred the bill, but refrained from attacking the quota. The Council annulled it anyway, relying on Article 6 (1789), guaranteeing equality under the law; it ignored entirely the 1946 principle of 'equality of the sexes', which might have led it to decide otherwise (Conseil 1982c).

The university reform bill established a number of co-determination mechanisms, including a single electoral body in which all teachers, from professors to assistants, would elect representatives to university councils.

On the first day of debate, the right threatened referral to the Council, bluntly declaring that the petition had already been written. The opposition complained that the reform constituted an affront to professors of 'magisterial rank' and would result in a dangerous 'politicization' of university life. 'After the flight of capital [after nationalizations]', another deputy stated, 'you want to encourage the flight of brains' (National Assembly Debates, 24 May 1983: 1360-8).

The Council, arguing that the voting system 'would threaten the independence of the professors' by weakening their control, annulled the co-determination provisions, relying on a newly discovered principle of 'professional independence', an FPRLR, which it said could be found in laws governing the status of public servants (Conseil 1984a). The opinion, denounced as a 'political' decision by the minister of education (Le Monde 1984a), is one of the more imaginative Council rulings. In effect, the Council had 'constitutionalized' a principle—professorial independence—which cannot be found in any constitutional text. It bears mentioning that the Council's preferred policy, if not its jurisprudence—the Council inexplicably chose not to rely on the FPRLR 'freedom of education', which it had found in 1977—is remarkably similar to the German court's.

After nationalizations, the 1984 press law was the most controversial law adopted during the 1981-5 period (see case study in Stone 1992a: Ch. 7). The purpose of the legislation was to establish an enforceable antitrust policy to counter increasing concentration in the newspaper industry. The rules then in place—a one person-one paper standard—had never been enforced. Indeed, the rules had been openly flouted by the rightist deputy, Robert Hersant, who had built a press empire of 19 dailies, seven weeklies, and eleven periodicals in a series of shady deals. After the 1981 elections, Hersant mobilized his papers to oppose the Socialist government and to promote the right's emerging neo-liberal agenda. Although the government could justly claim that its bill was designed to protect 'press pluralism' and to restore respect for law, its partisan aspects were obvious.

The legislative battle was waged in the language of constitutional law, but arguments were no less recognizably pro- or anti-Hersant. For Socialists, freedom of the press was conceived as the right of readers to choose from offerings representing the diversity of opinion existent within society. This right could no longer be guaranteed, claimed a minister, because 'certain men' had engaged in 'fraud, cheating, and embezzlement'. The opposition argued that talk of rights only obscured the government's true motive, namely, to take revenge on Hersant. Freedom of the press was conceived in terms of ownership and free enterprise. The bill, under the threat of referral, lost much of its teeth in a massive auto-limitation process. Nevertheless, in its final form, Hersant would still have been forced to choose between his regional papers and the national *Figaro*.

In one of the most complex decisions in its history, the Council annulled parts of ten different articles of the law (Conseil 1984b). Most important, the Council declared that the antitrust rules could not be applied to 'existing situations' unless (1) these situations had been illegally acquired or (2) pluralism was actually threatened. The Council then declared that neither condition had been met, thus destroying the bill and saving the Hersant empire; further, the decision had the perverse effect of freezing Hersant's dominance because the antitrust rules applied in full to competitors. In so ruling, the judges wilfully ignored the lengthy parliamentary discussions of (1) the illegality of Hersant's situation, pending in several courts, and (2) the evolution of concentration in the industry. At no point in the decision did the Council explain on what basis it determined that pluralism was not threatened, or why it judged Hersant's situation to have been legally acquired. The decision provoked denunciations from Socialist politicians as well as the unions and newspapers' owners and editors. A former member of the Council of State—France's highest administrative court—even published a dissent in a leading daily, concluding that the Constitutional Council had begun 'to behave like a third legislative chamber, remaking laws . . . according to options more political than judicial' (*Le Monde* 1984b).

Assessment

I have argued elsewhere that, for students of policy-making at least, constitutional courts ought to be conceptualized as specialized third legislative chambers, specialized because their legislative powers are meaningfully restricted to decisions on constitutionality (Stone 1990; 1992b). To this I would add the following: the more any given legislative process is judicialized, the less that restriction matters. In highly judicialized processes, constitutional debate tends to overwhelm all other aspects of debate. Once aired in both chambers of parliament, the debate is transferred to constitutional courts for a third, authoritative judgment.

In traditional separation of powers schemes, common to both Anglo and Continental theory, legislatures differ from courts in that the former make law generally and prospectively. In contrast, judicial lawmaking is said to be particular and retrospective because it is a by-product of case-by-case adjudication and applies to past or existing situations. In abstract review processes, courts make law outside of the judicial process and according to law-making techniques more legislative—prospective—than judicial—retrospective. In the French press pluralism case, the Council overrode Parliament's judgment that press pluralism was threatened, and then went on to specify how pluralism should be protected in the event that a threat might develop. In the German abortion case, the FCC ruling is indistinguishable from draft legislation, with constitutional commentary attached. Abstract review process regularly leads courts to behave unambiguously as third chambers. The effects of concrete review of legislation, however, are not necessarily less legislative or prospective. Management's legal attack on co-determination, for example, was animated not by expectations of annulment but by hopes that the FCC would fix limits on future attempts to extend co-determination (Markovitz 1986: 140). In corrective revision processes, the distinction between parliamentary and constitutional court lawmaking breaks down entirely. In these, policies that have been laid down by constitutional courts—how stockholders shall be paid, how the penal code must treat the crime of abortion—are sent to governments and parliaments for ratification. Finally, once policy space has been pre-empted by relevant jurisprudence, there might be no need for a further decision: existing jurisprudence, given agency through the medium of judicialized legislative politics, determines general outcomes.

Each of the legislative processes examined here included upper-house vetoes and final readings by constitutional courts (Table 3.4). Although the 1969–76 period was one of relatively high FCC activism—the standard against which other periods must be measured—the FCC's overall impact on the SPD-FDP programme was less systematic and extensive than that of the French Council. The exigencies of coalition combined with constitutional politics to gut the industrial co-determination and vocational training bills. The Bundesrat, whose support was required for passage of the university framework and, originally, vocational training legislation, was easily able to structure auto-limitation and corrective revision processes, enforcing strict compliance with FCC rulings. Absent the effects of these filters, the FCC would certainly have faced far more constitutionally complex and politically difficult tasks, comparable to what the Council faced. Only for the *Ostpolitik* and abortion cases was there both SPD-FDP congruence and no need to obtain Bundesrat approval. In the latter case, the FCC engaged in extensive constitutional lawmaking. In France, nationalizations being only the most spectacular example, the Council's impact on Socialist legislation was often far higher than that of either chamber of Parliament.

Table 3.4. The impact of constitutional politics on selected reforms in France and Germany

	Auto-limitation	Upper House veto	Court referral	Court annulment	Corrective revision
France					
Nationalizations	No	Yes	Deputies, senators	Yes	Yes
Decentralization	Yes	Yes	Deputies, senators	Yes	Yes
Electoral reform (sex quota)	No	Yes	Deputies, senators	Yes[a]	No
University reform (co-determination)	No	Yes	Deputies, senators	Yes[a]	No
Press (anti-trust)	Yes	Yes	Deputies, senators	Yes[a]	No
Germany					
Ostpolitik treaties	No	Yes	Bavaria	No (SGIs)	No
University reform (co-determination)	Yes	Yes	*	*	*
Abortion reform	No	Yes	5 *Länder*, deputies	Yes	Yes
Co-determination	Yes	Yes	Constitutional complaint	No	No
Vocational training	Yes	Yes	Bavaria	Yes	No

SGIs: strict guidelines of interpretation. *Legislative process placed under FCC tutelage as a result of a prior annulment of related Lower Saxony legislation; the federal law was thus adopted in what was in effect a corrective revision process. [a] Law was promulgated absent vetoed provisions.

The Coordinate Construction of the Constitution

In judicialized environments, constitutional courts behave legislatively. But the following is also true: the degree to which any legislative process is judicialized is equivalent to the degree to which parliament behaves judicially. In France and Germany, the building of constitutional law, like the making of public policy, is participatory.

This simple truth is fiercely resisted by the doctrinal community. European academic lawyers labour continuously to separate law from politics and, by extension, to distinguish what constitutional courts do from what political institutions do. This distinction functions to insulate scholarly activity, and to some extent courts, from the vagaries of politics, providing a stable setting for the scholarly synthesis of doctrine and law. Although something of a disciplinary article of faith, the distinction is supported by a number of concrete arguments (see Gusy 1985; Luchaire 1979). According to the most important of these, constitutional courts are particular in that (1) they are charged with determining constitutionality, (2) they function to protect fundamental rights, and (3) their review authority is determinative and final.

The first argument is most often invoked by legal scholars and the courts themselves to counter charges of usurpation: because the constitution provides for constitutional review and locates its exercise in a constitutional court, attacks on the conduct of review are easily dismissed as attacks on the constitution itself, and thus illegitimate. The next step, the assertion that the constitutional court possesses the exclusive power to determine constitutionality, comes easily. But it cannot be accepted. In judicialized settings, legislators, too, determine constitutionality. A court's monopoly on constitutional interpretation can be argued to exist, if at all, only with respect to the judicial system.

The point can be pushed further. In France, deputies and senators are required to behave as constitutional judges whenever a motion of unconstitutionality is raised. Such motions, which are written in the form of a judicial decision, are debated 'in order to determine if the proposed text is contrary to one or more constitutional provisions' (Règlement de l'Assemblée nationale 1986: 94).[4] During these debates, legislators cite constitutional provisions, original intent, past Council decisions, and the work of respected law professors. If the motion is adopted by a majority, the bill is declared unconstitutional and it dies. The Senate, declaring itself to have a special role in the protection of public liberties, has adopted a number of such motions. Table 3.5 shows the remarkable increase in their popularity on the floor of the assembly. Although the argument has now been forgotten, it was once widely accepted by the most qualified French public law scholars that Parliament constituted a constitutional court whenever it debated such motions (Waline 1928).

German parliamentarians possess no such procedural manoeuvre. Nonetheless, constitutional debates can be highly structured. Bundestag committee hearings regularly invite legal experts and former constitutional judges to advise them as well as to engage in 'Karlsruhe-astrology'[5]—attempts to predict the future position of the court (Landfried 1989). The concern for

---

[4] The Senate's standing orders are similar.
[5] The FCC is located in the town of Karlsruhe.

Table 3.5. Motions of unconstitutionality in the French National Assembly, 1967–1990

	1967–73	1974–80	1981–7	1988–90
Motions raised	2	35	203	35
Average per year	0.29	5	29	11.7
Motions voted	1	35	93	23
Average per year	0.14	5	13.2	7.7

Motions of unconstitutionality are requests for debate and then a vote on the allegation that a bill is unconstitutional. If a majority supports such a motion, the bill in question is rejected. Motions are virtually always raised by the opposition, and the vote is virtually always along party lines.

Source: Statistiques, Bulletin de l'Assemblée nationale, numero speciale for each of the years cited. The statistical bulletin does not present figures for the pre-1967 period, probably because no such motions were raised.

constitutionality is, however, not generated by fear of FCC censure alone. As observers of German politics unanimously agree, political elites share a deeply rooted commitment to *Rechtsstaat* ideology, a commitment which has been at the heart of state theory for more than a century. In consequence, legislators are unusually willing, even anxious, to rely on law and legal scholarship to guide their work (Blair 1978; Brinkman 1981; Dyson 1982; Johnson 1978; 1982). Due to the consolidation of constitutional review in the Federal Republic, the *Rechtsstaat* is today a constitutional *Rechtsstaat*, and legislators naturally draft legislation according to their understanding of it.

The second argument—that constitutional courts function to protect individual rights—should also not obscure another reality of constitutional politics: under judicialized conditions, the work of parliament, too, is dominated by the question of how best to protect and to balance rights claims. In the cases examined here, governments and their majorities never denied the constitutional status of such principles as equality under the law, freedom of education, fair compensation for expropriation, or the right to human life. On the contrary, they worked to uphold or extend these principles, as they understood them. They also sought to establish others for the first time: worker's participation, equality of the sexes, press pluralism. Oppositions countered with rights arguments of their own. Once settled by Parliament, these constitutional debates about the legislative application of rights were transferred to constitutional judges for yet another constitutional deliberation. The argument that these courts function to protect rights boils down not only to an admission that courts sometimes make law, but that they make better law than do legislators.

Do judges in fact protect rights better than do parliamentarians? No structured, systematic research on this question exists, in spite of its obvious importance.[6] My own view is that, in judicialized environments, courts do not protect rights better than do legislators. There are few—I doubt that there are any—constitutional rulings under judicialized conditions that unambiguously prove the contrary. Leading decisions do not force legislators to pay attention to rights that would otherwise be ignored and do not raise issues which had not already been raised in legislative debate. Leading decisions are legislative choices, replacing those of the parliamentary majority, about how constitutional rights must be protected.

Partly because rights are neither self-evident nor self-actualizing, constitutional courts are at times led to balance contending rights claims, and therefore to legislate. In the German abortion case, the balancing act was a subtle one. The dissenting opinion nevertheless focused on the fact that the FCC's ruling would force Parliament to renounce a liberalization of the penal code and to require a more repressive law. Courts, the dissenters wrote, fulfil their duty to extend liberties only when they require the state to liberalize. The 1981–5 period in France provides an extraordinary example of what can be done by a government committed to the extension of fundamental rights and liberties (see Safran 1988). It did so on its own, outside of the requirements of constitutional politics. In contrast, it can easily be demonstrated that many of the Council's most important decisions during this period served not only to consecrate the opposition's version of rights, but to protect those in privileged social and economic positions (see Keeler and Stone 1987). The same can be said for several key decisions of the FCC during the SPD-FDP governing period 1969–83.

My point is not to belittle the role of constitutional courts. The FCC and the French *Conseil d'état* often protect, in individual complaints and concrete or administrative review processes, the constitutional rights of individuals in interactions with the state. The protection is unambiguous and can be observed and measured. My argument is that constitutional review processes under judicialized conditions do not necessarily function to protect rights in the same unambiguous way. Constitutional judges and legislators are partners—in cooperation or rivalry—in the development of constitutional rights.

---

[6] One would be faced with a range of exceedingly complex ideological issues.

The third argument, essentially that constitutional courts have the final say on constitutional matters, is more structural than ideological, and unassailable. But the argument cannot in itself distinguish what constitutional courts do from what legislators do. Indeed, one might respond as follows: when legislators behave judicially, constitutional courts constitute their appellate jurisdiction. During the process of adopting the industrial co-determination law, eleven different constitutional lawyers and former FCC judges testified on the constitutionality of worker-management parity. After months of debate, one such expert told the Bundestag:

by now you have heard more or less everything which could be defended . . . absolute opposition, absolute support, and everything in between. You'll have to form your own opinion about how legal science ought to be put to work. (quoted in Landfried 1984: 54)

In its decision, the FCC made it clear that it had studied the Bundestag's debates in great detail. In France, parliamentarians recognize that their decisions at times constitute distinctly separate acts of judicial authority. Here is how Étienne Dailly put it during the Senate's debate on a motion of unconstitutionality against the nationalization bill:

I repeat: I have never said that we would refer this bill [to the Council]. I have limited myself to arguing that it is unconstitutional. Personally, I consider that we [in parliament] are judges of the first instance. But we are under the control of the Council, just as judges of first instance are under the control of the Court of Appeal. (Senate Debates, 20 November 1981)

Conclusion

The French and German constitutional courts are powerful policy-makers whose impact on legislative process and outcome is extensive and multidimensional. Constitutional judges are more than simply 'negative legislators' empowered to veto legislative provisions (Stone 1992a: 228–31). They also exercise creative legislative powers: to recast policy-making environments, to encourage certain legislative solutions while undermining others, and to have the precise terms of their decisions written directly into legislative provisions. The judicialization of policy-making is, in essence, the formalization of an extensive and intimate form of what in American parlance has been called 'coordinate construction'. Ministers and parliamentarians deliberate in the language of constitutional law and make reasoned decisions about the constitutionality of legislation; these deliberations then structure both judicial legislative behaviour and constitutional lawmaking processes. If I have pushed the argument too far, there are sound reasons. Students of public policy, and especially comparativists, all too often ignore the crucial role of law and courts. Legal scholars all too often assume that constitutional interpretation is the exclusive prerogative of judges. In France and Germany, at least, the making of public policy and the development of constitutional law are often one and the same.

4

Testing, Comparison, Prediction

To sustain a viable social science of law and courts, we need to generate testable propositions, develop appropriate research designs to test those hypotheses, and engage comparative materials.[1] In this chapter, we discuss and use three strategies for building theory through testing and comparing, each of which follows from the construction of an a priori, deductive model of various aspects of adjudication.

The first strategy, adopted by Stone Sweet in 'The European Court and Integration', employs econometric and other modes of statistical analysis as well as qualitative 'process tracing' to evaluate specific causal propositions about how European integration and the construction of the legal system have proceeded. This research design, quite rare in the social sciences, constitutes a mixed means of testing: the analyst (1) derives hypotheses deductively from materials developed in prior comparative research, (2) collects data to operationalize the theorized variables, (3) tests the hypotheses through analysing the data quantitatively, and (4) cross-checks these results and explores other theorized relationships or dynamics, qualitatively. As discussed briefly below, good fortune and collaboration made such research possible.

The other two strategies are associated with the comparative method and the crucial case study. Both designs are particularly useful for building a social science of law and courts, since the experimental and statistical methods are often unfeasible. As adopted in Shapiro's book *Courts* (1981a), the 'crucial case method' (see Eckstein 1975) involves searching the literature of comparative law to identify that historical situation most likely to falsify a given proposition, that is, one where Shapiro's theory would predict an outcome quite contrary to that described in the existing, authoritative literature.

---

[1] The behavioural work that followed from the move to 'Political Jurisprudence' showed that the activities of judges and other legal elites could be usefully quantified, and hypotheses about this behaviour could be evaluated using statistical methods. The *American Political Science Review* and the *American Journal of Political Science* regularly publish such work, with a heavy focus on US federal courts.

A third mode of testing involves constructing causal hypotheses to explain a major change that has occurred in one particular part of one particular legal system. These hypotheses can then be tested comparatively by predicting future developments in the same legal system—a diachronic, comparative design—or by predicting that another legal system now displaying the same hypothesized conditions will experience in the future those results that occurred in the first system, akin to what George (1979) calls a 'structured-focused comparison'. Shapiro's contribution to this chapter, 'Giving Reasons in European Law', does just this, by deriving predictions about Europe from the evolution of American judicial review of administrative acts.

The Comparative Case Study

In our view, comparative research on courts can be useful for two broad theoretical purposes. First, the analyst engages comparative materials to refine concepts or candidate hypotheses from hunches that had emerged in prior research on another legal system. Single case studies, as Eckstein (1975) argued in an influential paper, could be justified as a kind of preliminary social science *only* to the extent that they could be used to build causal theory in areas where clear, falsifiable propositions did not yet exist. This is the most common method of comparative politics—although it rarely results in falsifiable theories—and it underpins the articles on constitutional law and politics offered in Chapter 3 of this volume. In his research on the French Fifth Republic, for example, Stone Sweet found legislative bargaining 'in the shadow' of the constitutional court (Stone 1989a), from which he developed a typology of different bargaining structures as well as methods by which to study them. He then began to study the judicialization of politics across Europe (Stone Sweet 2000). Inductive, case-by-case methods can become the basis for theorizing in a deductive mode once concepts have been sufficiently refined, the relationship between variables theorized, and hypotheses have demonstrated reasonable plausibility. The model presented in 'Judicialization and the Construction of Governance', for example, is expressed in a general, abstract, and deductive form, which hides the fact that it developed only piecemeal, through the interpretation of accumulated data. As Stone Sweet's paper in this chapter shows, once the model was in place, hypotheses to guide further research could be relatively easily derived.

Second, as Eckstein emphasized, the comparative case study is an unassailable method of social science when, informed by falsifiable theory, it is designed to test causal claims. This is the basic method Shapiro adopts in *Courts*. Here, we summarize the approach and findings of that book and related research at some length, since we do not include a full-text example otherwise.

We begin with the basic theoretical formulation set out in the first pages of Shapiro's *Courts*, one that is deliberately taken up by the model of judicialization and governance that Stone Sweet presents in Chapter 1 of this volume. This formulation is actually a very simple and reductive one, precisely because only very basic and reductive concepts could have any hope of general application to a phenomenon such as courts, which has been so universal across time, places, and circumstances. In Shapiro's hands, the theory is also built up reactively: it seeks to reverse the orthodox view of courts while at the same time explaining why that view is so prevalent.

The theory begins with what we call the social logic of courts. If a conflict arises between two persons and they cannot resolve it themselves, then in all cultures and societies it is logical for those two persons to call upon a third to assist in its resolution. That assistance falls along a spectrum that stretches from the mediator to the arbitrator to the judge. This spectrum is defined by the degree to which the third party moves from eliciting a mutually consensual resolution to imposing or coercing a resolution. The triad contains a basic tension. To the extent that the triadic figure appears to intervene in favour of one of the two disputants and against the other, the perception of the situation will shift from the fairest to the most unfair of configurations: two against one. Therefore the principal characteristics of all triadic conflict resolvers will be determined by the need to avoid the perception of two against one, for only then can they rely on their basic social logic.

Thus all triadic figures everywhere along the spectrum will seek to elicit to the greatest degree possible the consent of the two conflicting parties both to their jurisdiction and to the substance of a resolution. For mutual consent can help avoid the perception of two against one. The go-between who simply shuttles back and forth between two parties until they themselves resolve their differences or choose to go elsewhere operates in a situation of pure, immediate, moment-by-moment consent. His only intervention is in the recasting of messages as he delivers them. The mediator intervenes more, perhaps proposing various resolutions to the parties for their mutual consent. The judge intervenes the most, formulating a single resolution and imposing it on the parties. Like every other triadic figure along the spectrum, however, the judge confronts the two-against-one problem and thus will seek to elicit consent.

Two principal devices are employed to supplement or replace the pure, immediate moment-to-moment consent of the go-between. They are office and rules. The judge seeks to avoid the perception of two against one by asserting his neutrality between the two disputants, in the sense both of his personal neutrality and of his employment of a decision rule that appears to take discretion out of his hands, while dictating a resolution quite independent of his personal preferences for either party. In the early Roman law the two parties mutually chose the judge, and mutually chose the decision rule or law which the judge was to apply to their particular dispute. If either party claimed the judicial decision was two against one, the response was: 'How could it be? You chose the judge and you chose the law.' The *Lex Mercatoria* examined in Chapter 5 works in much the same way.

Over time, the particular and immediate consent by parties is formalized, or institutionalized, as office and law. The politically organized society appoints official judges and enacts general decision rules or law. That shift reduces the element of consent and increases the element of third-party imposition. Societies move to this level of imposition both because it remains in their general interest that conflicts be resolved, because they organize exchange in more complex and impersonal ways, and also because they may wish to see certain types of conflict resolved in certain ways, with reference to certain kinds of political values. But in moving away from pure consent, the problem of perceived two against one is aggravated.

This is where the orthodox prototype of courts comes in. That prototype calls for an independent judge, who applies pre-existing legal rules, following adversary proceedings that enable him to arrive at a decision in which one party is declared legally right and the other legally wrong. The prototype says to the loser: do not perceive the outcome as two against one. You did not choose the judge, but appointment by the state assures that he or she did not favour your opponent. You did not choose the law, but that it was enacted by the state before your dispute arose assures that the judge did not simply make up a rule favouring your opponent. Furthermore, you have participated equally with your opponent, according to procedures also laid down by the law. And finally the obligation of the judge to find a legal winner and loser assures you that the legal rule which exists above and beyond either party, rather than the judge's attitude to you or your opponent, will determine the outcome. In a sense the whole history of legal orthodoxy, and all the ritual and paraphernalia of courts, is an endless attempt to address the two-against-one problem.

These ideas play a central part in a general theory of governance developed in this volume. Anticipating the much-cited work *Bargaining in the Shadow of the Law* (Mnookin and Kornhauser 1979), the original *Handbook of Political Science* entry on courts, which became the first chapter of *Courts*, speaks of 'legalized bargaining under the shadow supervision of an available court' (Shapiro 1975: 329; see also Stone Sweet's article in Chapter 3). Such bargaining is facilitated by the knowledge of each party that, if the two do not reach a consensual resolution to the conflict, the other may go to court and seek an imposed outcome. Just as important, the previously judicially announced rules that will determine what a court will impose if litigation does occur fix the parameters within which the two parties bargain even if neither ever goes to court. The relative legal strengths of the two parties, as defined by those rules judicially announced to resolve *previously litigated* disputes, are crucial factors in determining the bargaining strengths of negotiating parties in other disputes that are *not* litigated but, in form, are resolved by purely private, consensual agreements. Thus courts generate a huge hinterland of resolutions whose private, mediatory character is actually crucially determined by the rules judicially imposed upon others. Indeed, by strictly limiting the number of questions on which the parties are free to initially disagree as bargaining begins, such rules not only constrain but facilitate the bargaining process.

The basic theory propounded here points us to various mis-statements or overstatements in the orthodox prototype while also explaining the persistent vigorous allegiance to that prototype.

First, courts may be, or seek to be, independent and neutral at retail, but not at wholesale. Judges may seek not to favour any particular party on a person-to-person basis. They may also seek to isolate themselves from particular interference from other particular government officials in particular cases. However, precisely because we have made them government officers and charged them to employ government-made rules, they are not, and are not supposed to be, independent of the law and neutral toward its purposes. On the contrary, we expect them to be servants of the law. A common tactic for defending the legitimacy of courts is to deliberately confuse these two levels of independence and neutrality. By doing so we seek to finesse the stark fact that court decisions will indeed be two against one in the sense of deciding in favour of litigants who are members of a class of persons favoured by the law and against those disfavoured. In burglary cases we do not expect judges to be neutral as between home dwellers and thieves, even though we would condemn them for taking orders from the police as to whether a particular burglary defendant should be convicted.

Second, the theory recognizes the appeal of pre-existing rules or laws governing judges' decisions as a mode of avoiding perceptions of two against one. 'You have lost not because I the judge don't like you, but because the law, which is master of us all, commands it.' However, precisely because of the consent eliciting potential of this kind of stance, the theory would lead us to expect that, where no pre-existing rule actually does dictate the outcome in a particular case, judges will make up their own new rule or law in the course of that case and pretend that their new rule was a pre-existing one. If obvious, such judicial lawmaking would raise the suspicion that the judge has deliberately made up a rule that favours the party he or she favours. So judicial lawmaking will usually be camouflaged by the claim that judges only interpret or discover pre-existing legal rules or objectively derive particular legal rules from underlying legal principles. Writ large, as it is elsewhere in this volume, this argument suggests that any government organ or government as a whole that seeks to ameliorate individual conflict will make laws quite apart from any desire it may have to dictate what individuals should and should not do.

Third, there are consequences for the fact that any judicially imposed compromise between two litigants will reveal judicial discretion, and the accompanying risk of judicial favouritism, because any compromise involves some discretionary choice among alternative potential compromises. There may be a single, correct, right, and a single correct, wrong, legal resolution, but by definition there cannot be a single right compromise. Mediators work by the direct, personal consent of the parties, and their proposed resolutions are adopted only by the mutual consent of the parties. For judges, who do not enjoy such consent, undoubtedly it is better to present their decisions as legally right. Losers are told that they lose not because the judge favoured their opponent but because, no matter what their good intentions, the law says they were wrong. But arranging it so that the winner wins everything and the loser loses everything is not calculated to elicit full consent from the loser, no matter how much the judge talks of legal right and wrong. So, as Stone Sweet's 'dispute resolver's calculus' (Chapter 1) suggests, we expect that judges will seek to elicit some degree of loser consent through giving the losers something as well as telling them something. We should expect some element of compromise even in judicially imposed outcomes expressed as right versus wrong, with right party taking all. Common law courts famously prefer money damage remedies to others because a judge can award the 'right' litigant less money than he has asked for, and take from the 'wrong' litigant more money than he wants to pay. Likewise, administrative and constitutional law judges inevitably generate balancing and proportionality tests, partly to be able to say to classes of litigants: each of your legal interests in the case before us is a legitimate one; the court has taken a decision by weighing these interests, one against the other, given the facts; but, in future cases that pit the same two legal interests against one another, we may well decide differently, depending upon new facts and circumstances (Stone Sweet 2000: 97–9; 142–3). The theory expects to find intimate judicial mixture of mediation, compromise, and consent with the imposition of right-wrong, win-lose, outcomes. Flexible techniques of determining outcomes, like balancing tests and discretion over damages, allow the judge a means not only of dealing with present dangers of perceived two against one, but also of signalling to future litigants that outcomes do not freeze in place judicial bias (see also Stone Sweet's paper in Chapter 2).

Courts also adopted a theory of appeal as a corollary to its basic view of courts as subject to dynamics common to all parts of government. Here again the theory of appeal is a deliberate attempt to adopt a simple, child-like, view of complex legal political phenomena. Conventionally, appeals are seen from the bottom up as a mechanism for protecting individuals who have been the victims of mistakes by trial courts. Even a cursory acquaintance with the global history of law reveals the incompleteness of this view. Appellate mechanisms are costly for the political regimes that finance them. Many political regimes that care little or nothing for individual rights, notably the historical Chinese and Japanese empires, have financed quite elaborate appeals mechanisms. Suppose we look at appeals from the top down instead of from the bottom up. What's in it for the top?

Elsewhere in this volume, we treat courts in terms of a general Weberian view of hierarchical, and sometimes non-hierarchical, organizations. A quick look at the court organization chart of most countries reveals a standard hierarchical pattern. At the bottom are many trial courts, usually territorially distributed. At the top is a highest appellate court. Often there are a number of intermediate appellate courts, each supervising a number of trial courts, and they themselves are subject to the highest appellate courts. Most more or less advanced political regimes are arranged in such hierarchies. These hierarchies are designed to take more or less general commands from the top and translate them into more and more particularized instructions as they are transmitted downward. The bottom units of these hierarchies not only receive the increasingly detailed instructions, but each collects detailed local information that is transmitted upwards. As it moves upwards from the very large number of bottom units to intermediate and then highest levels, this information is progressively more and more edited and summarized. The top does not have the capacity to generate thousands of detailed commands for each and every bottom unit and so depends on intermediate lower units to fill in the details. Similarly the top does not have the capacity to absorb and use the mass of bits of information gathered at the bottom and so depends on intermediate layers to successively filter and synthesize information so that it reaches the top in a form the top can comprehend.

Treating courts as an isolated organization, the functions of appeal as far as the top is concerned are easy to discern. Top courts can announce general laws or rules of decision or legal doctrines. Through the practice of vertical *stare decisis* (see Chapter 2), these announcements are commands to lower courts. Losers in trial courts have a high incentive to bring bottom-court disobedience to those orders to the attention of higher courts by appealing. Thus appeals create a host of monitors of bottom obedience to the top, most of whom the government doesn't have to pay. Through their appeals decisions, higher courts discipline their subordinate courts to obey their commands. As appeals move upwards, a lot of detailed information drops out and attention is increasingly focused on major legal problems or issues. The final appeals decision is designed both to state the governing legal rule generally and to ensure its application to the particular situation that gave rise to the appeal. In future cases all the bottom courts are bound to make the necessary particular applications of the appeals court's general doctrinal pronouncements in earlier cases. In short, through the appeals process the highest level of courts gives commands to its subordinates that they are bound to elaborate into detailed applications and receives selective information about whether the lower courts are obeying and whether the legal rules made at the top are working down in the real world.

In all relatively centralized political regimes, one of the biggest problems lies along the information channel of hierarchy. Because the top needs digested information, at each level of hierarchy from the bottom to the top some detailed information must be dropped out. It is natural in this process for each level to drop data on its failures and disobedience, and document upward its obedient successes. Here we can see why appeal is so concerned with individual losers, even in a regime that cares little about individuals. Appeals are not only reports upwards by the lowest courts, they are reports upwards by non-court officials which stress the failures of trial courts to follow the commands of higher courts.

More generally, hierarchical regimes may combat these information problems in a number of special ways. One is to construct a number of separate hierarchies reporting on the same local matters to a single top. Regimes may finance an appellate court hierarchy alongside a separate administrative hierarchy because judicial appeals are a vehicle through which the top can learn about failures in its administrative hierarchy that are edited out of upward-flowing administrative communication. Thus the current Chinese interest in an independent judiciary.

Another device is slice-of-life or product sampling. In addition to hierarchical, and thus pre-digested, information gathering, every once in a while the highest authorities may reach down into the local world, pluck up some particular happening, and do a detailed examination of the particular successes and failures there of subordinate governors and the governed. Such sampling tactics work, of course, if the bottom cannot know in advance which particular thing the top is going to pluck up. They work best if the plucking looks random to the bottom but nonetheless somehow routinely picks up failures. Appeals cases pluck particular sets of events and circumstances from the bottom and ship them up to the top for a detailed re-evaluation of what went on at the bottom. Local governors are unlikely to be able to anticipate well what cases will get appealed how far up the hierarchy, and so cannot anticipate and concentrate on doing unusually well on the slices of life the top is going to see. And, as we note in Chapter 2 of this volume, judges are most likely to move away from the status quo when they see failure in the status quo. Appeals are most likely when trial court judges move away from the status quo. From the viewpoint of the top of a political regime especially looking for failures unreported by subordinate governors, judicial appeals mechanisms are particular attractive because they are an unpredictable central government sampling of local performance biased toward picking up failures that are otherwise suppressed by other reporting hierarchies.

The theory then argues that, in spite of its expense, appeal will be virtually universal because it is advantageous to political regimes quite apart from any advantage it yields to losers at trial. How can one go about testing such a proposition?

Experiment can rarely be employed in the law and courts field as a mode of testing hypotheses, and the use of robust statistical methods is hampered by small-n problems, the absence of comparable data on legal systems, and in various other ways. As noted, comparative case study may be used for many purposes. One is hypothesis testing: the analyst generates hypotheses on the basis of limited and scattered data and then tests them against particular fields of data, more deeply considered. An economizing device is to choose data most likely to falsify the offered hypothesis. When possible, the hypothesis ought to be constructed so that it will generate predictions that can then be shown to be accurate or inaccurate for the body of data most likely to falsify the hypothesis.

Prediction itself is quite difficult in the social sciences, in part because we are not willing to defer our understanding of vital political matters until the predictions have time to play out. Thus in social science, as in physics, predictions of the past as well as of the future may be useful. Prediction of the future is obvious. Prediction of the past requires a further word. If the past is unknown now but may be discovered by new investigation, then hypotheses may be tested by predicting that something happened in the past; we then conduct new historical investigations to see whether it in fact did. Cosmology proceeds in this way, hypothesizing about what happened at the beginning of the universe, then seeking new evidence about what happened by observing sources so distant that signals sent early in the history of the universe are just reaching us now. More often, in social as opposed to physical studies, a slightly different method may be employed. We can predict the past on matters that have been very little studied and/or predict past outcomes that run quite contrary to the consensus of received scholarly opinion on what happened in the past.

Courts sought to test each of its offered hypotheses by examining the major legal system most likely to falsify it. In two of its chapters, Shapiro simply tried to show that existing data and past scholarship tend to confirm rather than disconfirm offered hypotheses on judicial independence and judicial lawmaking. His subjects were England and France. Two other chapters attempted the stronger technique of predicting the past, and this is where the theoretical materials just surveyed came in. The subject of one is imperial Chinese law. The consensus of traditional scholarship on Chinese law was that a sharp distinction existed between mediation on the one hand and, on the other, litigation before a government judge enforcing law. Commended by the dominant Confucian ideology, nearly all conflicts not resolved by the parties themselves supposedly went to informal mediation where an intermediate solution was achieved wholly favourable to neither party. These mediations were conducted by socially esteemed private persons, not by government officials. Judicial decisions under formal law were disesteemed, avoided whenever possible, and thus largely reserved for serious crimes. The theory set out in *Courts*, however, would predict that no such deep divide would exist, that mediation and judging would be located quite close to one another on the triadic spectrum, and both would mix consent and coercion. Thus, Shapiro argued, against traditional wisdom and on the basis of the sparse data available at the time, that imperial Chinese law and courts did handle a great many property, contract, and commercial disputes as well as criminal ones, and that what might appear to be mediation was often actually non-governmentally appointed judges applying rules imposed not by government, but by non-governmental entities such as villages, clans, and guilds. Shapiro also argued that Chinese litigation or judging itself often involved strong mediatory consent-eliciting elements. Far from facing each other across a deep chasm, one esteemed by dominant Confusion ideology and the other, therefore, reserved for crime, as depicted by conventional scholarship, mediation and judging must have been intimately interconnected and interdependent.

When *Courts* was written, relatively little was known about the substance of actual trial as opposed to appellate litigation in imperial China. Research of the last two decades conducted on only recently available trial records tends to confirm that litigation was used frequently in a wide range of civil as well as criminal matters (see Macauley 1998: 14–15 and literature cited) and that mediation and litigation were strongly interactive and interconnected. We now know that lawsuits were often threatened or actually filed to press opponents to mediate; that, once filed, many, probably most, lawsuits ended in pre-trial settlements; and that judges, faced with crowded calendars, pressed parties to settle. Recent writings by Chinese specialists remains divided on how often government judges—district magistrates—actually themselves engaged in mediation or imposed compromise as opposed to winner-take-all solutions in litigation. But it is agreed that they sometimes did in spite of formal legal prohibitions on doing so. Little research has yet been done on village, clan, and guild private judging (Huang 1996).

The *Courts* chapter on traditional Islamic law offers the most striking use of social science prediction of the past. As just argued, appeal should appear in all legal systems. The unchallenged consensus in Islamic scholarship was that there was no appeal in orthodox Islamic law, although modern Islamic states had introduced appeal when they partially Westernized their particular national legal systems. The Islamic chapter in *Courts* made the relatively weak argument that the theory offered can explain this absence of appeal. If, as the theory proposes, appeal is a function of hierarchy, then we would not expect to find appeal in orthodox Islamic law, the *shariah*. In orthodox Islam no distinction is really made between law and theology. All law is religious law. Islam is a notably non-hierarchical religion. There is no pope. The religion is divided into a number of competing schools each of which is conceded to be orthodox by the others. Much reliance is placed on the consensus of the whole body of the faithful. Disagreement between and within sects is a divine gift showing the many branches of the great tree of Islam. If Islam is essentially a non-hierarchical religion, and all law is religious law, then we would expect that appeal would be absent.

The *Courts* chapter goes on, however, to employ the stronger predictive technique. The proposed theory of appeal would predict that, in spite of the then consensus of Islamic scholars, appeal would be found, even in Islam, where a strong element of governmental hierarchy had existed over an extended period of time. Shapiro then sought and did find appeal in the Ottoman empire, a long-lasting, Islamic, but very hierarchical polity. The Ottoman sultans created a graded hierarchy of judges—*khadis* or *quadis*—appointed by themselves, with themselves and their immediate subordinates as the highest judges. Depending on the status of the litigants, initial trials might be held at any level of the hierarchy. But where losing parties had the status and wealth to move upwards, they could appeal from lower-rank to higher-rank *khadis*. There was appeal in Islam if you looked for it in the places where the theory predicted it would be.

Why had conventional Islamic scholarship missed this appeal, even when fully aware that the Ottoman judges were marshalled in a ranked hierarchy of the normal Weberian pyramidal kind? Unlike Western legal systems, Islam has no *res judicata*, that is, no notion that, once a trial has been concluded and a decision reached by one judge, no second trial may occur. Of course, in Western law, while no second trial may occur, appeal may occur. Typically, although not always, in the West appeal is 'on the record', that is, the appeals court does not retry the case seeing the evidence and hearing the witnesses but instead conducts its inquiry on the basis of the trial court record of fact and law sent up to it. In Islam there is no appeal on the record. Appeal is by trial *de novo*, that is, a complete retrial of the legal and factual issues, a method rare but not unknown in the West, but unlikely to be much known to Islamic specialists. Thus, unlike the normal Western practice, Islam has no special appellate procedures. Viewed individually, every legal proceeding, whether an initial trial or an appeal to a higher *khadi* from a lower one, will look exactly alike. Moreover, because higher-status litigants will seek even initial trials from higher-ranked *khadis*, even high Ottoman *khadis* will conduct many initial trials. If one combines the theory of appeal offered in *Courts* with a consciousness of appeal by trial *de novo* practices—present but non-obvious in Western law—then one's attention is drawn not to individual trials but to sequences of trials moving from lower-ranked to-higher ranked *khadis*. These sequences are Ottoman, Islamic appeal.

Thus, by employing a predictive approach to historical data and a body of scholarly commentary most likely to falsify the proffered hypothesis, some support for the hypothesis may be acquired. Recent research by Islamic specialists has tended to confirm the existence of appeal in Islam, but to discover some non-hierarchical appeal (Powers 1992). Thus doubt is thrown on a purely hierarchical theory of appeal. Even if the theory eventually must be modified or abandoned, however, it has served to transform Islamic appeal from an oxymoron to a recognized field of research.

Even better than prediction of the past, of course, is prediction of the future. For then there is no chance that the proponent of a particular theory has peeked at the predicted outcomes before predicting them. The trick, or the blind luck, is to predict something that either happens or fails to happen soon enough to help in theory testing. The law and courts of the European Union are, therefore, an attractive data set for prediction because they are evolving so rapidly. Shapiro's article on 'giving reasons' in EU law, presented in this chapter, involved one piece of good luck after another.

In brief, this article makes the following argument. Judicial review of administrative agencies by US federal courts went from very passive in the 1940s and 1950s to very active by the late 1960s. Judges reinterpreted the language of the Administrative Procedures Act (APA) to require the agencies to offer exhaustive explanations and defences of their decisions. This change in US judicial behaviour can be attributed to a number of mutually reinforcing causes that the article specifies. The treaties constituting the European Union contain a clause requiring EU organs to 'give reasons' for their decisions, and this clause parallels the US APA language. The conditions that existed earlier in the US now exist in Europe. Therefore, in spite of its past passivity, it may be predicted that the European Court of Justice (ECJ) will move in the same direction as the US federal courts did, from passive to more active judicial review of administrative decision-making.

When Shapiro began work on this piece, the prediction that the EU courts would become active in reviewing administrative decisions was derived from a theory based entirely on American materials. Only after deriving the prediction did he look at EU case law at all. The first piece of luck was that the past case law flatly contradicted the prediction. Thus, Shapiro could not be accused of predicting what he already knew had occurred.

The second piece of luck had to do with legal technicalities. The courts of the EU follow the general Continental practice of not openly engaging in *stare decisis*. Although the reality is different, European courts purport not to follow case precedents. Instead, they claim to return each time to a new interpretation of the original, governing legal text, such as a statute or constitutional provision, unfettered by past interpretations by earlier judges. Because they pretend not to follow precedent, in a case decision they never announce formally that they are breaking with precedent. Yet the prediction offered was that the EU courts would break with their own past precedents of passivity in reviewing administrative decisions. The luck was that the particular form of proceedings followed by the ECJ in this instance yielded about as clear a reversal of the previous case law as can ever have been seen on the Continent. The Court's own Advocate General, himself ranked as a judicial official of the Court, offers a formal address to the Court in each case. It is published along with the Court's opinion. In the case employed in this article to verify the offered prediction, the Advocate General's address states that a long line of previous Court of Justice decisions, if followed in the instant case, would lead the Court not to move to activist review. He then urges the Court to break with the past precedents, engage in more demanding judicial review of administrative action and, in this case, find against the administrators. Following the usual, although not invariable, practice, the Court's opinion does not state that it is breaking with precedent, but it engages in more activist review, and it finds against the administrators.

The third piece of luck was timing. The initial giving-reasons paper was written for a conference. As the participants were heading into the conference hall, one of them, Judge Lenaerts of the European Court of First Instance, said to Shapiro, 'You can't know it yet, because the opinions aren't published yet, but my court and the Court of Justice have just done what you predicted.' Outside of election studies, political scientists rarely get, or even hope to get, such rapid outcomes against which to check predictions.

Although the predictive aspects of this study turned out very neatly, the comparative aspects were weaker. This study was not one in which very general hypotheses were generated and then tested against whatever experience was most likely to falsify them. Instead it was a more conventional 'two-country study'. First. a particular dynamic of causes and effects was hypothesized for one segment of US legal experience. Then it was assumed that, if like causes existed in the EU, then there would be like effects. On this assumption, and after finding like causes in the EU, predictions were made about future developments in Europe on the basis of past developments in the US. If the predictions proved to be wrong, then one of three errors must have occurred. The hypothesized cause and effect relationships could have been wrong for the US. Or they were correct, but the finding of similar causes in Europe might have been wrong. Or other conditions in Europe were sufficiently different from those in the US so that like causes would not necessarily produce like effects. If the prediction turned out to be correct, then there would be some confirmation of the cause and effect analysis of the US and of the finding of similar European causes, and some reason to believe that conditions in the US and the EU were sufficiently similar to make this kind of comparative method of hypothesis testing feasible.

Two interconnected points should be emphasized. Such a study should be of as of great an interest to 'American politics' specialists as to a 'comparative politics' specialist. It is, after all, a test, using a comparative technique, of causal hypothesis about American politics. Second, the study is intended to challenge the traditional division in American political science between the American politics people who study only America and the comparative politics people who are entitled to study any place other than the US. Why should political scientists refuse to use for comparative purposes the one country they know most about (Shapiro 2002)? The current fad in 'globalization' studies may finally provide us with a path to US-European comparisons, because at least in law and politics 'global' phenomena usually turn out to be developments common to North America and Western Europe, sometimes with Japan and a few other post-industrial states thrown in (see also Chapter 5).

The American side of the giving reasons article is derived from a long series of studies of US judicial review of administrative action (Shapiro 1968; 1982; 1983; 1986d; 1988). The root premise of this research challenged the conventional wisdom that each of the three great branches of American government has its own peculiar function, performed in its own peculiar way (see also Chapter 6). Instead, it argued that the only way a court could review an agency decision effectively would be to go through for a second time essentially the same decision-making process that the agency has already pursued. Moreover, it was argued that both agencies and courts must interpret the statute enacted by the legislature that had authorized agency action. Statutory interpretation invariably involves lawmaking. Both agencies and reviewing courts are secondary or supplementary lawmakers. Thus the paradox stated in the title of Shapiro's *Who Guards the Guardians* (1988): if Congress provides for judicial review to police the lawmaking discretion it grants administrative agencies, it does so at the cost of granting the same kind of lawmaking discretion to the courts. Elsewhere in this volume (Chapter 3) the same kind of argument writ large emerges as a 'junkyard dog' theory of constitutional judicial review.[2]

Of course, the whole argument goes back to the initial stance of political jurisprudence. Courts are not special, set-aside, non-political places. They do the same jobs in roughly, but not exactly, the same ways as the rest of government.

A final cautionary point about the Shapiro piece reprinted in this chapter. The argument there is that a certain cause-and-effect story first played out in the US. So if later we discover the same causes in Europe we may expect the same effects later in Europe. The argument is not that American law is more advanced or in any way better than European law or that EU law has

---

[2] These issues are found in English and French administrative law as well (Shapiro 2002).

copied, or should copy, American law. Indeed, one element of the argument is that the most direct influence of American on European legal developments is European awareness of the severe down-side of American-style judicial review of administrative action. This is a time-staged, like causes produce like effect, predictive study, not an assertion of diffusion from the US to Europe nor a prescription that Europeans adopt an American practice.

What was predicted in 'The Giving-reasons requirement' was a change in direction by the European courts, not how far they would go. There were good reasons to believe that they would not go as far as the extreme demands that had been made by the US Courts of Appeal which are outlined in the article. In the US there had been increasing criticism of those demands because of the high costs and regulatory delays they have imposed on the regulatory agencies. While there is no direct evidence in their decisions, we do know that many judges of the European courts are knowledgeable about American developments (see Lenaerts 1988).

Subsequent to the European courts' initial change of direction as predicted in the article, work has been done tracing further developments (for example, Nehl 1999; Shapiro 2001c; 2001d). Recent findings can be summarized briefly. First, the ECJ has continued to repeat old formulae and invent new ones to indirectly convey the message that it does not want to go as far as the US. It particularly wants to avoid a situation in which the giving-reasons requirement will be used strategically, that is, where regulated firms will barrage EU administrators with endless claims and questions and then seek reversal of administrative decisions on the ground that each and every point they raised was not responded to. Second, in addition to basing themselves on the giving-reasons requirement of the treaties, the European courts have also grounded their more vigorous review of administrative action on a 'duty of good administration' which they find implicit in the treaties. Third, the ECJ appears to be attempting to rein in what it may regard as somewhat too vigorous review by the Court of First Instance but doing so without itself going back to its own previous passivity.

Judicialization and Supranational Governance

When the first draft of 'Judicialization and the Construction of Governance' was completed in 1996, Harry Eckstein invited Stone Sweet into his office, which was adjacent to Stone Sweet's at the School of Social Sciences in Irvine. Eckstein wanted to say that the 'Judicialization' project had just begun. It was time to develop a series of empirical research projects on new—or historical—systems of triadic governance, capable of assessing the theory.

Stone Sweet had been thinking along the same lines, and replied that the European Community (EC) looked like a promising start: the EC was a relatively new polity, with a novel legal system and a clear beginning point. Comprehensive data were, at least in principle, available. And, as Eckstein had suggested, the research could be organized by hypotheses easily and directly derivable from the deductive theory elaborated in the first part of the 'Judicialization' piece.[3]

Over the next several months, Stone Sweet developed the project as a grant proposal, which the Law and Social Science Division of the National Science Foundation agreed to fund over five years. This funding enabled the collecting and processing of basic data on the EC polity, including on the legal system.[4] These data, which had not been gathered before, were then used to test a theory of European integration in a series of papers, including the one presented here (see also Stone Sweet and Caporaso 1998a, b; Fligstein and Stone Sweet 2001). As Eckstein later noted, the opportunity to advance in this clean, positivist way—from abstract theory to causal propositions, and then from data collection to testing and analysis—might come along only once in a lifetime, with luck.

The theory in Stone Sweet's 'Judicialization' piece is expressed deductively and in the abstract, without reference to time or place. It elaborates a model of triadic dispute resolution (TDR), including adjudication, focusing on two sets of linked processes. The first set of hypotheses concerns the relationship between dyadic contracting, or social exchange, and TDR: as social exchange rises and becomes more complex and differentiated, triadic dispute resolution will be increasingly activated and thereby implicated in governance. The second set of hypotheses concerns the sources and consequences of judicial lawmaking. Critical to the theory (Chapters 1 and 2) is the propensity of judges to give reasons to justify their decisions—and to insist that other government officials do so as well—and the tendency of the judges' audience to interpret any such justification as a clarification, modification, or

[3] The paper 'The European Court and Integration' owes a great deal to discussions Stone Sweet had with others, especially James Caporaso, Russell Dalton, Neil Fligstein, Ronald Jepperson, Paul Pierson, Wayne Sandholtz, and Martin Shapiro. Their reading of his papers on judicialization provoked many important changes, and always in the direction of making the arguments more general, more causal, and more testable. It was a great advantage that only one of these scholars works on law and courts. Most important, these discussions reinforced Stone Sweet's own view that he was building a theory of a certain mode of governance per se, and not simply an approach to judicial politics.

[4] The data are mounted on various websites, including of the Robert Schuman Centre, the European University Institute, San Domenico di Fiesole, Italy <http://www.iue.it/RSC/> and of Stone Sweet <http://www.nuff.ox.ac.uk/Users/Sweet/index.html/> These data are analyzed, for varying purposes, elsewhere (for example, Stone Sweet and Brunell 1998b; 2000a, b).

creation of legal norms. Taken together, the model shows how triadic governance can organize institutional change and polity-building by linking the evolution of rule structures to individual and collective decision-making. Although Stone Sweet's immediate purpose was to explain the evolution of the GATT-WTO and the French Fifth Republic, he adapted the theory to the particulars of the EC, deriving testable propositions about how the construction of supranational governance would proceed.

The theory proposes that an expansive, dynamic form of governance—the triadic—will increasingly condition integration and polity-building in Europe to the extent that three factors, transnational exchange—the dyad—organizational capacity to respond to social exchange—the triad—and legal rules—the normative structure—become linked in a mutually reinforcing system of causal interdependence. Stone Sweet recognized certain necessary but not sufficient conditions for such a causal system to emerge. The most important of these were supplied by the preliminary reference procedure, put in place by the Treaty of Rome, and the announcement, on the part of the ECJ, of the doctrines of supremacy and direct effect. The so-called 'constitutionalization' of the treaty system (Weiler 1991) did indeed transform governance in the EC, by creating the conditions for its own judicialization. The aggregate data analysis finds overwhelming support for the hypotheses offered, across the life of the EC. The qualitative analysis then explores the impact—feedback effects—of litigation and judicial rule-making on policy-making processes and outcomes at both the national and the supranational levels. As the theory predicted, triadic governance in the EC operates to saturate the 'political' arenas with rules and with rule-oriented modes of deliberating, a process that advances gradually, but inevitably, in areas of sustained litigation. Judicialization accelerates and reinforces what Haas (1958; 1961) characterized as 'the expansive logic' of European integration, reducing the intergovernmental elements of EC governance, and enhancing supranationalism.

'The European Court and Integration' paper does not dwell on the theory of judicialization; after hypotheses are derived, it goes on to analyze the data and engage the central theoretical debates on integration. When Stone Sweet turned his attention to the EC, it quickly became obvious that there was significant overlap between 'Judicialization and Construction of Governance' and certain aspects of Ernst Haas' regional integration theory (see Stone Sweet and Sandholtz 1998). Unfortunately, the decline of Haas's neo-functionalist project in the mid-1970s robbed the study of European integration of its theoretical aims and vitality. Research on integration, post-Haas, had proceeded on a piecemeal basis: the description of specific episodes of treaty-making, legislating, and litigating. There was little development of causal theory on the dynamics of integration, virtually no systematic data collection, and efforts to develop and test causal propositions slowed to nothing. Sandholtz and Zysman (1989) revived the field in a paper that echoed Haas in important respects. In the 1990s, the claims of 'intergovernmentalists' (Garrett 1992; Moravcsik 1991; 1993; 1995), overtly hostile to neo-functionalist ideas, dominated what passed for theoretical debate, although not without important challenges (for example, Burley and Mattli 1993; Sandholtz 1992; 1993; 1996). Although the nature of their argument kept changing,[5] intergovernmentalists asserted that the executives of member states, or of the most powerful member states, effectively controlled the pace and scope of integration through their control of treaty-interpretation and the legislative process, and down-played the causal significance of supranational organizations and trans-national actors. Stone Sweet believed that, if he had correctly specified the dynamics of how new systems of governance emerge and evolve, then either the intergovernmentalist propositions or his had to be wrong when it came to Europe. The paper sought to assess these various claims in light of the overall development of the EC.[6] During this same period, Stone Sweet convened two long-running collaborative research projects on the dynamics of European integration, both of which focused on theorized connections between social exchange, organization, and institutions. This work self-consciously tried to synthesize the 'Judicialization' model with a modified neo-functionalism and other institutionalist materials. The volumes, *European Integration and Supranational Governance* (Sandholtz and Stone Sweet 1998), and *The Institutionalization of Europe* (Stone Sweet, Sandholtz, and Fligstein 2001), are the result. If a theory of how judicial authority emerges and evolves can generate an approach to European integration, then perhaps courts are microcosms of political systems in some significant respect. At any rate, that was what the 'Judicialization' paper argued and what Harry Eckstein wanted Stone Sweet to find out.

---

[5] Moravcsik (1998) retreated into a position broadly consistent with much of neo-functionalism, as the latter theory was modified post-Sandholtz and Zysman (1989), and Garrett abandoned his claims altogether.

[6] A more detailed empirical critique of intergovernmentalism appears in Stone Sweet and Caporaso (1998a).

The Giving Reasons Requirement

Martin Shapiro

> Article 190 (now 253) of the EEC Treaty provides that: Regulations, directives and decisions of the Council and of the Commission shall state the reasons on which they are based...

Giving reasons might appear to be a rather simple and common-sense requirement. In reality it is densely packed with past legal and constitutional experience and replete with potential for development, particularly for development of a pervasive and deeply intrusive style of judicial review of administrative and legislative decision-making.

This article will first consider the various streams of past experience and then examine future implications. Much of our attention will focus on the American experience. In both evaluating US experience and speculating on the potential for further growth in the European Community (EC or Community) that this experience might imply, many European readers will say to themselves, 'This may work perhaps for American or for common law judges, but never for Continental or Civil Law judges.' Let me ask now that my reader willingly suspend disbelief in the comparability of American and Continental judicial mind-sets until fairly late in this piece, where we can begin to address the actual European experience. Beyond this suspension of disbelief, perhaps it is enough to note post-Second World War developments in European judicial review. Constitutional courts in Germany, Italy, and even in that seemingly unbreachable bastion of judicial self-restraint, France, as well as the European Court of Human Rights, the European Court of Justice (ECJ), and British courts reviewing administrative decisions have reached levels of judicial activism quite American in style. A plausible premise exists for European judiciaries to adopt more and more of the American style.

Reprinted from the *University of Chicago Law Forum 1992*, 179. Reproduced by kind permission.

Giving Reasons and Reasonableness: A Comparative Law Approach

Giving Reasons and Administrative Discretion

The American welfare and regulatory state has grown largely through the delegation of legislative powers to administrative agencies that generate vast bodies of regulations, rules, and decisions under the authority of statutes. The authorizing statutes themselves often are worded so generally as to place few constraints on administrative lawmakers. If the statutes are more detailed, they usually establish a pattern of generally stated aspirations combined with complex, yet incomplete and potentially conflicting, specific commands that yield as much administrative discretion as do New Deal-style 'standardless' delegations. Moreover, the welfare state requires millions of small decisions tailored to the individual needs of particular claimants. Decisions such as when a single parent on welfare ought to be required to work, as opposed to being urged to go back to school, are not easily encapsulated in statutory language or even detailed agency regulations. Finally, the same welfare state requires that government engage in myriad management decisions about resource allocation, decisions that experience has shown are best left to the sort of management discretion that exists in large private enterprises.

Rule-making discretion, the discretion to treat unlike cases in unlike ways, and resource management discretion are, therefore, not only inevitable but welcomed features of contemporary administration. However, since the 1960s there has been increasing pressure to constrain that discretion. All sorts of devices for attenuating the potential evils of administrative discretion have been suggested. Many ideas involve improvements on the legislative side, through either better statute drafting or more active and informed legislative oversight. Other proposals involve improving the organization, staffing, and operations of the agencies themselves.

Giving-reasons requirements are a form of internal improvement for administrators. A decision-maker required to give reasons will be more likely to weigh pros and cons carefully before reaching a decision than will a decision-maker able to proceed by simple fiat. In another aspect, giving reasons is a device for enhancing democratic influences on administration by making government more transparent. Such requirements are often closely brigaded, as they are in the American Administrative Procedures Act (APA, 5 USC. Secs 551–706 (1988)), with requirements of notice of pending government actions, public consultation, and publication of final decisions.

In these aspects, giving-reasons requirements are not 'giving reasons to judges' requirements but 'giving reasons to the public' requirements. Administrators must inform the citizens of what they are doing and why. Such requirements are a mild self-enforcing mechanism for controlling discretion. The reason-giving administrator is likely to make more reasonable decisions than he or she otherwise might and is more subject to general public surveillance.

Giving Reasons and Judicial Review of Administrative Action

In another respect, however, giving reasons has been deeply entangled with judicial review. If administrative discretion is inevitable and desirable, then one obvious mode of denaturing discretion of its poisons is to set judges to watch administrators.

Giving reasons is one of the mildest forms of judicial supervision of administrative discretion. Its deepest roots are in political theory. As Carl Friedrich (1958) noted long before the recent focus on reason giving, in the Western tradition the very concept of political authority, or indeed any kind of authority, implies the capacity to give reasons. When we impute authority, as opposed to merely acknowledging power, we are asserting our belief that the persons or entities making statements or rendering decisions could, if called upon, give good reasons for what they have said or done. It is natural, then, to ask administrative authorities actually to give reasons and to view such a request as the mildest of all constraints on administrative discretion. Such a request is not a limitation on the scope or substance of the discretion but merely a test of the authority of the administrator to wield discretion. Administrators may still arrive at whatever decisions they think best; they must merely give reasons for the decision at which they did arrive.

Precisely because giving reasons constitutes the mildest form of judicial intrusion, this constraint on discretion has been particularly popular in systems of cabinet government, where legislative and executive power are theoretically merged in a sovereign parliament. In such systems, judicial review of the executive is highly suspect as an invasion of parliamentary sovereignty. At the same time American conservatives sought to rein in the New Deal by the judicially announced 'non-delegation' doctrine in such cases as *Carter v. Carter Coal Co.* (USSC 1936) and *Schechter Poultry Corp. v. United States* (USSC 1935). British conservatives sought to constrain their growing administrative state by pushing giving-reasons requirements. They urged that parliamentary statutes giving ministers standardless discretion to act as they thought best should not foreclose judicial review and should require 'speaking orders', that is, government decisions containing reasons as well as conclusions and commands.

The Growth of Giving Reasons into a 'Record' Requirement

The evolution of the giving-reasons requirement in US administrative law dramatically illustrates its potential for growth. Giving reasons has served as a judicial constraint on administrative discretion, even when that discretion appears to be subject only to the broadest and vaguest statutory standards. Most fundamentally, if there is no record of agency deliberation, an administrative agency wielding its discretion is impervious to judicial review. If the court sees only the agency's final decision, the judge has a difficult time raising even jurisdictional questions. In the absence of any rationale at all, for example, horses may fall under the jurisdiction of the agency administering the chicken statute. In some way or another, after all, horses may impinge upon chickens in the barnyard.

A giving-reasons requirement generates a record. And once a judge has a record, anything is possible. At their most modestly restrained, British judges even in the 1950s could bring themselves to quash an administrative decision when it showed an 'error of law on the face of the record' (Harlow and Rawlings 1984). Could it be, after all, that the requirement to give reasons was a purely formal one: that so long as the administrator gave some reason, no matter how bad or how wrong, he or she was home free? Giving reasons, of course, creates a record consisting literally of the reasons given but also of the statutes and/or regulations that those reasons elaborate. Thus, the giving-reasons requirement opens the door to rival statutory interpretation by court and agency.

Where statutes are generally or vaguely worded to grant broad administrative discretion, administrators can easily avoid such manifest errors of law by adopting boilerplate[1] statements of reasons that do nothing more than state the statutory language as a 'whereas' and decisions as a 'therefore'. This tactic becomes less successful the more complex and specific the statute is, and reviewing courts continuously address the question of how accepting they should be of such boilerplate.

Moreover, most administrative implementations of statutory norms involve applications to fact situations sufficiently complex and sufficiently in dispute that a giving-reasons requirement inevitably imposes some

---

[1] That is, fixed or stock verbal formulae that appear regularly in contracts regardless of the specific agreements being made.

pressure on the administrator to offer at least summary findings of fact. Giving reasons of fact renders administrators much less vulnerable to judicial review than giving reasons of law. Courts must respond to manifest errors of law because their most fundamental duty is to uphold law. Their access to and expertise in the law is as good as or superior to that of the agencies. After all, even extrinsic aids to statutory interpretation, like legislative history, are as available to judges as administrators.

On the other hand, administrators enjoy superior expertise and access with respect to facts. Judges have no special duty to facts as they do the law. Moreover, under some conditions, and particularly in the area of individual welfare claims, the factual dimension of giving reasons is just as open to the boilerplate tactic as is the legal dimension. Administrators test various factual reasons on the courts. Those receiving judicial approval become a catalogue of fixed formulae from which the one that best fits the individual or situation before the decision-maker, and most nearly matches the decision he or she intends to make, can be plucked and tendered. Here again, courts must decide whether they find such pre-prepared reasons palatable.

Nevertheless, if giving reasons engenders giving facts, the giving-reasons requirement at the very minimum turns into an embryonic 'record' requirement. Giving reasons allows judges to run through, replay, or reconstruct the decision-making process that led to the policy decision under review. I have argued elsewhere that retracing the administrators' decision-making process is the essence of all judicial review of administration (Shapiro 1968). Surely the more the judge can replay the administrator's game, the more tempted he or she will be to do so.

Giving-reasons requirements, then, have this 'record' potential for moving beyond the mildest level of judicial review to a level at which judges match their own policy analyses against those of the agencies. But that is not the only such potential of giving-reasons requirements.

The Evolution of Giving Reasons into a Means of
Substantive Judicial Review

It may well be that, initially, giving-reasons requirements were less about creating a mild form of judicial review than they were about creating an internal check on administrative discretion. As we have noted, any decision-maker under an obligation to give reasons may be less prone to arbitrary, capricious, self-interested, or otherwise unfair judgment than one under no such obligation. Perhaps establishing an enforcement mechanism for the giving-reasons requirement itself, not creating an entering wedge for judicial review of agency procedures or decisions, provided the original purpose behind judicial enforcement of the reason-giving requirement. The judge may have been perceived as a mere enforcement agent for the requirement, and the requirement itself may have been thought of as improving the intrinsic performance of administration, not subjecting it to outside supervision. If this was the initial intention, in the United States at least, the outcome has often been quite the contrary.

The most prominent giving-reasons requirement in an American statute is the Administrative Procedures Act requirement that informal rules be accompanied by a 'concise general statement of their basis and purpose' (USC Sec. 553(c) 1988). The statute also provides an explicit judicial review standard. Informal rules may not be unlawful or 'arbitrary and capricious', nor may they be an 'abuse of agency discretion' (USC Sec. 553(c) 1988).

The relation of judicial review to giving reasons shifts dramatically depending upon the context. In the English system, for instance, judicial review may be seen as essentially a means of enforcing the giving-reasons requirement. The judge merely acts as a policeman, reviewing to ensure that the administrator obeys the statutory command to give reasons. When combined with a substantive review standard, however, means and ends dramatically reverse. Instead of the court reviewing to ensure that the agency gives reasons, the agency must give reasons to ensure that the court can review. Judges begin to say to agencies, 'You must give us enough reasons to enable us to tell whether you have acted reasonably or arbitrarily and capriciously.' As this dynamic unfolds, giving reasons moves from a mild and self-enforcing restraint on administrative discretion to a quite severe, judicially enforced set of procedural and substantive restraints—or at least so it has in the American context.

This story has been told at length elsewhere, and only a brief summary should suffice here (Shapiro 1988). The APA roughly distinguishes two types of administrative agency rule-making. Formal rules are to be made by rather rigid court-like procedures, with a complete record culminating in findings of fact and law supporting the rule announced. Informal rule-making requires that the agency give notice of its intention to make a rule, then accept comments by the public, and ultimately publish its rule accompanied by a concise and general statement of its basis and purpose. As we have already noted, this latter requirement is the giving-reasons component. The APA makes no mention of a record requirement for informal rule-making. Juxtaposing the provisions on formal and informal rules makes clear that the central difference intended between them was that the former was to have formal findings based on a formal record and the latter was not.

The Act was passed in 1946 and, until at least the mid-1960s, that distinction was maintained. By the 1980s, the federal courts had invented, supposedly by statutory interpretation, the concept of the rule-making record. Informal rules had to be accompanied by records and findings even more detailed and elaborate than had been initially envisaged for formal rule-making. The courts performed this feat largely by elaborating the giving-reasons requirement along three dimensions.

First, the courts converted the purpose of giving reasons from informing the public to allowing judicial review to determine whether a rule was either arbitrary and capricious or an abuse of discretion. The courts turned the notion of 'arbitrary and capricious' on its head by arguing that a rule was not arbitrary and capricious only when it was well-reasoned and well-supported by facts. Although initially only formal rules required grounding in 'substantial evidence in the record as a whole', eventually courts expanded the concise and general statement of basis and purpose accompanying informal rules into an enormously elaborate justification of the rule the agency had adopted. Only then could the judges determine whether the rule was properly reasoned rather than arbitrary.

Second, the courts expanded the APA's notice and comment provisions into the dialogue requirement. Requiring an agency to invite comment would mean little if the agency did not listen seriously to those comments it received. After all, courts had a duty to enforce the APA. The only way judges could know whether the agencies were listening seriously was by requiring the agencies to reply to each and every argument offered by interested parties. Giving reasons thus became an agency obligation to respond to each and every comment made with regard to a proposed rule.

The third dimension is a subtle variant of the second. By the 1970s, federal courts were saying that agencies had to respond to all issues raised by participating parties in the informal rule-making proceedings. By the 1980s, they were saying that agencies had to respond to all issues, not just those issues raised by the parties. The agencies now not only were required to engage in a serious dialogue and prove it by giving reasons about each point raised by the participants, but they were also required to make synoptic decisions, that is, to set clear policy priorities, consider all possible alternative rules for achieving those priorities, gather all relevant facts, and adopt the rule that had the very best chance of achieving the chosen priorities in light of the facts. In this context, the obligation to give reasons becomes the obligation to defend synoptically a synoptic decision—to offer every reason needed to resolve every issue of fact, value, and choice among alternative policies that could arise in making the optimal rule.

The movement from the second to the third dimension was hardly noticed. As environmental, health, and safety legislation raised the monetary stakes in rule-making higher and higher, regulated industries and their 'public interest' opponents poured more and more resources into raising ever more issues at rule-making hearings. They raised every issue that they could imagine. Therefore, the practical difference between responding to every point made by the parties and responding to every point imaginable was not very great, though implications for judicial control were considerable. Now agencies had to prove to judges that the agency reasons were better than any other reasons. Giving reasons had changed from 'You can adopt any rule you please as long as you give reasons' to 'You must adopt the best-reasoned rule.'

Giving reasons had been converted from a very mild, essentially procedural requirement into a very draconian, substantive one. In a certain sense, such a conversion was both inevitable and peculiarly easy. Once giving reasons reaches far enough to require the agency to give a fairly full account of the factual basis for its decision, judges are in a position to second-guess administrators. The only way to cut judges off from such second-guessing is to cut them off from the facts. Judges then have no choice but to approve what administrators have done as long as it is based on any seemingly articulate statement of reasons. For without the facts, how can one tell whether the reasons make any sense—unless, of course, the administrators have made a manifest error of law on the face of their reasons? Moreover, if facts are available, how can a judge possibly assess the adequacy of the reasons given other than by examining those facts and seeing whether he reaches roughly the same conclusion that the agency has reached?

In reviewing the facts, judges will accept plausible reasons only for those outcomes that are reasonable. If on the facts the judges conclude that a given outcome is simply not defensible, they are not going to accept any set of reasons backing it, no matter how superficially plausible those reasons may be. Once a judge with a duty to enforce a reasons requirement has access to a factual record, even a rudimentary one, a giving-reasons requirement ceases to be purely procedural. The requirement then engenders some degree of substantive judicial review of the lawmaking discretion of others. Substantive review is, of course, a polite way of saying that, to some degree, judges substitute their own policy guesses for the policy guesses of others.

This inevitable shift of reason giving from procedure to substance in the presence of facts is smoothed, however, by the procedural veneer of reasons giving. Judges know that substantive review—that is, saying that a rule is unlawful just because it is poor—constitutes a substitution of their policy views for the views of others. The 'others', moreover, are legislatures or bureaucracies that enjoy policy-making resources and democratic authorization far superior to those of the courts. Thus, when judges engage in substantive review, they tend to seek some way to mask their resource and democracy deficits.

Giving-reasons review is an ideal cover. First, it is cast in the form of procedural, rather than substantive, review. Judges will tell the agency, 'It is not that the rule is necessarily unlawful, but rather that you have missed a procedural step. You have not given adequate reasons.' The emphasis is, of course, on the 'given', not on the 'adequate'—that is, on the failure to perform a required action, not on the badness of the action performed. Second, and more importantly, giving-reasons review provides judges with a suspensive, although very powerful, policy veto. The judge says, 'I reject your rule because you have not offered good reasons for it. Resubmit the rule with a better set of reasons. Of course, I reserve the right to reject your rule again if the second set of reasons are no better than the first.' In this situation, most prudent agencies will recognize the need to change the substance of their rule rather than simply change the rhetoric of the reasons. The agency's change in the rule, however, will be seen as 'voluntary'. Certainly in the 1980s, US appellate courts, and particularly the DC Circuit, performed extensive substantive review, routinely striking down rules that they considered less than the best policy. However, since most rules were sent back as 'inadequately reasoned', it is still possible to argue that nearly all American judicial review of rule-making has remained procedural.

In summary, then, the American experience at least argues that 'giving reasons' has a strong tendency for growth. It begins as a mild and self-enforcing restraint on administrative policy discretion. Anyone who must give reasons to anyone else is likely to be more circumspect than he or she otherwise would be, and anyone who has to give reasons to the public is more likely to be responsive to it than otherwise. When courts enforce giving reasons, however, the audience for the reasons shifts from the public to the judges. For the judges to evaluate the reasons given, they must have enough information to rule on the adequacy of those reasons. The judges are not there merely to bless false façades of reasons.

Given interest group participation in administrative decision-making, the audience for reasons further multiplies. Reasons must be given not only in general, and to the public, and to the judges, but to the participants. Moreover, the reasons the participants want are the reasons for the rejection or acceptance of each of their specific claims. All of this, finally, may lead 'giving reasons' to become a judicially enforced demand that the rule-maker prove that it has made the very best decision possible within its range of discretion. An administrator who must choose the 'best' rule, of course, has no discretion. He or she has no choice but to choose the best rule according to the reviewing court. Thus, a requirement that begins as a mild, generalized restraint on discretion may become the substitution of judicial discretion for administrative discretion.

This potential for growth is, nonetheless, just that—a potential. Such developments may not occur, or may take place only partially. And even if they go quite far, judges always have discretion over their own decisions. Individually, judges may be more or less easily satisfied by the reasons administrators give. Many factors no doubt impinge on the propensity of a judge at any particular time and place to push giving reasons into substantive judicial review. American judges may already be retreating from their stance of the 1980s. Yet offering, or imagining, the extreme extension of a legal doctrine sheds light on its current condition.

Giving Reasons in Community Law

Article 173 of the EEC Treaty provides that Community actions must satisfy 'essential procedural requirements'. The ECJ has repeatedly held that the giving-reasons provision of Art. 190 is an essential procedural requirement. Article 190 applies to regulations, directives, and decisions of both the Council and the Commission. Thus, giving reasons constitutes a procedural requirement for both administrators engaged in supplementary lawmaking and implementation and legislators engaged in primary lawmaking. Both the Council and the Commission exercise a mixture of executive and legislative functions. However, with some exceptions, the Council enacts primary legislation comparable to congressional statutes in the US, and the Commission issues secondary legislation roughly comparable to rule-making by American executive agencies and independent commissions and with roughly the same range from highly general to quite specific. Both bodies also make highly particularized administrative decisions. Thus, at the very minimum Art. 173 and Art. 190 ensure that the key decision-making bodies of the Community follow the procedural giving-reasons requirement. As a matter of both administrative and constitutional law, the requirement is roughly equivalent to the concise and general statement of basis and purpose of the APA and the requirement of due process of the Fifth Amendment.

The comparability of US and Community administrative law is obvious. The comparability in constitutional law exists only if the argument about reasonableness and reason giving that I made earlier is convincing. Even if the argument is convincing, however, a paradox must be noted. Substantive, not procedural, due process imposes a giving-reasons requirement on the US Congress. Further, the demand is not imposed directly on Congress as a formal procedural one, but instead is imposed only in the course of litigation subsequent to passage of the statute. If the statute faces a constitutional challenge, someone must give reasons for it. Ideally the someone will have been Congress, but sometimes the litigators defending the statute can successfully do the reason giving. Thus the constitutional imposition of a giving-reasons requirement on legislators is a formal, direct procedural requirement in the Community and is an indirect, substantive one in the US.

Pure Procedure

The American experience in both administrative and constitutional law raises the question of whether the Community giving-reasons requirement is substantive as well as procedural. Further, how extensive are the Community's procedural demands? We have seen that the APA reasons requirement has grown into a substantive demand that the agency give complete and even synoptically correct reasons. Further, the APA requires that the agency provide a counter-reason to match every reason offered by those opposing the agency's rule. We have seen that under constitutional due process or its contemporary twin, equal protection, the legislature is sometimes compelled to show that an adopted rule achieves legitimate goals with minimum cost to individual rights. Is Art. 190, as now construed by the ECJ, more than a purely procedural requirement, and is there room for future substantive growth?

First and foremost, Art. 190 is a pure procedural requirement. In theory, the ECJ will invalidate a Council or Commission action about which it has no substantive qualms whatsoever solely on the grounds that reasons have not been given. This procedural rigour is tempered in various ways. The ECJ has repeatedly held that the nature and extent of the reasons that must be given depend on the nature and circumstances or context of the particular action taken (ECJ 1981*a, b*; 1988*a*). Just as the 'concise and general statement of basis and purpose' language of the APA suggests, it is impractical and self-defeating for courts to demand that legislative bodies provide a detailed account of all the deliberative analysis that led to the final statutory outcome. All that a legislature could do to meet such a demand would be to pile up on the judicial rostrum all of the staff studies, internal memorandums, committee reports, and debate that led to the final outcome. At the other extreme, a particular administrative decision about the precise legal liability of a particular individual or enterprise should carry with it a set of quite particularized and detailed reasons. The ECJ tends to demand only general reasons for major legislation and to demand more detailed reasons for more circumscribed decisions.[2]

The requirements of Art. 190 are satisfied for measures of general application if the '[c]onsiderations upon which the defendant's decision rests are clear'.[3] Where general regulations take the form of a constantly changing series of decisions such as market quotas, detailed reasons need not be given for each change. Reference back to the reasons given in the preambles of the previous quotas may be sufficient if the ECJ could possibly deduce the general market organization scheme formed by the quotas.[4] The ECJ sometimes echoes the American APA language when dealing with major Commission or Council mandates:

[I]t is sufficient . . . to set out, in a concise but clear and relevant manner, the principal issues of law and of fact upon which [such action] is based and which are necessary in order that the reasoning which has led the Commission to its Decision may be understood. (ECJ 1963a)

As with APA courts, however, one should note that the language here lends itself potentially to a judicial demand for 'reasoned elaboration' by the Commission rather than a mere list of unrationalized assertions. Indeed, the Advocate General in *Consorzio Cooperative D'Abruzzo v. Commission* (ECJ 1987a) seems to be calling for some movement in that direction. On the other hand, although general acts require only reasons 'in essence', even where actions are general in form they trigger a necessity for more detailed reasons when the rules are not general and abstract but a series of individual decisions.[5]

In attempting to construct this gradation, the ECJ is clearly heavily influenced by the most basically procedural root of the giving-reasons requirement—the desire for transparency in government affairs. As we noted

---

[2] Thus, in ECJ (1968: 95) the Court held: 'It is a question in the present case of a regulation, that is to say, a measure intended to have general application, the preamble to which may be confined to indicating the general situation which led to its adoption, on the one hand, and the general objectives which it is intended to achieve on the other. Consequently, it is not possible to require that it should set out the various facts, which are often very numerous and complex, on the basis of which the regulation was adopted, or a fortiori that it should provide a more or less complete evaluation of those facts.'

[3] ECJ (1988b) (Advocate General's opinion) and the cases cited therein. For a useful summary of recent case law, see ECJ (1988c) (Advocate General's opinion).

[4] ECJ (1986a). See also ECJ (1989a), holding that a full statement of reasons is not required when 'regulations fall within the general scheme of the body of measures of which they form a part'. Id at 85.   [5] This is one Advocate General's opinion in ECJ (1984b;1987b).

earlier, quite apart from any desire we may have that government decisions be substantively correct or even lawful, we have a desire to know what the government decisions are and the reasons the government made them. After all, we often don't know what the decision is unless we are told the reasons for it.

Thus, in rejecting a member state's challenges to directives or other major Council actions, the ECJ has sometimes ruled that since the challenging member state participated, as a member of the Council, in the very process of reaching the decision, the member state's own participation must have revealed to it all of the reasons for the decision. In those circumstances, the complaining state has received all the reasons to which it is entitled, and Art. 190 requires only a highly general formal statement of reasons. The ECJ has even applied this logic to the less direct participation of member states in Commission decisions (ECJ 1987c; 1988a; 1988c). In cases involving individual enterprises that must have become familiar with the agency's reasoning in the course of the negotiations, the ECJ has held that a not very complete, formal statement of reasons accompanying a final decision will suffice (ECJ 1988a). In one rather curious case, the ECJ allowed an extremely cryptic Commission finding of law to pass muster under Art. 190. The ECJ apparently felt that any experienced Community lawyer could easily explain to his client the chain of legal reasoning that must have led to the conclusion reached (ECJ 1988a).

The Transition from Pure Procedure to Substance

The ECJ has adopted a standard formula for expressing the transparency requirement:

In imposing upon the Commission the obligation to state reasons for its decisions, Article 190 is not taking mere formal considerations into account but seeks to give an opportunity to the parties of defending their rights, to the Court of exercising its supervisory functions and to member-States and to all interested nationals of ascertaining the circumstances in which the Commission has applied the Treaty. (ECJ 1963a; see also ECJ 1985c)

That very formula, however, constitutes a transition from procedural to substantive reasons that is strikingly comparable to the American transition from procedural to substantive due process in the famous Minnesota Rate Case (USSC 1890). In that case, the Supreme Court held that a railroad rate statute violated due process because it did not provide for judicial review of the rate orders of the State railroad commission. At first glance, the case appears to be one of pure procedural due process. The statute falls because it fails to provide a procedure, namely, an appeals procedure. When one asks, however, why it is necessary to have an appeals procedure, and what the courts are to do when such a procedure is put in place, the substantive hook in the procedural case becomes clear. The Supreme Court insisted that judicial review is a necessary procedure because the Constitution demands that judges determine whether the rates initially set are substantively correct.

If the ECJ were concerned only with procedure and transparency then its rule would read, 'The Community organ must give sufficient reasons to allow relevant parties to know the basis of its decision.' There would, of course, be continuing quibbles about how much basis, but the goal of transparency would clearly be the sole good. By adopting the formula it does, however, the ECJ links the giving-reasons requirement firmly to judicial review. This is so not only in the specific invocation of review but also in the specification of transparency for the parties. For, in reality, the ECJ is saying that the Community organ must give the individual party sufficient information so that the party can make an informed judgment about whether to sue or not.

The paradox is a rather nice one. Suppose a court says: '(1) You must give reasons' and '(2) We have the power of judicial review.' The court is saying, 'We will review simply to see whether you have met a purely formal procedural requirement. If we see a list of reasons, you pass, unless of course someone can show that as a matter of fact these were not your real reasons.'

A court that says 'You must give reasons so that we can review' is, however, saying something quite different. Requiring an agency to give reasons in order for a court to review the agency's decision allows the court to decide whether the agency was justified in reaching the decision it reached. The reasons demanded after all are reasons about substance as well as procedure. It would not be a sufficient reason for the agency to say, 'Well, the reason for this rule is that we met on Tuesday and passed it by majority vote.' The agency must offer substantive reasons for what it did. Lo and behold, procedure has turned into substance. Article 190 becomes not only a guarantee to the citizens of the transparency of their government but also a guarantee to the ECJ of its powers of substantive judicial review.

I am not claiming that this point is a big revelation. Unlike the US Supreme Court, which had to transpose the purely procedural language of the due process clauses into substantive reasonableness review, the ECJ had plenty of constitutional authority for substantive judicial review even without Art. 173 and Art. 190. The ECJ's reading of Art. 190 as instrumental to its review powers granted elsewhere is unexceptionable. However, Art. 190 now mandates not only that Community organs give reasons but that they give good reasons.

In American administrative law, the movement from procedural to substantive review has come through a middle ground. That middle ground was the expansion of the APA's 'concise and general statement' reasons requirement into the requirements of rule-making record, dialogue, and reasoned elaboration. So when a transition from procedure to substance inheres in Art. 190, we are alerted to look for similar movements in the giving-reasons law of the Community. However, the nature of the Council as a general legislature would lead us to expect that, if a movement comparable to the DC Circuit's transformation of the APA is occurring in the Community, the movement will probably be most evident in review of Commission actions.

The ECJ does not begin where the DC Circuit did, with an APA that on its face distinguished between formal rule-making where a record was required and informal rule-making. Article 190 would certainly allow the ECJ to require as much of a record as it wanted for Commission decisions, to create a situation where the rulemaking record requirement in an informal rule-making is just as elaborate as that in a formal rulemaking or adjudication. In fact, the Commission has always been in the habit of compiling rather elaborate records.[6] Thus, the ECJ has not had to go through the struggle that the DC Circuit did to get the kind of extended substantive record before it that a court needs to second-guess agency lawmakers. The ECJ sees relatively full records and has the clear authority to ask for even more extended records if it reads Art. 190 as requiring them.

The dialogue dimension of giving reasons is extremely prominent in EC case law, but in the plaintiffs' pleadings rather than the ECJ's opinions. Especially in cases involving Commission decisions concerning particular enterprises or product lines, complaining parties frequently invoke Art. 190 and point to particular unanswered arguments they have raised with the Commission. While rarely successful, this demand for dialogue can be met in one of two ways: either the ECJ finds that the Commission has in fact responded to the particular argument, or the Court finds that the Commission has given a sufficient response in the matter as a whole to allow the party to determine whether its legal rights have been violated. In *Stichting Sigarettenindustrie v. Commission* the ECJ (1985*b*) says:

The Court has consistently held that, although under Article 190 of the Treaty the Commission is obliged to state the reasons on which its decisions are based, mentioning the factual and legal elements which provide the legal basis for the measure and the considerations which have led it to adopt its decision, it is not required to

---

[6] The interpretation of the Council and the Commission pushes in that direction quite apart from judicial review.

discuss all the issues of fact and law raised by every party during the administrative proceedings.

Of course, each time the ECJ resolves an Art. 190 complaint by finding that the Commission actually did respond to the point raised, the ECJ acknowledges, in a sense, the validity of interpreting Art. 190 as requiring dialogue. For instance, in *Remia BV and Others v. Commission* (ECJ 1985c), the ECJ stated that, with regard to the duty to state reasons, the contested decision clearly contains a sufficient answer to the arguments put forward by the applicants. In *Technointorg v. Commission and Council* (ECJ 1988e) the complaining party pushed an extreme form of the dialogue requirement. The Advocate General rejected the Art. 190 complaint, but he did so by showing in considerable detail that there really was all the dialogue to which a party would be reasonably entitled. The ECJ adopts the same approach, although it provides a little less detail than the Advocate General.[7]

Yet a Court acknowledgement of a dialogue requirement would be complete only if there were at least a few major cases in which the Commission decisions were invalidated for failure to make an adequate response to the regulated parties. Such cases do not exist. In this sense, though Community law reflects pressure toward a dialogue requirement, the ECJ has yet to move decisively to such a requirement.

The basic reason that the parties push and the ECJ resists dialogue lies in the difference between transparency and participation. Courts are likely to be initially hostile to demands for dialogue. Such requests are the last resort of regulated parties who have no substantive arguments left. Moreover, if dialogue claims are judicially accepted, they lead to a more and more cumbersome administrative process because the regulated parties will be encouraged to raise more and more arguments to which the regulating agency will have to respond. If the only instrumental value for giving reasons is transparency, the courts will resist dialogue demands. One can discover an agency's actions and purposes without the agency rebutting every opposing argument.

The dialogue requirement has come into American law because American courts have been in pursuit not only of transparency but participation in the regulatory process. The notice and comment requirements of the APA incorporate this participation value into American administrative law. The

---

[7] See also ECJ (1988a); both the Advocate General and the court excused the paucity of reasons given on the grounds that the complaining party had been fully informed and fully responded to participant in the decision process; ECJ (1987d), excusing a similar paucity on the ground that the Community had requested a dialogue with the complaining party and that the party did not seize the opportunity.

pluralist political theory that has been the guiding orthodoxy of post-war American politics demanded that every group with an interest be allowed to participate in every governmental process affecting that interest. American courts adopt the dialogue requirement as a device for facilitating judicial review of regulating agencies' commitment to group participation. The notice and comment demands of the APA can be met merely by allowing the interest groups to speak. The agency need not really listen. If, however, the agency is required to respond to each thing the groups say, then the agency must at least listen enough to make a response. Courts invented the dialogue requirement to ensure that the agencies were not only receiving the arguments of non-governmental participants but really taking them seriously.

If the ECJ sticks closely to transparency as the sole goal of Art. 190, the ECJ is unlikely to move towards a dialogue requirement. Yet participation in government by interests affected by government decisions presents an increasingly compelling value in contemporary society, particularly where environmental matters are involved. The ECJ has already, however unintentionally, opened one avenue for linking participation to Art. 190 by stating that the Council need not give full reasons to the member states where they have participated in the decisions. To be sure, these ECJ opinions are transparency-based. They require that those member states already know what was going on because they were there. Nevertheless, they create an opening for counter-arguments from complainants who were not present and claim that, therefore, they need the Commission to be responsive. In short, full transparency can be achieved only through participation or through dialogue as a form of participation.

Complainants have pushed not only for dialogue but for reasoned elaboration under Art. 190. If the Council gave wrong reasons, it must fail the test of Art. 190, at least if Art. 190 is more than a purely formal demand that reasons, even wrong ones, be given. The ECJ's jurisprudence has firmly established that wrong reasons are not enough under Art. 190. Accordingly, someone invoking Art. 190 does not necessarily have to show that the Community organ offered reasons that were false in the sense of not being the real reasons for the Community's action. Further, such a showing may not be sufficient to invoke Art. 190. However, showing that the reason given is incorrect as to fact, law, or logic is sufficient.[8]

---

[8] For instance, if the principal claim is that the Council chose the wrong legal basis for a directive, that it acted under Art. 235 when it should have acted under some other article, then a subsidiary reasons claim is almost automatic. If the Council was wrong to act under Art. 235, then, whatever reasons it gave for acting under Art. 235 and/or the citation of Art. 235 as the reason for its action, must fail Art. 190.

In some cases the ECJ discusses the reasons given, showing that they are indeed good reasons. To be sure, cases in which the ECJ has found a Community organ in violation of Art. 190 because its reasons were not good enough are few and far between. Yet the ECJ's willingness not simply to count but to march through the reasons given, commenting on their adequacy, indicates that at least an embryonic reasoned-elaboration requirement already exists. Further, the requirement goes beyond transparency to a requirement of giving substantively good reasons. A substantive criterion of reasoned elaboration or giving good reasons is, of course, closely related to the ECJ's general inclination or disinclination to do substantive review of the Commission's work, a point we will return to later.

We have seen that the final stage in the evolution of the development in American administrative law was the judicial demand that the agencies engage in synoptic decision-making, that is, that they respond adequately not only to all issues actually raised by interested parties but also to all issues. In short, the demand is that the agency do a perfect job of decision-making with the strong implication that the agency must arrive at the perfect, or at least the best, decision. Obviously, if the ECJ has not moved even as far as a full dialogue standard, the ECJ is very far indeed from turning the requirement of giving reasons into synopticism. If any hints of a synoptic standard exist in the ECJ's jurisprudence, they lie not in Art. 190 review but in the ECJ's various assertions of substantive review per se, for instance, its claim to do 'comprehensive' review of the Commission's anti-competition decisions (ECJ 1989b).

In rejecting dialogue, there are a number of instances in which the ECJ has rather explicitly rejected synopticism. In *Re Skimmed Milk Powder: Netherlands v. Commission*, for instance, the court states that 'the obligation to state reasons relates to decisions that are actually adopted and in those decisions the Commission is not required to explain the reasons for which it did not adopt a suggestion made by its departments' (ECJ 1988a: 1207). In *Remia and Nutricia v. Commission*, the ECJ (1985c: 2545) states that Art. 190 'does not require the Commission to discuss all the matters of fact and of law which may have been dealt with during the administrative proceedings'.

Finally, the ECJ has given some hints as to whether giving *post hoc* reasons will suffice. As a general proposition, *post hoc* reasons, offered during litigation, would meet one prong of the ECJ's transparency requirement. Such reasons giving would allow the court to fulfil its review function. Only reasons contemporaneous to the initial government action, however, would seem to satisfy the other prong. Presumably, parties adversely affected by the government action would be in a position to calculate whether the government violated their rights—whether they should litigate—only if the parties were aware of the Community organ's reasons at the time the action occurred. Surely it would be unfair to require the information they need in order to decide whether to litigate to be supplied only in the course of litigation. Yet the ECJ's position on this question is not entirely clear.

In *Re The Protection of Battery Hens: United Kingdom v. Council* (ECJ 1988*f*), the ECJ ruled that the Council's secretariat may not make *post hoc* alterations in the reasons given in the preambles of Council directives on which the Council has voted. However, such alterations would not really appear to fail either prong of the transparency test. *Battery Hens* suggests quite a different aspect of the *post hoc* reasoning problem. At the deepest level, modern administrative law has left unresolved a basic tension between two approaches to governing authority. Under one approach we ask: 'Is the government action reasonable?' That is: 'Can good reasons be given for the action? Can it be justified?' Under the other approach we ask: 'Did the government act for good reasons?' That is: 'Did the government act out of legitimate or illegitimate motives? Did it have lawful or unlawful intentions?' Because the subjective intentions of government decision-makers are typically difficult to discern, particularly because most government actions are compromises among multiple goals and interests, reviewing courts are pushed toward 'can reasons be given' and, thus, toward accepting *post hoc* reasons. On the other hand, courts never quite abandon the notion of subject intent, as such doctrines as *détournement de pouvoir* suggest. *Post hoc* reasons that are obviously designed to mask, correct, or substitute for the real government motivation must be judicially scrutinized.

In *Re Generalised Tariff Preferences: Commission v. Council* (ECJ 1987*b*), the ECJ treats *post hoc* reasons unfavourably, but only to bolster its holding that the Council was really using the wrong legal basis for a directive in which the official preamble mentions no legal basis at all. Reference to *post hoc* reasons is used not to allow a *post hoc* screen for the subjective intent of the government organ but, instead, to penetrate to the actual subjective intentions.[9]

On the other hand, the ECJ does find acceptable one kind of *post hoc* reasoning particularly favoured by lawyers. Where a government organ has made a general finding of law, comparable to those made by courts, the

---

[9] In *Regina v. Minister of Agriculture, Fisheries and Food* (English High Court, Queen's Bench Division 1988), the plaintiff sought, unsuccessfully, to argue that the Council violated Art. 190 '[b]y indicating insubstantial or insufficient reasons . . . and omitting to state a further and substantial reason'. In essence the complaint was that the Council had not given its real reason.

government may be required to give the legal reasoning supporting that finding. One reason for this position may well be a transparency considera- tion. Confronted by a formal finding of law, the parties' lawyers can usually quickly reconstruct the legal reasons or arguments that lie behind it. Another basis for the ECJ's position is probably one of redundancy: where a general legal conclusion is involved, the question of whether the government organ meets the giving-reasons requirement and the question of whether the gov- ernment decision is substantively correct, or lawful, is the same question. The ECJ is content to hear the government's legal reasoning in the course of litigation; and if the reasoning fails, the government action fails. The Art. 190 question either need not be reached or is automatically answered.

American experience indicates that the most crucial aspect of the giving- reasons requirement may be that it serves as a way of softening and somewhat disguising substantive judicial review. Thus, the requirement softens and disguises the ultimate dilemma of judicial review. The ultimate dilemma is, of course, that judges feel a strong urge and are typically under a constitutional mandate, self-proclaimed or otherwise, to strike down wrong government decisions. At the same time, judges typically have no claim to the technical expertise necessary to declare a decision wrong in the face of the expert government agency's determination that it is right.

The ECJ clearly has encountered the problem. Article 33 of the European Coal and Steel Community Treaty provides:

The Court may not, however, examine the evaluation of the situation, resulting from economic facts or circumstances, in the light of which the High Authority took its decisions or made its recommendations, save where the High Authority is alleged to have misused its powers or to have manifestly failed to observe the provisions of this Treaty or any rule of law relating to its application.

Nothing could more clearly command the ECJ both to defer to adminis- trative expertise and, at the same time, not to defer. Complete deference to fact finding by another government organ would mean no judicial review at all. If the agency can allege any facts it wants, it can hardly lose on the law. The EEC Treaty contains no such provision. Early on, the ECJ staked out a strong substantive judicial review position. Subsequently, the ECJ has maintained this position, while also proclaiming a high degree of deference to Commission and Council fact finding (Hartley 1988).

The giving-reasons requirement provides a partial solution to this tension in two ways. First, the requirement can provide a halfway house between procedural review and substantive review in which judicial substantive objections are couched in procedural language and the Court exercises a suspensive rather than an absolute veto. The ECJ says, 'Because you did not give good enough reasons, your action fails to meet an "essential procedural requirement".' Presumably the Community organ may then proceed, without changing its substantive decision, to remedy its procedural fault by giving more and better reasons. Second, a giving-reasons requirement can become full-scale substantive review without quite full-scale challenge to the expertise of the expert government organs. The moves from 'did not give reasons' to 'did not give good reasons' to 'did not give good enough reasons' are easy and virtually indistinguishable moves. The difference between 'did not give good enough reasons' and 'did not adopt a good enough policy' is non-existent in many instances. Where the government organ did give reasons but the ECJ said the reasons are not good enough, the Court was often actually disagreeing with the government organ on the substance of the policy. Indeed, in rejecting various offered reasons, a court can usually signal what substantive policy it would accept.

Thus, if a court is inclined to hover somewhere between total deference and completely activist substantive review, the giving-reasons requirement provides a flexible tool of review. Furthermore, one measure of the degree of a court's exercise of substantive review is the number of times it finds that government organs have not given reasons.

The European Court of Justice Experience with Substantive Review

The ECJ has shown certain proclivities toward using giving reasons as a substantive review device, but the Court strikes down very few actions of the Commission and Council on Art. 190 grounds alone. A review of some recent cases indicates the substantive review potential of the giving-reasons doctrine.

For example, in *Generalised Tariff* (ECJ 1987*b*) both the Advocate General and the ECJ inextricably combine giving reasons and pure substantive review. In one directive, the Council simply does not cite any article of the treaties as the basis of its action. The Advocate General argues that the Council has not met an essential procedural requirement, but nonetheless the Council argues that the directives ought not to be invalidated because they are substantively acceptable. The ECJ notes that the Council did not cite any EEC Treaty article because the members could not agree on whether to cite Art. 113, which does not require a unanimous Council vote, or Art. 235, which does. The ECJ goes on to note that the Council then went to unanimous voting and so the Council must have been acting under Art. 235. The ECJ concludes that the Council action is invalid because it was based on Art. 235

when it should have been based on Art. 113. Accordingly, the ECJ invalidates the Council action on substantive grounds.

Here, the ECJ might have voided the Council's action under Art. 190 because the Council had failed to give any legal reason at all for its action, for example, the Council cited no legal basis for its action. Alternatively, the ECJ might have passed the Council's action under Art. 190 because its resort to unanimous voting signalled that the Council had in reality chosen Art. 235.[10] Instead, the ECJ (1987b: 1498) states that:

[T]he contested regulations are measures falling within the sphere of the common commercial policy and . . .since the Council had the power to adopt them pursuant to Art. 113 of the Treaty, it was not justified in taking as its basis Art. 235.

It is clear from the foregoing that the contested regulations do not satisfy the requirements laid down in Art. 190 of the Treaty with regard to the statement of reasons and that, moreover, they were not adopted on the correct legal basis. Consequently, they must be declared void.

We shall never know if the Council failed Art. 190 on the pure procedural ground of failing to state any reasons at all, or on a substantive ground, for having implicitly stated a wrong reason.[11]

In *Re Revaluation of the Green Mark: Germany v. Commission* (ECJ 1987e), the German government asserted that the Commission violated Art. 190 by issuing an internally contradictory regulation. Germany argued that the regulation treated market price and buying-in price as different from one another when in fact the buying-in price necessarily became the market price. The Advocate General responded with economic data showing that in the previous four months of 1984 the buying-in and market prices had in fact been different. The ECJ (1987e: 46–7) rejected the Art. 190 claim on the grounds that 'the German government has not shown that the calculation on which the provision . . . is based was unrealistic and thus that the regulation was self-contradictory'. This outcome may be taken as deference to Commission expertise. However, the outcome also may be taken as indicating that, if the Commission's calculation was shown to be substantively unsound, generating a self-contradiction, then the ECJ should have found a breach of Art. 190.

---

[10] In this case, the Commission argued that citation of a legal basis has to be explicit to satisfy Art. 190 (ECJ 1987b: 1497. The Council argued that implicit citation was sufficient under Art. 190 (ECJ 1987b: 1498).

[11] In a case in which the ECJ did not reach the Art. 190 issues, the Advocate General argues that if there is manifest error or abuse of discretion evident on the face of the reasons given, then Art. 190 has been violated. See ECJ (1988b). In ECJ (1987d), the ECJ suggests that a plaintiff may succeed under Art. 190 if it can show that the reasons given 'exceeded the margin of discretion. . . .'.

Re Roofing Felt Cartel: Belasco v. Commission also concerns alleged contradictions in reasons given. The complaining party alleges five such
contradictions in the Commission's reasons. In the portion of its opinion
labelled 'Inadequacy of the Statement of Reasons', the ECJ (1989*b*: 2194)
rejects the dialogue requirement urged upon it by *Belasco*:

As regards the alleged failure to reply to the applicants' arguments... although under
Article 190... the Commission is required to set out all the circumstances justifying
the adoption of a decision and the legal considerations which led the Commission to
adopt it, [Article 190] does not require the Commission to discuss all the matters of fact
and of law which may have been dealt with during the administrative proceedings.

Yet, in another portion of its decision, the ECJ nevertheless goes point by
point through each alleged contradiction and holds that the Commission
was substantively correct in each instance.

The upshot of *Belasco* may be important on the question of *post hoc* reasoning. The ECJ rejects dialogue but then examines substantively each point the
party seeking dialogue wished to raise. The ECJ implied that the Commission need not answer the regulated party at the time of its initial decision.
However, at the time of judicial review the Commission will have to respond
to whatever issues raised by the regulated party the ECJ thinks significant.
Belasco is not, of course, nearly as striking a case of using Art. 190 for substantive review as it would be if the ECJ had found against the Commission.
However, the ECJ clearly does state that the Commission passes Art. 190 not
simply because it gave reasons, but because it gave good and correct reasons.[12] The ECJ's message is that giving reasons is not merely a procedural
requirement but, rather, that good reasons must be given.[13]

The statement of reasons required by Art. 190 of the Treaty relates to the
decision actually adopted. In principle, it would be quite excessive to require
the Commission to explain the reasons for which it did not take alternative
decisions. In *Skimmed Milk Powder*, the Advocate General states that in his
view the applicant 'bears the onus of demonstrating that a different solution should have been adopted' (ECJ 1988*a*: 1065, 1080). Accordingly, the
Commission need not show that it has considered and rejected for good

[12] The ECJ reached a similar result in ECJ (1985*d*). In ECJ (1987*f*), the ECJ does strike down a
Commission action for failure to satisfy Art. 190. However, the holding is really based on clear
error of law on the face of the record rather than a substantive failure in the Commission's analysis
and is, in a sense, a pure procedural holding that the Commission fails Art. 190 because it gives
no reasons at all.

[13] This is clearly stated in the Advocate General's statement in ECJ (1988*a*). He firmly rejects
synoptic demands, but does suggest that under Art. 190 a complaining party may prevail if it
can show that the Commission was substantively wrong. 1988 ECR at 1191 (referring to Advocate
General's opinion in ECJ 1988*a*: 1065, 1080).

reasons each and every alternative other than the one it adopted, but the Commission must have good reasons for the one it did adopt.

Remia (ECJ 1985*c*) is an instance where the ECJ obviously does feel the conflict between substantive review and deference to technical expertise. Advocate General Lenz has clearly been seeking to move in the direction that US courts took in expanding the concise and general statement of basis and purpose requirement of the APA. In both *Remia* (ECJ 1985*c*) and *Akzo Chemie BV v. Commission* (ECJ 1986*b*), Lenz adopts the formula that Commission statements of reasons must be 'clear and relevant'. In both cases, in a rather conclusory way, he proposes that the Commission's reasons are concise but not 'clear and relevant' and so fail Art. 190. In both cases the ECJ rejects the 'clear and relevant' formula, and in both cases the ECJ upholds the Commission. In *Akzo*, the ECJ speaks of 'adequate' reasons and is far less conclusory than the Advocate General. The ECJ cites various paragraphs of the Commission's decision which it says give enough reasons.

Remia involves Art. 85(1), one of the 'anti-trust' or competition articles of the Treaty. The ECJ states:

The Court must therefore limit its review ... to verifying whether the relevant procedural rules have been complied with, whether the statement of the reasons for the decision is adequate, whether the facts have been accurately stated and whether there has been any manifest error of appraisal or a misuse of powers. (ECJ 1985*c*: 2575)

Here, the ECJ clearly is backing away from substantive review in the face of Commission economic expertise. As to Art. 190, the ECJ rejects 'clear and relevant' in favour of 'adequate' and finds the Commission's reasons adequate. However, the ECJ actually marches through the Commission's reasons, arguing that they were sufficiently responsive to the actual circumstances and met the normal transparency requirements. Yet the ECJ does not comment at all on whether the reasons were substantively correct.

In *Remia*, stating facts and giving reasons are tandem requirements. The ECJ does say that it exercises review to determine whether facts are accurately stated. Yet the court arranges its sentence structure so that facts must be accurate and reasons adequate. The reasons need not be accurate. This may appear to be splitting hairs. The point is, however, that the ECJ is actually claiming to review whether the simple, first-order facts are accurately stated, and whether the Commission's reasons indicate that the Commission has considered those facts, but the ECJ disclaims competence to review the economic analysis that the Commission applied to the facts in order to reach its decisions. Thus, the Commission must give responsive reasons but not necessarily good reasons. At the very least, the ECJ avoids judging the substance of the reasons. Instead, the Court retreats from 'comprehensive' to an 'arbitrary and capricious, abuse of discretion' style of review.[14]

Americans have recently observed two equal and opposite Supreme Court attitudes toward deference to agency expertise. In *Motor Vehicle Mfrs. Association of the United States Inc. v. State Farm Mutual Auto Insurance Co.* (USSC 1983), the Supreme Court seemed to demand that the agencies do synoptic decision-making subject to synoptic review. In *Chevron USA v. Natural Resources Defense Council* (USSC 1984), the Supreme Court seemed to defer completely to agency expertise. No such dramatic pair of opposing decisions exists in the ECJ's Art. 190 jurisprudence, but two relatively recent cases do seem to point in quite different directions.

Re Agricultural Hormones (ECJ 1988*d*) is a case in which the ECJ seems to take an extremely cavalier attitude to the giving-reasons requirement. A Council directive failed to make any precise identification of the Commission proposal providing one of the reasons for its enactment. The ECJ holds:

The applicant's third complaint with regard to the statement of reasons is that the directive fails to identify the Commission's proposal . . . It must be observed . . . that the directive in question does not in fact contain a precise reference enabling the Commission's proposal to be identified. However, that omission cannot be regarded as constituting an infringement of an essential procedural requirement, inasmuch as it is not denied that the directive was in fact adopted pursuant to a proposal from the Commission (ECJ 1988*d*: 899).

Accepted at face value, this passage says that so long as a Community organ in fact had a reason, it was under no obligation to say what the reason was. Such a position by the ECJ would nullify even the minimum transparency requirement of Article 190.

Agricultural Hormones is one of those cases in which one is sorely tempted to guess at the identity of the opinion writer. The opinion is very much in the traditional French style: cryptic, conclusory, and inexplicable in its own terms. One resorts then to the normal technique of dealing with French judicial opinions, moving from the opinion itself to the surrounding paraphernalia. Advocate General Lenz's opinion informs us that this case is one of the special category in which a member state pleads Art. 190 against

[14] In this context, Advocate General Lenz's opinion becomes clearer. He is seeking to tell the ECJ that it can deal with the tension between review and expertise in a more active way than by retreat to a lower than 'comprehensive' review standard. Confronted by the Commission's expertise, the ECJ can invoke the suspensive veto of Art. 190 rather than the complete, substantive veto of finding an Art. 85(1) violation. In this manner, the ECJ can use Art. 190 to voice substantive disagreement with Commission anti-trust decisions. Moreover, by using Art. 190, the court avoids claiming that it knows more economics than the Commission does. I do not know whether the ECJ rejects this approach because it prefers to retreat in anti-competition matters or simply because it agreed substantively with the Commission's decision.

a Council directive. In spite of the absence of a formal statement of reasons in the directives' preamble, the member state must have been made fully aware of the Council's reasons in the course of its own direct participation in the Council's decision. Thus, while a formal statement of reasons would be preferable, the member state has not been deprived of an essential procedural requirement because it had other means of knowing the Council's reasons.

In contrast, *Regina v. H. M. Commissioners of Customs and Excise ex parte the National Dried Fruit Trade Association* (ECJ 1988g) shows a court inclined to move in the direction of DC Circuit techniques. The case deals with Commission regulations of general application roughly comparable to American 'informal rules'. The complaining party clearly seeks to push the ECJ from its normal requirement of something like an old-style concise and general statement of basis and purpose to the more detailed requirement of 'reasoned elaboration'. Advocate General Slynn (ECJ 1988g: 778) is clearly somewhat tempted: 'I think the reasoning can be criticized for not making more explicit the Commission's reasons for applying the protective measures to other kinds of dried grapes not produced in the Community.' Yet, in the end, Mr Slynn opts for a rather minimal giving-reasons standard very close to the APA's concise and general statement of basis and purpose. He says Art. 190 is satisfied because '[t]he overall purpose and intention [are] clear'.

When the DC Circuit was transforming the 'concise and general' and 'arbitrary and capricious' wording of the APA into an aggressive substantive review standard, one of its major tactics was to shove the actual statutory language into footnotes and use expressions of its own coining like 'reasoned elaboration. In *National Dried Fruit*, the ECJ's judgment does not specifically invoke Art. 190 itself or its own previous Art. 190 formulae. Instead, the Court says only that 'the Commission's view . . . is sufficiently reasoned and is not to be regarded as incorrect'. Having said this, the ECJ nonetheless goes on to invalidate one of the regulations at issue on proportionality grounds and to uphold two others. The ECJ's discussion is cast in purely substantive economic analysis terms, and it lumps together proportionality and reasons-giving requirements in part of its analysis. In the end, the court upholds two Community regulations that it says make sense and strikes down one that does not.

Proportionality, like 'least means' analysis, is obviously the strongest form of substantive review. In effect, courts are saying, 'We invalidate the law you have made because we can think of a better law—one that achieves your goals at less cost to competing interests.' We should not make too much of *National Dried Fruit*, but it does show the potential that giving reasons exhibits for movement into substantive judicial review.

Agricola Commerciale Olio Srl v. Commission (ECJ 1984*b*) has some curious resonances with *National Dried Fruit*. The Advocate General proceeds carefully and methodically, treating *détournement de pouvoir*, lawfulness, and factual error as substantive questions and treating Art. 190 issues as separate and procedural questions. The ECJ does not explicitly mention Art. 190 at all. The court's opinion marches through the Commission's decision, finding that 'the only reason given' and 'the only ground relied upon . . . is vitiated by errors of fact' (ECJ 1984*b*: 3898). Taking the narrowest view, this case could be one in which the ECJ finds that the Commission has made an error of fact, thus falling foul of a purely substantive non-giving reasons aspect of review. Having invalidated the Commission decision on this ground, the ECJ need not reach the Art. 190 giving-reasons issue. In the actual opinion, however, giving reasons, giving good reasons, and reasonableness are conflated as they so often are in American law.

Conclusion

The American experience from the 1960s onward gives us a number of hints as to what to watch for in the Community's giving-reasons jurisprudence. We can see that an American-style dialogue requirement is being pushed hard by complaining parties who keep insisting that, if a Community organ has not responded to all the points they have raised, Art. 190 has not been satisfied. So far the ECJ has explicitly and repeatedly rejected the claim that Community organs must respond to all issues raised in the course of regulatory proceedings. At the same time, however, the ECJ has often answered claims that Community organs did not respond, not by saying simply that they had no obligation to respond, but by showing that they did actually respond. The more the ECJ answers Art. 190 charges by itemized lists of responses made to issues raised, the more it moves toward a dialogue requirement. It is one thing to reject an Art. 190 claim on the grounds that no dialogue is required and quite another to reject a claim because the dialogue actually occurred.

Similarly, complaining parties have urged a synoptic standard under Art. 190, requiring the Community organ both to give reasons for not having chosen the alternative policies it rejected and to give reasons for the one it selected. Here again the ECJ has rejected synoptic demands. Clearly such demands are hard to press on first-order legislative bodies. How could we possibly ask Congress or the Council to give reasons for all the statutory provisions it rejected as well as for all those it enacted? It is easier to press synoptic demands on subordinate lawmakers enacting supplementary legislation within the narrow range of alternatives established by the primary statute. Here cases like *National Dried Fruit* are suggestive. Mixing reason-giving and proportionality does yield something like synopticism. The supplementary lawmaker must give reasons why the regulatory alternative selected was chosen over other alternatives that would appear to achieve the statutory purpose less intrusively.

Finally, when considering Art. 190 issues, the ECJ often moves to legislative-style analysis. The court looks not only to the purely procedural question of whether reasons are given but also to the substantive question of whether the reasons are good, correct, persuasive, or make sense. If the ECJ seeks to maintain fairly aggressive review, while at the same time avoiding a challenge to the expertise of its coequal branches, then Art. 190 could provide a convenient halfway house. Many courts have found that telling experts that they cannot do something until they provide a better reason is easier than flatly rebuffing the expert.

Whether or not Art. 190 develops in the way due process and the cursory APA requirements for informal rule-making have developed depends, then, on how large a role the ECJ wants to play in assuring that Community primary and supplementary laws are reasonable. The Single European Act (1992) initiates rapidly accelerating Community-wide legislation and regulation. Thus, more aggressive substantive review is possible. What happens to Art. 190 will depend on the temper of the times and the temper of the judges.

As to the judges, I am in no position to speculate. *In the original article a footnote appeared at this point which is now elevated into the text in the bracketed passage that follows immediately.* [Since this article was written, two new and as yet unpublished decisions have appeared that would suggest that the judges are moving in the directions indicated here. Both opinions repeat the standard formula that the Commission need not respond to every issue raised by the parties but must give sufficient reasons to enable the ECJ to exercise its power of review and the parties to decide whether to seek review. Nevertheless, both seem to demand a far more extensive Commission reasoned elaboration than Community judges had previously required. In *Technische Universität München v. Hauptzollamt München-Mitte* (ECJ 1991a), Advocate General Jacobs admits that:

[A]t present the case-law of the Court is ... perfectly clear ... [that] ... a statement of reasons similar to the one contained [here], though laconic, was sufficient to comply with the minimum requirements of Article 190.... Notwithstanding the above case-law, I question whether the minimum reasoning used by the Commission in such cases ... satisfies the requirements of Article 190.... Id., p. 25 of preliminary photocopied version.

The ECJ found the Commission's statement of reasons insufficient to sat-isfy the demands of Article 190. Id., p. 11, § 27 of the French translation of the preliminary photocopied version.

The second case, *La Cinq SA v. Commission, T-44/90* (ECJ 1992, preliminary original French text), is a decision of the Court of First Instance. Although in form rejecting a giving-reasons challenge to a Commission ruling, the Court holds that the Commission failed to examine important facts and so has 'failed its legal obligation to take into account all the elements pertinent to the case' (Id., p. 32, § 94, author's translation). Most significantly for our purposes, in reaching this conclusion the Court stresses that a complaining party has repeatedly raised decisive points which the Commission has failed to address in its decision (Id., pp. 30–2, §§ 88, 91, 92). (I am indebted to Judge Koen Lenaerts of the Court of First Instance of the European Communities for pointing these cases out to me and providing me with the preliminary Xeroxes. Of course he bears no responsibility for my interpretation of the cases.)]

As to the times, developments are occurring that suggest a more expansive reading of Art. 190, at least for purposes of achieving greater transparency. When European regulation of business was national, it could be, and was, done by direct and intimate communication between French, Dutch, or Danish bureaucrats and business executives who spoke the same language, both literally and figuratively. They had been to the same schools, lived in the same neighbourhoods, and often had worked in the same govern-ment offices together in their youth. Intimacy, not transparency, was the preferred style. Indeed, transparency was shunned because it would have allowed meddlesome outsiders into the tight little island of the regulators and regulatees. Now more and more regulation is done not at home, but in Brussels. I do not wish to exaggerate the change. The Brussels bureaucracy is drawn from the national bureaucracies and shares their taste for intimacy. Moreover, the French, Dutch, or Danish business executive can still usually find some sympathetic compatriot and old friend somewhere in the Brussels establishment.

However, regulation is now one step removed and the old intimacy of direct dealings between government and business somewhat reduced. The growth of a huge lobbying industry in Brussels represents one manifesta-tion of this change: professional go-betweens are now necessary where at home they were not. In these circumstances transparency begins to appear attractive to the regulated, who sometimes see themselves on the outside looking in rather than on the inside and delighted to keep others out. Lately,

Europeans have shown a strange interest in the Administrative Procedures Act, in 'independent regulatory commissions', and in other American paraphernalia. At the same time, many Americans, tired of 'adversary legalism', are yearning for a touch of the European style.

Giving-reasons requirements are an obvious vehicle for transparency. Judicially enforced demands for transparency have a strong potential for translating themselves into vigorous, substantive judicial review of bureaucratic decision-making. Given the feelings of the times, this is a good time to start a fever chart for Art. 190, one of the world's central devices for judicial enforcement of bureaucratic transparency.

The European Court and Integration

Alec Stone Sweet and Thomas Brunell

No international organization in world history has attracted as much scholarly attention as the European Community (EC).[1] The reason is straightforward: the EC has evolved from a relatively traditional, albeit multi-faceted, inter-state system into a quasi-federal polity. In a word, Europe has *integrated*, as the linkages between politics on the EC level and politics on the member-state level have expanded in scope and deepened in intensity. Scholars working in diverse fields, including public law, international relations, and comparative politics, have been fascinated by the integration process, not least because of the challenge of understanding the reciprocal impact, over time, of international and domestic systems of governance.

Current disagreements about how to understand European integration are largely disputes between intergovernmentalists, whose imagery is drawn from the international regime literature (Garrett 1992; Keohane and Hoffmann 1991; Moravcsik 1991; 1993; Taylor 1983), and supranationalists, whose imagery is often federalist (Leibfried and Pierson 1995; Marks, Hooghe, and Blank 1996; Sandholtz 1993; 1996; Sbragia 1993). Intergovernmentalists accord relative priority to member-state governments—representatives of the national interest—who bargain with one another in EC forums to fix the terms and limits of integration. Supranationalists, especially the heirs of neo-functionalism (Sandholtz and Stone Sweet 1998), accord relative priority to EC institutions—representatives of the interests of a nascent transnational society—who work with public and private actors

Originally published as 'Constructing a Supranational Constitution: Dispute Resolution and Governance in the European Community' in *American Political Science Review*, 92 (1998), 63. Reproduced by kind permission.

[1] Although 'European Union' is now commonly used to denote the European polity, we use 'European Community' throughout the paper. Formally, the 'European Community' remains the most inclusive term for how the organization and its legal system function most of the time.

at both the European and the national levels to remove barriers to integration and to expand the domain of supranational governance. This paper is implicated in these disputes. One of our claims is that, on crucial points, the intergovernmentalists have got it wrong.

More important, we propose a theory of European legal integration, the process by which Europe has constructed a transnational rule-of-law polity. The theory integrates, as interdependent causal factors, contracting among individuals, third-party dispute resolution, and the production of legal norms. We test the theory with reference to the EC, in two stages. First, we explain the construction of the legal system and analyse the relationships between our three key variables over the life of the Community. Second, we examine the impact of the operation of the legal system on governance, that is, on policy processes and outcomes, at both the national and the supranational levels.

Contracting, Dispute Resolution, Law-making

Our theory relies on three analytically independent factors that we expect to be interdependent in their effect. Because we believe that the theory has general application—it helps us to understand how all rule of law, governmental systems might emerge and develop—we present it in an abstract form here. It has been elaborated more formally elsewhere (Stone Sweet, Chapter 1, this volume).

The first factor is a simple contract—an exchange relationship—between two persons. Contracts, codified promises, fix the rules for a given exchange, by establishing the rights and obligations of each contracting person with respect to the other. The contract is an inherently social institution, embedded as it is in a cultural—or normative—framework that enables individuals to conceive, pursue, and express their interests and desires, but also to coordinate those desires with other individuals. Further, to get to the very notion of a codified promise, we have to have language, notions of individual roles, commitment, reputation, and responsibility—which have no meaning outside of a social setting—and some set of collective expectations about the future. As exchange proceeds over the life of the contract, or as external circumstances change, the meanings attached to the same set of rules by the contractants may diverge. To the extent that such conflicts arise, contracting generates a social demand for third-party dispute resolution, for law and courts, the function of which is to sustain social exchange over time.

The second factor, then, is the operation of triadic dispute resolution (TDR). Without it, the costs of exchange may be prohibitive, since each prospective party may doubt that the other will abide by promises made over the life of the contract. A judicial system lowers these costs, providing a measure of certainty to each contractant and a means of reconsecrating the terms of the contract over time, given the certainty that differences in contractual interpretation will arise as unforeseen circumstances arise. Transaction costs are particularly high in situations in which strangers— those who do not share a common normative framework, whether cultural or law-based—contemplate exchange, and where effective TDR does not exist.

The triad—two disputants and a dispute resolver—constitutes a basic, probably primal, institution of governance (Simmel 1950: 145–69). In every human community that we know anything about, we find such triads, arrayed along a spectrum that stretches roughly from consent-based mediation to arbitration to coercive-based adjudication. Commonly, TDR performs profoundly political functions, including the construction, consolidation, and maintenance of political regimes (Shapiro 1981*a*: Ch. 1), functions inhere in the lawmaking dynamics of dispute resolution itself.

Consider formal adjudication, wherein judges are required, for legitimacy purposes among others, to provide legal reasons to support their decisions. When a judge decides, the lawmaking impact of the decision is always twofold. First, in settling the dispute at hand, the judge produces a legal act that is particular—it binds the two disputants—and retrospective—it resolves a pre-existing dispute. Second, in justifying the decision, the judge signals that she will settle similar cases similarly in the future; this legal act is a general and prospective one—it affects future and potential contractants. Thus, judges do not simply or only respond to demands generated by social exchange. Rather, they adapt, continuously, the abstract legal rules governing exchange in any given community to the concrete exigencies of those individuals engaged in exchange.

The third factor is legislating, the elaboration of legal rules. Rules facilitate, but also structure, exchange by restricting some practices while permitting others. Conceived in this way, the legislator serves a social function that is rather similar to that of the judge: both produce rules that serve to reduce the transaction costs, enhance the legal certainty, and stabilize the expectations of those engaged in or contemplating exchange. Legislating, of course, is a far more efficient means of coordinating activity than is case-by-case adjudication and rule-making. But because legal norms are so efficacious—immediately binding on broad classes of people and activities— their production poses a collective action problem. Partly for this reason, and partly due to the dynamics of judicial rule-making, judges may legislate on matters before legislators do. In any case, in polities that possess both a permanently constituted legislature and an independent judiciary, law-making powers are shared and boundaries allegedly separating institutional functions blur. Thus, the legislature relies on the legal system to enforce its law; and the judiciary possesses broad capacity to generate legal rules where none existed prior to a given dispute, and to reconstruct legislative norms in interstitial processes of interpretation.

Viewed in dynamic relation to one another, contracting, TDR, and legislating can evolve interdependently and, in so doing, constitute and reconstitute a polity. Thus, as the number of contracts increases, the legal system will increasingly be activated. To the extent that the legal system performs its dispute-resolution functions effectively, it reduces contracting costs, thus encouraging more exchange. As the scope of legislation widens and deepens, the conditions favouring the expansion of exchange are con-structed, the potential for legal disputes increases, and the grounds available for judicial lawmaking expands. New collective action problems are posed as older barriers to exchange are removed, and these problems push for normative solutions.

Components of the virtuous circle just described have been identified empirically and theorized by scholars working in diverse fields. North (1981; 1990) has argued that differential rates of national economic development are in large part explained by the relative effectiveness of legal systems in reducing the costs of exchange among strangers. Although they did not focus on law and courts, Haas (1958; 1961) and Deutsch *et al.* (1957) understood, somewhat differently, that sovereign states would respond to increasing levels of transnational interactions by integrating politically, that is, by creating common institutional and normative frameworks that would, in effect, give birth to new systems of transnational governance. Haas used the term 'spillover' to capture the expansive logic of integration. In their studies of the birth and subsequent development of legal systems, Kommers (1994), Landfried (1984; 1992), Stone (1992*a*), and Burley and Mattli (1993) have shown that tight linkages can develop between self-interested litigants and judges, and that these interactions generate a self-sustaining dynamic which, by feeding back onto the greater political environment, can recon-figure the inner workings of the polity itself. These sorts of 'policy feedbacks' and their political consequences are also familiar to historical institution-alists, who give them pride of place (Pierson 1993; Steinmo, Thelen, and Longstreth 1992).

In the rest of this paper, we examine the development of the European polity, focusing on the construction and operation of the legal system.

Constructing the Supranational Polity

The emergence of a transnational, rule-of-law governmental system cannot be presumed. Our theory suggests that transnational exchange would be a critical catalyst for such an event, generating a social demand for dispute resolution—transnational TDR—revealing important collective action problems that beg for normative solutions—transnational rules—and thereby pushing for modes of supranational governance. The theory further suggests that, once the causal connections between exchange, TDR, and rules are forged, the legal system will operate according to a self-sustaining and expansionary dynamic. But the development of causal linkages between our three variables implies the existence of, respectively, some measure of individual property rights, some form of adjudication, and a lawgiver. For well-known reasons (for example, Waltz 1979), these conditions have been notoriously difficult to achieve and sustain in the inter-state system.

In Europe, the six states that signed the Treaty of Rome in 1958, establishing the European Economic Community, were able to overcome some of these difficulties, but only partly. The Rome Treaty contains important restrictions on state sovereignty, such as the prohibition, within the territory constituted by the EC, of tariffs, quantitative restrictions, and national measures 'having equivalent effect' on trade after 31 December 1969. It enables the pooling of state sovereignty by establishing legislative institutions and a process for elaborating common European policies. And it establishes 'supranational' institutions, including the European Commission and the European Court of Justice, to help the Council of Ministers—the EC institution that is controlled by member-state governments—legislate and to resolve disputes about the meaning of EC law. Nevertheless, despite these and other important innovations, the member states founded an international organization, not a transnational, rule-of-law polity. Some treaty provisions announced principles that, if implemented, would directly impact individuals—for example, free movement of workers, equal pay for equal work among the sexes—but the Treaty did not confer on individuals judicially enforceable rights.

Even within a European free trade zone we would expect the transaction costs facing transnational exchange to be higher than costs faced by those who contract within a single member state's jurisdiction, other things equal, to the extent that at the supranational level there exists no secure common legal framework comparable in its efficacy to that furnished by national legal systems. In the absence of such a framework, those who exchange cross-nationally would face a kaleidoscope of idiosyncratic national rules and practices that would act as hindrances. The establishment of an effective European system of dispute resolution, and a means of overcoming national barriers to exchange, is therefore a crucial first step.

In the next section, we briefly examine the European Court of Justice (ECJ) 'constitutional' case law. These judgments recast the normative foundations of the Community, radically upgrading the capacity of the legal system to respond to the demands of transnational society. It bears emphasis that this case law constitutes a necessary condition that underlies all of the causal models tested in this paper.

The Constitutionalization of the Treaty System

The 'constitutionalization of the treaty system' refers to the process by which the EC treaties have evolved from a set of legal arrangements binding upon sovereign states into a vertically integrated legal regime conferring judicially enforceable rights and obligations on all legal persons and entities, public and private, within EC territory. The phrase thus captures the transformation of an intergovernmental organization, governed by international law, into a multi-tiered system of governance founded on higher-law constitutionalism. Today, legal scholars and judges conceptualize the EC as a constitutional polity, and this is the orthodox position (Lenaerts 1990; Mancini 1991; Shapiro 1992; Weiler 1981; 1991); international relations scholars are more reticent to do so, for reasons that are internal to the development of international relations theory (Stone 1994). In its decisions, the ECJ has implicitly treated its terms of reference as a constitutional text since the 1960s and, today, explicitly refers to the treaties as a 'constitutional charter' or as 'the constitution of the Community' (Fernandez Esteban 1994).

The ECJ, the 'constitutional court' of the Community (Shapiro and Stone 1994), is the supreme interpreter of this constitution. The Court's function is to enforce compliance with EC law. Although the outcome was not anticipated, the greater bulk of the Court's case load is generated by preliminary references from national judges responding to claims made by private actors. The preliminary reference procedure is governed by Art. 177 of the EEC Treaty (1958). According to that article, when EC law is material to the resolution of a dispute being heard in a national court, the presiding judge may—and in some cases must—ask the ECJ for a correct interpretation of that law. This interpretation, called a 'preliminary ruling', shall then be applied by the national judge when settling the case. Article 177 was designed to promote the consistent application of EC law in the member states. The member states did not mean to provide a mechanism by which individual litigants would be able to sue their own member states, nor did they mean to confer on national judges the power of judicial review of national legislation. Both of these outcomes, however, inhere in the ECJ's vision of the Community as a constitutional polity.

The constitutionalization process has been driven, almost entirely, by the relationship between private litigants, national judges, and the ECJ, interacting within the framework provided by Art. 177. The process has proceeded in two phases. In the 1962–79 period, the Court secured the core, constitutional principles of supremacy and direct effect. The Court made these moves without the express authorization of treaty law and despite the declared opposition of the member states (Stein 1981). The doctrine of supremacy, announced in *Costa* (ECJ 1964), lays down the rule that, in any conflict between an EC legal rule and a rule of national law, the former must be given primacy. Indeed, according to the Court, every EC rule, from the moment of entry into force, 'renders automatically inapplicable any conflicting provision of . . . national law' (*Simmenthal*, ECJ 1978). The doctrine of direct effect holds that provisions of EC law can confer on individuals legal rights that public authorities must respect, and which may be protected by national courts. During this period, the ECJ found that certain treaty provisions (*Van Gend en Loos*, ECJ 1963*b*) and a class of secondary legislation, called 'directives' (*Van Duyn*, ECJ 1974*a*), were directly effective. The 'regulation', the other major type of secondary legislation, is the only class of Euro-rule that was meant—by the member states—to be directly applicable in national law.

These moves integrated national and supranational legal systems, establishing a decentralized enforcement mechanism for EC law. The mechanism relies on the initiative of private actors. The doctrine of direct effect empowers individuals and companies to sue member-state governments or other public authorities either for not conforming to obligations contained in the treaties or regulations, or for not properly transposing provisions of directives into national law. The doctrine of supremacy prohibits public authorities from relying on national law to justify their failure to comply with EC law, and requires national judges to resolve conflicts between national and EC law in favour of the latter.

In a second wave of constitutionalization, the Court supplied national courts with enhanced means of guaranteeing the effectiveness of EC law. In *Von Colson* (ECJ 1984*c*), the doctrine of indirect effect was established, according to which national judges must interpret national law in conformity with EC law. In *Marleasing* (ECJ 1990*a*) the Court clarified the meaning of indirect effect, ruling that, when a directive has either not been transposed or has been transposed incorrectly into national law, national judges are obliged to interpret national law as if it were in conformity with European law. The doctrine thus empowers national judges to rewrite national legislation—in processes of 'principled construction'—in order to render EC law applicable, in the absence of implementing measures. Once national law has been so (re)constructed, EC law, in the guise of a de facto national rule, can be applied in legal disputes between private legal persons—that is, non-governmental entities. Thus, indirect effect substantially reduces the problem that the Court's doctrine of direct effect covers only disputes between a private person and a governmental entity. Finally, in *Francovich* (ECJ 1991*b*), the Court declared the doctrine of governmental liability. According to this rule, a national court can hold a member state liable for damages caused to individuals due to the failure on the part of the member state to properly implement a directive. The national court may then require member states to compensate such individuals for their financial losses.

In this case law, the ECJ has imagined a particular type of relationship between the European and national courts: a working partnership in the construction of a constitutional, rule-of-law Community. In that partnership, national judges become agents of the Community order—they become Community judges—whenever they resolve disputes governed by EC law. The Court obliges national judges to uphold the supremacy of EC law, even against conflicting subsequent national law; encourages them to make references concerning the proper interpretation of EC law to the Court; and empowers them, even without a referral, to interpret national rules so that these rules will conform to EC law and to refuse to apply national rules when they do not.

The effectiveness of the EC legal system thus depends critically on the willingness of national judges to refer disputes about EC law to the ECJ, and to settle those disputes in conformity with the Court's case law. Although national judges embraced the logic of supremacy with differing degrees of enthusiasm, by the end of the 1980s every national supreme court had formally accepted the doctrine (Slaughter, Stone Sweet, and Weiler 1998). National judges, persuaded by compelling legal arguments in support of supremacy, empowered themselves by, among other things, appropriating the power of judicial review of national legislation (Burley and Mattli 1993; Weiler 1991; 1994). The ease with which European judges at the member-state level were able to accommodate supremacy contrasts with the slower

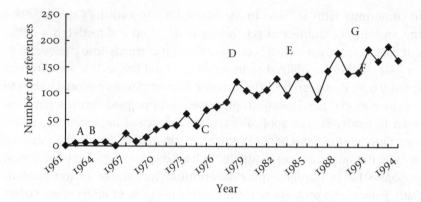

Fig. 4.1. Annual number of Article 177 references to the European Court of Justice, 1961–1994

The line plots the annual number of Art. 177 references to the ECJ. The source for Art. 177 references is data collected by the authors and the ECJ. Landmark decisions are highlighted in the graph. A: Doctrine of Direct Effect of Treaty Provisions (1963); B: Doctrine of Supremacy (1964); C: Doctrine of Direct Effect of Directives (1974); D: Simmenthal Doctrine (1978); E: Doctrine of Indirect Effect (1984); F: Marleasing Doctrine (1990); G: Doctrine of State Liability (1991)

and more conflictual consolidation of the US federal system (Goldstein 1994).[2]

Figure 4.1 plots the annual rate of Art. 177 references beginning with the first reference in 1961. It also temporally locates the leading constitutional decisions discussed here. The growth in the number of references is steady and dramatic. Without the doctrines of supremacy and direct effect, the level of preliminary references would doubtlessly have remained stable and low. In proclaiming supremacy and direct effect, the Court broadcast the message that EC law could be used, by individuals, businesses, and interest groups, to obtain policy outcomes that might otherwise be impossible or more costly to obtain by way of national policy processes. It is evident from the graph that litigants and national judges heard this message and responded.

Finally, it cannot be stressed enough that the EC legal system was constructed without the explicit consent of the member states. Member states possessed the means to reverse constitutionalization, but only by revising the EC's constitution. Treaty revision requires the unanimous vote of the member states, acting as a constituent assembly, followed by ratification in each member state, according to diverse procedures, including referendums.

[2] In the nineteenth century, transformations in the common law, rather than in constitutional law, were fundamental to American economic development, and therefore to American integration (Horwitz 1977).

Given this decision-making rule, it is unsurprising that the member states have never overturned an ECJ interpretation of the treaties.

Data Analysis

Our theory yields a set of testable propositions. First, transnational exchange generates social demands for transnational TDR. Specifically, higher levels of cross-national activity will produce more conflicts between national and EC law, and therefore more Art. 177 references. Second, higher levels of transnational activity will push for supranational rules—judicial or legislative—to replace national rules. Third, to the extent that European judicial and legislative institutions function with minimal effectiveness, European integration—as evidenced by the rising tide of the ECJ's case law and of EC legislation—will feed back onto society. The consolidation and expansion of European governance will fuel more transnational activity and provide the normative context for more Art. 177 references, in an increasing number of domains. The source of references, at this stage, will not be limited to those engaged in transnational exchange, but will include those who seek to impose or make more effective European rules within national regimes. Fourth, to the extent that the above propositions hold, transnational activity, transnational TDR, and the production of European legislation will develop interdependently, and this interdependence will drive European integration in predictable ways. That is, once the causal linkages among these three factors have been constructed, a dynamic, self-reinforcing process will push for the progressive expansion of supranational governance. These propositions, of course, depend critically on the prior announcement, by the Court, of supremacy and direct effect.

We tested our theory with data collected in 1995, at the ECJ in Luxembourg. With the help of the Court, we gathered information on Art. 177 reference activity from 1961 to mid-1995, for a total of 2,978 references. We then coded each reference, among other things, by country of origin, year of referral, the national court making the reference, and the subject matter of the dispute.[3] These data had never before been compiled. We also compiled data on transnational exchange and the production of European legal rules; for the former, we make heavy use of data on intra-EC trade because it is the only reasonable indicator of transnational exchange on

---

[3] Although most references are limited to a single subject matter of EC law, some references contain claims based on as many as five subject matters. This accounts for the difference between the total number of references and the total number of subject matters invoked in references in the data presented below.

which we have reliable data that are reported annually, partner by partner, for the life of the Community.[4]

We have argued that transnational exchange is fundamental to the construction of a transnational legal system. To begin testing the proposition, we confronted one of the deepest mysteries of European legal integration, namely: what accounts for the wide cross-national variation in the number of Art. 177 references? The scholarly literature on the problem has produced a handful of reasonable candidate explanations, including the role of legal culture, the bureaucratic organization of the courts, the extent of constitutional monism or dualism, and the length of a judiciary's experience with judicial review. Two recent studies—Dehousse (1996) and a collaborative research project that focused on the reception of supremacy by the national courts (Slaughter, Stone, and Weiler 1998)—assessed these and other factors in comparative perspective. Both studies generally concluded that variation in the intensity of the ECJ-national court relationship is overdetermined and/or explained by factors operating with different effects across the member states.[5]

Our theory provides an alternative explanation, one based on cross-national activity. Figure 4.2 depicts the correlation of the average level of intra-EC trade over the years 1961–92 on the average number of Art. 177 references per year from the national courts of each of the twelve member states.[6] We averaged the number of references annually in order to correct for the fact that some member states joined the EC later than other member states; and we have combined reference data for Belgium and Luxembourg

[4] We are not arguing that intra-EC trade, one type of transnational activity, subsumes other important forms of exchange, such as labour and capital flows and the formation of EC interest groups and social movements. Unfortunately, data on these and other forms of exchange are incomplete and often unreliable. We would expect that increasing transnational activity of a particular type, within a given domain, would drive integration processes in that area: for example, patterns in cross-national flows of workers will drive litigation in social security. Generally, we had good reason to expect that trade would dominate the construction of Europe since, for most of the life of the Community, the core of the European integration project has been the creation of a common market for goods and agriculture. For further discussion of this point, see Tables 4.3 and 4.4.

[5] There is little point in formally testing these explanations. We know, by simply looking at the raw data on references comparatively, that alleged relationships between the factors cited above and national levels of Art. 177 references—for example, the more monist the constitutional order, the fewer Art. 177 references will be generated—do not hold. If these factors do impact levels of Art. 177 references, they must operate with different effects across the EC.

[6] In 1995, the Eurostat reporting service furnished annual intra-EC trade figures for the 1958–92 period. Because the service has not yet updated these figures, and because subsequent data are reported on different scales, we have not used post-1992 data in any of the regression models reported here.

because the trade data for those member states are combined by Eurostat reporting services. The linear relationship between intra-EC trade and references is nearly perfect, with countries that trade more with their partners in the EC generating higher levels of Art. 177 references; the adjusted $R^2 = .92$, SEE $= 2.46$, n $= 11$. These results confer rather startling confirmation of the abstract model. We also examined the effect on references of other plausible and quantifiable independent variables, including cross-national measurements of 'diffuse popular support' for the EC legal system, population, and GDP; but none came close to performing as well as intra-EC trade.[7]

Figure 4.2 depicts the relationship between intra-EC trade and Art. 177 references cross-nationally, with no time element. Figure 4.3 depicts the relationship between the same two variables over time, since the first Art. 177 reference in 1961, with no cross-national element. In this model, we include a dummy variable to account for (1) the constitutionalization of the Treaties and (2) the prohibition of national restrictions on intra-EC trade (Art. 30 EEC) that took effect on 1 January 1970. As we have seen, the doctrines of supremacy and direct effect made it possible for individuals to have their rights under EC law protected before their own national courts; and, as of 1970, Art. 30, which proclaims the free movement of goods, provided the legal basis for traders to claim those rights (Poiares Maduro 1997).[8] We coded the dummy variable '0' from 1961 to 1969, and '1' from 1970 to 1992; the variable is hereafter referred to as the 'post-1969 dummy'.

---

[7] We tested whether, respectively, (1) higher levels of diffuse support for the European legal system—measures developed by Caldeira and Gibson (1995), (2) larger populations, aggregated as the average population for each member state 1961–93, and (3) larger economies, aggregated as the average GDP for each member state 1961–93, generate higher levels of references per member state. The dependent variable for each model is the average number of Art. 177 references per member state, and n $= 11$. Our results are summarized as follows:

	Intercept	t-stat	Coefficient	t-stat	Adj. R^2	SEE
Diffuse support	10.08	3.92	19.88	1.18	.04	8.54
Population	6.4	1.55	$9.43 \, (10^{-8})$	1.16	.03	8.55
GDP	3.33	1.48	$1.48 \, (10^{-11})$	4.3	.63	5.27

Sources: The index of diffuse support for the ECJ is from Caldeira and Gibson (1995: 364). Population data are from World Bank (1990). GDP data for 1960–9 are from Banks (1976); and GDP data for 1970–94 are from World Bank (1995).

[8] In addition—pursuant to Art. 33 EEC—in 1970 the European Commission produced a directive clarifying the meaning of the principle of free movement of goods and the lawful exceptions to it.

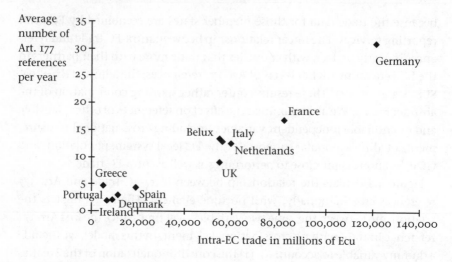

Fig. 4.2. Intra-EC trade and average number of Article 177 references, 1960–1993

For each member state, the total number of Art. 177 references was divided by the number of years in which that member state had been making references to the ECJ. Belux is Belgium and Luxembourg combined. Trade figures are the annual average of intra-EC imports and exports for each member state measured in European currency unit Ecu, 1960–93. Trade data are from Eurostat (1995). The source for Art. 177 references is data collected by the authors and the ECJ. The regression equation is $y = .2105 + .0002247$ (Trade) + e. Adjusted $R^2 = .92$, n = 11, and the SEE = 2.46. The t-statistics are: .178 for the constant; and 10.8 for intra-EC trade.

Figure 4.3 plots the actual and predicted annual levels of Art. 177 references for the EC as a whole. The Predicted line—generated by a regression analysis in which the dependent variable is the yearly number of Art. 177 references, and the independent variables are annual intra-EC trade and the post-1969 dummy—plots the level of references predicted by the independent variables. The adjusted $R^2 = .91$, SEE = 17.92, and n = 32. The coefficients for both intra-EC trade and the dummy variable are positive and statistically significant.

Our time-series data for intra-EC trade and Art. 177 references are non-stationary—the augmented Dickey-Fuller test—a common problem for data containing a strong trend. We argue that our results are nevertheless valid for two reasons. First, the data on intra-EC trade and Art. 177 references are co-integrated, indicating that a linear combination of the two variables is stationary.[9] Second, we checked for serial auto-correlation in the error terms, and found none.[10]

[9] Using the Johansen co-integration test, we reject the hypothesis of no co-integration at the .01 level.

[10] Using Econometric Views 2.0, we examined the correlogram. All of the autocorrelations of the residuals, with the exception of one, at t-8, were within plus or minus 2 standard errors of zero.

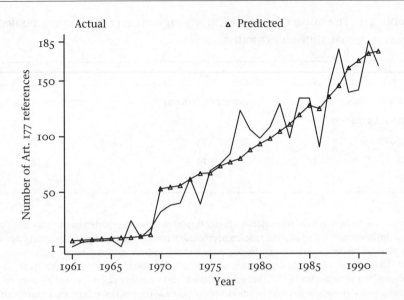

Fig. 4.3. Actual and predicted annual levels of Article 177 references from intra-EC trade, 1961–1992

The Actual line plots the yearly number of Art. 177 references by national courts to the ECJ, 1961–92. The Predicted line plots the number of annual references predicted by the regression analysis in which intra-EC trade and a post-1969 Dummy variable—coded 'o' from 1961 to 1969, and '1' from 1970 to 1992—are the independent variables, and the annual number of Art. 177 references for the EC as a whole is the dependent variable. Levels of aggregate trade begin with the original six member states—Belgium, France, Germany, Italy, Luxembourg, and the Netherlands—and, as new member states join the EC, their trade figures are included. Trade data are from Eurostat (1995). The source for 177 references is data collected by the authors and the ECJ. The regression equation is $y = 3.56 + .0000938$ (intra-EC Trade) $+ 39.93$ (post-1969 Dummy) $+ e$. The adjusted $R^2 = .91$, $n = 32$, SEE $= 17.92$, and the Durbin–Waston statistic for the regression equation $= 1.85$. The t-statistics are: 0.59 for the constant; 10.59 for intra-EC Trade; and 4.52 for the post-1969 Dummy.

We would be more confident in our results if we had more observations. By using our time series and our cross-national data together, we were able to increase the number of observations and provide a more stringent test of the impact of transnational exchange on judicial activity. Table 4.1 presents the results of two pooled models. The first examines the impact of intra-EC trade on Art. 177 references, cross-nationally and over time; the second examines this same relationship, but with the post-1969 dummy included as a second independent variable. The adjusted R^2 for these models is, respectively, .73 and .77; the SEE for these models is, respectively, 6.19 and 5.74; and n = 246. The trade variable in both models is positive and highly statistically significant. Following the advice of Stimson (1985) and King (1986), after

Table 4.1. The impact of intra-EC trade on Article 177 references: pooled, cross-sectional, time series models

	Model 1	Model 2
Intra-EC trade	.000126***(18.89)	.0000995***(13.29)
Post-1969 dummy		7.64***(6.25)
Adjusted R^2	.73	.77
SEE	6.19	5.74
N	246	246

*** p < .001

Entries are unstandardized regression coefficients, with t-statistics reported in parentheses. The dependent variable is annual Art. 177 references for each member state per year. The independent variable for Model 1 is intra-EC trade, the value of both imports and exports for each member state (Belgium and Luxembourg combined) with all other member states, for each year. The independent variables for Model 2 are intra-EC trade and a dummy variable coded '0' from 1961 to 1969 and '1' from 1970 to 1992. The model consists of 246 observations: Belgium–Luxembourg 1961–92; Denmark 1973–92; France 1961–92; Germany 1961–92; Greece 1981–92; Ireland 1973–92; Italy 1961–92; Netherlands 1961–92; Portugal 1986–92; Spain 1986–92; UK 1973–92. The source for the trade data is *Eurostat* (1995). The source for Art. 177 references is data collected by the authors and the ECJ. Econometric Views 2.0 was used to estimate a fixed effects model. See Stimson (1985) and Sayrs (1989) for a discussion of pooled models.

estimating the models, we ensured that no serial auto-correlation of the errors existed.[11]

Thus, we find overwhelming support for our claim that transnational exchange has been a crucial factor driving the construction of the EC's legal system.[12] Further, our analysis does not conflict with—indeed it builds on—the basic narrative, told by legal scholars, of how the Court constitutionalized the treaties.

We have also argued that the emergence of effective transnational TDR is seminal to the emergence of supranational governance. Our theory suggests that the operation of the legal system will produce powerful feedback effects, the most important of which are normative—that is, rule-based. One crucial function of TDR is to produce stable, normative solutions to collective action

[11] Using Econometric Views 2.0, we examined the correlograms for each panel. All of the auto-correlations of the residuals were within plus or minus 2 standard errors of zero, and no significant patterns were found.

[12] We expect that, as the European polity matures, the litigation of EC legal disputes will increase. We do not expect that Art. 177 references will continue to rise indefinitely. The capacity of the ECJ to process references is limited. We predict that national judges themselves will increasingly resolve EC legal disputes on their own, without a prior reference. For a discussion of the problem of Art. 177 and the overloaded docket of the ECJ, see Weiler (1987).

problems. In principle, a governmental system could be constituted entirely by judicial rule-making: the dispute resolver governs by the pedagogical authority of its decisions. In practice, courts share governmental authority with legislative bodies, not least because legislating is a more efficient way to produce legal rules than is adjudicating. Once a transnational legal system has been consolidated, the production of European legal rules, whether by judicial or legislative processes, will facilitate the expansion of transnational exchange.

To evaluate the interrelationships that may have developed among our three variables, we collected data on the annual production of the two general categories of EC legislation: regulations and directives, hereafter called 'Euro-rules'. Both types of legislation are drafted and proposed by the European Commission, a supranational body that blends legislative and administrative functions (Ludlow 1991). To simplify a complicated process, these proposals can be amended in interactions involving the European Parliament, the Commission, and the Council of Ministers (Tsebelis 1994). Euro-rules are finally adopted by the Council of Ministers, a body composed of ministers from member-state governments, the exact composition of which is determined by the subject matter of EC law under discussion (Wessels 1991).

Figure 4.4 plots the actual and predicted annual levels of Art. 177 references for the EC as a whole. The Predicted line—generated by a regression analysis in which the dependent variable is the yearly number of Art. 177 references, and the independent variables are annual intra-EC trade, the annual number of Euro-rules promulgated, and the post-1969 dummy—plots the level of references predicted by the independent variables. The adjusted $R^2 = .92$, SEE $= 17.01$, and n $= 32$. The coefficients for all three variables are positive and significant as expected.

Figure 4.5 depicts the growth of transnational exchange—in the form of intra-EC trade; the evolution of transnational TDR—in the form of Art. 177 references; and the development of transnational legal norms—in the form of Euro-rules. It thus depicts the development of the European polity. The high inter-correlation among the three variables is another way of describing the virtuous circle at the core of our theory.

Do European integration processes serve to expand transnational activity? To answer the question, we compared annual rates of growth in trade, for the life of the Community, among (1) EC member states with each other, and (2) non-EC member states with EC member states. In order to maximize comparability, we focused on two groupings: the original six members, and three states—Denmark, Ireland, and the UK—which joined the EC in 1973.

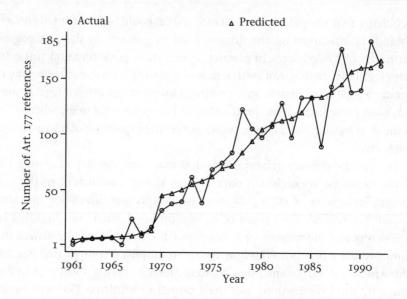

Fig. 4.4. Actual and predicted annual levels of Article 177 references from intra-EC trade and Euro-rules, 1961–1992

The Actual line plots the yearly number of Art. 177 references by national courts to the ECJ, 1961–92. The Predicted line plots the number of annual references predicted by the regression analysis in which intra-EC trade, Euro-rules, and a post-1969 Dummy variable—coded 'o' from 1961 to 1969, and '1' from 1970 to 1992—are the independent variables, and the annual number of Art. 177 references for the EC as a whole is the dependent variable. Levels of aggregate trade begin with the original six member states—Belgium, France, Germany, Italy, Luxembourg, and the Netherlands—and, as new member states join the EC, their trade figures are included. Trade data are from Eurostat (1995). Euro-rules are the annual number of directives and regulations promulgated by the EC. The source for Art. 177 references is data collected by the authors and the ECJ. The regression equation is y = 2.84 + .0000731(intra-EC Trade) + 2.04 (Euro-rules) + 31.35 (post-1969 Dummy) + e. The adjusted R^2 = .92, n = 32, SEE = 17.01, and the Durbin-Watson for the regression equation = 2.18. The t-statistics are: 0.50 for the constant, 5.55 for intra-EC Trade, 2.04 for Euro-rules, and 3.34 for the post-1969 Dummy.

As the numbers in Table 4.2 show, in the pre-1973 period, the growth in trade among EC member states was far higher than growth rates achieved between EC member-states and neighbouring, non-EC member states. Once these latter states joined the EC, their growth rates rose above levels achieved by the original six. Although trade is a crucial measure of the degree of integration among the member states, its relative importance in activating the legal system must also be evaluated in terms of changes in the density and scope of European rules.

The theory, after all, posits an expansive logic to integration processes. According to this logic, the growing interdependence of transnational

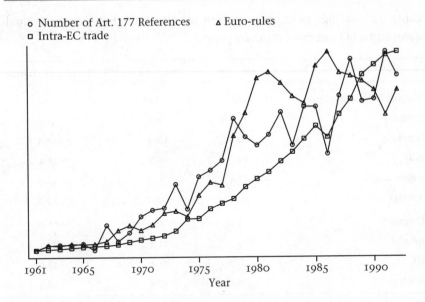

Fig. 4.5. Annual levels of intra-EC trade, Euro-rules, and Article 177 references, 1961–1992

The Number of Art. 177 references line plots the yearly number of Art. 177 references for the EC as a whole, 1961–92. The Euro-rules line plots the annual number of directives and regulations promulgated by the EC. The Intra-EC trade line plots levels of aggregate intra-EC trade for the EC as a whole. The graph has been re-scaled since the variables are on different scales.

exchange, TDR, and Euro-rules drives the progressive construction of the supranational polity. By the construction of a supranational polity we mean the process by which governmental competences, in an increasing number of domains, are transferred from the national to the supranational level. Simply put, as TDR and other processes remove the most obvious hindrances to transnational exchange—such as border inspections, fees and duties, and so on—and as supranational coordinative rules replace the disparate rules in place in the member states, new obstacles to integration are revealed and become salient—such as regulations protecting consumers, the environment, and so on. These national rules and practices will be targeted by litigants, and pressure will be exerted on EC legislative institutions to widen the jurisdiction of EC governance into new domains. We think of this dynamic as a kind of legal 'spillover.' Thus, as EC rule-making proceeds, a second logic to references asserts itself: the more individuals have an interest in subverting national legal regimes and substituting EC regulations for national ones, the more they will litigate, whether or not they engage in cross-border economic exchange.

Table 4.2. Average percentage growth rates in trade between individual states and all EC member states by period

	1961–72	1973–92	Percentage change
Belgium and Luxembourg	11.8	9.4	−20.1
France	13.5	9.2	−31.7
Germany	12.1	10.4	−14.3
Italy	13.3	10.8	−18.2
Netherlands	11.3	9.4	−16.9
Average	12.4	9.8	−20.2
Denmark	6.0	9.9	+65.0
Ireland	9.3	11.4	+22.1
UK	8.8	11.3	+28.0
Average	8.0	10.9	+38.4

Entries under the 1961-72 and 1973-92 columns are the average rate of growth in trade between each member state listed with all members of the EC. Entries under the Percentage change column are the change registered, between the two periods, in the growth rates in trade between each state listed with all members of the EC. Denmark, Ireland, and the UK entered the EC in January 1973. *Source:* Eurostat (1995).

Our data provide some preliminary support for our contention. First, we examined the evolution of the substantive content of Art. 177 references. Recall that these claims constitute allegations, by private litigants, that rules or practices in place in an individual member state conflict with Euro-rules. Litigants have therefore requested national judges to enforce EC law by, in effect, eliminating conflicting national rules or practices. Table 4.3 charts this evolution, vividly recording the extent to which the domain of EC law has expanded.[13] The percentage of claims involving the direct exchange of goods—the free movement of goods and agricultural products—has steadily declined, from over 50 per cent in the 1971–5 period to 27 per cent in

---

[13] We coded references by subject matter and relevant provision of the EEC Treaty. Each of the legal subject matters listed in the first column corresponds to the sections of the EEC Treaty following in parentheses: agriculture (arts. 38–47); free movement of goods (9–37); social security (51); taxes (95–99); competition (85–94); approximation of laws (100–102); transportation (74–84); establishment (52–66); social provisions (117–122); external—a miscellaneous category including all EC economic policies affecting the European Free Trade Area, the GATT, food aid, and special agreements with non-EC states; free movement of workers (48–50); environment (130R-T); commercial policy and dumping (110–116). Of the 3,855 EC subject matters implicated in references, more than 80% fall within the 13 domains listed in Table 4.2.

Table 4.3. Distribution of legal claims by subject matter, Article 177 references

Subject matter	1961–70	1971–5	1976–80	1981–5	1986–90	1991–5
Agriculture	% 20.4 n (30)	30.9 (109)	25.1 (176)	20.3 (153)	19.6 (160)	12.5 (135)
Free movement of goods	13.6 (20)	19.6 (69)	17.1 (120)	19.8 (149)	18.5 (151)	14.9 (161)
Social security	19.7 (29)	12.5 (44)	10.3 (72)	8.4 (63)	9.1 (74)	10 (108)
Taxes	11.6 (17)	2 (7)	4.6 (32)	4.8 (36)	8 (65)	8.5 (92)
Competition	8.8 (13)	6.3 (22)	3.6 (25)	4.5 (34)	5 (41)	8.2 (89)
Approximation of laws	2.8 (4)	0.3 (1)	1.9 (13)	4.9 (37)	3.8 (31)	5.1 (55)
Transportation	2 (3)	0.6 (2)	1.4 (10)	1.3 (10)	1.5 (12)	2.9 (31)
Establishment	0.7 (1)	2.6 (9)	2.3 (16)	2.7 (20)	5.6 (46)	6.6 (72)
Social provisions	0.7 (1)	0.3 (1)	1.1 (8)	3.7 (28)	4.2 (34)	8.8 (95)
External	0.7 (1)	2.8 (10)	1.7 (11)	2.4 (18)	0.9 (7)	1.5 (16)
Free movement of workers	0.7 (1)	4.3 (15)	2 (14)	4.1 (31)	5 (41)	3.2 (35)
Environment	0	0	0.4 (3)	1.6 (12)	0.9 (7)	2 (22)
Commercial policy and dumping	0	0.6 (2)	1.4 (10)	0.9 (7)	0.9 (7)	1.8 (19)
Total claims	147	352	702	754	816	1,084
% of total claims by period	3.8	9.1	18.2	19.6	21.2	28.1

Table constructed from data compiled by the authors with the help the Court of Justice. The table lists only the 13 most important legal domains which, combined, comprise more than 80% of total claims. We coded references by subject matter and relevant provision of the EEC Treaty. Each of the legal subject matters listed in the first column corresponds to the sections of the EEC Treaty following in parentheses: agriculture (Arts. 38–47); free movement of goods (9–37); social security (51); taxes (95–9); competition (85–94); approximation of laws (100–2); transportation (74–84); establishment: the freedom to establish undertakings and to provide services (52–66); social provisions (117–22); external (a miscellaneous category including all EC economic policies affecting the European Free Trade Area, the GATT, food aid, and special agreements with non-EC states); free movement of workers (48–50); environment (130R–T); commercial policy and dumping (110–16). Of the 3,855 EC subject matters implicated in references, more than 80% fall within the 13 domains listed in Table 4.3. Although most references are limited to a single subject matter of EC law, some references contain claims based on as many as five subject matters. This accounts for the difference between the total number of references and the total number of subject matters invoked in references.

Table 4.4. The declining impact of intra-EC trade on Article 177 references: pooled, cross-sectional, time series models

Intra-EC trade	.000283*** (5.26)
Post-1969 dummy	4.62** (3.11)
Trade* interaction	−.00000554** (−3.44)
Adjusted R²	.78
SEE	5.61
N	246

** p < .01 ***p < .001 Entries are unstandardized regression coefficients, with t-statistices reported in parentheses. The dependent variable is annual Art. 177 references for each member state, per year. The independent variables are intra-EC trade, the value of both imports and exports for each member state (Belgium and Luxembourg combined) with all other member states, for each year; a dummy variable coded 'o' from 1961 to 1969, and '1' from 1970 to 1992; and an interaction variable which is intra-EC trade multiplied by year. The model consists of 246 observations: Belgium–Luxembourg 1961–92; Denmark 1973–92; France 1961–92; Germany 1961–92; Greece 1981–92; Ireland 1973–92; Italy 1961–92; Netherlands 1961–92; Portugal 1986–92; Spain 1986–92; UK 1973–92. The source for the trade data is Eurostat (1995). The source for Art. 177 references is data collected by the authors and the ECJ. Econometric Views 2.0 was used to estimate a fixed effects model. See Stimson (1985) and Sayrs (1989) for a discussion of pooled models.

the 1991–5 period. At the same time, more indirect hindrances to trade, such as national rules governing equal pay for equal work—coded as social provisions—environmental protection, and taxation policy, have become important sites of contestation.

Second, we assessed the relationship between trade and Art. 177 references over time by including a variable to capture the interaction of intra-EC trade and time. Table 4.4 presents the results of this model. Our a priori expectation about the interaction variable was that the coefficient would be negative, indicating a declining impact of trade on Art. 177 references over time. The coefficient for the interaction variable is indeed negative and statistically significant. We believe that the growing articulation and differentiation of the Euro-rules that constitute the EC's normative structure will, increasingly, generate Art. 177 references. Thus, as the scope of EU rules expand, the legal system will not simply be a vehicle for trading interests, but also for more diffuse 'public' interests.

In the next section, we examine more closely our contention that the operation of the EC legal system both provokes and reinforces the spillover effects that partly drive the construction of supranational governance.

Dispute Resolution and the Dynamics of Supranational Governance

We have argued that integration processes are generally driven by transnational activity, by the transaction cost-reducing behaviour of supranational institutions, and by the positive feedback effects of lawmaking onto society. In this section, we cross-check our theory by, among other things, examining concrete policy outcomes in specific domains of EC law. We therefore shift the perspective from the broad relationships depicted in the statistical analysis to a more fine-grained examination of how, and to what effect, the legal system operates. Because our theory fundamentally conflicts with the dominant framework for understanding how the EC and its legal system operates, that of intergovernmentalism, we begin by summarizing our differences with intergovernmentalists.

Intergovernmentalists argue that national executives are in control of every crucial step in the construction of the European polity. Employing a logic derived from two-level game imagery (Evans, Jacobson, and Putnam 1993), Moravcsik (1993; 1994), for example, claims that governments, acting in the Council of Ministers and in summit meetings, establish the parameters that determine the content, scope, and pace of integration. Governments cooperate to achieve their policy goals and to enhance their autonomy in domestic politics. Due to the decision-making rules in place in most EC legislative processes—unanimity and super-majority voting—the Euro-rules produced typically reflect the preferences of those governments that support the least amount of integration in any given area—the lowest common denominator. The behaviour of private actors, sub-national public authorities, and the Community's organs are secondary; they serve to consolidate new levels of integration (Moravcsik 1995).

Intergovernmentalists have also sought to explain the operation of the legal system. Employing a logic derived from principal-agent theories of delegation (Kiewiet and McCubbins 1991), Garrett (1992), and Garrett, Keleman, and Schultz (1996) argue that the European Court—the agent—serves the interests of the dominant member states in the EC—the Court's principals. The ECJ, intergovernmentalists claim, codifies the preferences of these states in its case law. The Court does so in order to avoid court-curbing measures and to secure compliance with its rulings.

In contrast to intergovernmentalists, we argue that governments do not control legal integration in any determinative sense, and therefore cannot control European integration more broadly. We do not want to be misunderstood. The EC polity contains strong 'intergovernmental' components; that is, EC politics are partly constituted by the interactions between representatives of the member-state governments. But it is our contention that 'intergovernmentalism', when that term is used to denote the existing body of theory and causal propositions about how the European integration process has proceeded, is deeply flawed. In using the word 'intergovernmentalism' we need to distinguish the descriptive from the theoretical label. Moreover, any theory of European integration must notice and take account of the role of governments, clearly stating how that role is conceptualized.

The Council of Ministers and representatives of the member states are important actors in European politics. We understand their impact on integration to be positive when they (1) work with supranational institutions to adopt, at the supranational level, Euro-rules, and (2) transpose, on the national level, European directives into national law. They have a negative impact on integration when they (1) block EC legislation, in their capacity as members of the Council, and (2) refuse to comply with Euro-rules that they do not like, in their capacity as national governments.

Generally, we expect governments to be more reactive than proactive within integration processes. European integration facilitates not only transnational trade, but also the construction of associations and social movements, and this exchange, as it rises, puts pressure on governments to act in pro-integrative ways. At any point in time, and in any particular area, governments can fail to respond to transnational interests, and they can ignore increasingly mobilized domestic interests but only at ever-increasing cost. Thus, we expect that the pace of integration will vary across issue-area, partly as a function of the relative intensity of transnational activity and litigating in that area. And we expect the EC's legal system to serve the interests of transnational society, not individual governments, or even a consortium of powerful governments (see Stone Sweet and Sandholtz 1997). Judges are agents of the Treaty, not of governments.

Empirically, our differences with intergovernmentalists must begin with the challenge of explaining the constitutionalization of the treaty system. Constitutionalization, as we have tried to demonstrate, profoundly transformed the EC polity. As discussed above, the Court, activated by Art. 177 references, constructed the EC legal system: it worked to diffuse the doctrines of supremacy and direct effect, and to provide national judges with the means to enforce EC law, even against member-state governments and the legislatures that governments control. Further constitutionalization did not take place surreptitiously. During the proceedings that directly preceded the Court's announcements of supremacy and direct effect, various member-state governments argued, in formal 'observations'—briefs advising the Court how it should decide—that the Treaty could not be interpreted so as to support either doctrine (Burley and Mattli 1993; Stein 1981). Nevertheless, the Court revised the Treaty by authoritatively interpreting it, and these interpretations transformed the nature of Community governance. Governments agreed to this transformation, but only after the fact and only tacitly, by progressively adjusting their behaviour to the emergence of new rules.

We view the Court not unlike Weiler (1981; 1991; 1994) as generally working to enhance its own autonomy, autonomy that is then exercised to promote the interests of transnational society and to facilitate the construction of supranational governance (see also Burley and Mattli 1993). The Court does not work in the interests of member-state governments, except in the very loose sense in which those interests can be construed as being in conformity with the Treaty's purposes broadly—not narrowly—conceived. The move to supremacy and direct effect must be understood as audacious acts of agency. The Court could afford to move aggressively to revise the Treaty on its own because its formal relationship with the member states is a permissive one. Given the decision-making rule in place—unanimity among the member states—the credibility of the threat that the member states would reverse constitutionalization or any ECJ treaty interpretation was, and remains, low.

We now examine the dynamics of integration in two very different areas: the free movement of goods and the Europeanization of social provisions. While we cannot claim a representative sample, the cases selected vary along a number of dimensions, several of which deserve emphasis. The free movement of goods domain constitutes negative integration, the removal of national rules that hinder transnational exchange. A core value of the EC polity, the domain is the most highly developed of European law. The production of EC social provisions constitutes positive integration, the elaboration of positive, supranational rules that replace, or fix standards for, national rules governing in a particular area. Such rules regulate exchange among individuals and between individuals and their governments. Unlike negative integration processes, wherein the dominance of the ECJ and its case law is virtually total, the competence to make rules in the social provisions area is shared by the Court and the EC's legislative institutions, including the Council of Ministers, which has generally had the last word. Since the late 1970s, the EC legislator has produced five major directives on equal treatment and non-discrimination among the sexes in the workplace and in benefits. In negative integration processes, the potential for large collective gains from trade is obvious; in positive integration processes, the efficiency logic of integration is greatly reduced. Given these and other important differences, to the extent that the EC legal system operates in invariant, or similar, ways, our claims are better supported or undermined.

We begin with Art. 177 references. Recall that most references are triggered by litigants who claim that rules or practices in place in a member state are in non-compliance with EC law and request, nevertheless, that a national judge enforce EC law. Activated by these references, the ECJ was able to construct the EC legal system by taking decisions that voided the application of national rules and practices in favour of Euro-rules. Thus, most rulings are rendered in the bright light of clearly revealed preferences on the part of member states not to comply. This dynamic belies, on its face, intergovernmentalist assertions, like those of Garrett's (1992) and Garrett, Keleman, and Schultz (1996). And, as mentioned above, member-state governments participate directly in Art. 177 processes by regularly filing with the Court legal briefs defending the legality of their own, or any other member state's, rule, and indicating to the Court how they believe the dispute ought to be decided. Thus, in advance of any important decision, the ECJ is normally well informed of member-states preferences.

Congruent with our theory, we expect Art. 177 litigation to be patterned in predictable ways. In stating these expectations as testable propositions, we further clarify our differences with intergovernmentalists. First, other things being equal, references will target, disproportionately, those national barriers to transnational activity which hinder access to larger markets relative to smaller markets. The hypothesis can be tested by examining the impact of litigation on negative integration, that is, the removal of barriers to trade and other activity. Second, other things being equal, references will target, disproportionately, those national rules and practices that operate to downgrade the effect and application of European secondary rules. The legal system will operate to push lowest common denominator outcomes upwards—in a progressive, pro-integrative direction—nullifying the lawmaking effects of unanimity voting in the Council. The hypothesis can be tested by examining the affect of litigation on positive integration, via the production of harmonized European rules and their transposition into national legal regimes. Our general claim is, therefore, that the EC legal system works to dismantle barriers to transnational activity in place in the dominant member states, and to ratchet upwards lowest common denominator Euro-rules. If we are right, another proposition follows logically: governments' preferences will not have a significant impact on judicial outcomes. These claims and predictions conflict, fundamentally, with intergovernmentalist expectations.

Table 4.5. Article 177 references for free movement of goods and social provisions: percentage difference, actual number, and proportional share

Member state	Free movement of goods			Social provisions		
	Percentage difference	Actual number	Proportional share	Percentage difference	Actual number	Proportional share
Austria	−0.05	0	0.4	0.55	1	0.1
Belgium	−4.89	42	74.8	0.22	19	18.36
Denmark	−0.57	10	13.8	6.92	15	3.4
France	0.23	116	114.3	−12.90	7	28.5
Germany	9.32	265	202.3	−6.28	40	50.3
Greece	−0.73	3	7.9	−0.58	1	2.0
Ireland	−0.38	5	7.5	1.87	5	1.9
Italy	−0.82	84	89.4	−7.97	9	22.2
Luxembourg	−0.30	5	8.8	−0.45	1	2.2
Netherlands	−1.43	86	95.5	2.50	28	23.8
Portugal	0.51	7	3.6	−0.54	0	0.9
Spain	0.27	11	9.2	−0.77	1	2.3
Sweden	0.19	2	0.7	−0.11	0	0.1
UK	−1.34	34	42.9	17.54	40	10.7

Table excerpted from Table 4.6, produced in the Appendix. The Percentage difference column indicates the positive or negative extent to which litigants are attacking the rules of a particular member state in a particular legal domain relative to other member states and other areas. The Actual number column indicates the number of Art. 177 references in that legal domain in each member state. The Proportional share column indicates the number of references each member state *would have registered* if there were no difference between overall litigation rates for each member state and rates of litigation for each member state in each policy area. For instance, France accounts for slightly less than 17.1% of all references. Thus, France's Proportional share of Free movement of goods references is 17.1% of 670 total references in that category (114.3). In other words, the proportional share entries are from the table of no association (the basis for the chi-squared test). French courts made 116 references in this same legal domain. The French entry in the Percentage difference column is calculated as follows: (116 − 114.3)/670. Entries may differ slightly due to rounding.

Table 4.5 depicts cross-national patterns of litigation in the legal domains of free movement of goods and social provisions—the table excerpts material contained in Table 4.6, produced in the Appendix. The 'percentage difference' column provides us with a rough benchmark for evaluating these patterns. The 'actual' number column indicates the total number of

Art. 177 references registered in each member state per legal domain. The 'proportional share' column indicates the number of references each member state would have generated if there were no difference between overall litigation rates and rates of litigation in specific legal areas. Thus, if a member state accounted for 12 per cent of total references, we assigned a proportional share of 12 per cent of the references in each domain to that member state: in other words, they are entries from the table of no-association, the basis of the chi-squared test. Then we subtracted, for each category and for each member state, the predicted number of references from the actual number of references, and standardized the difference by percentage. Thus, the entries contained in the 'percentage difference' column consist of positive and negative percentages: a high positive value indicates that litigants are attacking the rules and practices of a particular country in a particular legal domain relative to other countries and other areas; a negative value indicates that a country is not being dragged to the ECJ as often as we might expect based on overall litigation rates relative to other member states and policy areas.

Note that in the free movement of goods domain accusations of German non-compliance dominate EC litigation. Of 670 references concerning the free movement of goods, 265—40 per cent—target German laws. This high percentage does not mean that Germany has been more protectionist than every other member state. It does mean that the German market, the largest EC market, is the key prize of free traders. Further, it means that the matrix of trade-relevant rules in place in Germany has provided the predominant context for the Court's construction of an integrative case law.

Confidence in our theory is further strengthened by empirical studies of outcomes. Kilroy (1996), in her analysis of free movement of goods cases, assessed the relationship between observations—the briefs filed by the Commission and the member states in pending cases—and the ECJ's rulings. She found that in 81 decisions—two-thirds of her pool—the Court struck down national rules as treaty violations, and that in 41 cases—a third of her pool—the Court upheld national rules as permissible under EC law. She further found that, in 98 of 114 cases in which the Commission intervened, the Court sided with the Commission. The Commission's position therefore 'predicted' the Court's decision 86 per cent of the time. Member-state interventions utterly failed to predict the Court's rulings; German interventions were found to be particularly ineffectual in generating outcomes. Following the logic of Garrett (1992), Kilroy (1996: 23) finds it 'surprising that Germany has a relatively lower impact on the Court'. But we do not. The Community's supranational institutions, especially the Commission and the Court, operate to facilitate transnational activity and to expand the effectiveness of

EC law, not to codify or give legal comfort to the preferences of dominant member states.

These numbers tell only a part of the story. As important has been the positive feedback of the Court's case law on integration processes. The free movement case law, initiated in 1974 with the *Dassonville* case (ECJ 1974*b*), sustained the integration project at a time when the legislative process was stalled by disputes between member states and between the Council of Ministers and the Commission (Gormley 1985; Oliver 1988). Out of this case law came the famous principle of mutual recognition of national standards, which the ECJ used to help construct the common market. In developing this principle, the Court demonstrated how member states might retain their own national rules, capable of being applied to the production and sale of domestic goods within the domestic market, while prohibiting the member states from applying these same rules to goods originating elsewhere in the Community. The ECJ's case law also placed member-state regulations in 'the shadow of the law', raising the spectre of relentless litigation against national rules that did not comply with the dictates of mutual recognition.

Simplifying a complex chain of events, the adjudication of free movement of goods disputes between traders and member states triggered a political process by which the Commission, in alliance with transnational business coalitions, converted mutual recognition into a general strategy that could be extended beyond free movement. That strategy ultimately resulted in the 1986 Single European Act. The literature on the Single Act has sufficiently demonstrated that member-state governments did not meaningfully control this process (Alter and Meunier-Aitshalia 1994; Dehousse 1994; Sandholtz and Zysman 1989). Instead, member-state governments were forced to adapt to it. Governments did act, of course, in negotiating a treaty that codified pro-integrative solutions to collective action problems (Moravcsik 1991), including the principle of mutual recognition. But most of these solutions had already emerged, out of the structured interactions between transnational actors, the Court, and the Commission.

We turn now to social provisions, the cluster of treaty rules and directives governing non-discrimination on the basis of sex in pay and employment benefits. Table 4.5 shows that litigation originating in the UK judiciary has driven the ECJ's docket in this area of the law. Fully 40 out of 167—24 per cent—of all references in the sector have attacked, as inconsistent with EC law, legal rules and administrative practices in the UK. It is well known that the UK government has constituted the crucial veto point in legislative deliberations within the Council of Ministers on social provisions (Pillinger 1992: 85–101). Indeed, since the first directive was adopted by the Council of Ministers in 1975, the UK government has not wavered in its intention, publicly declared, to veto any European proposal that would enshrine, in EC law, rules not already present in existing UK parliamentary statutes (Kenney 1992). The data show that, in this sector, litigation has disproportionately attacked the national rules and practices that represented the lowest common denominator position on EC secondary legislation adopted by the Council. Of course, this result depends as well on the fact that women workers are well supported through trade unions and special labour courts.

We then tested our predictions concerning outcomes and the impact of observations made by the Commission and the member-state governments, by examining all of the Court's judgments pursuant to Art. 177 references in the social provisions area from 1970—the date of the first reference in the area—through 1992.[14] Rulings were coded into one of two categories: either the Court had accepted a national rule or practice as consistent with EC law, or it had declared it to be in violation of EC law. Of the 91 judgments[15] that could be unambiguously coded into one of the two categories, the Court made declarations of violation of EC law in 48, a success rate for plaintiffs, individuals who had attacked the rules or practices in place in their own member-states, of 53 per cent. The ECJ considered the lawfulness of UK practices in 24 rulings, declaring violations in 13. If we aggregate results from litigation involving the big three—France, Germany, and the UK—the Court declared violations in 24 of 41 decisions: 59 per cent. We also found, as Kilroy had in the free movement area, that the Commission's observations tracked results far better than did the observations filed by governments. The Commission's success rate is a whopping 88 per cent: 73 of 83 observations predict the direction of the final ruling. The UK's rate of success was 58 per cent—31 of 54 observations tracked final results. These findings challenge the intergovernmentalist's assertion that the preferences of the most powerful member states constrain the Court in a systematic manner.

The impact of the ECJ's case law on national and supranational policy processes and outcomes in this area has been deep and pervasive. A large body of scholarship (for example, Ellis 1991; Harvey 1990; Kenney 1994; 1996; Pierson 1996a; Pillinger 1992; Prechal and Burrows 1990) has documented the extraordinary extent to which the ECJ has used its powers to creatively

[14] We were forced to exclude data that could otherwise have been collected from ECJ judgments rendered in 1993 (14 cases); as of December 1996, the European Court Reports for 1993 were unavailable, having been recalled to correct errors.

[15] We were forced to exclude data from ECJ judgments rendered in 1993, some 14 cases; the Court reports were unavailable, having been recalled to correct for errors.

interpret EC secondary legislation, like directives, and to ratchet up lowest common denominator positions taken in the Council of Ministers. Kenney, who has examined the relationship between EC and British sex discrimination law in great detail, has shown that by the mid-1980s 'the EC [had] eclipsed the British parliament as the arena of innovation' in sex discrimination law (1992: Ch. 3). British Conservative governments have been forced by national court decisions to ask Parliament, on successive occasions over the past 15 years, to amend British statutes to conform to the ECJ's evolving case law.[16] In this area, at least, lowest common denominator bargains struck in the Council of Ministers have not stuck. Instead, the Court has, more or less systematically, ratcheted obligations upwards in a pro-integration direction.

Finally, we examined the relationship between this case law and the work of the Council of Ministers. We found that the ECJ has used Art. 177 references to legislate, by judicial fiat, provisions vetoed in the Council of Ministers. In a wave of cases decided in 1990 and 1991, the ECJ boldly usurped the Council's legislative primacy by enacting, as a matter of treaty interpretation, the substance of provisions contained in three different legislative proposals.[17] Each of these bills had been drafted by the Commission either to extend non-discrimination provisions to new areas or to enhance the enforceability of Euro-rules on equal treatment in the national courts. And each had been vetoed by the UK, among other governments, in the Council.

Thus, outcomes in both of the legal domains examined are broadly consistent with predictions derived from our theory, but are inconsistent with intergovernmentalist propositions and expectations. Although our analysis does not constitute a definitive test, we are confident that our theory outperforms intergovernmentalism more generally.[18] Again, we have not argued

---

[16] Relative to other European judiciaries, one would expect the UK courts to enforce EC law only with great difficulty. The doctrine of parliamentary sovereignty formally prohibits judicial review of legislation, on any grounds, and doctrines governing the resolution of conflicts between treaty law and parliamentary statutes conflict with the ECJ's doctrine of supremacy. Both of these long-lived orthodoxies have been swept aside in areas governed by EC law, as the UK judiciary has incorporated as national law the doctrines of supremacy, direct effect, and indirect effect (Craig 1991; Levitsky 1994).

[17] The Court enacted: (1) in *Barber* (ECJ 1990*b*), abrogations of those provisions of the Equal Treatment (1976) and Social Security (1979) Directives that had permitted member states to derogate from principles of equal treatment in retirement pensions; (2) in *Dekker* (ECJ 1991*c*), the main provisions of the 'pregnancy directive', which were designed to protect pregnant women from discrimination; and (3) in *Hertz* (ECJ 1991*d*), the core elements of the proposed 'burden of proof' directive, which was designed to shift the burden to the member states in cases involving sex discrimination.

[18] Garrett (1992), Garrett, Keleman, and Schultz (1996), and Kilroy (1996) have seriously misspecified the Eurolaw 'game'. In their model, the game is dyadic, played by member states in one seat and the European Court in another. Inexplicably, they ignore two actors—private litigants

that member-state governments are irrelevant. It is our contention, however, that governments do not meaningfully control integration processes. Existing intergovernmentalist theories of integration may well help us to understand the bargaining processes that goes on in the Council of Ministers and in European summits. But this bargaining takes place within contexts constructed by processes explained by our theory.

In summary, we believe that the EC legal system operates according to a generalizeable dynamic. Individuals ask national judges to void national rules or practices in favour of EC legal rules within a particular domain of activity. Transnational dispute resolution—the interaction between litigants, national courts, and the ECJ—recasts the law governing that domain of activity, and therefore recasts the policy-making environment. As new rules are generated and existing rules are reinterpreted, member states whose national rules or practices are now out of step with EC rules are placed in an ever-creeping, ever-darker 'shadow of the law'. The Court's case law provides the Commission with the constitutional backing for its own policy-making goals to the extent that these goals are themselves integrative. And this case law enhances the capacity of individuals to initiate future litigation by providing potential litigants with more precise information about the content and scope of European law. Thus, in process tracing, we see again the self-sustaining dynamic that we theorized and that we found in the quantitative analysis.

Conclusion

We have proposed a theory of how a transnational, rule-of-law polity may emerge. This emergence, the theory implies, depends critically on the construction of causal linkages among three factors: exchange, triadic dispute resolution, and the production of legal rules. We derived a set of propositions from the theory, and tested them in the case of the European Community. We then cross-checked our quantitative results by process-tracing in two discrete areas of EC law. We found broad support for the general theory and for specific claims about how the EC legal system operates.

and national judges—who are crucial to how the legal system functions. Moravcsik (1993: 513) openly admits that his intergovernmentalism cannot explain the construction of the legal system. It is our contention that the operation of the legal system—highly structured interactions between private litigants, national judges, and ECJ—is at the very core of European integration processes writ large. Political scientists cannot begin to explain the dynamics of European integration without a coherent account of legal integration.

We emphasized the transformative effect of the ECJ's early case law, which 'constitutionalized' the treaty system. Relative to the EC as originally conceived by the member states, and relative to pure intergovernmental forums, constitutionalization made the Community far more responsive to the demands of transnational society—those who exchange across borders. In the EC, individuals can activate transnational adjudication processes on their own. In virtually all other international regimes, individuals must rely on intermediaries—usually representatives of governments—to press their claims and to pursue their other interests. But, in the EC, the operation of the legal system has progressively reduced the capacity of member-state governments to control policy outcomes, while enhancing the policy influence of the EC's supranational institutions, national judges, and private actors.

We end by suggesting that our theory may help us to understand the evolution of rule-of-law systems more generally. North (1990) has shown us that individual behaviour, governmental organizations, and rules often evolve symbiotically, determining a great deal of what is most important about modern economic and political systems. North has further argued that 'impersonal exchange with third party enforcement ... has been the critical underpinning' of successful modernization and political development (North 1990: 35). Shapiro (1981a) has demonstrated that courts are crucial to regime formation, state building, and the consolidation of political legitimacy. Judges, because they are agents of normative—rule-oriented— change in rule-of-law societies, possess the broad capacity to configure and to reconfigure the polity. Certainly they have done so in North America (for example, Horwitz 1977; Wolfe 1986; Russell, Knopff, and Morton 1989), in Europe (for example, Kommers 1989; Stone 1992a; Weiler 1991), and in some international regimes (for example, Hudec 1993). As we are now experiencing a 'global expansion of judicial power' (Tate and Vallinder 1995), we have every reason to theorize more rigorously the political impact of triadic dispute resolution.

Appendix

Table 4.6. Article 177 references: actual number, proportional share, and percentage difference by legal subject matter

	A	B	C	D	E	F	G	H	I	J	K	L	M	N
Austria	−0.05%	−0.05%	−0.05%	−0.05%	−0.05%	0.55%	−0.05%	−0.05%	−0.05%	−0.05%	1.42%	−0.05%	−0.05%	−0.05%
Actual number	0	0	0	0	0	1	0	0	0	0	1	0	0	0
Proportional share	0.4	0.4	0.1	0.3	0.2	0.1	0.2	0.1	0.1	0.1	0.04	0.2	0.1	0.3
Belgium	−4.89%	−6.83%	1.79%	−3.22%	17.56%	0.22%	−6.61%	5.91%	11.47%	−3.13%	7.96%	−8.94%	−0.52%	−0.21%
Actual number	42	33	29	5	112	19	2	28	31	20	13	1	15	66
Proportional share	74.8	85.1	25.0	7.0	43.5	18.4	4.9	18.3	15.3	27.8	7.6	5.0	16.8	67.3
Denmark	−0.57%	−0.10%	0.17%	−2.07%	−1.81%	6.92%	0.21%	−1.46%	−2.07%	4.36%	6.76%	0.16%	0.06%	−1.57%
Actual number	10	15	5	0	1	15	1	1	0	16	6	1	3	3
Proportional share	13.8	15.7	4.6	1.3	8.0	3.4	0.9	3.4	2.8	5.1	1.4	0.9	3.1	12.4
France	0.23%	−3.72%	13.72%	−1.21%	−4.01%	−12.90%	5.64%	0.60%	−5.41%	−3.43%	−5.32%	−8.20%	−0.07%	8.95%
Actual number	116	102	69	10	51	7	10	29	16	34	8	4	24	157
Proportional share	114.3	130.0	38.2	10.7	66.4	28.5	7.5	27.9	23.3	42.4	11.6	7.7	25.7	102.7
Germany	9.32%	13.54%	−11.03%	15.80%	−5.62%	−6.28%	−27.96%	−14.99%	0.43%	−0.91%	−2.29%	9.77%	−9.66%	−11.49%
Actual number	265	334	43	29	96	40	1	25	42	73	19	18	29	113
Proportional share	202.3	230.0	67.5	18.9	117.6	50.3	13.3	49.4	41.3	75.1	20.5	13.6	45.5	181.8
Greece	−0.73%	−0.26%	−0.29%	−1.18%	−0.67%	−0.58%	−1.18%	3.70%	−0.45%	−0.38%	−1.18%	−1.18%	−1.18%	−1.80%
Actual number	3	7	2	0	2	1	0	8	1	2	0	0	0	8
Proportional share	7.9	8.9	2.6	0.8	4.6	2.0	0.5	1.9	1.6	2.9	0.8	0.5	1.8	7.1
Ireland	−0.38%	1.23%	0.66%	−1.13%	−0.61%	1.87%	−1.13%	0.09%	−0.40%	−1.13%	−1.13%	3.32%	−1.13%	−0.63%
Actual number	5	18	4	0	2	5	0	2	1	0	0	2	0	3
Proportional share	7.5	8.6	2.5	0.7	4.4	1.9	0.5	1.8	1.5	2.8	0.8	0.5	1.7	6.8
Italy	−0.82%	1.71%	2.27%	−0.66%	−11.82%	−7.97%	32.10%	1.89%	−6.06%	2.30%	−7.48%	4.42%	10.05%	3.56%
Actual number	84	115	35	8	6	9	20	25	10	39	4	8	33	102
Proportional share	89.4	101.6	29.9	8.4	51.9	22.2	5.9	21.8	18.3	33.2	9.1	6.0	20.1	80.3

	A	B	C	D	E	F	G	H	I	J	K	L	M	N
Luxembourg	**−0.30%**	**−0.39%**	**−0.60%**	**−1.05%**	**−0.28%**	**−0.45%**	**−1.05%**	**1.39%**	**1.87%**	**−0.64%**	**0.42%**	**−1.05%**	**0.37%**	**0.94%**
Actual number	5	5	1	0	3	1	0	4	4	1	1	0	2	12
Proportional share	8.8	10.0	2.9	0.8	5.1	2.2	0.6	2.2	1.8	3.3	0.9	0.6	1.9	7.9
Netherlands	**−1.43%**	**−2.34%**	**−4.45%**	**0.02%**	**5.73%**	**2.50%**	**1.64%**	**−2.08%**	**−3.32%**	**3.00%**	**−2.51%**	**−0.94%**	**2.04%**	**1.65%**
Actual number	86	91	22	9	78	28	7	20	15	43	8	6	23	96
Proportional share	95.5	108.6	31.9	8.9	55.5	23.8	6.3	23.3	19.5	35.4	9.7	6.4	21.5	85.8
Portugal	**0.51%**	**−0.54**	**1.25**	**−0.54**	**−0.28**	**−0.54**	**−0.54**	**0.07%**	**−0.54%**	**0.67%**	**0.93%**	**1.69%**	**0.17%**	**−0.37%**
Actual number	7	0	4	0	1	0	0	1	0	3	1	1	1	1
Proportional share	3.6	4.1	1.2	0.3	2.1	0.9	0.2	0.9	0.7	1.3	0.4	0.2	0.8	3.2
Spain	**0.27%**	**−1.11**	**1.31**	**−1.37**	**−0.09**	**−0.77**	**−1.37**	**4.73%**	**−0.64%**	**−0.16%**	**−1.37%**	**−1.37%**	**1.47%**	**−0.04%**
Actual number	11	2	6	0	5	1	0	10	1	3	0	0	4	8
Proportional share	9.2	10.4	3.1	0.9	5.3	2.3	0.6	2.2	1.9	3.4	0.9	0.6	2.1	8.2
Sweden	**0.19%**	**−0.11%**	**−0.11%**	**−0.11%**	**−0.11%**	**−0.11%**	**−0.11%**	**0.50%**	**−0.11%**	**−0.11%**	**−0.11%**	**−0.11%**	**−0.11%**	**0.06%**
Actual number	2	0	0	0	0	1	0	1	0	0	0	0	0	1
Proportional share	0.7	0.8	0.2	0.1	0.4	0.1	0.1	0.2	0.2	0.3	0.1	0.1	0.2	0.7
UK	**−1.34%**	**−1.04%**	**−4.63%**	**−3.24%**	**2.05%**	**17.54%**	**0.41%**	**−0.31%**	**5.27%**	**−0.39%**	**3.88%**	**2.48%**	**−1.45%**	**−2.60%**
Actual number	34	41	4	2	33	40	3	10	16	15	7	4	7	23
Proportional share	42.9	48.8	14.3	4.0	24.9	10.7	2.8	10.5	8.8	15.9	4.4	2.9	9.7	38.5

A = Free Movement of Goods; B = Agriculture; C = Competition & Dumping; D = External Policy; E = Social Security; F = Social Provisions; G = Environment; H = Establishment; I = Free Movement of Workers; J = Taxes; K = Transportation; L = Common Policy; M = Approximation of Laws; N = Other. Actual number indicates the number of Art. 177 references in that legal domain for each member state. Proportional share entries are the number of cases that each member state *would have registered* in each legal domain if there were no difference between overall litigation rates for each member state and rates of litigation for each policy area. Thus, if Germany accounts for 30% of the references overall we assigned a Proportional share of 30% of the references in each policy area to Germany. In other words, Proportional share is the 'table of no association'—the basis of the chi-squared test. Bold entries are 'Percentage differences', which are calculated the following way: (Actual number-Proportional share)/total number of references in the legal domain. These entries are indicative of the positive or negative extent to which litigants are attacking the rules of a particular member state in a particular legal domain relative to other member states and other areas.

5

Judges and Company

In this chapter, we examine how lawyers and law professors, operating in private arenas, successfully revived a pre-modern legal system, the *Lex Mercatoria*. Shapiro's 'The Globalization of Freedom of Contract' deals, first, with the unification of private law in the United States in the 1920s, which he then uses as a benchmark to assess the massive post-Second World War movement to a global law of contract. Stone Sweet's 'Islands of Transnational Governance' traces the development of a transnational legal system, comprised of anational contract law and a network of arbitration houses that compete to supply third-party dispute resolution to the international commercial world. In addition to the more specific arguments made in the papers, we are attracted to the new Law Merchant for some more general reasons worth noting.

First, the rise of commercial arbitration offers an opportunity, always unusual, to explore further questions of how new judicial systems emerge and institutionalize. Because arbitration falls between mediation and adjudication on the continuum of triadic dispute resolution (TDR) (see Chapters 1 and 4), it allows us to treat the dynamics of TDR and judicialization in their more general guises, without having to start or end with state courts.

Second, the new *Lex Mercatoria* is a hugely significant fact of globalization, an example of the successful construction of a transnational political system by private actors. Political science's focus on public, to the exclusion of private, forms of governance seems to us unjustified, unjustifiable, and self-defeating.[1] The calls for more general theory, and recurrent complaints of an alleged 'small-n problem', cannot be squared with the discipline's embarrassing failure to expand its own property space to include private institutions, organizations, authority relations (Eckstein 1973). As these papers suggest, the *Lex Mercatoria* is rapidly emerging as a relatively comprehensive system of governance, one that will increasingly condition how state actors, including courts, manage markets.

---

[1] See also Chapter 2.

Third, we are sympathetic to the goals of those seeking to develop more sociologically based and political understanding of the relationship between institutions, firms, and markets—the manifesto of 'economic sociology' is Fligstein (2001). With the decline of such projects in political science, exemplified by the Yale school and Lindblom's *Politics and Markets* (1977), economists have enjoyed something of a monopoly on this topic, to the detriment of social science as a whole. We can hardly study how institutions and markets influence one another without the notions of efficiency and equilibria, the logics of which economists have done so much to elucidate. Yet how these logics operate may vary across time and space; and they may interact with other logics to produce quite different outcomes. These issues are as empirical as they are theoretical, and they deserve much more attention from students of law and courts.

In turning to public law political science, this chapter touches on crucial aspects of politics and governance that are rarely noticed by the sub-field: the relationship between law firms, their corporate clients, and judges. One early lesson of political jurisprudence was that judges could not be considered in isolation from broader networks of legal elites. More generally, we have argued that social scientists need to pay careful attention to what happens both before and after judicial decisions, through the activities of litigators and professors of law (for example, Shapiro 1990*b*; Shapiro and Stone 1994; Stone 1992: Ch. 4; Stone Sweet 2000: Ch. 5). At a minimum, litigants activate courts, and thus it is obvious that patterns of litigation partly fix the parameters for how judges impact politics. Further, courts really never have 'the last word' on any important legal question. Judges redistribute values and resources with their decisions, and thereby create categories of winners and losers within society. People react to what courts do, and often enough they react by reactivating the courts. Apart from a concern for litigants past and future, both of us view legal scholars as political actors who are *always* of potential import. There are deep symbiotic relationships between courts and the legal academy, and these help to legitimize judicial power and to shape legal outcomes in other ways. As a research strategy, we always assume that if we see lawyers and law professors begin to behave differently, then something of interest just may be afoot.

The practice of lawyers is less visible than the very public and heavily documented output of judges and law professors, and therefore marginally more difficult to study. In their ground-breaking study of divorce lawyers, Sarat and Felsteiner (1995) used as an epigram at the head of one of their chapters a quotation from an old Shapiro piece: 'law is not what judges say in the reports but what lawyers say to one another and to clients in their offices' (Shapiro

1981*b*: 1201). The borrowing from Justice Holmes is obvious. In another, even older, article, Shapiro (1971*b*) attempted to persuade academic lawyers that they ought to study lawyering as well as law in the formal sense. At the time, the response was that lawyering was human behaviour rather than law, and therefore ought to be studied by social scientists, not by lawyers. Subsequently some of them began to study lawyers (for example, Gibson and Mnookin 1989). Political scientists who studied law and courts ignored lawyering because they were fixated on government officials, and most lawyers were private actors. Under the rubric 'sociology of professions', lawyers, like doctors and army officers, were left to sociologists. Although a few political scientists produced studies of government lawyers (for example, Irons 1982; Kagan 1978; Weaver 1977), it has taken until quite recently for some political scientists to begin to study private lawyers (for example, Kagan 1985; Kritger 1990; Mather 1998; Sarat and Scheingold 1998).

Litigation markets are a complex form of governance (see Chapters 2 and 4). If litigation markets help legal actors achieve effective levels of communication and coordination between non-hierarchically organized courts, lawyers are the prospective buyers in that market. If appeal is a mode of insuring the control of top courts over bottom ones and more generally of improving central government control over its local operatives, lawyers actually drive the system by counselling clients on whether an appeal is worthwhile. On the basis of their reading of previous court decisions, it is lawyers who initially decide what new legal arguments are plausible, activate courts, establish the menu of options from which judges normally select, and thus help to trace the paths along which judicial lawmaking moves. Lawyers provide a support group that turns out to be crucial to successful judicial review.

In a review article of a massive, comparative sociological study of lawyers, Shapiro (1990*b*) mustered some of these same arguments. We ought to concentrate on the study of big firms and lawyers who serve corporate clients, that is, on 'business lawyers', because they are far more significant to both lawmaking and the health of the profession than are, say, suburban divorce lawyers. The simple-minded proposition was then offered that, in studying business lawyers, looking at business was probably more important than looking at lawyers. The ways and means of big corporate organizations would determine the fate of the lawyers that served them. As big corporations turned from vertical integration, in which coordination problems were internalized, to conceiving of themselves as pure bundles of management skill and capital seeking profit, business lawyers would wield greater influence and enjoy greater prosperity. For such corporations would seek profit by any arrangement that was appropriate to a particular profitable task, including mergers and acquisitions, partnership, franchising, joint ventures, concession management, research grants, subcontracting, short- and long-term leasing, supply arrangements, and so on. All of these involve external rather than purely internal coordination, and so are accomplished by contract rather than hierarchical command. If business thrived on contracts then it followed that lawyers would thrive on business.

In a number of Shapiro's (1993*b*; 1996*a*) pieces on the 'globalization of law', it was pointed out that, while globalization had some public law aspects, its principal manifestation in law was probably in the transnational contract and commercial law required by the big multinational organizations. Contract law is an arena where, within the overarching law and office imposed by political regimes, private parties do continue to choose their own consensual triadic conflict resolvers and their own rules of decision to be employed by that resolver. That is contracts, by mutual consent of the signatories, create the body of rules under which conflicts that arise between the parties will be resolved. Many contracts also provide that the triadic figure shall not be a government judge but a private arbitrator specified by mutual agreement of the signatories. In transnational contracts, the parties may even choose by mutual consent what nation's law shall provide the overarching rules under which the private rules written into the contract shall operate, or even that a national, general principles of contract law shall provide the overarching rules.

All of this leads on to the papers on transnational law presented here. Clearly, 'global' harmonization of contract law is occurring faster by the evolution of the contract-writing practices of big law firms writing big contracts for big business than it is by international agreements among sovereign states (Shapiro 2000). This chapter seeks to catch in mid-stream a rapidly developing political process in which law is made by the interaction of government officials, including judges, organized interests, particularly multinational corporations, *and* an array of networks or epistemic communities, particularly business lawyers, international arbitrators, and legal scholars. This is one of the central stories of *governance*—as opposed to government—in the contemporary world. Put differently, it is a central story of international 'regime building' in which states are major, but not the sole major or even the dominant, participants. Shapiro's paper on transnational lawyer contract practice as the vehicle of lawmaking goes hand in hand with Stone Sweet's paper on arbitration as private international governance structures. They illustrate how *government* turns into *governance*.

Globalization of Freedom of Contract

Martin Shapiro

The expression 'freedom of contract' means a number of different things in different contexts. In American constitutional history, freedom of contract is a constitutional icon of laissez faire having nothing particularly to do with contract. In this context, freedom of contract stands for a substantive due-process right of entrepreneurs to be free of government regulation in all their business activities, contractual and otherwise, or at least free of unreasonable government regulation. It was particularly invoked against government wages and hours regulation (see Currie 1985). In contexts other than the American constitutional one, and particularly in the context of the nineteenth century civil law, freedom of contract was the banner of a theory of contract law, and of private law more generally, that emphasized the free will of individuals and the role of law in facilitating and supporting the freedom of individuals to make whatever social and economic arrangements among themselves they wish to make. In the twentieth century the civil law world, and the common law as well, speaks more of contract than freedom of contact. And contract law is seen not only as facilitative and supportive of freedom of contract but of the regulation of contract behaviour as well (see Eisenberg 1997). In this sense contract law is subtractive from as well as additive to the 'natural' freedom to contract.

Most of this is no doubt better and more completely rehearsed by those who have gone before me, but the regulative aspects of contract law are particularly important when we move to something referred to as the globalization of freedom of contract. So is the distinction between the legal practice of contracting and contract law. I will treat contract law as a form of government regulation of contract practice. Most forms of regulation actually involve the government in both fostering and restricting the regulated activity. We can certainly see 'globalized' contract law as both fostering and restricting the freedom of contract.

If 'freedom of contact' contains a number of ambiguities and cross currents, 'globalization' contains even more. 'Globalization' is a current catchphrase apparently coined either for sheer glamour or because someone thought that 'international' and 'internationalization' was, in its very announcement of the transcendence of nation, still redolent of our obsolescent fascination with the nation state (Dellbruck 1993; Shapiro 1993*b*; Wiegand 1996; Shapiro 1996*a*). The globalization of contracts would mean contracting behaviour that, more or less, treated national boundaries as irrelevant. And the globalization of contract law would be a body of law that, more or less, operated without reference to national legal systems.

The Law of Merchants

The 'globalization' of contract—not contract law, but the practice of contracting—is a fairly easy matter to get a handle on. There is, of course, a very long history of international trade and of the invention by merchants, bankers, and carriers of forms of agreement to facilitate that trade. Perhaps in this area of human endeavour, more than most, the sequence of chicken and egg involving social practices and law is clear. Here, the social practice comes first and the law comes tumbling after. The endlessly recalled merchants and money lenders of the medieval fairs, Hanseatic navigators, and so on create business customs, usages, practices, and written instruments that the law subsequently absorbs. Much of the law, indeed, is not nationally enacted statutory law but the mere recognition and adoption of business practices by courts called upon the settle disputes between merchants (Trakman 1983). Furthermore, many of the courts that do the adopting are not themselves purely organs of national or other governments but rather are pie powder or fair courts—courts in which the judges are themselves merchants to whom government powers are delegated to enforce their own practices (see Constable 1993; Milgrom, North, and Weingast 1990).

Given the history, the notions of globalization of freedom of contact or contract law, then, are fairly easy to follow. First, markets become global, and businesses become transnational. The transnational businesses engaging in global transactions perforce must enter into global agreements or local agreements that are globally similar. The law then globalizes to meet these practical business needs. Globalization of law in this context is simply the story of the Law Merchant all over again. We can expect that the globalization of contact law will simply be the writing into court practice of whatever business practices the global economy throws up. The legal materials—that is, the statutes, treaties, judicially and academically announced legal doctrines, model codes, and so on and so forth, will simply formalize that which the entrepreneurs and their customers have freely arrived at. Freedom of contract comes first and the law of contracts comes after.

Only one black mark seems to mar this historical picture. Historically the *Lex Mercatoria*, the international body of trade law, derived from merchant practice, came to be enforced mostly by regular national courts, not special merchant courts (Goldman 1984). 'Private international law' did not come to include a substantive body of contract law. Instead, private international law responded to international contracting practices by evolving a huge body of procedural law, 'conflict of laws', designed to shove disputes arising under international commercial agreements into one or another of the national court systems and under one or another of the national bodies of contract law (see Webb 1985). It is true that national courts hearing such disputes would take into account all sorts of particular and peculiar international trade practices and the various legal materials that encapsulated them, but alternatively they remained national courts enforcing national law. Indeed, much of the current concern with globalizing, harmonizing, and/or unifying contract law arises from the palpable inconveniences that continue to arise when transnational business disputes must be resolved by national courts applying national law.

Beyond this one little cloud, there is another and larger problem that causes some disturbance to the picture of pure freedom of contract, that is, of business evolving its own agreements practices with the law merely following on to confirm them. Throughout its history in the Western world a fundamental tension has existed between a norm of contract as signifying the free will of the parties and contract as achieving a just, fair, or equitable exchange. Again, this story has been so often told so well by scholars so much better equipped to do so that I need hardly rehearse it again here. Particularly in the first half of the twentieth century, by court decision and often by statute, new contract law was created that did not simply reflect evolving contracting practices. Instead, this new law was specifically designed to counter evolving contracting practices that increasingly favoured the more over the less economically powerful. Labour contracts, consumer credit contracts, leases, and so on became the targets of law reform that demanded that contracts be fair even when the parties were 'willing' to enter into unfair ones. Thus by the time we begin to speak of the globalization of contract law, contract law itself involves not only facilitating the freedom of contract but impinging on that freedom in the name of fairness (see Eisenberg 1976).

As we all know, most of these regulative aspects of contact law are conceived as attempts to remedy unfairness arising from radical disparities in the economic power of certain classes of contracting parties such as creditors and debtors. Globalization of contract law particularly involves contracting between business enterprises, so that the context is not one of radical disparities between the parties. Nevertheless, where globalization takes the form of transnational harmonizations or unifications of existing bodies of national contract law, the regulative aspects already introduced into those bodies of national law are likely to be introduced into the global law as well simply because they are there. Moreover the 'North–South' or 'developed–developing' dimensions of the international economic arena are likely to trigger fairness concerns and thus interest in the regulative as well as the supportive aspects of contract law. Even where most of the contracting parties are corporations and governments, on the current international scheme some contracting parties are clearly more equal than others (see Laing 1993).

To the extent that the globalization of contract law is about harmonization and/or unification of national contract law and also about the further development of the traditional *Lex Mercatoria*, the story to be told is fairly simple. Globalizing markets lead to global contracting. Global contracting practices then call forth global contracting law. But as contract law globalizes, it not only concerns itself with fostering and facilitating contracting across national boundaries but also concerns itself with insuring that such contracts will be fair.

The story is not as simple as this, however, because the globalization of contract practice involves not only the projection of former domestic contract practices onto a global screen but also a more or less radical change in contracting practices themselves. To put the matter crudely, globalization of contact practices is, to a very great degree, the spread of the American style of long, detailed contract, concocted by large American law firms for a very high fee, to the rest of the world. This contract gigantism is further aggravated by, or indeed perhaps even caused by, the increasingly complex interrelationships that business enterprises have invented. The more complex the relationships, necessarily the more complex are the contracts governing them—at least, so it can be argued.

Conflict of Laws, *Lex Mercatoria*, General Principles, and Arbitration

Legal scholarship has always found it easier to note and describe what legislatures and courts do, and what legal scholars themselves do, than to describe what lawyers and clients do. Accordingly I will go at contract matters backwards, first looking at globalizing tendencies in contract law, doctrine, and jurisprudence where it is relatively easy to pin down what is going on and then moving to globalizing tendencies in contract practice where what I have to say is far more speculative and unsupported by scholarly studies.

Contract law is, first and foremost, an authorization or acknowledgement of a realm of private lawmaking in which by mutual agreement parties create their own law to govern some mutual undertaking (Goetz and Scott 1980). Precisely because the realm is one of private lawmaking, it has always seemed appropriate that the parties also structure a private mechanism for resolving conflicts that arise under the private law and within the private endeavour they are jointly undertaking.

The base line from which recent globalization tendencies can be measured is conflict of laws (see ' Symposium: Conflict of Laws in the Global Village' 1995). Much of the body of legal doctrine we know as 'conflict of laws' has been engendered in the context of contract litigation. Where contracting parties or contracted transactions straddle legal jurisdictional boundaries, to the courts of which jurisdiction and which state or national body of contract law should contract litigation be assigned? Conflict of laws is a set of non-consensual responses to this problem. The law itself, not the parties, chooses the jurisdiction for litigation. Conflict of laws is a great traditional and continuing mode of facilitating cross-boundary contracting.

Conflict of laws, however, runs against the grain of the consensual nature of contacting. Thus contracting parties frequently seek to substitute their own consensual choices of jurisdiction for those imposed by conflict of laws.

The most familiar form of such jurisdiction by contract provisions is that which explicitly provides that litigation concerning the contract shall take place in the courts and under the law of a specified state. Here is the paradox that parties contracting across boundaries can, to a degree, defeat the boundary problem by themselves localizing the dispute resolution process. But parties may choose to push even further along the private and consensual route. Thus mediation or arbitration clauses frequently appear in contracts. If we conceive of triadic conflict resolution as arranged along a continuum from go-between through mediator to arbitrator and judge (Shapiro 1981a), contract provisions invoke a rather broad range of the continuum. Some contracts invoke more or less pure mediation, in which the triadic figure is substantively unbound by the law of the contract and simply proposes or assists the parties in proposing various alternative resolutions until one is struck to which both parties will agree. Further up the spectrum toward judging, we encounter arbitration clauses in which the arbiter is bound by the substantive law of the contract but, by the terms of the contract, is placed in a 'paternal' relationship to the parties enjoined to impose a resolution that will be benevolent to both the conflicting parties. Contracts may provide that the arbitrator act as an 'amiable compositor' guided by equity (Lando 1985). Next comes the arbitrator who is in reality merely a privately employed judge who is enjoined to enforce upon the parties the substantive law of the contract. And, of course, finally we encounter contracts that deviate from a regime of free litigation by the parties only to the extent of constraining them to bring their lawsuits within a particular jurisdiction.

Where pure mediation is involved, it may be argued that contract law as such, globalized or otherwise, is irrelevant because the mediator is concerned only with eliciting the consent of the parties, not in enforcing legal obligations upon them. In the language sometimes used for labour contracts, this is pure 'interest mediation'. Even here, however, the more widely accepted various principles and doctrines of contract law become, the more easily the two parties may come to a common understanding of what is fair under the contract. And, of course, if such mediation is done 'under the shadow of the law' or 'under the shadow jurisdiction of a court', that is, if it is done under the threat of future litigation if the mediation fails, then such principles may loom even larger for the parties. Where we move to amiable compositor-style arbitration, shared principles and doctrines may play an even larger role because arbitrators often find citation of shared principles to be a successful route to benevolent conflict resolution. Where arbitration is private judging, such shared principles are even more powerful, indeed, more powerful than they are for state judges. For the private judge is likely to feel somewhat less bound by the particulars of any one state's formal contract law than is the judge on the state's payroll.

All this is preliminary to saying that the Lex Mercatoria often plays a substantial part in the resolution of contract disputes particularly where arbitration is involved. A strong argument can be made that the Lex Mercatoria has been acquiring growing status among arbitrators (Lando 1985) and even that 'general principles' of contract law are increasingly employed by arbitrators (Note 1988). The more conservative position is that the Lex Mercatoria or general principles of law may be employed only in conjunction with and as a supplement to some national system of contract law. The more 'globalized' perspective would hold that arbitrators may consider some contracts to be totally stateless and appropriate for arbitral judgments derived entirely from non-national sources (see Carbonneau 1990).

Whatever the theory, in actual practice a large number of international contracts with arbitration clauses now either remain entirely silent about the choice of substantive law or invoke the *Lex Mercatoria* or general principles of law without any invocation of any particular national law of contract. Or having specified some national law, or some national body of conflict-of-law rules that can be used to choose the appropriate national substantive law, they then go on to specify *Lex Mercatoria* or general principles of law as additional sources of law for the arbitrator. Perhaps the increasing popularity of such non-national government or globalized substantive law has its origins in the many situations where one of the parties is private and the other is a government or one of its instruments. The private party does not wish the contract governed by either the national law or the national courts of the national contracting party. The national government finds it beneath its dignity to submit to the law and courts of another nation state. Arbitration under the *Lex Mercatoria* and/or general principles of law may then be appealing to both parties.

In general, even in arbitrations, and even where the parties have remained silent or even explicitly sought to avoid all national law, the decision maker will employ some rather traditional choice of law process to implicate some national body of substantive contact law, or perhaps the sum of several bodies of such law, because the *Lex Mercatoria* and general principles are both admittedly rather uncertain and incomplete bodies of law. Nevertheless, particularly where the parties themselves have given prominence to these bodies of law in their contract provisions on substantive law and/or have chosen an amiable compositor style for arbitration, arbitration is likely to involve a legal technique that is far more global than national.

A further complexity is added, of course, by the need to achieve the enforcement of arbitral awards by national courts (see Volz and Haydock 1996). Presumably no national court will enforce an arbitral award that violates strong national public policy whether it is based on non-national or national law. Some national courts, most notably those of France, will enforce arbitral awards based solely on the *Lex Mercatoria*. While the courts of some other states may explicitly decline to do so, the general tendency of courts to avoid searching review of an arbiter's substantive judgments, together with the arbitral practice of mixing global and national sources in various ways, means that arbitrators may rely fairly heavily on non-national law without much fear that their awards will be unenforceable. For instance, where arbitrators interpret contract provisions or a provision of national contract law itself 'in the light of' the *Lex Mercatoria* or as incorporating certain general principles of law, their awards are hardly likely to be refused national court enforcement on that ground.

If we look at the broad picture of globalization here, there is an obvious tension not so much between globalization and nationalism as between certainty and equity. And that tension runs along two contrary vectors. *Lex Mercatoria*, trade practices, and general principles promise the parties and the arbitrators some flexibility in achieving fair outcomes where explicit national contract rules might do otherwise in a particular fact situation. The potential for fairness, however, is bought at the cost of increasing uncertainty of the law as we move from the specificity and relative completeness of national contract law to the vagaries of 'general principles'. Along a quite different vector the movement is the opposite. When contracting with certain governments, private parties may believe that the *Lex Mercatoria* yields both greater certainty and fairness than the law of the host state even when applied by an outside arbitrator.

In spite of the uncertainties it creates, movement toward the *Lex Mercatoria* or general principles, particularly in contracts with arbitration clauses, is fuelled both by the general international inclination towards granting the parties the broadest freedom in choosing the substantive law of their contracts and by the appeal of 'lottery' solutions to the bargaining problems encountered by certain contracting parties in certain situations. Where any national law chosen appears to give undue advantage to one or the other of the parties, and both wish to avoid the high transaction costs of seeking to write a whole scheme of fundamental contract law into the contract itself, then invoking an arbitrator and the *Lex Mercatoria* and/or general principles allows the contract to be completed now with legal questions deferred to a future black box. The two parties share the uncertainty costs, and hope that future legal costs will never be incurred. The extreme solution of this sort is, of course, the provisions for an amiable compositor.

It should also be noted that the desire of some academics and arbitration specialists to emphasize the *Lex Mercatoria*, like the various European and UN efforts to draft model contract laws which we are about to look at, constitute a counter-current to the Americanization of transnational contract practice and contact law that appears to be a major feature of globalization. If the *Lex Mercatoria* achieves a central importance in the law that international commercial arbitrators employ, that is really to say that an essentially civilian, Continental body of learning largely cultivated by European academics becomes a central source of law (Dezelay and Garth 1996).

Trans-State Harmonization of Contract Law and Doctrine

The pattern that emerges from the development of the *Lex Mercatoria*, particularly at the least judge-like end of the arbitration range but even at the more judge-like end and in the work of national judges themselves, is one of relatively general principles of contract law along with some specific practices that have developed into such settled expectations that they can be used as legal rules. Either alternative to, or growing out of, or formalizing the *Lex Mercatoria* are various formal bodies of written transnational or multinational contract law enacted or announced by various transnational or multinational bodies, governmental or otherwise. The US Uniform Commercial Code (UCC) is the most familiar of these. Composed by a quasi-official body, the Commission on Uniform State Laws, it is a model code which State legislatures were free to adopt or not. Eventually most States adopted the Code in whole or in part, and it has been highly influential in judicial lawmaking as well. It consists in part of relatively specific legal formalizations for particular commercial practices and in part of much more general principles and rules. Its companion is the Restatement (Second) of Contracts, the product of a private body, the American Law Institute. These two efforts play out the globalization theme in miniature—if something as large as the US can ever be called miniature. Contract law remains State law. Contract disputes remain subject to conflict of laws assignment to one State or another. But trans-State models for parallel or harmonized State contract law are offered and widely accepted.

Since the Second World War a spate of international endeavours of a comparable kind have been launched. There was the Uniform Sales Law of the Hague of 1964, which was subscribed to almost exclusively by Western European states. It was followed by the 1986 Hague Convention on the Law Applicable to Contracts for the International Sale of Goods, which has been joined by a wider range of states.[1] The United Nations Commission on International Trade Law has produced the UNCITRAL Legal Guide on Drawing Up International Contracts for the Construction of Industrial Works (1988). There is a UNCITRAL Model Law on International Commercial Arbitration (1980).[2] The European Communities produced a convention on the Law Applicable to Contractual Obligations (1980). An array of model contract provisions of various specialized kinds such as the Conditions of Contract

---

[1] See also The United Nations Convention on the Contracts for the International Sale of Goods 1980.

[2] UNCITRAL publishes an annual yearbook in which its various legal guides and model laws can be followed.

for Works of Civil Engineering Construction have been produced by private groups (Fédération Internationale des Ingenieurs-Conseils 1987). The EEC funds a project by the International Institute for the Unification for Private Law that prepared a number of drafts of 'Principles for International Commercial Contracts'(see 'Symposium: Contract Law in a Changing World' 1992). It has now completed a major project on principles of European contract law (Lando 1995).

From all of these endeavours certain basic strands emerge. First, there appears to be no inclination to create larger-than-traditional jurisdictions to match the increasing geographic reach of contracting. The American states and the nation-states of the rest of the world are to remain the basic jurisdictions for the resolution of contract disputes, at least when the resolutions take place in formal courts. Globalization only means a multiplication of model provisions, international conventions, and so on, which individual states may choose to adopt *in toto* or in part or particular parties may choose to introduce into their contracts. Only if and when particular contracting parties choose to bind themselves by arbitration clauses that establish an arbitrator not bound by the contract law of a particular state would we have something like a conflict resolution jurisdiction that ran as wide as the contract runs.

Second, all of the attempts to do contract law on a larger scale incorporate the basic tensions, dialectics, and antinomies that surface within particular states when contract restatement, codification, or systematization are in the wind. While much effort is spent in careful collection and systematization of existing law, elements of reform or change are also present. The usual debate rages about whether contract law should merely formalize successful business practices or accept some and reject others. The familiar tension is evident between meeting of the minds theories and fairness theories, and between moral or keeping promises theories and economic or risk-bearing or efficient breach theories of contract. Some approaches to contract emphasize the goal of each party fully understanding exactly what he is promising and being promised. Others emphasize a normative concern for fairness even if the parties seem to have clearly agreed to some things that are unfair. Some emphasize a moral norm of keeping the promises made in contracts. Others see nothing wrong in promises being broken so long as the breaker compensates the other party for any injuries he suffers from the failure to keep the promise. Thus some bodies of contract law are especially concerned that the contract be objectively fair to both sides while others are especially concerned that the contrast accurately expresses what each party wants and attains subjective agreement between the two.

One approach emphasizes the facilitative side of contract law. If the parties really want something, and truly understand what they are getting, then it is the business of government to assure they get it even if it is actually unfair to one of them. The other emphasizes the regulative role of government. The government ought not to enforce unfairness even if the parties seem to have wanted it. Along another dimension, some contract regimes place great emphasis on what was promised actually being done. They incline toward authorizing judges to order the parties to do what they have promised to do. Other regimes are inclined towards allowing parties not to keep their promises when it would cost them more to keep the promise than to compensate the other party for their failure to do so. They incline towards authorizing judges to award monetary damages against those who break promises but not authorizing judges to order those who break promises to do what they have promised to do. The differences between the two approaches rest in part on a disagreement about morality. Should the state enforce a morality of promise keeping? Or should it pursue economic efficiency as the primary value behind contract law? In part the difference arises out of differing estimates of the long-term public interest. Will the society flourish best if the government intervenes to enforce promises or intervenes to ensure efficiency? Because common law generally has been loath to require specific performance, instead favouring money damages, and civil law has been much more favourable to performance remedies, these debates over fundamental contract questions are often expressed as differences between civil law and common law theories or between performance or damage remedies. But the basic tensions are to be found within as well as between the common law and civil law families.

Third, partly as a result of these tensions and partly as a result of the universal consciousness that the details of contracting and broader commercial practices are complex and constantly changing, all the efforts at composing harmonized or globalized contract law tend to run heavily toward a mix of rather generally stated principles and what amount to capsules of well-settled particular practices. There seems to be fairly widespread agreement that a detailed international code of contract law cannot and should not be written (Joerges 1995).

Fourth, these attempts at harmonized law tend to vest judges with a good deal of discretion. In part such judicial discretion is inevitable if harmonized law is to be a set of general principles. In part, however, the resort to judicial discretion represents a rather strong current in legal scholarship, at least among the scholars who pursue these efforts towards an increasingly moral theory of contracts. No doubt because of the preponderance of civil lawyers involved, the emphasis tends to be on *pacta sunt servanda*, that is, that contract promises must be kept. Theories of risk allocation or efficient breach, which, in effect, say that you may break contract promises if you are willing to pay the costs to others generated by your doing so, are banished (Cooter and Ulen 1988: Chapter 6). Therefore specific performance is typically incorporated in parallel to money damages. The very same academic lawyers, however, do not subscribe to a pure meeting of the minds theory of contract. Instead they are much concerned with reasonableness, equitableness, and fairness. These concerns increase if those in breach cannot even choose to pay and walk away. As a result, the new drafting efforts are full of escape hatches for situations in which what the words of the contract seem to compel would result in grave injustice to one of the parties. Given the complex and changing circumstances attendant on contemporary contracts, these escape hatches tend to be written as discretions vested in judges to mitigate contract-compelled injustices rather than detailed rules for contract escape. The result necessarily is not only judicial discretion for individual cases but a kind of declaration by drafters that in spite of their best efforts much of the law will continue to be judge-made case law (Lando 1995).

Perhaps the most interesting feature of the globalization efforts flows directly from those already noted. There is the strong sense, based on historical knowledge, that whatever the law written by legislators, judges, and lawyers says, actual business practices will be the principal source of contract law. To the extent that certain of those practices become global, the law will follow suit as to both geographic reach and substance. On the other hand, there is the strong sense that if global contract law is to be a set of general principles and a call for just and fair results, then judges of different national or sub-national legal cultures will decide contract cases to a significant degree in the light of those differing cultures. Perhaps it take a good deal of optimism to engage in trans-cultural lawmaking efforts, but there certainly is a kind of Pollyanna-ish quality to what is going on. In spite of the endless debates one would expect among academic lawyers, there is the almost open declaration that, no matter what we do, we cannot do any real damage, because business practice will overwhelm any mistake we make in formal law-writing and judges will prevent the law we write both from generating serious injustice in individual cases and from excessively disturbing long-standing national contract law expectations (see Rosett 1992).

The two central model law-building enterprises have been the European Convention on Contracts for the Sale of Goods and the UN Convention on Contracts for the International Sale for Goods which succeeds it

('Symposium: Contract Law in a Changing World' 1992). Both have been subscribed to by a substantial number of states. Here, rather than the Americanization that we encounter in much contract practice and arbitration, we encounter a slight Europeanization of contract law. Specific performance remedies are much more available than under the UCC. The civil law concepts of 'avoidance' for 'fundamental breach' rather than 'revocation of acceptance' are employed. Failure of the buyer to pay probably cannot trigger as rapid a response from the buyer as may occur under the UCC. And seller's failure to perform promptly may be cured by a further agreement between buyer and seller extending the time for performance. In an explicit compromise between common and civil law traditions, 'good faith' is mentioned only in the interpretation provisions of the UN Convention and not in its performance and enforcement provisions.

Both conventions also exhibit a particular dedication to freedom of contract, to the belief that law should follow practice, and to stating the law in terms of general principles leaving room for much spontaneous growth in practice. The Conventions are even more liberal than the UCC or the Restatement (Second) of Conflict of Laws (see p. 304 above) in allowing the parties autonomy in choosing the law applicable to their contract. The UN Convention offers a very broad opt-out clause from almost any or all of its particulars. Many of the UN Convention rules are default rules that govern only in the absence of specific agreement between the parties. Article 9 provides that trade usages and the prior practices of the parties derogate from the rules of the Convention. The Convention specifically does not cover validity. It conspicuously avoids regulatory provisions such as reasonableness and unconscionability—but is must be noted that much of the new UNIDROIT drafting of Principles for Commercial Contracts and that of the Principles of European Contract Law project place considerable emphasis on 'reasonableness' (see, for example, 'Principles for International Commercial Contracts' 1992). And it provides that matters 'governed by' but 'not expressly settled in it' are to be decided in conformity with 'the general principles on which it is based' (p. 707). One could hardly encounter a more favourable balance of freedom of contract over regulation of contract than is to be found in the two Conventions. Both are, of course, aimed primarily at the contractual relationships between business firms and so we would expect to encounter less concern for regulation than might be encountered in consumer sales or credit contract law. The European Union has recently issued a major harmonization directive on some aspects of consumer contracts that does take a much more regulatory stance but is very limited in scope (Joerges 1995).

Globalizing Contract Practice

The most obvious globalization of contract law phenomenon then, and the one most easily observed by its detritus of law review articles, conference reports, year book volumes, and circulated draft codes, is this flourishing industry of model contract, model statute, and model code writing. The next globalizing phenomenon I wish to note is far more difficult to document from traditional scholarly sources. It is, however, a phenomenon I wish to assert must be very evident to both transnational contracting parties and to their lawyers. If my assertions about globalizing contract practices are incorrect, there should be no shortage of voices to correct me.

The American-Style Contract

For quite a long time now there appears to have been a relatively distinct style of American contracting among large business enterprises. No doubt it arose gradually, but it must go back at least as far as the turn of the century. American contracts tended to be long, detailed, and designed as much as humanly possible to anticipate the possible vicissitudes of future business relationships under the contract. One can argue that such a development is inevitable in a capitalist, free enterprise—but regulated—large-scale, rapidly growing economy deploying huge amounts of capital and labour and enjoying rapid technological progress. If the same development was not occurring in Europe, for instance, in the same time frame, the explanation might be more cartelized economies with lesser geographic reach.

The growth of the long, detailed American contract style also has two chicken and egg aspects particularly related to the American scene. Long, detailed contracts might be written because the lawyers involved saw litigation as frequent and inevitable and were writing contract provisions to provide and close off defences at trial. Or, frightened by the ever-present spectre of litigation, contract writers might be seeking to anticipate and avoid every possible misunderstanding that might trigger litigation. One way or another, long, detailed contracts, in some mixture of cause and effect, are probably related to the American style of litigation.

Interrelated to the connection between contracts and litigation is a connection between contracts and law firms. Big law firms have the resources to write long, detailed contracts and to litigate issues that arise under them if necessary. Big law firms also have strong economic incentives to persuade clients to demand such contacts. And, of course, the inclination to use such contracts, from wherever the inclination is derived, fuels the growth of large law firms.

American businessmen often can be heard wondering at how 'what used to be done with a handshake' now requires an army of lawyers and how legal expenses have somehow grown into a significant part of their business expenses. It makes little difference to my argument whether the American businessmen are right or wrong in complaining about all this having happened recently. It is important to my argument that long, detailed contracts became prevalent far earlier in America than elsewhere. If I am wrong about that then much of my subsequent argument about globalization fails.

The simplest way to tell my globalization story would be to say that, for whatever reasons, a certain American style of contracting arose and then spread to Europe and the rest of the world as American companies doing business abroad insisted on contracting that business in the style to which they had become accustomed. I think that story is essentially true at least in some sectors of business, a point I will illustrate later with worldwide developments in franchise law. An alternative story would be that transnational business, American-based and otherwise, began to encounter worldwide the same phenomena that had earlier fostered American-style contracting, that as it encountered these phenomena it was also aware of the existence of American contracting practices, and so borrowed from that ready-made body of contract technology. Perhaps this story is best illustrated by developments in large-scale mineral development agreements that I will turn to later.

Franchising Law

The[3] worldwide development of business format, that is, McDonald's-style franchise contracting practice and law, illustrates many of the features of the globalization of freedom of contract. Franchising flourished in the US for many years. Most American states produced special franchise contract law provisions and the Federal Trade Commission issued a set of regulations. American franchise operations then experienced an enormous burst of international growth. The simplest story would then be that there followed a globalization by way of Americanization, that, as American franchising travelled around the world, it took the American franchise law with it. The real story is a little more complex but not essentially different. First of all the French went into franchising in wedding, maternity, and children's clothing retailing quite early and many of the European legal responses are to this French rather than American franchising. Second, although between 1988

---

[3] This section draws heavily on Campbell (1994).

and now the number of nations with explicit franchising laws has gone from one—the US—to 18, most nations still do not have much explicit franchising law. Yet the pattern of working law among the rest is basically the same as that among the 18 and a general description of what has occurred can be offered without distinguishing between the 18 and the others.

In general, at least in the realm of contract law, most nations and the European Community have adopted a stance of benevolent neutrality toward business format franchising. They have recognized its economic benefits in the US and allowed the market to decide its fate in their own domestic economies. Opposition to franchising, and particularly to American franchising, has expressed itself not in contract law but in such arenas as local land-use planning and business licensing.

The most typical pattern in contract law has not been rapid response of law to practice. Particularly as American franchisers expanded abroad, they offered foreign franchisees their American form franchise contracts. These contracts are the most American of the American-style contracts. That is, in contemplation of long continuing business relationships, they seek to nail down every last contingency that could arise in such situations and thus are extremely long and detailed, often incorporating a whole operations manual into the contract itself. In addition, and this is not so American perhaps, the very essence of their success is that they are uniform and dictated by one of the parties, the franchiser, to the other on a more or less take-it-or-leave-it basis. The response of academic lawyers throughout the world to this huge new contract phenomenon has been the usual response of academic contract lawyers to anything new. For as long as they could they studiously ignored it, continuing to slice thinner and thinner the dozen or so traditional topics of contract law scholarship. The initial response of lawmakers has been that to the 2,000 pound gorilla: they let it sit anywhere it wants. More specifically the response largely has been to treat the business format franchise contract as an 'innominate' or 'mixed' contract having some of the features of each of a number of kinds of contract previously known by the particular legal system and thus to be dealt with under the general law of contract and, segment by segment, by analogy to the existing variety of contacts that its various parts resemble. As noted, some countries then eventually enact a statute that in effect systematizes this application of general contract principles plus disaggregation. With or without statutes, what most national law has done is essentially to normalize the American-style contract practice.

Thus the globalized contract law has been almost entirely supportive of the private contract practices developed by the franchisers. The new franchise law has been regulative, in the sense of seeking to impose government policies on contracting parties, only in a few areas. It is impossible to resist noting that among the few specific regulatory responses to franchising is a French decree requiring that French language endings rather than English be coupled to the root 'franch'. Earlier we noted that modern contract law has been particularly regulatory with regard to situations in which form contract language is imposed by a stronger party and repeat player on a weaker, sporadically playing, party, most often in consumer sales and consumer credit contracting. The franchise contract seems to be one of those situations. Yet there are several good reasons for staying the regulatory hand here. First and foremost uniformity is precisely the valuable economic good being created and sold to the public by the whole franchise arrangement and the public, the ultimate consumer, seems to benefit greatly from it. Boilerplate, which may appear to be a vice in other contract settings, is the very heart of virtue in this one. Second, the franchisee is not exactly that poor thing, the idiot consumer, who needs the especial guardianship of the state. The franchisee is presumably a knowledgeable entrepreneur in his or her own right.

Therefore, in both the statutory and the non-statutory states, the regulatory thrust, to the extent that it has developed at all, largely has taken the form not of limiting form contracting but of being meticulous about disclosure requirements. The franchiser is in a far better position than the franchisee to know the significance of each uniform bit of the contract and is placed under an appropriate burden to disclose.

Several areas of non-contract law are far more likely to impede franchise contracting than is contract law itself, at least as it is being construed today in most of the world. And it is in some of these areas that the 2,000 pound gorilla phenomenon is most evident. Business format franchising collides with the anti-trust or competition law of many nations and most notably of the European Union. The response of the EU was to issue a 'Block Exemption' from its competition laws for business format franchising along with a special individual waiver process for franchises that could not qualify for the block exemption. While, as a matter of legal practice, much attention must be paid to adjusting global franchise contracts to national competition laws, the response of most nations, like the response of the EU, has been to mute competition law in favour of franchising. Most typical anti-competitive business format franchise contract practices can be successfully defended as essential to protecting the trademark or other economic efficiencies of the basic franchise arrangement.

Trademark is a second area of law to which special attention must be paid in writing global franchise contracts. Here the general movements towards internationalizing or globalizing trademark law itself have tended to ease the path of the global franchiser.

Thus the basic story is that American plus franchise contracting practices have been accepted largely by inaction in most of the legal systems of the world and by special accommodation when inaction would not have been enough. Franchise contracting is, of course, subsumed under the general contract law of the particular state, but the only major, specific regulatory move has been the beefing up of disclosure requirements. Indeed, the most typical move of those political entities that have made a special lawmaking effort to confront franchising has been the enactment of statutes or regulations which allow or require private associations of franchisers-franchisees to write voluntary codes of ethics for their sector.

Business format franchising can no doubt be cited as one of the great globalizing of freedom of contract stories in which globalizing contract law has been essentially supportive of globalizing contract practice. Certainly an enormous amount of contract language and an enormous number of contract provisions first developed in the United States have been exported around the world. And certainly such business format franchising contracts tend to be long and detailed.

Mineral (Non-Oil) Development Contracts

The[4] much touted flexibility of contract as a legal instrument is dramatically shown in a range of international contracts that deviate sharply from the standard repertoire because a sovereign state is one of the parties. Perhaps among the most interesting of these deviations is the joint venture agreement for mineral development. In such agreements the regulatory potential of contract law comes to the fore, and, as is often true, regulation is exercised in behalf of the 'weaker' party. In older times mineral development in developing states by First World investors usually took the form of a 'concession' agreement. At least from the point of view of the developing states, such concession agreements were not very complex. The cost of luring job- and tax revenue-creating projects into destitute countries was the grant of nearly sovereign powers to foreign investors to exploit a particular stretch of land in return for a small share of the profits. In more recent, post-colonial, days, the opposite extreme has been the service contract in which the outside investor merely contracts with the host state to provide

---

[4] Most of the information for this section has been obtained from Schanze (1981) and Smith and Wells (1975).

management of the day-to-day mining operations at a government-owned site. Such arrangements have flourished in the oil industry where competition among oil companies and high market demand give the governments of the oil states an overwhelming bargaining advantage. In solid minerals, however, the situation is less advantageous to the host states which must give potential exploiters of mineral resources a better deal.

The better deal that has evolved is essentially ultimate relatively long-term management control to the investors but a far greater share in management and in management-acquired information to the host country than occurred under the concession arrangement, or even under the service contract. Most interesting is that much of the increased host state control can be achieved either through state mining, tax, environmental, health, and corporation law or through contractual agreements between the state and the foreign investors. Contracts and regulatory statutes become alternative modes of increasing state control.

This balance of interests between investors and host states is achieved through mining agreements that create joint-venture corporations to conduct the actual mining operations. A very wide range of alternative corporate structures, powers, decision-making processes, and shareholding patterns are available through such agreements. The host state may be the majority or minority shareholder. Whoever is the minority shareholder may or may not be given a veto over the corporation's management decisions. The basic agreement may provide very detailed provisions of exactly what the management of the joint venture may do or not do, may do with or without the authorization of the board of directors, and/or may do or not do with or without the authorization of an executive committee of the board whose voting is structured differently from the board itself. By a careful and complex delineation of the joint venture's corporate structure and processes, the master agreement, the articles of incorporation, and a project management contract between the joint venture and an investor-controlled entity can arrive at nearly any mix of investor and host government day-to-day and long-term control of management.

A key element of the master contract may be an extremely complex specification of the powers and the boundaries between the authority of a set of managing directors and a board of directors. In addition, the master contracts may provide for renegotiation of various specific goals of the joint venture over time. And these mixes can be very subtle. They are not only about who has the final say about what but who gets to participate how much before the final say is said and who gets how much of the information on which the final say is based.

In short, here we have not only a contract establishing a substantive exchange between the investors and the host state but a contract that establishes the details of the organization of an operating corporation that finely meshes investor and host country interests and management participation. Here contracts are used to fashion ongoing structures of state regulation of private endeavours and/or private participation in state enterprises. Joint participation is seen as an optimum mode of adjusting the interests of the two parties both because it can lead to a regime of reciprocal influence rather than all or nothing vetoes and because it assures each side access to the information necessary to protect its interests. Such joint participation contracts are necessarily quite long and detailed.

Business Organization and the Law

Somehow attendant on both the franchising and mineral development stories is also a story about the worldwide evolution of business organization which can also be seen as either America diffusion or parallel development.

If we are interested in the globalization of commercial contracting practice and law, or simply in business law, obviously we must be concerned about developments in both business and law institutions and their ways of thinking and doing. My argument here, in brief, is that the theory and practice of business organization has moved toward the externalized complex big deal as central to success and that American law practice has moved toward the large law firm bent on manufacturing large, complex law.[5] The result of the two movements is a globalization of the long, extremely complex, and detailed 'American' form of business contracting.

To turn first to the business side, business theory and practice at one time heavily favoured the vertically integrated, oligopolistic firm. In such firms most relationships of production and distribution are internalized, the firm ideally touching the outside world only in its employment of labour, its purchase of sites, and its ultimate sale to consumers. Norms are enunciated in internal directives and manuals. Disputes among individual executives or units are administrative problems to be solved by administrative techniques. Relations with rival oligopolies were to be handled by secret and direct contact at the highest executive levels.

---

[5] I am not concerned here with the standard chicken and egg problem. Did American big-firm practice develop in response to business needs or did the lawyers themselves create business demand for their increasingly complex and costly services?

More recently business theory and practice has tended toward a view of the firm as a bundle of capital and intelligence seeking profit by whatever arrangements will yield profit. Rather than the rigidities and clear boundaries between the internal and external of the vertically integrated firm, the new firm proactively seeks every sort of joint venture, minority or majority participation, lead or subcontractor, licensing, franchising, leasing, concession, management, pooling, spin-off, subsidiary, partnership, and so on, arrangement that may be most feasible for meeting a particular business goal. The boundary between internal and external constantly shifts and is sometimes blurred. Many essential business relationships are externalized. As a result norms must be stated in contracts. Disputes become less a matter of internal administration and more a matter of bargaining, under the shadow of potential mediation, arbitration, and litigation. More relationships are handled through lawyers than executive-to-executive.

Added to this general tendency of business is a phenomenon that has particularly marked international business. The vertically integrated firm tended to ignore national boundaries in a classic 'imperialist' pattern of reaching abroad to secure its raw materials and/or its ultimate sales. In the post-imperial world, many large businesses found that their international business relationships could not be internalized. Third World governments nationalized major economic activities within their boundaries and/or demanded for themselves a major role in business activity. Often this role was played by way of intense regulatory regimes where government acted as government. Just as often, as we have seen in the minerals area, Third World governments demanded a place as business participants or partners. Big firms found many of their overseas activities externalized and legalized because Third World governments had become their collaborators in business activities and these collaborations were defined by contract between the firm and the host state.

On the law side the story is equally familiar. Where business consists of complex, often long-term, ongoing relationships between two or more entities in economic, legal, political, social, and technological environments that are rapidly changing, those entities can maintain their relationships either by intimate, fluid, constant, and highly discretionary collaborations among their principals or by highly detailed legal, contractual provisions that are carefully tailored to their particular current situations and fully anticipate future changes in those situations—or, of course, any mix of the two. The large American law firm has the resources to provide the extremely complex, detailed, and particularized contracts needed if the second option is chosen and also the resources to provide the large-scale, fact- and procedure-oriented litigation services necessary if trouble should arise under such contracts. Everyone is, of course, familiar with the paradox that, the more carefully and fully contracts seek to anticipate every potential nuance that may arise in a complex, ongoing business relationship, the more massive the litigation is likely to become if the anticipation fails.

Just as the size of litigations and the size of law firms grew in some interlocked way in the US business world, one would expect a similar growth internationally if for no other reason than because large American firms played a very large part in international business life and were likely to export their style. Even when American operating firms were not involved, American investment capital often was. American firms were likely to want the same kind of contracts with foreign firms as they had with domestic ones. American law firms representing American businesses were certainly ready, willing, and able to provide them. As we have noted, certain special features of the international business environment also seemed to require longer, more complex contracts.

And, at least once the resources and the habit were established, contracts were a natural place to pile all sorts of organizational and substantive rules and procedures that in another world would have gone into company manuals. As we have seen, the rules for cooking hamburgers get piled into the franchise contract. The rules for voting on the executive committee get piled into the mineral development contract. The contracts that govern bank financing agreements for large, new enterprises are notoriously long and detailed. But it can be argued that their great complexity is far less a result of the work of lawyers seeking to avoid problems that lead to litigation or seeking to gain advantage for their clients should litigation arise than it is the result of bankers writing into the contracts themselves the internal manuals that are to guide bank employees administering the loans.[6]

In any event, it may well be that a disproportionately large share of international contracting business now goes to large American law firms to write large American-style contracts. Perhaps most revealing is the situation within Europe. The customs and mores of the legal professions of most European countries have always made it difficult for Continental lawyers to provide the legal services that large corporations need, and, until very recently, there were essentially no large European law firms. For reasons peculiar to the evolution of the English legal profession, there have been large solicitors' firms in London for a long time. Continental lawyers are now experiencing considerable angst at what they see as a flow of European

---

[6] I owe this point to Professor Buxbaum. See also Peter (1995).

contract business to London, because the large firms there can give the customers what they want. What is most notable, however, is that, although the English firms have been large for some time, and for reasons that have nothing in particular to do with contracting, traditionally they were accustomed to writing relatively brief, 'heads of agreement' style contracts. They have now shifted to writing far more detailed contracts and their new Continental business is often attributed to that shift. It may be that here we encounter a situation of globalization as Americanization in which English lawyers gain an advantage over their European Union competitors because they are better placed to quickly adopt American practices and are willing to Americanize.

While no hard quantitative evidence exists, it is clear to practitioners that the typical big-deal contract is long, is drafted in New York or London by big firms that can 'pick' the contract provisions 'off the shelf', that is, out of their own institutional memories built up in hundreds of previous deals, and provides for arbitration and/or litigation under New York or English contract law, which is, of course, the law reflected in the stock of contract provisions on the New York and London shelves.

It should be underlined, however, that the whole story of the 'globalization' of the complex, detailed, litigation-oriented American contract style is very weakly documented in empirical studies or even studies of the spread of doctrine. Wolfgang Wiegand's (1991) writing on the Americanization of European law is certainly pioneering and Yves Dezalay (1992) has done a major empirical study of European law practice that certainly supports this story. But until a great deal more real work is done, the notion of a globalized American-style contract law remains a hypothesis that I am pleased to offer but can barely begin to confirm.

Luckily Dezalay and Garth have now published their in-depth empirical study of international contract arbitration (Dezalay and Garth 1996; Lillich and Brower 1994). As they argue, arbitration clauses have become nearly universal in international business contracts; and international contract arbitration has been growing by leaps and bounds. So what they are up to is clearly at the very centre of whatever globalization of contract law is occurring. Along one dimension what they discover is a globalization of contract law in the sense of the creation of a global forum or set of institutions and a global set of arbitral practices or a global arbitration style and a relatively small, relatively coherent community of global arbitrators. And 'global' here means not only all European—including eastern Europe—and transatlantic but also North-South—developed and developing nations—and to some degree even East-West. Along another dimension, however, what they depict is a conflict between Europeanization and Americanization of the globe with Americanization winning the upper hand.

Their story begins as one of Europeanized globalization. A small group of very senior, highly esteemed European academic lawyers and judges of particularly scholarly bent establish an intellectual discourse or body of legal lore of international arbitration and a number of European centres for the conduct of an international arbitration practice. While few of the initiators of this movement probably consciously saw it this way, this move to arbitration largely consists of a set of anti-Americanization moves. First, it offered contracting parties the choice of specifying a European site of dispute resolution to counter the increasing tendency of international contracts, particularly those in which one firm was American, to explicitly choose New York law and either New York courts or the well-developed arbitration system in New York as the site of resolution. Second, it sought to substitute a more informal, less adversarial mode of resolution for more formal, adversarial litigation. Third, it sought to move the resolution process away from elaborate procedural manoeuvring, and more particularly the complex wrangling over conflict of laws problems that had come to characterize much international contract litigation, towards a simple and direct confrontation with the basic substantive issues. Fourth, it sought to reduce the degree to which the parties' lawyers controlled the resolution process and increase the degree of control of the third member of the triad—the arbitrator. The arbitrator was to be a person of far greater knowledge and far greater prestige than the lawyers, the true master of the transnational law of contract and the wise old man devoted to substantive justice rather than the referee between two contesting lawyers. In part this enhanced role for the triadic figure stems from the very choice of arbitration over litigation which can be taken as implying a certain rejection by the parties themselves of the excessive legalism and accentuated adversarialism of the regular courts. In part the boosting of the triadic figures was a function of the specific historical circumstances. International contract arbitration was largely created by a small community of academics and judges closely allied to academics and was based on their uniquely vast grasp both of the most erudite and universal theories of contract and of comparative law. International arbitration was built up on this charisma of scholarly prowess. The environment created was one in which the 'grand old man' doing the arbitrating knew everything. The very legitimacy of the arbitration rested on his knowledge which had, in effect, created the whole arbitrating institution. And the arbitrator was a repeat player legitimizing his work partly by reference to his own previous experience. The lawyers for the parties, on the other hand, were mere technicians, occasional interlopers into this scholarly realm from their mundane, professional, parochially national law practices.

Fifth, because international contract arbitration grew up as a European movement, it tended towards the very limited discovery practices common in Europe. Thus arbitration was far, far less involved in the enormous machinery of fact gathering, organization, analysis, and presentation than is American corporate litigation. Sixth, the leaders of this European arbitration movement were, for the most part, boosters of the *Lex Mercatoria* and some sort of modern version of the *ius gentium*. They much preferred to decide cases by reference to general legal principles and common principles discerned by comparative analysis of national legal traditions than by reference to the particular law of a particular state. And as we have already seen the *Lex Mercatoria* and the various European and UN contract conventions that are seen as growing out of it and becoming a part of it tend to adhere to European rather than American traditions and theories of contract law.

Having depicted this Europeanized origin of the globalization of contract arbitration, Dezaley and Garth go on to depict a stage of Americanization. Large American law firms become deeply involved in the arbitrations in European cities and bring with them their hardball style and their capacity to marshal facts. A generation of practitioners arises who specialize in representing clients in international arbitration and then themselves begin to replace the grand old men who are, after all, not only grand but old. As the lawyers for the parties also become repeat players and possessors of high levels of knowledge of transnational contract law, the relative power of the triadic figure and the lawyer for the parties shifts in favour of the lawyers. As a result of all these phenomena there is a shift back towards concern for conflict of laws and a renewed preference for finding concrete legal rules rather than relying on general principles, theory, and comparative method. Arbitration comes to look more and more like litigation, and indeed litigation American-style. The arbitrator looks less and less like mediator and more and more like privately hired judge. As international contract arbitration becomes more and more dominant and globalized, it comes more and more to look like American-style adversarial litigation.

As Dezaley and Garth emphasize, their findings are even harder to support directly than would be findings about contract litigation in regular courts. For most contract arbitration clauses contain secrecy provisions that prohibit the publication of arbitral awards and the opinions supporting them. Of course this practice not only hampers the researcher but also must, to some unknown degree, favour the European over the American style. For the secrecy cuts off the American-style lawyer from one of his favourite practices, searching out cases 'on all fours' on their facts to the one being decided and the citation of those cases in precedential arguments. Where case particulars are hard to come by, academic writings and the theories and general principles they propound—in other words the world of the European grand old men—almost necessarily play a disproportionate role. Of course, those wedded to the American style will respond by treating published court precedents as authoritative for arbitrations and so drive arbitration further into the litigation mode.

If we put together the business firms externalizing many of their relationships and the penchant of large law firms to write long, detailed contracts that seek to anticipate every imaginable factual situation that may arise over a long future time span and then to threaten to fiercely litigate every detail, two chicken and egg stories may be told. And the two constitute the crux of the modern, scholarly debate about what the law is really like. In one story the large law firm and its extreme adversarial legal practices have themselves been created by the needs and demands of business. Society calls and the law responds. In the other story, the lawyers have been busily constituting legal practice to their own advantage, creating business for themselves rather than serving the needs of business. The lawyers say they are serving the clients. And the businessmen say that they have become the prisoners of law firms that complicate their lives and take an enormous ransom for doing so.

These two stories, so often told for the American scene, now seem to be equally at large in the global context. In one of the stories, contracting parties are freer and freer to make the law that governs themselves. In the other, contracting parties are freer and freer to subject themselves to the pathologies of the American legal profession.

Conclusion

Most students of law would agree that there has been an enormous growth in contacting between firms sited in different countries. There is a great deal of documentation of the growth of a body of model transnational contract principles, rules, and statutes and of international contract arbitration institutions, processes, and personnel. I have certainly insufficiently documented the spread of the long, detailed, litigation-oriented 'American'-style contract as a major feature of the globalization of contract practice, but nonetheless assert it with some confidence until contradicted by contract specialists. Dezalay and Garth are at least on the way to documenting an Americanization of the international arbitration processes that clearly are a major feature of the globalization of contract practice and law.

All of this may lead to either some very straightforward or rather paradoxical conclusions about the globalization of freedom of contract depending on one's point of view and on a number of wild guesses unsupported by hard data. If freedom of contract is entirely a matter of how free *governments* allow private enterprises to be in making contracts, then globalization is surely a story of increasing freedom. There is a growing body of practice and law that make it possible for private parties resident in different states to make and anticipate enforcement of contracts with relatively few barriers created by national sovereignty itself. There may even be a growing capacity for private parties to make contracts with governments that enjoy a strong chance of performance. There is considerable growth in a global law of contracts and global forums for the enforcement of that law that provide the legal support for global growth in contracting. Leaving aside the waxing and waning of government regulations that constrain the choices of contracting parties (Vogel 1998), the capacity for and the practice of contracting freely across the globe has certainly increased since the Second World War.

If, however, we look at the world as containing not just two players—those who wish to contract and governments—but instead three players, those who wish to contract, governments, and the legal profession—the freedom picture may not be as clear. It is here that the arguable, but not proved, thesis of globalization as Americanization becomes relevant. To the extent that the American style of contract writing and disputing is becoming global, global freedom of contract may be, along a certain dimension, illusory or purchased at a very high cost. The lawyers may have become far freer than the contracting parties.

Islands of Transnational Governance

Alec Stone Sweet

The Westphalian state, at least in its ideal-typical form, provides a model of political organization that resolves many of the fundamental questions concerning the relationship between boundaries, territory, jurisdiction, citizenship, and nationhood. It does so by equating state sovereignty with the internal control and external autonomy of national governments. Among other things, this formulation implies the organizational capacity to police borders, to determine what moves in and out. It implies that the state's law and organizations authoritatively govern the activities of those who live or act within state territory. And it implies that the state is legally constrained, in its relations with other states, only by rules upon which it and other states have agreed.

The Westphalian state may never have actually existed. Conceptually, political control—an actual or an asserted state of affairs—and sovereignty—a purely juridical concept—are not one and the same; empirically, they need not be related at all. In this paper, I argue that sovereignty and control are detaching from one another rapidly, at least with respect to transnational commercial activity. In the past three decades, a growing and increasingly cohesive community of actors—including firms, their lawyers, and arbitration houses—have successfully created a transnational space.[1] The space is comprised of a patchwork of private jurisdictions, of rules and organizations without territory, an offshore yet virtual space. These are islands of private, transnational governance.

The paper is divided into two parts. In the first, I discuss, in an abstract way, obstacles to the emergence of a stable network of traders engaged in relatively

---

[1] The transnational space described in this paper must not be confused with the supranational space constituted by arenas of governance within the European Community or Union. The latter is public space, constructed by and from the jurisdiction of the member states, and the sovereignty claims—for example, the supremacy of EC law—are delimited by state boundaries. The former makes no sovereignty claims.

long-range, impersonal exchange. I focus on three generic problems of human community: commitment, transaction costs, and institutional choice. In the second, I examine three quite different regimes that have governed transnational commercial activity: the medieval law merchant, the Westphalian state system, and—my principal focus—the new *Lex Mercatoria*.

Theoretical Considerations

Let us begin by positing the existence of a pool of actors who would engage in trade with one another if it were profitable. I assume that these individuals are strangers to one another in the sense that no pairing of them has had prior dealings, and no pairing shares a comprehensive normative system, such as a common culture or another institutional structure, to guide their relations.

There are good theoretical reasons to believe that extensive networks of impersonal exchange will emerge, and institutionalize as stable systems of commerce, only if a set of linked social problems can be overcome. These problems, which are present in all commercial settings, are all the more acute for strangers who wish to trade with one another. First, although our pool of potential contractors share, a priori, a common interest in constructing trading relationships with one another, they may nonetheless fail to do so if temptations to renege on exchange commitments remain powerful. Second, transaction costs are almost always higher for long distance than for local trade. Most important for us, existing institutions, by which I mean the rules and organizational practices governing interactions in a specific social setting, may not favour the expansion of private commerce outside of the local boundaries drawn by these rules. That is, separate systems of parochial rules may impose, rather than reduce, transaction costs on long-distance trade. Third, to the extent that our pool of traders does exchange with one another, issues concerning collective agreements about the nature and meaning of contractual instruments are inevitably raised. Actors will need to choose or develop rules of contract, as well as techniques for resolving contractual disputes. As with trade-relevant institutions more generally, how such systems of governance are organized and operate will help to shape both the nature and the scope of impersonal exchange into the future.

Problem 1: Cooperation and Commitment

The Prisoner's Dilemma (PD) game captures certain core elements of the situation confronting strangers who would exchange with one another, namely, a strategic choice context in which the dominant move is to cheat. To the extent that traders in our pool fail to live up to their contractual commitments, dyadic exchanges will tend to be one-shot deals. To the extent that this is so, conditional strategies, such as tit for tat (Axelrod 1986), do not emerge, and the trading system is stillborn.

Where contractants are not strangers, that is, where a pool of potential traders enjoys ongoing, face-to-face relations with each other within a shared normative framework, collective action problems and Prisoner's Dilemmas are more easily overcome (Hardin 1982; Taylor 1976). If communities are small and cohesive enough, social order can be constituted as a public good, and profitable individual exchange relationships can be sustained, without the prior construction of public authority or the state (Taylor 1982; Stone Sweet 1999b: 160–1).

Game theorists make a related point in models of n-person, iterated PD games, and in elaboration of the Folk theorem (Fudenberg and Maskin 1986; Kandori 1992). Cooperation can be achieved by individuals, and diffuse within a group, if each player possesses some knowledge about the preferences of other players (Schofield 1985) or some means of assessing individual reputations for trustworthiness (Kreps and Wilson 1982; Milgrom, North, and Weingast 1990).

The individuals in our pool know that they can make themselves better off through exchange. At the same time, trader X recognizes that cheating trader Y can be advantageous if Y abides by the contract made—the Prisoner's Dilemma. On the other hand, *given adequate information about the past behaviour of potential contractants*, X may choose not to cheat. Instead, X may figure that cheating Y today would make it more difficult to find new trading partners tomorrow, to the extent that cheating damages one's reputation for trustworthiness. Once any group of traders establish trustworthy reputations with each other, they will trade only among themselves. And traders that fail to establish good reputations will be punished by being excluded from the arrangement. This solution, of course, depends entirely on the organization of information and monitoring capacities, a collective good that, given the myriad costs involved, may or may not be generated by the traders themselves.

Similarly, a group could seek to impose rules, that is, to create an institutional solution *ab initio*. Assume that, within our pool, a group of traders adopts the rule 'one must not cheat' along with a set of corollaries designed to give it life and agency. Like all norms, the rule would provide behavioural guidance, generate common expectations, and facilitate the monitoring of compliance. Nevertheless, the establishment of a new norm, being itself an act of cooperation, is subject to the same potentially insurmountable obstacles all such efforts face. This is the Prisoner's Dilemma again, in the guise of an institutional design game (Tsebelis 1990: Ch. 4). Further, once this or any rule has been established, problems do not go away. The critical test of a norm's robustness, or legitimacy, occurs when the social interest embodied in the norm comes into evident conflict with the private interests, or interest-driven objectives, of any given trader. In such a case, an individual may well choose to behave in contravention of a norm, especially if the probable outcome of conforming to it would be to leave that individual worse off. So, even after norms have been created, the linked problems of how to ensure compliance and to punish non-compliance persist.

Of course, if we assume that the social interest has been clearly expressed, that some mechanism of letting everyone know who is and who is not a cheater has been put into place, and that everyone will eschew trading with cheaters, cooperation will be the likely outcome. But assuming such things does not explain them.[2]

Problem 2: Transaction Costs

Now let us assume that our pool of long-distance traders have established a regime bounded by robust norms that stigmatize cheating. All potential contractants share a commitment to the rule that trade promises shall be made and kept in good faith—in this sense, they are no longer quite 'strangers' to one another. The second set of problems our traders face is relatively high, and potentially prohibitive, transaction costs. Following North (1990; 1991), I understand the costs associated with any dyadic commercial exchange in a broad way, to include all of expenses incurred to complete that exchange.

If the potential gains to be had from long-distance exchange are outweighed by these costs, or are smaller than the gains to be had from local exchange, trade will remain local. The transaction costs of long-distance trade are likely to be far higher than those of local trade within long-standing communities. Two parties to any commercial contract face bargaining costs, which are increased if no common language, common understandings of

---

[2] Game theorists have not explained in any generally compelling way how cooperation emerges. When two individuals interact with each other over an indefinite period, it is possible that cooperation may arise between them. Yet it is equally possible that they will fail to cooperate at all, or that they will find themselves in a situation where one gains more than the other from the relationship, leading it to break down. At the moment, rationalists have no convincing means of predicting when cooperation will arise or when it will not, unless they assume pre-existing norms and institutions. The outcome discussed in this paragraph, for example, depends entirely on a rule 'don't trade with those who cheat', to which actors adapt in particular ways.

how to measure the relative value of goods, or common currency or payment system exist. Contracting costs are transactions costs, and they are higher where a secure system of property rights and enforcement mechanisms has not already been established. Further, expenses related to the transport of goods, communications, insurance, letters of credit, other financial instruments, and the payment of agents—middlemen—will almost always be less avoidable, and the outlays higher, for long-distance than for local exchange.

For most of human history, most commercial activity has not been long-distance and impersonal, but rather local or autarkic. The models typically employed by economists to explain the logic of impersonal exchange—increased specialization through comparative advantage, and growing interdependence within and between markets—rests on a set of assumptions that ignore transaction costs. On the one hand, individuals and firms possess perfect information—an assumption that bundles together, makes anonymous, and then denies the real significance of a long list of such costs; on the other hand, the only real constraints on trading activities, and the only structural determinants of outcomes, are the distribution of tastes for consumption and natural endowments.

North (1990) has argued that differences in national economic growth and development, whether measured cross-nationally or across time within the same state, are due in large part to the relative capacity of institutions—for example, contract law—and of governmental organizations—for example, courts—to respond to the needs of those willing to engage in impersonal exchange, most importantly by lowering the costs of such exchange. In North's account, which relies on complex feedback mechanisms that manifest themselves in lock-in and path-dependence, either a virtuous or a vicious circle is possible. Where institutions themselves impose higher transaction costs, impersonal exchange is stifled and economic growth is stunted. The question of whether or not a community can construct or adapt institutions capable of responding to the needs of traders is therefore critical to the successful consolidation of a cosmopolitan trading system—across localities or regions in a given national territory, or across state boundaries. Exactly how institutions are constructed will also matter. Traders can be expected to adapt their own practices to institutions that are in place, thus reinforcing them. And they will seek to evolve new institutions, or abandon trade altogether, if they find their activities governed by dysfunctional rules. Finally, there are individual actors who are advantaged by maintaining local hindrances to outside trading and whose behaviour and interactions have been tailored to these local rules, thus making the institutional setting more resistant to changes desired by cosmopolitans.

Problem 3: Institutional Choice and Governance

Finally, let us assume that our pool of traders has found ways to overcome the basic hindrances to long-distance trade discussed to this point: traders enter into contracts in good faith, expecting that the benefits from exchange with one another will exceed the costs. The third problem our group faces is one of institutional choice. How shall the new trading regime be governed?

In a world of competing sovereigns, where jurisdictions may overlap—medieval Europe—or where jurisdiction constitutes and more or less maps onto territorial boundaries—the Westphalian world—long-distance traders may have a choice of arrangements to govern their interactions. If they do have choice, they may decide to assign an already existing set of authoritative institutions to their contract, or they may decide to build their own institutions and organizations in order to consolidate their regime. There is little social science theorizing about, and still less theoretically inspired empirical attention paid to, how such decisions are made or their consequences (see the important paper by Mattli 2001). Nonetheless, I would emphasize the following three points.

First, our pool of traders cannot avoid the problem of institutional choice. Some—at least rudimentary—system of governance is required if an extensive network of long-distance exchange is to be constructed. For reasons already discussed, our traders require principles to govern their activities, such as rules of contract. Further, even if traders enter into agreements fully expecting to meet their own obligations, the contracts themselves are never complete. Most agreements of any complexity are 'relational' contracts. The parties to an agreement seek to broadly frame their relationship by agreeing on core commitments, but otherwise fixing outer limits on acceptable behaviour and establishing procedures for completing the contract over time (Milgrom and Roberts 1992: 127–33). Just as important, contracting within our pool of traders will generate a massive social demand for third-party dispute resolution, to settle conflicts involving interpretation of, and compliance, with agreements (Stone Sweet 1999b). In the absence of rules of contract and organizational capacity to resolve disputes, our traders face fearsome uncertainties that may keep them from building and sustaining exchange relationships.

Second, our traders may choose to select an existing local—that is, national—regime on efficiency grounds, since start-up costs are low or non-existent and the organizational infrastructure is already in place. The downside is that courts do not simply behave as neutral third parties vis-à-vis the contracting parties and their negotiated instrument. They also bring to bear on the proceedings the interests of another party, that of the regime itself (Shapiro 1981a). In resolving disputes, judges typically enforce the law of the regime. In the case of national courts, judges engage in norm enforcement, boundary maintenance, and social control through their interpretation of the sovereign's statutes and through their own rule-making, as registered in case law. For long-distance traders, local statutes and pre-existing judicial precedent may not be well-adapted to their activities. Instead, national regimes may impose, rather than reduce, the transaction costs of transnational commercial activity.

Third, despite the evident costs of creating their own body of principles to govern contracts and of establishing an organizational—third-party— means of resolving contractual disputes, our traders may nonetheless seek to do so, primarily in order to enhance their own autonomy vis-à-vis pre-existing jurisdictional authority. In escaping the control of national jurisdiction, for example, the traders can hope to create a more flexible regime adapted to their own specific needs. Yet, in constructing a new system of governance, they face a dilemma inherent in all institutional design, namely, how best to keep it operating in light of their priorities. Unintended consequences are to be expected. Those who design new legal systems, for example, regularly find themselves in worlds that judges have constructed to the extent that judges do their jobs effectively. Yet these worlds were never imagined at the *ex ante* constitutional moment by the designers (Stone Sweet 2000; Stone Sweet and Caporaso 1998b).

Transnational Exchange and Governance

My focus in the rest of the paper will be on the renaissance of the Law Merchant during the last decades of the twentieth century. I nonetheless begin by summarizing, for comparative purposes, how the problems surveyed in the first part of the paper were resolved prior to the emergence of the Westphalian state and then by the Westphalian state.[3]

The Medieval Law Merchant

The Law Merchant, or *Lex Mercatoria*, is a multi-faceted term which serves both to draw boundaries around a community and its practices, and to denote a legal system. It describes the totality of actors, usages,

---

[3] These first two accounts grossly simplify what are enormously complex histories and realities.

organizational techniques, and guiding principles that animate private, transnational trading relations. And it refers to the body of substantive law and dispute resolution rules and procedures that govern these relations. I will use the term in the second, more narrow sense. In doing so, I assert that the Law Merchant possesses meaningful, but not absolute, autonomy from traditional, public sources of law, such as national statute and public international law. This view, which is rapidly gaining more and more adherents, provokes deep controversy among scholars, arbitrators, and municipal law judges (Berger 1999; Berman and Dasser 1998; Booysen 1995: 45–7; Carbonneau 1998; Jin 1996; Rensmann 1998; Yu 1998).

The Medieval Law Merchant (MLM), which emerged and institutionalized between the eleventh and the twelfth centuries, comprised a relatively comprehensive, relatively efficient, legal regime for trade beyond 'local' borders (Berman 1983). This legal system was constructed and operated by the traders themselves. The functional logic of the MLM is straightforward: it enabled merchants to escape conflicts between various local customs and rules, and to avoid submitting to the authority of judges attached to pre-existing jurisdictions: the courts of feudal manors, city states, local gilds, the church. By the close of the twelfth century, the MLM governed virtually all long-distance trade in Europe and, through middlemen and their codes of conduct, at critical points along the great Mediterranean and eastern trading routes (Greif 1989; 1993).

The MLM regime was 'voluntarily produced, voluntarily adjudicated, and voluntarily enforced' (Benson 1992: 15–19). The regime embodied certain constitutive principles, including: *good faith*—promises made must be kept; *reciprocity, non-discrimination* between 'foreigners' and 'locals' at the site of exchange; third party *dispute settlement*; and conflict resolution favouring *equity* settlements. In practice, the MLM required traders to use contractual instruments, which were gradually standardized, and to settle their disputes in courts staffed by other merchants: experts, not generalists. Traders and their merchant judges placed a premium on quick judgments, and de-emphasized adversarial procedure. The function of dispute resolution was not so much to declare a winner and punish a loser, but to resuscitate the contractual agreement and cajole the parties to get on with their business.

The effectiveness of the MLM depended critically on reputation effects and the general fear of being ostracized from the trading community. As Milgrom, North, and Weingast (1990) have it, the crucial problem facing medieval long-range trade was not the infrequency of relations between any two traders but the 'costliness of generating and communication information' about the histories of potential trading partners. In their model (see also Greif, Milgrom, and Weingast 1994), the MLM acts as a kind of information clearing house about trading relations, making of reputations a transferable good, or 'bond', within the community of traders. The MLM also provides a forum for third-party dispute resolution, reinforcing the 'reputation system'. Because the results of the merchant judge's decisions are recorded, traders' past compliance with decisions can be monitored. The Nash equilibrium of the incomplete information, n-person PD, is that no player honours the contract. The institutional setting supplied by the MLM, however, creates the conditions necessary for constructing social order without a coercive state apparatus by making promises self-enforcing and by placing future contracting in the shadow of the law.

Milgrom, North, and Weingast recognize that to gather and disseminate relevant trading information and to provide dispute resolution is a costly organizational undertaking, but they nevertheless imply that the MLM was a uniquely efficient solution to the traders' problem. While one could take issue with this part of the analysis and conclusion, it would seem to make little difference whether the MLM was the most efficient regime possible as long as it performed more efficiently than existing institutional alternatives. However, it does warrant emphasis that, in addition to the costs of paying those who run the system, the substance of a third party's decisions itself may prove costly, especially if decisions are treated as having some precedential status.

The Westphalian State

Until well into the fifteenth century, the Law Merchant provided the institutional underpinning for most long-distance exchange in the trading world. As early as the twelfth century in England, and thereafter on the Continent, governments of states consciously sought, first, to emulate the main features of the MLM and, second, to subordinate the merchant's regime to state control (Berman 1983: 339–42). New statutes designed to 'move merchants into royal courts, and/or make merchant's courts less desirable' (Benson 1992: 19) absorbed large parts of the merchant's law into the state's commercial law.[4] At the same time, the European state gradually weaned itself from its more rapacious practices, such as repudiation of public debt and confiscations of property (Veitch 1986). By the close of the sixteenth century, the private commercial law of the nation state and the state's law courts had reduced the significance and scope of the Law Merchant, while never quite replacing it. During the nineteenth century, which witnessed

---

[4] Important innovations include the possibility of appeal.

waves of nation-building—and nationalism—extensive market integration, and huge reductions in transaction costs, due to improvements in transportation and communication and to the emergence of modern banking and insurance practices, the salience of national regimes to transnational commercial activity was at its zenith.

Thousands of volumes have been written about how national judges resolve conflicts involving transnational business deals. In a world of sovereign states, each of which supplies its own authoritative law of contract and forums for dispute resolution, it is not always obvious and may be a point of contention as to which body of legal rules is meant to govern a transaction or a dispute that arises from it. Due to the complexity of the topic and to the basic normative incoherence of the solutions at which judges have arrived, there is little point in going into great detail, beyond the following remarks.

For one or more reasons—which can fall within dozens of categories—a legal dispute may arise that involves the law of two or more jurisdictions. If that dispute comes before a national judge sitting on a law court of, say, state X, that judge may choose to assign the law of nation-state X to the case and then proceed to resolve the dispute accordingly. Frequently, however, the national law of the presiding judge is very obviously not the appropriate law. The parties may have solemnly agreed, for example, that the contract law of nation-state Y would govern their relationship; the material dispute may involve business that was concluded according to very specific commercial rules provided by the law of two or more other states, rather than X's; and the business may have been, or was meant to have been, conducted outside of the territory of state X—and Y. In such cases, our judge must determine which legal system will provide the substantive rules to bear on specific aspects of the dispute, and then proceed to settle the case.

These practices go by two names, 'Private International Law' and 'Conflict of Laws', which for our purposes are synonyms. I use the word 'practices' because conflict of laws has virtually no substantive content—although it is often portrayed as a branch of law. The private international law is, rather, a set of *techniques* or *doctrines* that are employed by the municipal law judge to enable the resolution of certain kinds of disputes. These techniques first developed in Italian city states from the twelfth to the fourteenth centuries, in France from the fourteenth to the sixteenth centuries, and the Netherlands in the seventeenth century; with the expansion of markets and trade, became widespread across Europe and North America in the nineteenth and twentieth centuries (Lipstein 1981).

Transnational actors today consciously work to avoid conflict of laws problems in national courts because such problems generate uncertainty.

They can do so in two main ways. First, they may incorporate specific national rules and procedures directly into their contract, in choice-of-law and choice-of-forum clauses (Farnsworth 1985). An American firm is likely to prefer this solution as long as the law chosen is American. Traders may also allow their lawyers to select the law with which the latter are most familiar. And it may be that, for some kinds of business, there is a substantive advantage for one or both contracting parties to selecting one, rather than another, national law and forum.[5] The second technique is to avoid national law altogether by explicitly referencing the *Lex Mercatoria* in choice-of-law clauses, and arbitration houses in choice-of-forum provisions (see below).

Institutional Failings

In the early modern period, when regional, let alone national, markets were not well integrated, state building, market formation, the elaboration of codes of commercial conduct, and the construction of legal systems were tightly linked activities. For long-range merchants, there were obvious advantages to adapting their own activities to those of the state, including enhanced security and enforceability of agreements. Nonetheless, as transnational activity expanded, especially in the nineteenth century, it put pressure on states to recognize and adapt to the special needs of long-distance trade. The development of conflict of laws techniques represents one crucial way in which state organizations adapted.

State-supplied institutions probably reached their functional limits by the 1950s at the latest, prompting transnational commercial society to reinvent itself and, at the same time, to construct a new social order. In fact, institutions provided by the state system have lost their dominance and are now being gradually displaced.

Transnational actors' priorities remain autonomy, security, certainty, and efficiency, but actors increasingly believe that they can, on their own, do better than states. The indicators of dysfunction in national regimes are clear enough. The various commercial codes and laws of contract are now deeply entrenched, slow to change to inputs from more cosmopolitan environments, and have a lock on too many national judges' imaginations. Further, conflict of laws techniques are in deep crisis. In the absence of such techniques, judges simply nationalize transnational disputes, which is unacceptable to traders. Yet the use of such techniques may be even worse for traders. In private international law adjudication, judges must decide

---

[5] These logics probably explain a great deal why a big part of the 'globalization of freedom of contract' (Shapiro, this chapter) is the Americanization/Anglicization of transnational business.

which foreign law is to be assigned to the case according to a complex set of criteria including policy considerations, which normally leads the litigants to solicit advice on the relative advantages of various regimes.

Once judges have decided to apply the law of a jurisdiction not their own, they have to behave as if they were trained in another national legal system. In essence, they 'jump into the dark' and hope they can land upright. In the past two decades, a substantial literature has appeared showing that existing conflict of laws techniques lead to wholly unpredictable decisions, even within the same jurisdiction (surveyed in Berger 1999: 9–31).[6] Finally, litigation is increasingly costly and time-consuming, whereas the trading environment can change in a matter of hours.

Not surprisingly, transnational economic actors increasingly take for granted the notion that national regimes make it more, not less, difficult for them to achieve efficiency and predictability in their relations with one another.

The New *Lex Mercatoria*

In the past three decades, transnational commercial activity itself has generated more and more of its own institutions. The trading community now commonly sees national legal systems as constituting an obstacle to doing business, which it seeks to avoid. With the help of lawyers and academics, this community is now engaged in the effort to 'unify' or standardize contract law; and various standardized, anational model contracts are in fact being intensively used. A system of private, competing transnational arbitration houses has emerged, providing traders with a range of alternatives to litigating their disputes in state courts. In consequence, national courts and legislators have adapted, most notably, by gradually but inexorably reducing the scope of their authority to regulate contracting and arbitration.

Transnational Contract Law

It has become easier and increasingly common for traders to select the new *Lex Mercatoria*, rather than national law, to govern their relationships. By

---

[6] Berger cites literature that characterizes conflict of laws 'an inveterate evil', 'a murky maze', 'creative chaos', 'alchemy', and a 'dismal swamp filled with quaking quagmires and inhabited by learned but eccentric professors who theorize about mysterious matters in a strange and incomprehensible jargon'. Juenger (1998: 277) bluntly states that, for the *Lex Mercatoria*, 'it is a happy coincidence that at this time in United States legal history the conflict of laws lies in shambles'.

doing so, they gain maximum control over their own relations. This control, and the centrality of the *Lex Mercatoria* as a mode of governance, is partly enabled by the 'creeping codification' (Berger 1999; Ferrari1998) of transnational commercial law. As this law is codified and used, its autonomy from national and public international sources of law is enhanced.

Projects to unify and codify transnational contract law have proliferated in recent years. The most important of these, which are run by independent institutes of practitioners and academics, have produced draft commercial codes of global and regional reach. Beginning in the 1970s, for example, the International Institute for the Unification of Private Law began work on what would become the UNIDROIT Principles of International Commercial Contracts, which purports to be a comprehensive code for international commerce (Berger 1998: Chs 3 and 4; Bonell 1998).[7] The Code, adopted by the Governing Council in 1994, organized in seven chapters and 119 articles, deals with the fundamental notions of contract, including *pacta sunt servanda*, good faith and fair dealing, validity, interpretation, performance and non-performance, choice of law and forum, and so on. Significantly, the Institute decided not to submit the code to governments or to intergovernmental bodies for fear that rounds of treaty negotiations would lead to changes and the reassertion of states', rather than traders', priorities. In Europe, various projects designed to unify European private law have been put forward (discussed by Berger 1999; Lando 1998; Bussani and Mattei 1997/98; Ferrari 1998), including the European Civil Code, which emerged in the 1990s and which has been submitted to EU governments and the European Parliament. Although actual practice has outpaced such efforts, what is important is that the UNIDROIT and European codes are increasingly being referenced expressly as the controlling law underpinning transnational contracts.

Opponents of the *Lex Mercatoria* have questioned whether *general principles* constitute *law*, at least as they understand *law* in their own national context. General principles, by their very nature, are abstract, if not vague; but abstractness has its advantages. National contract law, when read as black-letter law, suffers from the same alleged problems. But codified private

---

[7] The inspiration for the UNIDROIT project was the unification of US contract law that took place through the American Law Institute's Restatement of the Law of Contracts, as published first in 1932 and updated thereafter. The ALI's restatements, which appear in the form of black-letter law, both codify existing law—including settled case law—and creatively push solutions to unsettled questions, against a background of conflict-of-laws pathology. Like the ALI, UNIDROIT uses both comparative methodology and a functional analysis of problems and solutions to arrive at codification. The US example, due to the federalist nature of American private law, is functionally equivalent to, and a microcosm of, the present transnational situation.

law has already been substantially 'completed' by judicial lawmaking, which is partly what makes it ill-adapted to the needs of modern business. Further, general principles of contract are functional for traders in that they give wide latitude to private arbitrators to tailor arbitration to the specific needs and wishes of the parties. After all, through contracts, parties create their own law; the *Lex Mercatoria* is meant to provide an institutional foundation for this law, not to replace it.

Last, these projects can substantially lower the bargaining and transaction costs of doing transnational business relative to contracting under domestic law. Not only can traders avoid the myriad costs that inhere in using national law, including bargaining stalemates wherein neither party will agree to assign the contract to the specific national jurisdiction preferred by the other party; they can also easily access lawyers and contractual instruments that now comprise and occupy the virtual space of the transnational community. The International Chamber of Commerce (ICC), for example, sells inexpensive model contracts in the form of a booklet and a floppy disk; the software allows the contract to be customizing to specific needs. The introductory remarks to the ICC's (1997: 6) model international sale contract bluntly states: 'parties are encouraged not to choose a domestic law of sale to govern the contract.'

Transnational Dispute Resolution

Traders want dispute resolution that will enforce, as the controlling law, the rules traders have selected themselves. Further, because traders want to maximize their autonomy, including at the dispute settlement stage, they are attracted to arbitration. As Juenger (1998: 266) has it, 'the tendency to keep transnational commercial disputes out of the courts, and thereby beyond the reach of local laws, is nearly universal'. Higher levels of transnational activity have pushed arbitral practice to organize and to formalize; and as the institutionalization of global arbitration of private commercial disputes has proceeded, the autonomy of the *Lex Mercatoria* has, again, been enhanced.

The 'transnationalization of arbitration' story has a similar plot, many of the same characters, and much the same ending as the story just told about contracts. In the 1950s, UNIDROIT produced a Draft Uniform Law of Arbitration. This project was followed by UN Commission on International Trade Law's (UNCITRAL's) Model Law on International Commercial Arbitration of 1985. While there are differences, both are model codes meant to unify national rules concerning arbitration through adoption as national legislation. Both emphasize what transnational business most desires from the *Lex Mercatoria*: the freedom of the parties to contract, to choose arbitration and their arbitrators, to arbitral discretion in tailoring the law to the case, to procedural fairness on terms acceptable to the traders themselves, and to restricted national judicial review of arbitral awards.

Some states have in fact adopted parts of these—and other—model laws in their own internal reforms of codes governing commercial transaction, reforms all but required by the explosion of global trade (see discussion below). As important, the trading community has increasingly treated these rules as themselves part of the customary law governing their relations (*Lex Mercatoria*).

In any case, the number of arbitral centres that handle transnational business disputes has grown at an astounding pace. In 1910, there were ten arbitration houses; there were over 100 by 1985; today there are more than 150. For the biggest houses, the American Arbitration Association, the London Court of International Arbitration, and the International Chamber of Commerce, activity has tripled in just the past 25 years. The ICC, for example, processed 3,000 disputes during the 1920–80 period, but decided 3,500 during the 1980s alone. In the 1990s, the annual number of filings of arbitral cases reached 500. From the point of view of traders, arbitration in an established house like the ICC makes good sense. In addition to the advantages already discussed, an arbitration can normally be completed within six months, and the price of arbitration can be selected according to the size of the financial stakes at issue or the desired complexity of the arbitral procedures.

The Nation State Adapts

The rise of the new *Lex Mercatoria* raises deep questions about the nature of law and about the relationship of law to state power. To simplify a very complex set of issues, traditionalists tend to portray the *Lex Mercatoria* as a set of practices enabled by states. Over time, states have granted, within realms constructed through treaty law and national statute, more rather than less contractual autonomy to transnational economic actors, while retaining ultimate regulatory authority over these practices. Underlying this view lies a theory of law according to which only public authority—the commands of a sovereign—can produce law or confer upon private acts legal validity. In contrast, proponents of the *Lex Mercatoria* argue that state authorities have largely 'relinquished their authority to regulate' transnational contracting and arbitration, permitting both 'to function autonomously' in what is, in effect, an 'a-national' way (Carbonneau 1997: 293).

Traditionalists tend to focus less on what traders, their lawyers, and arbitrators are actually doing, and more on the linked problems of validity and enforcement of contracts and arbitral decisions. Their strongest argument for the continuing relevance of national law and courts to transnational commercial activity is a straightforward one: traders need the coercive state for enforcement purposes. Through various international instruments, the most important of which is the 1958 New York Convention on the Recognition and Enforcement of Foreign Arbitral Awards, states have agreed to limits on the reach of their own jurisdictions in order to collectively resolve a host of collective action problems associated with soaring trade and the popularity of arbitration. The New York Convention is a short treaty, with narrow but important purposes. It provides that states 'shall recognize' the validity of arbitral agreements and that states shall, through their courts, enforce arbitral judgments subject, *inter alia*, to the exceptions of 'inarbitrability' and 'public policy'.[8] Today, some 110 states have ratified the Convention.

Clearly the development of the *Lex Mercatoria* has been spurred by ratification of the New York Convention. Its broad function has been, in Carbonneau's words (1997: 392), to 'eradicate systemic hostility to arbitration ... stemming from the view that arbitration amounts to a usurpation of judicial adjudicatory authority'. At the same time, the nation-state has adapted far more to the *Lex Mercatoria* than vice versa, going far beyond the black-letter dictates of the Convention. A broad pattern of ongoing 'sovereign acquiescence' to the construction of the new Law Merchant has emerged (Carbonneau 1992: 119).

While I will turn to the specific situations in Europe and the United States shortly, three general trends deserve emphasis. First, in the national law of most advanced industrial states, the recognition and validity of a contract before a national judge are now presumed, even if the contract law in question has no relationship to law of that judge's jurisdiction. Second, national legislative provisions and judicial case law concerning arbitration have been dramatically transformed in ways that enhance the autonomy of the Law Merchant. To take three examples: arbitral clauses are today commonly treated as separable from the main contract,[9] the scope of judicial review

---

[8] Article V.2 of the Convention states that 'Recognition and enforcement of an arbitral award may also be refused if the competent authority in the country where recognition is sought finds that: (a) the subject matter of the difference is not capable of settlements by arbitration under the law of that country; or (b) the recognition or enforcement of the award would be contrary to the public policy of that country.'

[9] National legislation increasingly accepts what is known as the 'separability doctrine', according to which the validity of the arbitral clause is not affected by the legal nullity of the contract of

of arbitral awards has been radically reduced,[10] and issues of *Kompetenz-Kompetenz* have been largely resolved in arbitrators' favour.[11] Third, the public policy and inarbitrability exceptions to the recognition and enforcement of arbitral awards, contained in the New York Convention and thus in most national statutes, are being constructed narrowly by national courts and, in some countries like the United States, no longer have any practical relevance.

The United States

In the United States, the law on international commercial arbitration is entirely a matter of how the Federal courts have interpreted the New York Convention, which the US ratified in 1970. In this case law, American judges have appeared anxious to support arbitrators vis-à-vis disgruntled parties and to reduce the scope of substantive review afforded the latter in American courts. The leading cases show the courts to be favouring the wider interests of transnational society rather than the specific interests of American business in any given case, even when public policy considerations raised by the dispute could be interpreted as overlapping with national security interests. Two examples will suffice to make the point.

In 1974, the Court of Appeal for the Second Circuit decided litigation involving a challenge, by an American company Parson's Overseas, of an ICC arbitral tribunal decision to award an Egyptian company some $ US350,000 for breach of contract (*Parsons v. RAKTA*, USCA Second Circuit 1974). The dispute involved failure on the part of Parson's to complete the construction of a paper mill in Alexandria, Egypt, a mill which the company had also agreed to manage for the period of one year after construction. In May 1967, as building was in its final stages, Arab-Israeli relations rapidly deteriorated, and the American company decided to evacuate its workers; the Six Day War erupted a few weeks later. When Parson's subsequently decided to pull out of the project definitively, the Egyptian company activated the arbitration clause of the contract, and an ICC tribunal found in its favour.

Parson's sought to have the award vacated on public policy grounds and, indeed, the dispute had policy implications. The US Agency for International

which it is a part. In essence, the doctrine forecloses moves by one of the parties to the contract to avoid arbitration by pleading the contract's nullity.

[10] That is, the legal validity, in national law, of arbitral awards is presumed.

[11] *Kompetenz-Kompetenz* refers to the formal competence of a jurisdiction to determine its own jurisdiction or the jurisdiction of another organ. Modern arbitration statutes and case law largely accept that the arbitrator possesses the authority to fix the scope of its own jurisdiction, subject of course to the will of the contracting parties.

Development had agreed to finance a portion of the mill's construction, but financing was terminated with the US government's decision to break diplomatic relations with Cairo. Parson's argued that US foreign policy 'required' it, 'as a loyal American citizen, to abandon the project'. The Court dismissed this argument with a broad statement of policy of its own:

We conclude that the Convention's public policy defense should be construed narrowly. Enforcement of foreign arbitral awards may be denied on this basis only where enforcement would violate the forum state's most basic notions of morality and justice.... To read the public policy defense as a parochial device protective of national political interests would seriously undermine the Convention's utility. This provision was not meant to enshrine the vagaries of international politics under the rubric of 'public policy'.

American courts have hardly wavered in their support of foreign arbitrators since. In 1990, for example, a Federal District Court forced an American company, Sun Oil, to pay a $20 million ICC award to a Libyan company, although Sun's inability to perform its contractual obligations stemmed from decisions taken by the US government in pursuit of its anti-terrorism policy (*National Oil v. Libyan Sun*, US District Court 1990). The dispute involved Sun's decision to cease its participation in an oil exploration programme in Libya, after the US State Department prohibited travel to that country on US passports. Shortly thereafter, the US government banned imports from Libya—including of oil—and exports of goods and technical information, and Sun Oil's application for a licence to export data and technology to Libya was denied. After Sun refused to abide by the ICC tribunal's decision, the Libyan company asked American courts to enforce the award.

The District Court sided with the Libyans. The Court rejected Sun's claim that to affirm the award would effectively 'penalize Sun for obeying ... its government' and weaken 'the ability of the U.S. government to make and enforce policies with economic costs to U.S. citizens and corporations', flatly declaring that 'public policy' and 'foreign policy' are 'not synonymous'. The Court admitted that 'Libya itself is not a signatory to the Convention ... and [that] if the tables were turned, ... a U.S. company would not necessarily be able to enforce an arbitral award against a [Libyan company] in Libyan courts'. But, the Court continued, 'Libya's terrorist tactics and opportunistic attitude towards international commerce are simply beside the point'.

The Supreme Court has pushed even further, all but abolishing the role of American courts in regulating what arbitrators do. In *Mitsubishi v. Soler Chrysler* (USSC 1985a), the Supreme Court recognized the authority of arbitrators to interpret and apply American statutes when these can be shown to affect the rights and claims of one or more of the parties to the dispute. In *Mitsubishi*, the Court refused to review the merits of an award of the Japan Commercial Arbitration Association, an arbitration that turned in large part on how the arbitrator would apply US anti-trust laws to resolve the conflict. Declaring that arbitration represents an autonomous system of dispute resolution available to the parties, the Court went on to assert its functionality and underlying legitimacy:

By agreeing to arbitrate a statutory claim, a party does not forgo the substantive rights afforded by statute; it only submits to their resolution in an arbitral, rather than a judicial, forum. It trades the procedures and opportunity for review of the courtroom for the simplicity, informality, and expedition of arbitration.

. . . As international trade has expanded in recent decades, so too has the use of international arbitration to resolve disputes arising in the course of that trade. The controversies that international arbitral institutions are called upon to resolve have increased in diversity as well as complexity. Yet the potential of these tribunals for efficient disposition of these legal disagreements has not yet been [fully] tested. If they are to take their place in the international legal order, national courts will need to 'shake off the old judicial hostility to arbitration' . . . and also their customary and understandable unwillingness to cede jurisdiction to a claim arising under domestic law to a foreign or transnational tribunal. To this extent, it will be necessary for national courts to subordinate domestic notions of arbitrability to the international policy favouring commercial arbitration.

Since 1970, it appears that US courts have only twice refused to enforce foreign arbitral awards, and then only in part (reported in Stewart 1992: 191–2).

Europe

In Europe, national adaptation to the *Lex Mercatoria* is most visible in legislative revisions to the relevant code law (commentaries and assessments in Drobnig 1998; Hill 1997; Lörchner 1998; Rubino-Sammartano 1995). In the 1990s, the parliaments of England and Wales, Germany, and Italy have adopted statutes extensively revising the law on arbitration, whereas the French regime was reconfigured in the 1980s. Reforms have been in one direction: to deregulate international commercial arbitration by enhancing the autonomy and anational character of the Law Merchant. While there remain important technical differences, the new statutes: treat international arbitration more liberally than they do domestic arbitration; confer upon the contracting parties a wider scope to choose procedures and the controlling law of contract and arbitration; codify a doctrine of separability (note 10); recognize at least implicitly the *Kompetenz-Kompetenz* of arbitrators as well as their capacity to resolve conflict of laws issues (note 12); and reduce the grounds for judicial review of awards to a bare minimum. In France, the new code aligned itself with ICC priorities (Carbonneau 1992: 121), even placing the *Lex Mercatoria* on 'equal footing' with national and international sources of law as legitimate bases for awards (see Delaume 1995: 9–10).

There are at least three underlying motivations for deregulation. First, legislators and judges find it in the national interest to encourage transnational commerce. Second, court systems are overloaded. Providing for the autonomy of private international law arbitration drains off much complex litigation for which national law is less and less relevant. Third, there is now international 'competition for the "business" of ... international arbitration', and liberalizing is essential to attracting this business (Drobnig 1998: 196). In updating their own codes, German and Italian legislators claimed to be working to make their systems as hospitable to arbitration as England, France, and the United States.

The Institutionalization of the *Lex Mercatoria*

Although seriously under-studied, there is incontrovertible evidence that arbitration is becoming more cumbersome and costly, mostly due to the fact that some companies and their lawyers have come to treat it as a form of adjudication. Indeed, arbitration is in the process of *judicialization*. Lawyers now use techniques more associated with adversarial legalism than with procedural informality; and arbitration houses have had to replace trade generalists with technical experts and develop more formal and complex procedures to deal with the demands being placed on them (Dezelay and Garth 1996). Awards are longer and more closely argued; some of the most important awards are published, argued about in commentaries, and then used by trade lawyers and arbitrators as model precedents in subsequent disputes. Clearly, the balance between the general arbitral values of 'flexibility' and 'legal certainty' is being recalibrated in favour of the latter (Holtzmann 1992). Significantly, noisy calls for the creation of appellate courts for the arbitral system are being heard and actively debated (Seventh Geneva Global Arbitration Forum 1999). Of course, just how this new legal system responds to these pressure—how its organizational capacities are institutionalized—will determine a great deal of the future.

6

Abstract Review and Judicial Law-making

The diffusion of constitutional judicial review over the past half-century has resulted in the emergence of two dominant 'models' of review: the American and the European. In Europe, successive generations of politicians, constitution-makers, and legal scholars intensively debated but ultimately rejected importing American-style judicial review. They chose, instead, variations on a system that Hans Kelsen designed to 'fit' with existing parliamentary institutions, separation of powers ideologies, and a legacy of constitutional, but not 'judicial', review (Favoreu 1990; 1996; Kelsen 1928; Stone Sweet 2000: Ch. 2; von Beyme 1989). After the French Revolution, across much of the Continent parliamentary democracy had come to mean legislative supremacy; legislative supremacy implied separation of powers; and separation of powers meant the subjugation of the 'judicial function' to the 'political function'. Constitutional and statutory provisions codified these dogmas in diverse ways but to the same end: to make of the judge the 'slave of the legislator'. With the move to codifying constitutional rights, Kelsen's court spread across Europe because it enabled rights and other provisions to be enforced, as higher law, while maintaining—at least formally—the general prohibition against *judicial* review.[1]

The European model of constitutional review can be broken down into four constituent components (Stone Sweet 2000: Ch. 2). First, constitutional judges alone exercise constitutional review authority; the ordinary, non-constitutional judiciary remains precluded from engaging in review. Second, terms of jurisdiction restrict constitutional courts to processing constitutional disputes. Constitutional judges do not preside over judicial disputes or litigation or judicial appeals, which remain the purview of the judiciary; and the judiciary has its own appellate, supreme courts. Instead,

---

[1] In Europe, the creation of specialized jurisdictions, courts with specialized powers, has long substituted for grants of general jurisdiction to a unified judiciary, and Kelsen continued the tradition.

constitutional judges answer the *constitutional questions* that are referred to them by, among others, elected politicians and ordinary judges. Third, constitutional courts have links with, but are detached from, the judiciary and legislature. They occupy their own 'constitutional' space, a space neither 'judicial' nor 'political'. Fourth, most constitutional courts are empowered to judge the constitutionality of statutes before they have been applied. This mode of review, called 'abstract review', is typically defended as guaranteeing a more complete system of constitutional justice than does the American model, since it can eliminate unconstitutional legislation and practices before they can do harm. Thus, in the European model, the ordinary courts enforce the supremacy of statute in the juridical order, while the constitutional court is charged with reviewing statutes and authoritatively interpreting the constitution.

In American judicial review, by contrast, 'any judge of any court, in any case, at any time, at the behest of any litigating party, has the power to declare a law unconstitutional' (Shapiro and Stone 1994: 400). The power was derived by Chief Justice Marshall (USSC 1803) from the US Constitution, which confers on the judicial branch jurisdiction over 'cases' and 'controversies' that 'arise' under the 'Constitution' and the 'Laws'. If all American judges may enforce the constitution, it is typically assumed that they do so only in order to resolve specific 'cases'. For our purposes, a case is defined as litigation in which one of the disputing parties alleges to have been directly damaged by the enforcement of an unconstitutional law or other public act. American judicial review appears perfectly *concrete*, in European terms, in so far as it is activated by a claim that the enforcement of an unconstitutional law caused a real person—one of the litigants—actual injury. Advisory opinions on the constitutionality of statutes and other acts are precluded by the 'cases and controversies' requirement. Likewise, American courts will deny standing to parties that fail to show some degree of direct interest in the review of a public act, although doctrines governing standing have been famously unclear and unstable. In any event, even if it is impossible to deny that American courts will sometimes be required to participate in the work of the legislative or executive branches, it is still possible to claim that American review remains inherently 'judicial' to the extent that it is inherently 'concrete', because based on a case or controversy.

From the point of view of the American model, European constitutional review interjects elements of abstraction into the proceedings. 'Abstract review' is politically initiated, pre-enforcement review of legislation (see Stone Sweet's contribution to Chapter 3). It is *abstract* because it proceeds in the absence of litigation: the judges read the legislative text against the constitutional law, and then decide. There is no storyline or, if there is, the story is an imaginary or hypothetical one told to highlight the constitutional moral that comes at the end. 'Concrete review' is activated by a preliminary reference from a judge to the constitutional court, or a national judge to the European Court of Justice. What makes concrete review nominally *concrete* is its connection to—a stage in—a pre-existing judicial process. Concrete review is activated when a judge sends a question to the constitutional court; she does so when it is thought that one or more provisions of the constitutional law are material to the case, that is, that there is some reason to think that the controlling statutory norm or other public act is unconstitutional. Concrete review remains, nonetheless, meaningfully abstract in an overt and formal way. Technically, the task of the constitutional court is to answer the constitutional question posed—for example, is a provision of the code unconstitutional?—not to try the case or dispose of it. The task of the presiding/referring judge is to determine the facts, properly frame the question to the constitutional court, and then to resolve the dispute in light of the answer given. The remaining basic type of review—the individual constitutional complaint—is the least abstract in the sense that an individual must have exhausted all other remedies before turning to the constitutional court. In sum, even compared with other supreme courts, Kelsenian constitutional courts were designed as relatively pure oracles of the constitutional law. Their express function is to interpret the constitution and thereby to resolve disputes about the meaning of the constitution rather than to preside over concrete 'cases' in the American sense.

Orthodoxy has it, then, that in the United States the 'case and controversy requirement' enables judicial—concrete—review while prohibiting abstract review. It does so in the name of peculiarly American separation of powers ideas. In the European model of constitutional review, a different mix of peculiar ideas not only permits purely abstract review but insists that concrete review, too, be meaningfully abstract. Both models expressly defend the primacy of one mode of review as being necessary to preserve distinctions between the 'political' and the 'judicial' functions, as these distinctions are understood locally. And both attack the other mode as establishing a 'confusion' or powers, a usurpation of the legislator.

In the paper that follows, we use this orthodoxy as a reference point to ground a discussion about the essentially abstract nature of all judicial law-making. Every chapter of this book explores, in more or less depth and for various purposes, the fact that judges routinely select rules, not just to settle a particular dispute between two parties but to govern future interactions in a given domain of activity. Judges effectively make law through a combination of choice—the use of discretion—and justification—giving reasons—in light of their understanding of generic, not just particular, situations. Yet, unlike legislatures, courts do not activate themselves. One crucial set of questions confronting students of judicial lawmaking, then, concerns the extent to which this limitation actually matters and the extent to which different forms of jurisdiction and modes of review matter.

In the paper presented here, we respond to some of these questions with reference to the United States, using Europe as a backdrop. Parts of the paper were first published by Stone Sweet (1998b) as 'What is Concrete about Abstract Review in the United States?', in the *Revue Française de Droit Constitutionnel*. The article responded to the widespread belief, held on both sides of the Atlantic, that American courts did not engage in abstract review. The previous year, at a conference in Paris on comparative judicial review, Stone Sweet argued, with no noticeable effect, that the gulf between the American and the European models was much smaller than commonly assumed, given that American courts used abstract review techniques routinely, and given that constitutional courts, including the European Court of Justice, increasingly operated as appellate jurisdictions.[2] A few months later, two American supreme courts declared important statutes unconstitutional, although these laws had yet to be enforced. These decisions provided an opening into our topic. The piece was ultimately published with the strong encouragement of leading constitutional scholars, who read it in the light of their own self-interest in mitigating differences between the French system and the rest of the civilized world. The article was read as countering the widespread view that the French system, which allows only for abstract review, constitutes the least 'judicial' format for review in Europe and North America, and also the most 'political', while the American system, uncontaminated by Kelsenian elements, anchored the other opposite end on the continuum.

---

[2] For a more detailed discussion of this latter point, see Stone Sweet (2000: Ch. 4).

Abstract and Concrete Review in the United States

Alec Stone Sweet and Martin Shapiro

In the summer of 1997, two American supreme courts invalidated legislation before them after having suspended the application of these statutes pending a ruling on their constitutionality. In June, the US Supreme Court annulled key provisions of the Communications Decency Act, federal legislation that sought to regulate 'indecent' and 'offensive' expression on the Internet (USSC 1997). And in August, the Supreme Court of the State of California blocked the State assembly's attempt to require pregnant minors to obtain parental consent before receiving an abortion (CSC 1997). The decisions, which major American newspapers reported on their front pages, sparked debate in legislatures and on television and talk radio. While the rulings were viewed as important political events in their own right, we focus on them here in order to organize a discussion of the following two questions. In the United States, do courts exercise abstract constitutional review of statutes and other rules? The answer: an emphatic 'yes'. Given the 'case or controversy' rule, a rule established by the US Constitution, how 'concrete' is American abstract review? The answer: not much.

We begin by discussing how and under what conditions abstract review of statutes is exercised in the United States. The two decisions just mentioned are then examined, showing how such review operates in practice. We then pursue a more general discussion of judicial lawmaking in light of orthodox distinctions between different modes of review. The judicialization of politics proceeds through judicial lawmaking, which is always a blend of abstract and concrete.

Abstract Review of Statutes

In the jargon of European constitutional law, 'abstract review of legislation' refers to the control of the constitutionality of statutes, by a court or other jurisdiction, prior to their application or enforcement by public authorities. In American parlance, abstract review is review in the absence of a concrete 'case or controversy', the pure form of which is pre-enforcement review. In the US, abstract review occurs most often in one of the following two situations.[1] First, under certain circumstances, plaintiffs may seek declaratory or injunctive relief by a judge which, if granted, suspends the application of the law in question pending a judicial determination of its constitutionality. Plaintiffs commonly file such requests immediately after the statute has been signed into law by the appropriate authority. Second, under judicial doctrines developed by the US Supreme Court pursuant to litigation of First Amendment freedoms, plaintiffs may attack a law on its face, called a 'facial challenge', and plead the rights of third parties. Although there is often overlap between these two situations—a plaintiff mounting a facial challenge to a law will typically ask for preliminary relief—each deserves to be analysed on its own.

Preliminary Injunctions and Declaratory Judgments

Preliminary injunctions and declaratory judgments are legal remedies that have been developed by courts of equity. In the past 50 years or so, these techniques have penetrated into the constitutional law, becoming instruments of rights adjudication. Preliminary injunctions are court orders taken to preserve the *status quo ante litem* pending a judicial resolution of the dispute on the merits. Declaratory judgments are used by judges to clarify the rights of one of the parties to a dispute, prior to that dispute's resolution. Although the law of remedies distinguishes the preliminary injunction from the declaratory judgment in various ways,[2] these distinctions are of little relevance here. When exercising judicial review, US federal courts, including the US Supreme Court, commonly treat these forms of relief interchangeably. From the point of view of the plaintiff, moreover, there appears to be little difference in their relative effectiveness (Laylock 1994: 497). The criteria that govern the granting of preliminary injunctions also apply to the rendering of declaratory judgments. Judges will give relief where a plaintiff's constitutional rights are at issue, where the plaintiff is likely to prevail on

---

[1] Federal courts also continuously exercise abstract review of the rule-making of federal agencies, as discussed below.

[2] The traditional view is that the declaratory judgment is relatively less intrusive on the administration of the laws, especially criminal statutes. The purpose of the declaratory judgment is to clarify the rights of one litigant in a particular dispute, whereas the preliminary injunction enjoins a statute's enforcement altogether. In constitutional law, however, this distinction is breaking down (see USSC 1974b).

the merits, and where the plaintiff may suffer irreparable injury if relief is not granted.[3]

Facial Overbreadth and Vagueness

The US Supreme Court has, since *Thornhill* (1940), consistently held that a statute that extends government authority to activities protected by the First Amendment is presumptively overbroad, and therefore unconstitutional on its face, regardless of whether, or how, the statute has been applied in concrete situations. Put differently, the Court views the normal methods of constitutional adjudication—which proceeds on a case by-case basis, and enables the judicial branch to correct the law over time, with reference to problems raised as a result of the law's application—to be inappropriate for adjudicating violations of the First Amendment (Tribe 1988: 1023-4). Indeed, the Court treats the right of free expression as a 'preferred freedom' since it underpins democracy and the effective exercise of all other constitutional rights. In this area of the law, restrictive doctrines on standing and justiciability have therefore been relaxed. It is clear that the Court has been anxious to use its powers to protect the rights of individuals and groups who would normally not come before a court, in so far as they may refrain from exercising their rights for fear of punishment under a restrictive law. The negative impact of a law on speech is known as the 'deterrent effect' or the 'chilling effect'.

Thus, the doctrine of 'overbreadth' carves out an exception to the general rule, a corollary of the case or controversy requirement, that an individual cannot plead rights of other individuals not party to the action. In fact, a court that rules that a statute is overbroad may annul it, and reverse the conviction of the defendant in the case, without having to determine first whether the expressive conduct of the defendant falls under the protection of the first amendment. In *Spokane Arcades*, the Supreme Court summarized its approach to the problem of facial overbreadth and the rights of third parties in the following terms:

[A]n individual whose own speech or expressive conduct may validly be prohibited or sanctioned is permitted to challenge a statute on its face because it also threatens

---

[3] The rules are adapted from equity rules. In 1980, a US Circuit Court described 'the traditional equitable criteria for granting preliminary injunctive relief' to a plaintiff as fourfold: '(1) a strong likelihood of success on the merits, (2) the possibility of irreparable injury to plaintiff if the preliminary relief is not granted, (3) a balance of hardships favoring the plaintiff, and (4) advancement of the public interest [in certain cases]' (USCA Ninth Circuit 1980).

others not before the court—those who desire to engage in legally protected expression but who may refrain from doing so rather than risk prosecution or undertake to have the law declared partially invalid. If the overbreadth is 'substantial', the law may not be enforced against anyone, including the party before the court, until it is narrowed to reach only unprotected activity, whether by legislative action or by judicial construction of partial invalidation. (USSC 1985b: 491)

Courts resolve facial challenges in different ways. A court may render a decision that reduces the reach of a statute, without declaring its provisions unconstitutional. In such cases, the Court effectively interprets the statute in a particular way in order to make it constitutional. This 'saving construction' binds the judiciary. A court may also invalidate the statute as unconstitutional 'on its face'. A facial challenge will be successful if a court (1) agrees with the plaintiff that the law sweeps within its ambit activities protected by the First Amendment, thereby deterring these activities in a 'substantial' and 'socially significant' way, and (2) is unable or unwilling to construct a more narrow interpretation of the provisions being attacked, or to 'sever' potential constitutional applications of the law from unconstitutional applications. Of course, even if the appeal fails to result in a total invalidation of the law, a partial invalidation—an exercise in 'reconstructive surgery'—may be exactly the outcome the plaintiff wanted. To successfully defend a law, the government must demonstrate two things. First, it must show that whatever 'chilling effect' on speech the regulation might provoke will not be substantial but rather improbable and socially insignificant. Second, it must prove that the statute could not have been drafted more narrowly, that is, that there was no 'less restrictive alternative' statutory language available. A less restrictive alternative provision is one that it more likely to exclude unconstitutional applications and to reduce the deterrent effects of the regulation.

Most invalidations pursuant to judicial findings of overbreadth are partial invalidations: the court removes provisions that, in its view, would lead to unconstitutional applications of the law, allowing what remains of the law to be applied. However, 'severing' unconstitutional provisions from an otherwise constitutional statute is not always possible. If the offending provisions are central to the statute, benefits of severability are absent. In such cases, the court has little choice but to invalidate the statute, and no part of it will be enforceable (for example, USSC 1980).

Although plaintiffs who mount a facial challenge for overbreadth may claim that the same statute is also unconstitutionally vague, overbreadth and vagueness are distinguishable (see Tribe 1988: 1033–5). A statute is vague, and therefore unconstitutional, if persons 'of common intelligence must necessarily guess as its meanings and differ as to its application' (USSC 1926). A vague statute suffers from two interrelated flaws. First, it entails a high risk of discriminatory enforcement, raising concerns about due process and equal protection of the laws. Second, the risk of discriminatory enforcement may itself substantially deter or 'chill' the exercise of rights. To successfully defend a law attacked for vagueness, the government must show that the deterrent effect of the statute would not be substantial and that a more precise construction of its provisions, given the government's purposes, was not possible.

The 'Case or Controversy' Requirement

The abstract review of statutes conflicts with orthodox understandings of judicial authority in the US. The role of the judiciary, states the Constitution, is to resolve cases and controversies.[4] However, the precise, juridical meaning of the phrase 'case and controversy' has never been fixed, which has been all the more true when it comes to determining the compatibility of statutes with constitutional rights. In any event, the phrase cannot stand alone since it references doctrines related to separation of powers, standing to sue, and justiciability. Each of these legal frameworks has been constructed in complex lines of case law which are more or less incoherent. In what is arguably the most authoritative statement on the problem by the Supreme Court, Chief Justice Warren acknowledged this 'uncertainty':

Embodied in the words 'cases' and 'controversies' are two complementary but somewhat different limitations. In part these words limit the business of federal courts to questions presented in an adversary context and in a form historically viewed as capable of resolution through the judicial process. And in part these words define the role assigned to the judiciary in a tripartite allocation of power to assure that the federal courts will not intrude into areas committed to the other branches of government. Justiciability is the term of art employed to give expression to this dual limitation placed upon federal courts by the case or controversy doctrine.

Justiciability is itself a concept of uncertain meaning and scope.... [N]o justiciable controversy is presented when the parties seek adjudication of only a political question, when the parties are asking for an advisory opinion, when the question sought to be adjudicated has been mooted by subsequent developments, and when there is no standing to maintain the action. Yet it remains true that justiciability is not a legal

---

[4] The relevant provisions are the following: 'The judicial Power shall extend to all Cases, in Law and Equity, arising under this Constitution; the Laws of the United States... [and]... to Controversies to which the United States shall be a party; to Controversies between two or more States; between a State and Citizens of another State; [and] between Citizens of different States [...].

concept with a fixed content of susceptible or scientific verification. 'Its utilization is the resultant of subtle pressures' (USSC 1961).

... Additional uncertainty exists in the doctrine of justiciability because that doctrine has become a blend of constitutional requirements and policy considerations. And a policy limitation is 'not always clearly distinguished from the constitutional limitation' (Barrows v. Jackson 1953). ... The 'many subtle pressures' which cause policy considerations to blend into the constitutional limitation of Article III make the justiciability doctrine one of uncertain and shifting contours. (USSC 1968b)

No treatise on American constitutional law uses the term 'abstract review'. American constitutional practice and scholarship are largely ignorant of European constitutional law, where abstract review is ubiquitous. Confronted with a statement to the effect that American judges do indeed exercise abstract judicial review, an American judge or constitutional scholar would typically respond in one of two very different ways. First, the statement might be denied outright. Any law which substantially deters the exercise of some fundamental, constitutional right—such as the freedom of speech, or the right to privacy, including the right to control one's reproductive life—creates, by its very existence, a 'case or controversy' between those individuals so deterred and the government that deters them. This is the logic that underpins doctrines governing facial challenges and the granting of preliminary relief. Second, in contrast to the first response, the statement might be recast in terms that make sense to American judges and lawyers. It could be acknowledged that the practices described do indeed fall outside the case or controversy requirement but are relatively limited exceptions to the normal rules or are pathologies of American case law. Thus, a leading textbook (Cohen and Narat 1993: 122) states that preliminary relief 'takes a form suspiciously like that of an advisory opinion', which is prohibited. And Justice Black, in his opinion for the majority in *Younger* (USSC 1971), complained that 'facial challenges are fundamentally at odds with the function of the federal courts' to resolve cases and controversies.

However understood, the abstract review of statutes is alive and well in the United States. Indeed, it has become a 'normal' technique of judicial lawmaking in the areas of free speech and abortion rights.

Two Decisions

We now turn to recent judgments of two American Supreme Courts. In the first, the US Supreme Court adjudicated a facial challenge to a federal statute designed to prohibit pornography on the Internet. In the second, the

California Supreme Court reviewed the state legislature's attempt to restrict pregnant minors' access to abortion.

Regulating Offensive Speech in Cyberspace

The importance of the Internet and its interface system, the World Wide Web, to personal communications, commercial transactions, and advertising, has surged with the phenomenal growth of personal computing. At the beginning of the 1980s, about 300 'host' computers, most of which were owned and operated by American universities and government institutions, constituted the Internet, storing and relaying information among themselves. By 1996, the Net was comprised of some 10,000,000 host computers around the globe, about 60 per cent of which were based in the US. Until 1996, cyberspace, which had developed on its own with use, was left largely unregulated by the federal government.

The size of the Web, and its exact contours and content, are a mystery. What is clear is that the topic of *sex* takes up a huge proportion of cyberspace. The Web contains thousands of sites that perform useful public services, providing information about birth control, sexually transmitted diseases, homosexual support groups, and help for victims of rape and sexual harassment. But it also contains millions of sites that offer hard-core pornography, including photographs, film footage, and even video access to live 'performances'. Fearing government regulation of their activities, the majority of 'erotic' web site operators have set up a series of gate controls that (1) warn Web users that their site contains sexually explicit material and (2) require a statement that the user is 18 years or older. Some operators, who offer services for a fee, also require a credit card number or a special password which, they claim, is given only to adults. But many sites offering sexually explicit materials are free, and even the pay sites offer free 'previews' to anyone who states that they are 18 years or older. Because there yet exists no cost-efficient, technologically feasible way to verify the age of Web users, anyone with access to the Net has easy access to hard-core pornography. As worrisome, some of these sites offer child pornography and other illegal materials. But because operators can quickly and easily close down existing portals today and then open them up again with new coordinates tomorrow, policing the Internet remains desirable but virtually impossible, given the present state of technology.

In 1995, the US Congress began debating ways to regulate pornography on the Internet, finally producing the Communications Decency Act (CDA).[5]

---

[5] The act was one part of The Telecommunications Act of 1996, a long, complex statute designed to regulate telephone, cable television, radio broadcasting, and Internet services as one integrated sector.

Knowing that the constitutionality of the CDA would be litigated, legislators included a special provision, section 561, designed to expedite the review of the law's constitutionality in the event of a facial challenge. On 8 February 8 1996, the day the President signed the CDA into law, 20 public interest and business groups[6] did indeed file suit in a Federal District Court to prohibit the Federal Government from enforcing two of its key provisions. The plaintiffs claimed that two provisions of Title V violated the right of free expression guaranteed by the First Amendment to the US Constitution, and asked that the court enjoin the law's application. The two provisions (CDA 1996) read as follows:

Section 223 (a): ... Whoever –

(1) in interstate or foreign communications –
  (B) by means of a telecommunications device knowingly –
    (i) makes, creates, or solicits, and
    (ii) initiates the transmission of any comment, request, suggestion, proposal, image, or other communication which is obscene or indecent, knowing that the recipient of the communication is under 18 years of age, regardless of whether the maker of such communication placed the call or initiated the communication;
(2) knowingly permits any telecommunications facility under his control to be used for any activity prohibited by paragraph (1) with the intent that it be used for such activity, shall be fined under Title 18, or imprisoned not more than two years, or both.

Section 223 (d): ... Whoever –

(1) in interstate or foreign communications –
  (A) uses any interactive computer service to send to a specific person or persons under 18 years of age, or
  (B) uses any interactive computer service to display in a manner available to a person under 18 years of age, any comment, request, suggestion, proposal, image, or other communication that, in context, depicts or describes, in terms patently offensive as measured by contemporary community standards, sexual or excretory activities or organs, regardless of whether the user of such service placed the call or initiated the communication; or
(2) knowingly permits any telecommunications facility under such person's control to be used for an activity prohibited by paragraph (1) with the intent that it be used for such activity, shall be fined under Title 18, or imprisoned not more than two years, or both.

---

[6] Including the American Civil Liberties Union, Human Rights Watch, the National Writers Union, Stop Prisoner Rape, AIDS Education Global Information System, Queer Resources Directory, Safer Sex Web Page, and Planned Parenthood of America.

A District Court judge issued a temporary restraining order against the enforcement of these provisions and, shortly thereafter, 27 new plaintiffs filed a second suit.[7] After consolidating the actions, a three-judge District Court was convened pursuant to s.561 of the CDA. The panel found for the plaintiffs, and issued a preliminary injunction against the enforcement of the challenged provisions.

In her decision,[8] Chief Judge Sloviter declared that the CDA 'sweeps more broadly than necessary and thereby chills the expression of adults'. Further, she judged the terms 'patently offensive' and 'indecent' to be 'inherently vague'. The Court granted the injunction. The decision prohibited the government from enforcing violations of s.223(a.1.B) concerning indecent communications, while authorizing the government to prosecute child pornography activities; and it enjoined the enforcement of s.223(d.1.2), without qualification.

On appeal, the Supreme Court (1997) upheld the District Court's ruling, invalidating the law as unconstitutional for facial overbreadth and vagueness.[9] In its decision, the Court began by confronting the government's arguments to the effect that the CDA was 'plainly constitutional under three . . . prior decisions': *Ginsberg* (USSC 1968c), *Pacifica* (USSC 1978), and *Renton* (USSC 1986). In *Ginsberg*, the Court had upheld the constitutionality of a State law that prohibited the sale of sexually oriented material to minors, although such material could be lawfully purchased by adults. The authority of the Federal Communications Commission to regulate obscene content on the radio was upheld in *Pacifica*, on the grounds that the broadcast in question, a comedy routine, took place in the afternoon, 'when children were present'. And, in *Renton*, the Court allowed a municipal zoning rule prohibiting X-rated cinemas in certain neighbourhoods. In the present case, the government relied on these precedents to show: (1) that its interest in regulating obscene materials targeted at minors—or otherwise made available to them—was stronger than in cases in which such materials were marketed

[7] Plaintiffs in the second action included the American Library Association, America Online, American Booksellers Foundation for Free Expression, Citizens Internet Empowerment Association, CompuServe, Families Against Internet Censorship, Health Sciences Library Consortium, Magazine Publishers of America, Microsoft, Netcom On-Line, Newspaper Association of American, Opnet, Prodigy, and Society of Professional Journalists.

[8] Each of the three judges wrote a separate opinion, but all agreed that the act was unconstitutional on its face.

[9] Justice Stevens, joined by justices Scalia, Kennedy, Souter, Thomas, Ginsburg, Breyer, delivered the opinion of the Court. Justice O'Connor, joined by Chief Justice Rehnquist, concurred in part and dissented in part. O'Connor agreed with the majority that the act was unconstitutional, but would nevertheless allow the government greater flexibility in seeking to create separate adult and minor zones, and then to police more vigilantly the latter.

only to adults, and strong enough to cover the provisions under attack; and (2) that a scheme, which the government called 'cyberzoning', had constitutional support.

The Court rejected these arguments, distinguishing each of the cases from the dispute at hand. The New York statute upheld in *Ginsberg*, it argued, was more narrowly drawn than the CDA, since it applied only to commercial transactions and allowed parents to purchase magazines for their own children, despite the fact that public authorities might consider these same magazines to be too obscene for children to buy for themselves. The CDA, however, would apply to all transactions and would punish even those communications to which parents had consented. Further, the New York statute defined obscenity more carefully than did the CDA, as that which is 'utterly without redeeming social importance for minors'. In this and the two other cases cited by the government, the Court emphasized the crucial importance of context to its reasoning. In *Pacifica*, the Court had based its decision on the fact that children were most likely to be present in the audience during afternoon broadcasting. In addition, television and radio are, according to the Court, more 'invasive' than the cyberspace medium since a child would far more likely encounter an obscene television or radio broadcast by accident than he or she would accidentally encounter a sex-oriented website, given the warnings that precede entry into most sites. And in *Renton*, the city had justified its zoning regulations with reference to the public interest in combating the 'secondary effects' of adult movie theatres on neighbourhoods, such as a documented increase in crime. But, in the CDA, the Court stated, the government has produced a rule that is 'content' rather than 'context' based. Indeed, the rule all but ignores context, constituting a 'blanket restriction' on speech, and such restrictions are not permitted under the First Amendment.[10]

The Court then turned to a facial analysis of the statute itself, focusing on the word 'indecent' in s. 223(a) and the phrase 'patently offensive' in s. 223(d). The Court noted two fatal problems. First, 'each of the two parts of the CDA uses a different linguistic form', which 'will provoke uncertainty among speakers about how the two standards relate to one another and just what they mean'. The Court raised the second problem—overbreadth and vagueness—in the form of a question: 'Could a speaker confidently assume

[10] The government also defended the CDA with reference to the legal defences provided by s.223(e.5). Website operators could escape prosecution to the extent that they had (1) acted in 'good faith' and 'reasonably' to restrict access to minors' or, (2) required verification of minimum age. The Court dismissed the arguments on the grounds that such requirements placed too great a burden on operators, given the present state of the technology.

that serious discussion about birth control practices, homosexuality, [and] the consequences of prison rape would not violate the CDA?' Because the CDA is 'content-based' and because Congress had not adequately defined the words 'indecent' and 'patently offensive', the CDA 'raises special First Amendment concerns because of its obvious chilling effect on free speech'. Further, because the CDA contains criminal sanctions, it may well 'cause speakers to remain silent rather than communicate even arguably unlawful words, ideas, and images'. Thus: 'this increased deterrent effect coupled with the risk of discriminatory enforcement of vague regulations' imposes a special burden of the government to justify the law.

For its part, the government argued that s.223(a) and s.223(d) fell within the standard for defining 'obscenity' adopted by the Court in *Miller* (USSC 1973*a*). In that case, the Supreme Court established a three-part test for determining whether a given expressive act fell outside the purview of the First Amendment. If 'the average person, applying contemporary community standards, would find that the work, taken as a whole, appeals to the prurient interest'; 'if the work depicts or describes, in a patently offensive way, sexual conduct specifically defined by the applicable state law'; and 'if the work, taken as a whole, lacks serious literary, artistic, political, or scientific value', then it does not enjoy constitutional protection. Although each element of the *Miller* test clarifies, in some important manner, the meaning of 'obscene speech' for purposes of determining whether it may benefit from the shelter of the First Amendment, the CDA obviously contains no such clarifications, excepting the mention of 'descriptions of depictions' of 'sexual or excretory activities or organs' contained in s.223(d)—which may or may not be obscene under *Miller*. Whereas the *Miller* test was designed to restrict the scope of the obscenity exception to the First Amendment, the CDA is more open ended. Indeed, the Court ruled that: 'The breadth of CDA is wholly unprecedented . . . The general, undefined terms "indecent" and "patently offensive" cover large amounts of nonpornographic material with serious educational or other value'. Thus, as the Court moved to the final stage of the decision—determining (1) which provisions were 'severable' from the law and therefore incapable of being constitutionally enforced, and (2) which provisions, once reconstructed, could be applied—it was clear that the government had failed 'to explain why a less restrictive provision would not be as effective as the CDA'.

The Court upheld the District Court's ruling, removing the term 'indecent' from s.223(a), and leaving the term 'obscene' in place; but the judges insisted that 'in no other respect . . . can s.223(a) or s.223(d) be saved by such a textual surgery'. Thus, speech on the Internet is protected to the extent that it is not obscene, as governed by the *Miller* test.

Restricting Access to Abortion Services in California

Since the US Supreme Court's landmark decision in *Roe v. Wade* (USSC 1973*b*), the constitutional law and the legislative politics of reproductive rights have been intimately intertwined. In *Roe*, the Court ruled, among other things, that every woman possess the right to terminate her pregnancy, by appropriate medical procedures, during the first trimester of her pregnancy; after the first trimester, this right gradually yields to the government's interest in protecting the health of the woman and the life of the foetus. According to the Court, the 'right to choose' to terminate pregnancy inheres in the right of privacy, which, although not mentioned in the text of the US Constitution, was nonetheless found there in *Griswold* (USSC 1965). Far from settling or pacifying the abortion controversy in any meaningful sense, *Roe* provoked more of it, becoming the focus of unrelenting political opposition from some interest groups and State legislatures (Craig and O'Brien 1993). Some State legislatures adopted statutes they knew violated the rules laid down in *Roe* , fully expecting that the statutes would be the subject of litigation, and hoping that the US Supreme Court would overrule or soften these rules.[11]

Some States also sought to restrict the number of abortions performed by requiring the prior consent of spouses, and in the case of minors, the prior consent or notification of parents. In 1976, the Supreme Court, by a 5-4 vote, struck down a State law requiring the prior consent of spouses (USSC 1976*a*). That same year, in *Bellotti*, the Court (1976*b*) upheld a State law requiring a minor to obtain parental consent, but ruled that States must also provide minors who have been denied parental consent, or who do not wish to ask their parents for consent, the right to obtain such permission from a judicial authority. After *Bellotti*, 26 States, including California, passed laws requiring some form of prior parental notification or consent, and made provision for the 'judicial bypass' mandated by the Court.

In California, before 1967 abortions could be obtained legally only when necessary to preserve the life of the pregnant woman. In the Therapeutic Abortion Act of 1967, the State assembly made abortions lawful under either of two conditions: (1) when there was 'substantial risk' that continuation

---

[11] Such statutes are rarely enforced since they are usually immediately attacked before federal judges who usually grant preliminary relief. States, however, have been successful in watering down some of the rules announced in *Roe*, most prominently in *Casey* (USSC 1992*a*).

of the pregnancy would 'impair' the woman's physical or mental health, or (2) when pregnancy was the result of rape or incest. As a direct result of liberalization, the number of abortions performed in California rose from 5,018 in 1968 to 116,749 three years later (Luker 1984).

The legal capacity of minors to make direct decisions about their own health care also evolved rapidly during this period. Under the common law, doctors could be sued for battery if they provided medical services to minors without having obtained the prior consent of a parent or legal guardian. Beginning in the 1950s, however, the State legislature adopted a series of laws expanding the conditions under which minors could receive counselling, medical services, hospitalization, and surgery. Thus, laws permitted minors to seek and receive care—without having to obtain prior consent— concerning: any aspect of pregnancy and birth, including surgery (1953); sexually transmitted diseases (1968); rape (1977); and drug and alcohol problems (1977). In 1971, the California Supreme Court (CSC 1971) held that a minor could obtain an abortion, under a 1967 law, without the consent of her parents. The Court reasoned that if, under section 34.5 of the Civil Code, as amended in 1953, minors could receive the same care with respect to pregnancies as adults, then this capacity must extend to abortion services. In 1987, the State assembly enacted Bill 2274. The legislation added a clause to the Civil Code which stated that s.34.5 'does not authorize a . . . minor to receive an abortion without the consent of a parent or guardian other than as provided by Section 25958 of the Health and Safety Code'. For its part, s.25958 stated that:

(1) except in a medical emergency requiring immediate medical action, no abortion shall be performed upon a . . . minor unless she first has given her written consent to the abortion and has also obtained the written consent of one of her parents or legal guardian;
(2) if one or both of [the] pregnant minor's parents or her guardian refuse to consent to the performance of an abortion, or if the minor elects not to seek the consent . . . [the] minor may file a petition with the juvenile court . . . setting forth with specificity the minor's reasons for the request.

According to this provision, if the juvenile judge determines that the minor 'is sufficiently mature and sufficiently informed to make the decision on her own regarding an abortion, . . . the court shall grant the petition' but, if not, 'the court shall then consider whether the performance of the abortion would be in the best interest of the minor', granting or denying—subject to appeal—the petition accordingly. Doctors who performed abortions in contravention of these rules were to be subject to fines and imprisonment.

The legal history of Bill 2274 is a tortured one. After the statute was enacted in November 1987, but before it was to enter into force on 1 January 1988, several groups[12] representing physicians and women's reproductive rights sought a preliminary injunction against enforcement of the statute on the grounds that it violated the right to privacy contained in Article 1 of the California constitution.[13] In December 1987, the Superior Court granted the injunction, a ruling that was upheld by the Court of Appeal in October 1989. The Court of Appeal based its decision on the finding that the prior consent provisions would likely infringe on a 'pregnant minor's intimate and fundamental right to choose whether or not to continue her pregnancy'. After a trial based on the testimony of experts in health care, family counselling, the operation of similar systems in place in other States, and so on, the Superior Court struck down Bill 2274 as unconstitutional, a ruling which the Court of Appeal later affirmed. The California Supreme Court rendered two decisions on the bill. In the first, a 4-3 majority upheld the statute as constitutional but, shortly after the decision was reached, one of the justices died. After a new justice was appointed, the Court vacated its own judgment and decided to rehear the case. In its second decision, discussed here, a 4-3 majority invalidated Bill 2274 as unconstitutional.

In its defence of the statute, the State relied heavily on the case law of the US Supreme Court, initiated in *Bellotti*, which upheld governmental authority to require the prior consent of parents before minors could proceed to an abortion. In fact, legislators had drafted Bill 2274 on the basis of this case law, hoping to insulate the law from constitutional challenge. In its decision, the Court—the plurality[14]—began by distinguishing the scope of the State privacy right from the federal one. Noting that 'the California Constitution is and always has been a document of independent force... and that the rights embodied in and protected by the state of California are not invariably identical to the rights contained in the federal Constitution',[15] the Court declared that the California right to privacy 'is broader and more protective of privacy than the

---

[12] Plaintiffs included the American Academy of Pediatrics, the California Medical Association, the American College of Obstetricians, and Planned Parenthood of San Francisco.

[13] 'All people... have inalienable rights. Among these are... privacy'. Privacy was added to the list of 'inalienable rights' in California in 1972, by referendum.

[14] The decision, supported by a plurality of three justices, was delivered by Chief Justice George. A fourth justice filed a concurring opinion. Three dissents were also filed. To simplify, the dissenters argued that, in the controlling decision, the plurality had (1) lowered threshold requirements binding on the plaintiffs, (2) placed on the government an increased burden to justify the compelling interests embodied by the statute, and (3) violated the separation of powers.

[15] The Court emphasized that the California right to privacy had an explicit textual foundation, whereas the federal right had only been judicially 'discovered'.

federal constitutional right of privacy as interpreted by the federal courts'. Therefore, the constitutionality of Bill 2274 under federal constitutional law was not relevant to the present inquiry.

The Court then proceeded to examine the bill under the applicable threshold requirements. Threshold requirements are judicial standards to ensure that the power of judicial review will be used only to adjudicate serious rights claims, allowing the Court to filter out frivolous claims. In the area of privacy, a plaintiff shoulders the burden to demonstrate that (1) the claim implicates 'a specific, legally protected, privacy interest'; (2) 'a reasonable expectation of privacy' inheres in the context of the plaintiff's preferred choice of action; and (3) the 'invasion of privacy' is a 'serious' one. The Court ruled that the plaintiffs easily met these requirements:

[B]ecause the decision whether to continue or terminate has such a substantial effect on a pregnant minor's control over her personal bodily integrity, has such serious long-range consequences in determining her life choices, is so central to the preservation of her ability to define and adhere to her ultimate values regarding the meaning of human existence and life, and (unlike many other choices), is a decision that cannot be postponed until adulthood, we conclude that a minor who is pregnant has a protected privacy interest under the California Constitution . . . and that this interest is intruded upon by the provisions of Assembly Bill 2274.

A finding that the plaintiffs' privacy interests were substantial shifts the burden to the government to justify the statute in question. Thus, to prevail, the State would have to show that (1) it possessed a 'compelling state interest' in regulating the matter in question and (2) that this interest could not have been 'served by alternative means, less intrusive of fundamental rights'.[16] The constitutionality of Bill 2274 turned, therefore, on whether the State's 'compelling interests' in requiring parental consent were sufficiently important to support the restriction of the right to choose which would otherwise be possessed by pregnant minors. The State based its case on two such interests: (1) 'to protect the physical, emotional, and psychological health of minors'; and, (2) 'to preserve and protect the parent–child relationship'. The Court agreed that these interests 'rose to the level of compelling interests for purposes of constitutional analysis'. Nevertheless, it ruled that the statute at hand would actually harm, rather than further, the State's purposes. The State's claim that the bill would protect the health of minors was undermined by the fact that State law permits minors to make their own decisions regarding a host of other health matters, including whether or not to carry

---

[16] This is a version of the less 'restrictive alternative' doctrine developed by the US Supreme Court, and is broadly equivalent to proportionality tests developed in European administrative law.

the foetus to term and, after birth, to give the baby up for adoption. The Court saw no justification for this distinction.

Further, the statute would likely place minors at medical risk to the extent that they would not seek the consent of their parents. Likewise, the judicial bypass procedure would entail delays, and delays can complicate the provision of abortion procedures. Thus, Bill 2274, if enforced, 'is likely to impair, rather than to protect, the health of pregnant minors who do not wish to bear a child'. As to the second of the State's declared interests, the Court ruled that, far from promoting a closer parent-child relationship, the law would more likely 'exacerbate the instability and dysfunctional nature of the family' since the statute would most often come into play in those cases where the parent-child relationship was already under strain. Last, the Court noted that the State had not provided any empirical evidence to show that the capacity of minors to make their own decisions as to whether to terminate pregnancies had been detrimental to their health. In fact, the Court stated, the evidence pointed in the opposite direction.

Accordingly, the Court affirmed the judgments of the Superior Court and the Court of Appeal, and the law was annulled.

One other element of plurality's opinion is relevant to our concerns here, namely, the standards governing facial challenges. Recall that because plaintiffs had demonstrated that a substantial privacy interest was at stake, the Court had proceeded to a 'compelling interest' test. The state had argued—and the dissenters would agree—that, when a facial challenge was before the Court, the State enjoyed a reduced burden. Indeed, the State argued that it should be required to show only that the statute could be constitutionally applied in at least one circumstance. The dissenting justices argued at length that to require the government to justify the law under a compelling interest standard has led the Court to usurp the legislative function, that is, to substitute its policy judgment for that of the representative majority. The Court rejected this argument[17] on the grounds that, if accepted, the constitutional vice of overbreadth could no longer be controlled judicially. This part of the decision deserves to be quoted at length:

As a general rule, it is not the judiciary's function ... to reweigh the legislative acts underlying a legislative enactment. When an enactment intrudes upon a constitutional right, however, greater scrutiny is required. The ordinary deference a court owes to any legislative action vanishes when constitutionally protected rights are threatened. The rational connection between the remedy provided and the evil to be curbed, which might in other contexts insulate legislation against attack on due

---

[17] The California Court noted that the US Supreme Court, in its two leading decisions on abortion, *Roe* and *Casey*, had rejected similar arguments.

process grounds, will not suffice. We would abandon our constitutional duty if we took at face value the [legislative] determination . . . [citations removed]

The passage led one dissenter to respond that: 'Vanishing acts may be appropriate to the lexicon of a magician whose task it is to make things disappear. It cannot be used to describe the work of the judiciary cognizant of the inherent limits of our constitutional scheme. Smoke and mirrors should be no part of our repertoire'.[18]

Assessment

Few Europeans today argue that abstract review is little more than 'smoke and mirrors', and when they do almost no one listens. Yet only a few generations ago a similar view was the dominant, scholarly position in Europe. According to this position, American judicial review constituted the necessary and only acceptable means of ensuring stable, constitutional rule of law. During France's golden age of public law—the Third Republic—for example, the consensus scholarly position was that specialized, constitutional courts were inherently 'political' and legislative rather than 'judicial', precisely because the judicial function was understood in American 'case or controversy' terms (Stone 1992: Chs 1, 3, 9).

If today the legitimacy of the specialized constitutional court and of abstract review is beyond challenge, how do we explain the fact that the basic techniques of abstract review have infected American judicial review? This question raises important issues of theory and method in comparative law. Of course, we see the obvious institutional differences between, say, the French Constitutional Council and the US Supreme Court. But if we draw up a list of each court's respective duties and powers, and do not proceed further, we would miss the fact what the French Council actually does when it reviews the constitutionality of statutes looks a great deal like what American courts actually do when they engage in pre-enforcement review of statutes. In making this claim, we neither ignore nor minimize the formal, organic distinctions between constitutional review authority in France and the US. On the contrary, the greater these distinctions, the more theoretically relevant are findings of regularities. Put differently, the more we would expect, for formal 'comparative law' reasons, jurisdiction A and jurisdiction B to operate differently, the more significant is the finding that A and B operate similarly. In the face of such findings, the next step is to seek answers to two questions. First, what might explain these similarities?

---

[18] Dissenting opinion of Justice Brown.

Second, how general is the phenomenon in question and thus how generally applicable is our candidate explanation?

The development of abstract review in judicial systems in which such review is formally prohibited—for example, the American system—follows from an expansive understanding of the judicial role in protecting the constitutional rights of individuals from government incursion. A hypothesis: the more judges are asked to protect rights in an effective manner—the pan-European situation—or the more judges consider effective rights protection to be their constitutional duty—the American situation—the less likely judicial review will conform to, or be contained by, separation of powers doctrines that preclude abstract review. Put very differently, in systems in which the supremacy of the constitutional law within the general hierarchy of norms is defended by a jurisdictional authority, all separation of powers notions are contingent because they are secondary to, rather than constitutive of, the judicial function.

The American courts, in complicity with litigants, have carved out a place for abstract review by case law and precedent. The American doctrine of 'overbreadth' relies on a logic that is inherently the stuff of abstract review: a law that *could* substantially 'deter' the exercise of certain rights *is* null and void on its face. Today in the US all important statutes that would restrict free speech or the right to choose to terminate pregnancies are routinely attacked on their face and are candidates for preliminary relief. In such cases, what do American judges do? They make authoritative guesses about the future: guesses about how people would likely behave under the law; guesses about how a law would likely be enforced by public officials; guesses about how a statutory provision would likely be construed by the courts; and guesses about how many citizens would likely be hurt if the court permitted the law to be applied. European constitutional courts, when they exercise abstract review, make such determinations all of the time, informed, just as American judges are, by legislative histories and debates, and by their knowledge of how similar laws have been enforced and judicially interpreted in the past. Unlike the American courts, however, European constitutional judges do not have to perform doctrinal gymnastics to justify their abstract review powers, because European constitutions expressly confer these powers.

Everywhere it exists, rights adjudication proceeds through the elaborate construction of balancing tests, typically coupled with a proportionality—or 'least means'—requirement.[19] Inevitably, such tests organize the judicial construction of hypothetical situations, narratives with abstractions as

[19] In Europe, the development of balancing and proportionality tests has made review more concrete by leading constitutional courts, especially in Germany and Spain, to delve ever more

characters, stand-ins for real people facing challenging dilemmas. In the CDA decision, American judges imagined an average 'speaker' interested in 'serious discussion of prison rape, homosexuality, [or] birth control'. They read the text of the statute and decided that it would, if allowed to enter into force as written, have produced 'an obvious chilling effect'. The speaker would be led to keep silent, and the government failed to show that this cost was warranted, given its own policy interests. For the judges of the California informed-consent law, the stand-in character of the drama was a pregnant girl who, although 'sufficiently mature', came from an 'unstable and dysfunctional' family. The law, although defended by the State as furthering the protection of the family, would, according to the Court, have made it even more dysfunctional. There is nothing concrete in such review, except in so far as the decision reconfigures the constitutional environment for the legislature, for the future. If and when it does so, it will have to imagine the situation at least partly as the judges have.

The specific techniques of abstract review developed by American judges are strikingly similar, indeed virtually identical, to those developed by European judges. We will mention two of the most important of these here. First, once American judges have concluded that specific statutory provisions are unconstitutional, they then proceed to determine if these provisions can be severed from the statute to enable the constitutional, and thus uncontaminated, parts to be applied. In what is perhaps the leading constitutional law textbook in the US, Tribe (1988: 1027–33) characterizes this practice as 'surgery', or 'pruning the rotten branches from the tree'. European constitutional judges employ the same techniques, and judges and scholars use virtually the same language to describe the process. The French Council, for example, performs 'amputations' on provisions 'contaminated' by unconstitutionality, allowing what remains to be promulgated (Stone 1989). Second, both American judges and European constitutional courts routinely participate in the legislative function by using their review powers to give authoritative interpretations of statutes—the 'saving construction' in American parlance, and 'strict reserves of interpretation' in France; other phrases are used to describe the same things in Germany, Italy, and Spain.

deeply into the work of the ordinary judiciary pursuant to concrete review referrals. The phenomenon has provoked protests from ordinary judges and scholars, who lament that their constitutional court has become de facto a general appellate instance, or a cassation court, thus violating separation of powers (Stone Sweet 2001: Ch. 4). It could not have been otherwise. Once constitutional judges required the ordinary judge to engage in balancing, they made the latter's decision-making reviewable; and, in doing so, they empowered individuals, through the constitutional complaint procedure, to appeal *how* the ordinary judge has balanced directly to the constitutional court.

The judges do so in order (1) to permit the law to enter into force, and thus soften the impact of constitutional review on the legislature, and (2) to control how the law will be enforced by public authorities and applied by the judiciary in the future. These similarities deserves to be studied more closely by comparative constitutional scholars.

More generally, defining governance as the continuous adaptation of norms to situations brings the judge and legislator quite close to one another. Rights review of legislation, as Kelsen predicted, makes of the judge both a 'positive' and a 'negative' legislator. Turning the coin over, abstract review situations push legislatures into quasi-judicial behaviour.[20] The California State assembly tailored its law in strict accordance with the decision of the US Supreme Court in *Bellotti*, knowing full well that the law would be attacked in a facial challenge before a California or federal judge. The legislature presumed that the final word would be had by judicial, not legislative, authority. The US Congress was so sure that the CDA would be subjected to pre-enforcement review that it included a special provision in the law to put it on a fast track to the US Supreme Court.

The Abstract in Concrete Review

Just as we may uncover elements of concrete review within what appear to be relatively isolated American abstract review practices, we may also discover that the main stream of American concrete review contains many abstract counter-currents.

Our understanding of the fundamental similarities between US concrete and European abstract review has been confounded by a number of historical accidents. The US Constitution does not specifically authorize constitutional judicial review as do the contemporary constitutions of European states in which such review is practised. As a result, in the famous opinion in *Marbury v. Madison* on which US review is grounded, John Marshall (USSC 1803) was driven to a complex argument for review, an argument derived from the fundamental duty to decide 'cases and controversies' 'arising under' the Constitution that is specifically assigned to the Court by Art. III. Marshall argues that, where a constitutional norm and a statutory norm conflict, and the resolution of that conflict *is essential to the outcome* of the particular case before it, a court must decide that conflict. By defining and limiting constitutional judicial review in this way, Marshall succeeds in transmuting constitutional review into the kind of 'conflicts of law' problem that

[20] See Stone Sweet's paper in Chapter 3.

Anglo-American courts had always been required to resolve. Remember that Art. III vests the 'judicial power' in the federal courts. Surely any power that American judges, and English judges before them, had always exercised must be a judicial power. The power to choose between two conflicting laws, when such choice was necessary to the determination of which of two litigants would prevail, had always been exercised by such courts. Therefore it must be judicial. If constitutional review is, and is confined to, such a conflicts of law power, then it must be a judicial power. If it is a judicial power, it is authorized by Art. III: QED. Thus Marshall's confining of constitutional review to conflicts of law situations in genuine cases and controversies not only ties review to the specific cases and controversies language of the Constitution but, far more importantly, renders judicial review into a facet of the judicial power specifically granted to the federal courts by the Constitution. It is for this reason that American courts, lawyers, and scholars must cling so hard to the cases and controversies rationale, even after review has in reality moved into a phase that Europeans would label 'abstract'.

A kind of mirror image of the American historically generated anomaly exists in Europe. Europeans begin with the notion of statutory sovereignty, and so must reject diffuse judicial review, as well as review of individual rights claims against statute. The present-day constitutional court has its roots in the *Tribunat* of post-revolutionary France and the specialized jurisdictions of the Germanic federal states. In the nineteenth century, the purpose of constitutional review was to enforce the separation of powers provisions of constitutions, whether to preserve the powers of executives vis-à-vis parliaments or to police federal arrangements. The only true parties to a constitutional litigation were the separated powers, one of which was complaining of the invasion of its authority by another. That invasion occurred when the offending statute or executive act occurred. Its subsequent application or non-application to a particular citizen was irrelevant to the separation of powers issue that these jurisdictions were supposed to resolve. It was the offence of one governing institution against another that was significant, immediately vesting standing to seek review *in the officials* representing that institution, not in private parties before ordinary judges. The injury to the institution done by an incursion on its powers by another institution was real and immediate whether or not some individual citizens might sooner or later be harmed by it. In that sense, abstract review was concrete for the institution of government whose powers had been concretely invaded.

This relatively pure system of abstract review was most clearly reflected in the system of the French Fifth Republic pre-1974, in which review could be activated only by certain representative officials of the executive and the parliamentary chambers, at the instant at which the constitutional powers of their part were allegedly invaded by another part. However, once the Constitutional Council has discovered individual rights within the Constitution (1971), and once the power of referral was given to the parliamentary opposition (1974), the situation became absurd. French citizens now have constitutional rights, but neither they nor any other entity can ask the Constitutional Council to protect them. Moreover, all other judges remain precluded from hearing the individual's claim or engaging in the judicial review of statutes.

The abstract review category, used as Kelsen intended, as a limiting doctrine denying the judiciary jurisdiction over the constitution and keeping it out of rights review, thus becomes an embarrassment once individual constitutional rights were codified or discovered in constitutions. But it has an even more embarrassing feature in a number of European states other than France. If abstract review—that is, pre-enforcement review of legislation—is combined with, rather than maintained in opposition to, individual constitutional rights judicial review, then the courts are in danger of being flooded with every anti-government paranoid fantasy that any citizen can dream up. Indeed the courts of countries that allow individual constitutional complaints—for example, Germany, Spain, and many more in Eastern Europe—have been flooded, forcing constitutional judges to invent various practices designed to reduce the complaints actually reviewed to a trickle. In theory, individual complaints are meant to be the most concrete 'cases' European constitutional judges receive. In theory, individual complaints are meant to permit individuals to vindicate rights as a last resort, usually meaning once regular judicial remedies have been exhausted; but they were not meant to provide yet another means of attacking the constitutionality of statutes. Nonetheless, such attacks now occur regularly in Germany where individuals are able to show that a statute has hurt them in a 'direct' and 'personal' way (Schenke 1986); and the Spanish doctrine, according to which the *amparo* cannot be used to challenge a statute, is rapidly breaking down (see Guasch 1994). In fact, many of the most politically important complaints are, in fact if not in theory, completely abstract.[21]

---

[21] Indeed, abstract review and the constitutional complaint can at times become one and the same. In a striking example, the German statute ratifying the Maastricht Treaty—establishing European citizenship, monetary union, and a central bank—was suspended after four members of the German Green Party, joined by a former German EC Commissioner, attacked its constitutionality in separate constitutional complaints. Complainants focused on the alleged 'democratic deficit' afflicting the EC, and charged that the ratification had weakened German democracy. The German Court (GFCC 1993) dismissed the complaint but not before asserting its own powers to review claims based on the *ultra vires* nature of EU acts (Stone Sweet 2001: 175-7)

European courts hearing relatively 'abstract' individual complaints are likely to focus on the same questions as American courts do when deciding to grant preliminary injunctions or declaratory relief, or to act on facial overbreadth or vagueness claims. They will respond favourably where the plaintiff himself is likely to suffer irreparable injury even though the claim is technically abstract or where the statutory language on its face clearly will deter constitutionally protected conduct by others.

US courts have used standing rules to regulate the flow of more or less abstract cases. Recently, there has been some retreat from permissive standing doctrines. The Supreme Court is attempting to discourage individual complaints of government unlawfulness when such claims are unaccompanied by even a modicum of personal injury and when it is government failure to act that is at issue (see particularly USSC 1992b). The Court's narrowing of standing has been exaggerated by activist, interest-group oriented lawyers. Nevertheless, there is a US mood that reflects the same concerns as those of European and Latin American courts that, in theory, are required to take allegations of government unlawfulness seriously even when no harm to the individual complainant has taken place, and no concrete injury to anyone appears to be imminent. At a formal level, American lawyers must insist that there is no abstractness to review, and European lawyers must insist that there is. In both places, however, an individual constitutional complaint is more likely to be successful the more clearly some real injury to the constitutional rights of some particular person can be shown.

Anglo-American overt resistance to abstract review rests on more than the peculiar textual situation in which John Marshall found himself. It also rests on an asserted 'common law' virtue, that judges can make better decisions when confronted with concrete circumstances than with purely textual problems. As a well-known fictional English judge is wont to say, the common law is common sense. Common sense operates more easily on small, concrete, immediate problems than on large abstract ones, particularly large ones requiring much speculation about what might happen under many different circumstances at various future times. Yet this equation of concrete review with 'thinking small' is spurious.

In the first place, judicial policy-making may be more or less incremental or synoptic whether it occurs through abstract or concrete review (see Chapter 2). Under either, legal change may be accomplished more or less rapidly and/or radically. US Supreme Court decisions, such as *Brown v. Board of Education* (USSC 1954 on school desegregation), *Roe v. Wade* (USSC 1973b on abortion) and *Miranda v. Arizona* (USSC 1966 on admission of involuntary confessions) were all concrete review decisions, but they rival any abstract review decision ever issued anywhere in the magnitude of change in public policy introduced.

Second, the degree to which concrete review involves a small number of known, current circumstances rather than a broad range of unknown future ones is easily exaggerated. In theory the concrete reviewer is concerned only with current, real injury to one particular person, the named party in the lawsuit. Even when a US court is *not* dealing with a First Amendment 'facial' challenge to a statute, however, this limitation of judicial concern to a single party's alleged constitutional injury is largely fictional.

Gideon v. Wainwright (USSC 1963) is the case in which the Supreme Court announced that the American States must provide free legal counsel to criminal defendants when they could not afford to pay for such counsel themselves. This case converted what previously in the US had always been considered a negative constitutional right, that is, a guarantee that government could not prevent a criminal defendant from employing a lawyer, into a positive constitutional right, that is, a government obligation to provide criminal defendants with lawyers. At the time the case was decided, the justices were fully aware that a decision that Mr Gideon was constitutionally entitled to government-provided counsel would radically alter criminal justice processes in dozens of States and require many millions of dollars of new public expenditure throughout the United States. The notion that the *Gideon* decision resulted from nine judges thinking carefully about one man and his repeated arrests for drunkenness in Atlanta, Georgia, and what was happening to poor Mr Gideon in connection with one of those arrests, is bizarre. The *Gideon* case was simply a vehicle for, and Gideon himself only a personalization of, a massive public policy problem that was pervasive across the US, the plight of indigent defendants. It was not about a problem peculiar to one arrest of one person in one American city. The justices were clearly aware that what they should decide depended on their prediction of how local governments throughout the US would respond in the future to a Court-announced right to publicly provided counsel. It would be absurd to believe that the Court suddenly became sensitized to the problem of the indigent defendant by the plight of Mr Gideon. Indeed, it is not that they became concerned with the plight of indigent defendants by taking Mr Gideon's case, but that they took Mr Gideon's case because they were ready to announce a major, new national public policy on criminal defence—the US Supreme Court is free, with a few exceptions, to chose what cases it takes. Everyone involved in *Gideon* was aware that the issue was future, massive, nationwide government spending, not whether Mr Gideon yet again went to jail for a few days or weeks. Indeed, the value of Mr Gideon to the Court was not that the particular circumstances of his case assisted the justices in clarifying their thinking. Rather, Mr Gideon's circumstances were so typical of the circumstances faced by all indigent defendants that a decision in his favour would have massive, universal application, changing the public policy of many States and creating national uniformity in the treatment of indigent defendants.

This point can be made more generally. Every constitutional court inevitably announces that no particular constitutional right is absolute. All such courts eventually resort to some form of balancing or proportionality doctrine that proclaims that an individual right may be invaded when there is a sufficiently pressing countervailing right or public interest the protection of which requires such an invasion. Thus freedom of speech rights do not prevail when someone falsely shouts 'fire' in a crowded theatre, or falsely maligns the reputation of another, or truthfully broadcasts the details of troop movements in wartime. Just as inevitably, such courts arrive at a 'least means' corollary to balancing doctrines. Even when pressing public interests require some invasion of individual rights, only the minimum level of such invasion necessary to achieve the public purpose is constitutionally permissible.

Even in the most *concrete* of concrete review cases, balancing and least means or proportionality doctrines move courts far, far beyond the immediate circumstances of the named parties to the litigation. In defending the statute constitutionally attacked under a balancing standard, the state will bring before the court broad issues of public policy and public interest far removed from the immediate circumstances of the constitutional complainant. Whether or not this particular child pornographer actually abused some particular child in order to produce this particular piece of child pornography, the statute against child pornography is on balance constitutional because, although it interferes with freedom of expression, it deters the abuse of children. And when the government makes this argument in court, counsel for the child pornographer would be unwise to respond simply that his client produced his particular pornography without abusing any particular child. Surely counsel must go on to argue to the court that the statute does invade speech rights but does not really deter child abuse, and so the constitutional balance falls against it. Moreover, counsel with the least bit of sense will go on to argue that if what the government is concerned about is not censoring speech it does not like but preventing child abuse, it ought to pass and vigorously enforce child abuse statutes, that such statutes rather than child pornography statutes would achieve a legitimate state interest at the least cost to freedom of speech. The government will reply that vigorous enforcement of child abuse statutes is being done, but that standing alone, without supporting child pornography penalties, abuse statutes would not prove sufficient to achieve child protection. At this point, of course, the debate presented to the court has moved far, far beyond the particular and immediate circumstances of the particular case and the particular person alleging constitutional injury. The argument has moved to precisely the same broad, general, future probabilistic data and arguments that legislatures must examine in order to make a decision about whether to enact child pornography statutes in the first place. In the US tradition the case is technically a concrete review case, but the issue is not how the child pornography statute did, in the past, in fact operate in this one situation, but how it has in the past and will in the future operate in general across a wide range of predicted circumstances.

Finally, in any legal system that takes precedent seriously the claim that concrete review privileges particular circumstances is seriously undercut. If the concrete reviewer is aware that its decision will be treated as precedent not only in future cases in which the circumstances are exactly the same but in those with even roughly analogous circumstances, then the reviewer must take account not only of how the law now announced will affect the parties to the current case but what impact it will have in future cases and on the conduct of future potential parties seeking to avoid violating the law announced today. In short, to the degree constitutional reviewers are announcing a norm for the future in a present case, they would be foolish indeed not to consider the possible array of future circumstances in which the norm will be applied as well as the narrow set of past circumstances presented by the instant litigation.

In major US constitutional cases, the particular facts of the case become mere vehicles for the introduction of wide-ranging, future-regarding, predictive, probabilistic analysis. How can a court concentrate on what really happened to some old drunk when it knows that the decision it announces in the drunk's case will have far less impact on that drunk than it will on thousands of dope dealers and millions of taxpayers? The pathos of one episode of the human condition may, and perhaps should, touch even the judges of highest appeals courts (Noonan 1976). It may humanize the dull statistics of policy analysis. Nevertheless, no matter how formally concrete their review, US courts are fully aware that their major constitutional decisions are not simply 'doing justice' in particular, concrete past circumstances, but announcing general policy norms applicable to many different and not fully predictable circumstances in the future. They hear and attend to arguments about that future as well as those about current, particular injustice.

Today, what remains most concrete about concrete review in the US is a continuing, complex, often self-contradictory or inconsistent body of jurisprudence about standing that courts can sometimes use to narrow, reduce, or redirect the flow of constitutional litigation, use to avoid deciding particular controversies, and/or employ to legitimize a judicial review power not explicitly granted by the constitution. But, in many major constitutional litigations in the US, the concrete serves only to contain a great pool of general social data and policy analysis from which the courts derive general and forward-looking social policies that are far more politically significant than the concrete resolution of the particular case. Indeed, if that were not so the flood of ink spilled over the Supreme Court would be reduced to a trickle.

Just how unconcerned American jurisprudence is with the supposed virtues of reviewing a legal norm in the context of experience gained from its concrete implementation can be seen in a major area of non-constitutional American judicial review: the statutory review of administrative rules and regulations. Many Congressional statutes authorize administrative agencies to make supplementary rules to implement the statute. These rules have the force of law. These statutes almost always provide for pre-enforcement judicial review of such rules. This review can be sought only by private parties who can satisfy standing requirements. The review is abstract in the sense that the question of whether the rule challenged violates the Congressional statute authorizing the rule must be answered immediately after the rule has been promulgated and before it has been enforced on anyone. All the reviewing court has is the text of the statute and the text of the rule. This does not mean, however, that this abstract review is conducted solely, or even largely, by textual exegesis. Instead, the court hears all sorts of data, analysis, and argument about what the probable results of the projected future enforcement of the rule will be. Neither Congress, the courts, nor the targets or putative beneficiaries of these rules and regulations is willing to wait until a history of concrete enforcement has accumulated before review occurs. The stakes are too high. Instead, courts issue injunctions and declarations now, on the basis of their best guesses about how the rules would work out in the future if they were allowed to be applied in the future. This American confidence in abstract review is all the more notable because Congress has often resorted to delegating future lawmaking power to the agencies precisely because Congress is not confident it can predict how particular legal norms will work in the future. If it could, it would write them into the statute now rather than authorizing the agencies to make them in the future. We encounter the paradox that pre-enforcement judicial review which requires judicial predictions about the future is authorized by Congress as part of

Congress's response to its own perceived inability to predict the future. Paradox or no, American administrative law has firmly rejected the idea that judges can deal successfully only with situations in which legal norms have already been concretely enforced on particular people.

We may conclude this discussion of the crumbling of concrete review by a look at the most controversial of all areas of recent Supreme Court jurisprudence. As we have just seen in the example drawn from California, the abortion cases are a rather startling example of the interaction of the particular or concrete and the general. In *Roe v. Wade* and other such cases, the particular plights of the named—or, rather, unnamed—parties were certainly presented to the judges at length and may indeed have pushed them toward entering an arena that there were very good reasons for them to stay out of. Abstract arguments about life were countered by very concrete arguments about poverty and coat-hanger abortions. It might well be argued that seeing abstract constitutional arguments in the context of the concrete plight of particular parties here assisted judges or at least influenced outcomes.

The right to privacy, which is central to US abortion jurisprudence, first was announced not in the abortion cases themselves but in an earlier case, *Griswold v. Connecticut* (USSC 1965). *Griswold* involved a constitutional challenge to a Connecticut statute forbidding the provision of birth control services. The particular factual context emphasized by concrete review in this case would have made for an easy decision if the Supreme Court had been in the mood to really do concrete review. The Connecticut statute had been in place for many years. During those years private care physicians had been providing their patients with birth control information, and birth control supplies were available in pharmacies all over the State to whoever could afford to pay. No one was ever prosecuted. The only time prosecutions occurred was when someone tried to open a birth control clinic in New Haven to serve the poor. Then, under pressure from the Catholic Church, Catholic New Haven prosecutors elected by Catholic New Haven voters prosecuted the clinics. The particular facts, regard for which is supposed to be the special virtue of concrete review, screamed out for a constitutional equal-protection decision based on a finding of a long and consistent pattern of selective prosecution. Middle-class Connecticut women got all the birth control they wanted. Neither they nor their suppliers were ever prosecuted. Connecticut deprived only poor women of birth control by prosecuting only birth control clinics serving the poor.

In fact, this equal-protection argument and the facts behind it were emphasized to the Court, precisely because counsel believed that they would make it easier for the Court to take a small first step into the controversial procreation area, a step confined to the particular State fact situation and avoiding a direct general challenge to all State birth control and abortion laws. Within the Court itself such a narrow, fact-based, equal-protection draft opinion was produced but rejected. Instead the Court totally ignored the particular facts and produced an opinion based entirely on pure textual analysis of the Constitution itself. In short, the Court rejected concrete review and deliberately engaged in abstract review. Not only would concrete review have been easier strategically for the Court, but the abstract, textually focused review in which the Court engaged yielded a preposterous opinion that has been the butt of hostile analysis ever since. In fact there was selective, discriminatory prosecution that would have been easy to find. In text, there is no right of privacy in the Constitution. Yet Justice Douglas, for the majority, ignoring the concrete facts and the concrete parties, grimly set out to wring an abstract right to privacy from the constitutional text, so that he could then assert that because the Connecticut statute violated that right it was abstractly unconstitutional on its face whether enforced differentially or not. To do so Justice Douglas had to lean together five constitutional clauses, none of which mentioned privacy. Even then he could not assert that even the five together added up to a right to privacy. Instead, he had to assert that a constitutional right to privacy was to be found not inside the five-poled tepee he had constructed but outside the tent in the shadow or penumbra cast by the tent. This right to privacy was so much a product of textual torture that it couldn't even get in out of the rain.

Here is an instance in which the US Supreme Court engaged in what technically speaking was concrete review, totally ignored the enormous advantages that real concrete review could have offered, and chose instead to engage in an absurd, abstract textual analysis to arrive at a purely general, doctrinal conclusion. Whatever the Court's reasons for doing so, *Griswold* was concrete review that ended up in the most abstract of abstract reviews.

Certainly television has taught us that a single picture of a weeping child may move us more than a thousand words on the horrors of war. But, when we know that what we choose to do, or not do, about that particular child will become the norm for how we treat the next thousand children, we take the future of the thousand into account. So long as lawyers understand the emotional clout of concrete examples, real or imagined, they will introduce them into constitutional discourse. So long as judges know that their resolution of one present case will bear on the resolution of many future cases, they will consider the consequences of what they do.

As every architect knows, the abstract and the concrete are inseparable.

References

Law Cases

US Supreme Court Decisions

USSC (1803). *Marbury v. Madison*. 5 U.S. 137 (1803)

—— (1824). *Gibbons v. Ogden*. 9 Wheat. 1.

—— (1829). *Willson v. Blackbird Creek Marsh Co*. 2 Pet. 245.

—— (1833). *Barron v. Baltimore*. 32 U.S. 243 (1833)

—— (1852). *Cooley v. Board of Wardens*. 12 How. 299.

—— (1890). *Chicago, Milwaukee and St. Paul Ry. Co. v. Minnesota*. 134 U.S. 418.

—— (1926). *Connally v. General Construction*. 269 U.S. 385.

—— (1935). *Schechter Poultry Corp. v. United States*. 295 U.S. 495.

—— (1936). *Carter v. Carter Coal Co*. 298 U. S. 238 (1936).

—— (1940). *Thornhill v. Alabama*. 310 U.S. 88.

—— (1954). *Brown v. Board of Education*, 347 U.S. 483.

—— (1961). *Poe v. Ullman*. 367 US 497.

—— (1963). *Gideon v. Wainwright*. 372 U.S. 335.

—— (1965). *Griswold v. Connecticut*. 381 U.S. 479.

—— (1966). *Miranda v. Arizona*. 384 U.S. 436.

—— (1968a). *U.S. v. O'Brien*. 391 U.S. 367.

—— (1968b). *Flast v. Cohen*. 392 U.S. 83.

—— (1968c). *Ginsberg v. New York*. 390 U.S. 629.

—— (1969). *Tinker v. Des Moines School District*. 393 U.S. 503.

—— (1971). *Younger v. Harris*. 401 U.S. 37.

—— (1973a). *Miller v. California*. 413 U.S. 15.

—— (1973b). *Roe v. Wade*. 410 U.S. 113.

—— (1974a). *Spence v. State of Washington*. 418 U.S. 405.

—— (1974b). *Steffel v. Thompson*. 415 U.S. 452.

—— (1976a). *Planned Parenthood of Central Missouri v. Danforth*. 428 U.S. 552.

—— (1976b). *Bellotti v. Baird*. 428 U.S. 809.

—— (1978). *Federal Communications Commission v. Pacifica Foundation*. 438 U.S. 726.

—— (1980). *Schaumberg v. Citizens for a Better Environment*. 444 U.S. 620.

—— (1983). *Motor Vehicle Mfrs. Association of the United States, Inc. v. State Farm Mutual Auto Insurance Co*. 463 U.S. 29.

—— (1984). *Chevron USA v. Natural Resources Defense Council*. 467 U.S. 837.

—— (1985a). *Mitsubishi Motors Corp. v. Soler Chrysler-Plymouth, Inc*. 473 U.S. 614.

—— (1985b). *Brockett v. Spokane Arcades*. 472 U.S. 491.

—— (1986). *Renton v. Playtime Theaters*. 475 U.S. 41.

—— (1989). *State of Texas v. Johnson*. 491 U.S. 397.

—— (1992a). *Planned Parenthood of Southeastern Pennsylvania v. Casey*. 505 U.S. 833.

—— (1992b). *Lujan v. Defenders of Wildlife*. 504 U.S. 555.
—— (1997). *Reno v. the American Civil Liberties Union*. 65 U.S. Law Week 715-30 (June 24).

US District Courts Decision

US District Court (1990). *National Oil Corporation v. Libyan Sun Oil Co*. 733 F. Supp. 800 (D. Del. 1990).

US Courts of Appeals Decisions

USCA, Second Circuit (1974). *Parsons and Whitmore Overseas Co. v. Société Générale de l'Industrie du Papier*. 508 F.2d 969 521 U.S. 844.
—— Ninth Circuit (1980). *Los Angeles Memorial Coliseum Commission v. National Football League*. 623 F.2d 1197.

California Supreme Court Decisions

CSC (1971). *Ballard v. Anderson*. 4 Cal.3d 873.
—— (1997). *American Academy of Pediatrics, et al. v. Lungren*. 66 Cal.R.2d 210.

European Court of Justice Decisions

ECJ (1963a). *Germany v. Commission*. Case 24/62, ECR 1963: 63.
—— (1963b). *Van Gend en Loos v. Administratie der Belastingen*. Case 26/62, ECR 1963: 1.
—— (1964). *Costa v. ENEL*. Case 6/64, ECR 1964: 585.
—— (1968). *Beus v. Hauptzollampt München*. Case 5/67, ECR 1968: 83.
—— (1974a). *Van Duyn v. Home Office*. Case 41/74, ECR 1974: 1337.
—— (1974b). *Procureur du Roi v. Dassonville*. Case 8/74, ECR 1974: 837.
—— (1978). *Amministrazione delle finanze dello Stato v. Simmenthal*. Case 106/77, ECR 1978: 629.
—— (1981a). *Germany v. Commission*. Case 819/79, ECR 1981: 21.
—— (1981b). *Italy v. Commission*. Case 1251/79, ECR 1981: 205.
—— (1984a). *Rewe-Zentrale AG v. Direktor Der Landwirtschaftskammer Rheinland*. Case 37/83, ECR 1984: 1229.
—— (1984b). *Agricola Commerciale Olio Srl v. Commission*. Case 232/81, ECR 1984: 3881.
—— (1984c). *Von Colson v. Land Nordrhein-Westfalen*. Case 14/83, ECR 1984: 1891.
—— (1985a). *Re: British Telecommunications: Italy v. Commission*. Case 41/83, ECR 1985: 873.
—— (1985b). *Stichting Sigarettenindustrie v. Commission*. Joined Cases 240/82, 242/82, 261/82, 262/82, 268/82, 269/82, ECR 1985: 3831, 3882.
—— (1985c). *Remia BV and Others v. Commission*. Case 42/84, ECR 1985: 2545.
—— (1985d). *FRICO v. Voedselvoorziening In-en Verkoopbureau*. Joined Case 424/85, ECR 1985: 2755.
—— (1986a). *Eridania zuccherifici nazionali SpA v. Cassa Conguaglio Zucchero*. Case 250/84, ECR 1986: 117.

ECJ (1986b). *Akzo Chemie BV v. Commission.* Case 53/85, ECR 1986: 1965.

—— (1987a). *Consorzio Cooperative D'Abruzzo v. Commission.* Case 15/85, ECR 1987: 1005.

—— (1987b). *Re Generalised Tariff Preferences, Commission v. Council.* Case 45/86, ECR 1987: 1493.

—— (1987c). *Mannesmanröhren-Werke AG v. Council.* Case 333/85, ECR 1987: 1381.

—— (1987d). *NTN Toyo Bearing Co. Ltd v. Council.* Case 240/84, ECR 1987: 1809.

—— (1987e). *Re Reevaluation of the Green Mark: Germany v. Commission.* Case 278/84, ECR 1987: 1.

—— (1987f). *Re German Regional Aid Plans: Germany v. Commission.* Case 248/84, ECR 1987: 4013.

—— (1988a). *Re Skimmed Milk Powder, Netherlands v. Commission.* Case 238/86, ECR 1988: 1191.

—— (1988b). *Re Clawback on Export of Sheep: United Kingdom v. Commission.* Case 61/86, ECR 1988: 431.

—— (1988c). *Re Tuna Producers: France v. Commission.* Case 264/86, ECR 1988: 973.

—— (1988d). *Re Agricultural Hormones: United Kingdom v. Council.* Case 68/86, ECR 1988: 855.

—— (1988e). *Technointorg v. Commission and Council.* Joined Cases 294/86 and 77/87, ECR 1988: 6077.

—— (1988f). *Re The Protection of Battery Hens, UK v. Council.* Case 131/86, ECR 1988: 905.

—— (1988g). *Regina v. H. M. Commissioners of Customs and Excise ex parte v. The National Dried Fruit Trade Association.* Case 77/86, ECR 1988: 757.

—— (1989a). *Association Générale Producteurs De Ble (AGPB) v. Office National Interprofessionnel Des Cereales (ONIC).* Case 167/88, ECR 1989: 1653.

—— (1989b). *Re Roofing Felt Cartel: Société Coopérative Des Asphalteurs Belges ('Belasco') v. Commission.* Case 246/86, ECR 1989: 2117.

—— (1990a). *Marleasing v. Comercial Internacional de Alimentación.* Case C-106/89, ECR 1990: [I] 4135.

—— (1990b). *Barber v. Guardian Royal Exchange Assurance Group.* Case 262/88, ECR 190: [I] 1889.

—— (1991a) *Technische Universität München v. Hauptzollamt München-Mitte.* Case C-269/90, ECR [I] 1991: 5469.

—— (1991b). *Francovich and Bonifaci v. Italy.* Case C-6 and 9/90, ECR 1991: [I] 5357.

—— (1991c). *Dekker v. Stichting Vormingscentrum voor Jong Volwassenen.* Case 177/88, ECR 1991: [I] 3941.

—— (1991d). *Handels–og Kontorfunctionaerernes Forbund v. Dansk Arbejdsgiverforening (Hertz).* Case 179/88, ECR: [I] 3979.

—— (1992). *La Cinq SA v. Commission.* Case T-44/90, ECR 1992 [II]: 1.

French Constitutional Council Decisions

Conseil (1982a). Case 81-132: 1.

—— (1982b). Case 82-137: 38.

—— (1982c). Case 82-146: 66.

—— (1984*a*). Case 83-165: 30.
—— (1984*b*). Case 84-181: 73.
—— (1986*a*). Case 86-210: 110.
—— (1986*b*). Case 86-217: 141.
—— (1993). Case 93-325: 224.

English High Court Decision

Queen's Bench Division (1988). *Regina v. Minister of Agriculture Fisheries and Food and Sec'y of State for Health ex parte Fédération Européenne de la Santé Animale.* Common Market Law Review 3 (1988): 661.

German Federal Constitutional Court Decisions

FCC (1954). 4 BVerfGE .
—— (1956). 5 BVerfGE 85.
—— (1973*a*). 35 BVerfGE 79.
—— (1973*b*). 36 BVerfGE 1.
—— (1975). 39 BVerfGE 1.
—— (1979). 50 BVerfGE 290.
—— (1980). 55 BVerfGE 274.
—— (1993). 89 BverfGE 155.

Parliamentary Documents

France

National Assembly debates: 20 November 1980; 26 July 1982; 27 July 1982; 24 May 1983.
Senate debates: 20 November 1981.

Germany

Bundesrat debates: 21 February 1975; 12 December 1975.
Bundestag debates: 7 November 1975.
Bundestag reports: Drucksache 7/4462 (1975); 7/1328 (1972).

General

Alter, Karen (1998). 'Who are the "Masters of the Treaty"? European Governments and the European Court of Justice'. *International Organization*, 52: 121.
—— (2001). *Establishing the Supremacy of European Law.* Oxford: Oxford University Press.

Alter, Karen and Meunier-Aitshalia, Sophie (1994). 'Judicial Politics in the European Community: European Integration and the Pathbreaking Cassis de Dijon Decision'. *Comparative Political Studies*, 26: 535.

Aman, Alfred Jr. and Mayton, William (1993). *Administrative Law*. Saint Paul, MN: West.

Arrow, Kenneth (1974). *The Limits of Organization*. New York: Norton.

Arthur, W. Brian (1994). *Increasing Returns and Path Dependence in the Economy*. Ann Arbor, MI: University of Michigan Press.

Auerbach, Carl, Garrison, Lloyd, Hurst, Willard, and Mermin, Samuel (1961). *The Legal Process, An Introduction to Decision-Making by Judicial, Legislative, Executive and Administrative Agencies*. San Francisco: Chandler Publishing Co.

Axelrod, Robert (1986). 'An Evolutionary Approach to Norms'. *American Political Science Review*, 80: 1095.

Baird, Douglas, Gertner, Robert, and Picker, Randal (1994). *Game Theory and the Law*. Cambridge, MA: Harvard University Press.

Banks, Arthur (1976). *Cross-National Time Series, 1815–1973* (Inter-university Consortium for Political and Social Research #7412). Ann Arbor, MI:.

Baum, Lawrence (1997). *The Puzzle of Judicial Behavior*. Ann Arbor: University of Michigan Press: ICPSR.

Baumann, Alfons, Odening, Martin, Weikard, Hans-Peter, and Brandes, Wilhelm (1996). 'Path-Dependence Without Increasing Returns to Scale and Network Externalities'. *Journal of Economic Behaviour and Organization*, 29: 159.

Beck, Nathaniel and Katz, Jonathan N. (1995). 'What to Do (and Not to Do) with Time Series Cross-Section Data'. *American Political Science Review*, 89: 634.

Becker, Theodore and Feeley, M. (eds) (1973). *The Impact of Supreme Court Decisions: Empirical Studies*. New York: Oxford University Press.

Benson, Bruce L. (1992). 'Customary Law as a Social Contract: International Commercial Law'. *Constitutional Political Economy*, 3: 1–27.

Bentham, Jeremy (1988). *An Introduction to the Principles of Morals and Legislation*. London: Methuen.

Berger, Klaus Peter (1999). *The Creeping Codification of the Lex Mercatoria*. The Hague: Kluwer.

Berman, Harold J. and Dasser, Felix J. (1998). 'The "New" Law Merchant and the "Old": Sources, Content, and Legitimacy', in Thomas E. Carbonneau (ed.), *Lex Mercatoria and Arbitration: A Discussion of the New Law Merchant*. Yonkers: Juris.

Bickel, Alexander (1962). *The Least Dangerous Branch, The Supreme Court at the Bar of Politics*. Indianapolis: Bobbs-Merrill.

Black, Charles (1960). *The People and the Court*. New York: Macmillan.

Black, Donald (1998). *The Social Structure of Right and Wrong*. San Diego, CA: Academic Press.

Blair, Philip (1978). 'Law and Politics in West Germany'. *Political Studies*, 26: 348.

Blaurock, Uwe (1998). 'The Law of International Commerce', in Franco Ferrari (ed.), *The Unification of International Commercial Law*. Baden-Baden: Nomos.

Blessing, Marc (1997). 'Choice of Substantive Law in International Arbitration'. *Journal of International Arbitration*, 14: 39–65.

Bonell, Michael J. (1998). 'UNIDROIT Principles and the Lex Mercatoria', in Thomas E. Carbonneau (ed.), *Lex Mercatoria and Arbitration: A Discussion of the New Law Merchant*. Yonkers: Juris.

Booysen, Hercules (1995). *International Transactions and the International Law Merchant*. Pretoria: Interlegal.

Braunthal, Gerard (1983).*The West German Social Democrats: Profile of a Party in Power*. Boulder, CO: Westview.

Braybrooke, David and Lindblom, Charles (1963). *A Strategy of Decision*. New York: Free Press.

Brennan, Geoffrey and Buchanan, James M. (1985). *The Reason of Rules: Constitutional Political Economy*. Cambridge: Cambridge University Press.

Brinkman, G. (1981). 'The West German Federal Constitutional Court: Political Control through Judges'. *Public Law*, Spring: 83.

Burley, Anne-Marie and Mattli, Walter (1993). 'Europe Before the Court: A Political Theory of Legal Integration'. *International Organization*, 47: 41.

Bussani, Mauro and Ugo Mattei (1997/98). 'The Common Core Approach to European Private Law'. *Columbia Journal of European Law*, 3: 339.

Cadwallader, Mervyn L. (1959). 'Cybernetic Analysis of Change in Complex Social Organizations'. *American Journal of Sociology*, 65: 154.

Caldeira, Gregory (1994). 'Review of the Supreme Court and the Attitudinal Model'. *American Political Science Review*, 88: 483.

—— and Gibson, James L. (1995). 'The Legitimacy of the Court of Justice in the European Union: Models of Institutional Support'. *American Political Science Review*, 89: 356.

Calvert, Randall L. (1995). 'Rational Actors, Equilibrium, and Social Institutions', in Jack Knight and I. Sened (eds), *Explaining Social Institutions*. Ann Arbor: University of Michigan Press.

Campbell, Dennis (ed.) (1994). *International Franchising Law* (2 vols.). New York: Bender.

Cappelletti, Mauro (1980). 'The Mighty Problem of Judicial Review and the Contribution of Comparative Analysis'. *Southern California Law Review*, 53: 409.

Carbonneau, Thomas (ed.) (1990). *Lex Mercatoria and Arbitration*. Dobbs Ferry, NY: Oceana.

—— (1992). 'National Law and the Judicialization of Arbitration: Manifest Destiny, Manifest Disregard, or Manifest Error', in Richard B. Lillich and Charles N. Brower (eds), *International Arbitration in the 21st Century: Towards 'Judicialization' and Conformity?* Irvington, NY: Transnational.

—— (1995). 'Beyond Trilogies: A New Bill of Rights and Law Practice Through the Contract of Arbitration'. *American Journal of International Arbitration*, 6: 1–27.

—— (ed.) (1998). *Lex Mercatoria and Arbitration: A Discussion of the New Law Merchant*. Yonkers, N.Y.: Juris.

Cardozo, Benjamin N. (1921). *The Nature of the Judicial Process*. New Haven: Yale University Press.

Chapman, Bruce (1994). 'The Rational and the Reasonable: Social Choice Theory and Adjudication'. *The University of Chicago Law Review*, 61: 41.

Cherry, Colin (1957). *On Human Communications: A Review, a Survey, and a Criticism*. Cambridge, MA: MIT Press.

Cichowski, Rachel (1998). 'Integrating the Environment: the European Court and the Construction of Supranational Policy'. *Journal of European Public Policy*, 5: 387.

—— (2001). 'Judicial Rulemaking and the Institutionalization of EU Sex Equality Policy', in A. Stone Sweet, W. Sandholtz, and N. Fligstein (eds), *The Institutionalization of Europe*. Oxford: Oxford University Press.

—— (2002). 'Litigation, Mobilization and Governance in Europe' (Ph.D. thesis). Irvine: University of California.

Cohen, William and Narat, Jonathan (1993). *Constitutional Law*. Westbury, NY: Foundation Press.

Cole, Taylor (1959). 'Three Constitutional Courts: A Comparison'. *American Political Science Review*, 53: 963.

Collier, Jane Fishburne (1973). *Law and Social Change in Zinacantan*. Stanford, CA: Stanford University Press.

Collins, Hugh (1998). 'Formalism and Efficiency'. Paper presented at the Workshop, Private Law Adjudication in the European Multi-Level System, 2–3 October. San Domenico di Fiesole: Robert Schuman Centre, European University Institute.

Conant, Lisa (2002). *Requested info*. Ithaca, NY: Cornell University Press.

Constable, Marianne (1993). *The Law of the Other*. Chicago: University of Chicago Press.

Cooter, Robert and Ulen, Thomas (1988). *Law and Economics*. Glenview, Ill.: Scott Foresman.

Cour de Cassation (1995). *La Cour de Cassation et la Constitution de la République* [The Supreme Court and the Constitution of the Republic]. Aix-en-Provence: University Press of Aix-en-Provence.

Cox, Archibald (1976). *The Role of the Supreme Court in American Government*. Oxford: Oxford University Press.

Craig, Barbara and O'Brien, David (1993). *Abortion and American Politics*. Chatham, NJ: Chatham House.

Craig, Paul (1991). 'Sovereignty of the UK Parliament After Factortame'. *Yearbook of European Law*, 11: 221.

—— and De Burca, Grainne (1995). *EU Law*. Oxford: Oxford University Press.

Currie, David (1985). 'The Constitution and The Supreme Court: The Protection of Economic Interests, 1889–1910'. *University of Chicago Law Review*, 52: 324.

Cyert, Richard and March, James (1963). *A Behavioral Theory of the Firm*. Englewood Cliffs, NJ: Prentice Hall.

Dahl, Robert (1957). 'Decision-Making in a Democracy: The Supreme Court as a National Policy-Maker'. *Journal of Public Law*, 6: 297.

Danelski, David (1962). 'The Influence of the Chief Justice in the Decision Process, Court, Judges and Politics', in Walter Murphy and C. Herman Prichett (eds), *Courts, Judges and Politics: An Introduction to the Judicial Process*. New York: Random House.

David, Paul (1985). 'Clio and the Economics of QWERTY'. *American Economic Review*, 75: 332.

—— (1992). 'Path-Dependence and Predictability in Dynamic Systems with Local Network Externalities: A Paradigm for Historical Economics', in D. Foray and H. Freeman (eds), *Technology and the Wealth of Nations*. London: Pinter.

—— (1993). 'Historical Economics in the Long Run: Some Implications of Path Dependence', in G. Snacks (ed.), *Historical Analysis in Economics*. London: Routledge.

—— (1994). 'Why are Institutions the Carriers of History? Path Dependence and the Evolution of Conventions, Organizations, and Institutions'. *Structural Change and Economic Dynamics*, 5: 205.

—— (1997). *Path Dependence and the Quest for Historical Economics: One More Chorus of the Ballad of QWERTY* (Oxford Discussion Papers in Economic and Social History 20). Nuffield College, Oxford <http://www.nuff.ox.ac.uk/Economics/History>

—— and Greenstein, Shane (1990). 'The Economics of Compatibility Standards: An Introduction to Recent Research'. *Economic of Innovation and New Technology*, 1: 1.

Dehousse, Renaud (1994). *La Cour de justice des Communautés européennes* [The European Court of Justice]. Paris: Montchrestien.

—— (1996). 'Comparing National and EC Law: The Problem of the Level of Analysis'. *American Journal of Comparative Law*, 44: 761.

Delaume, Georges R. (1995). 'Reflections on the Effectiveness of International Arbitral Awards'. *Journal of International Arbitration*, 12: 5–19.

—— (1996). 'Choice-of-Forum and Arbitration Clauses in the United States: A Judicial Crusade'. *Journal of International Arbitration*, 13: 81–92.

Dellbruck, Jost (1993). 'Globalization of Law, Politics and Markets–Implications for Domestic Law–A European Perspective'. *Indiana Journal of Global Legal Studies*, 1: 5.

Deutsch, Karl W., Burrel, Sidney, Kann, Robert, Lee, Maurice, Lichterman, Martin, Lindgren, Raymond, Lowenheim, Francis, and Van Wagenen, Richard (1957). *Political Community and the North Atlantic Area: International Organization in the Light of Historical Experience*. Princeton: Princeton University Press.

Dezelay, Yves (1992). *Marchands de Droit*. Paris: Fayard.

—— and Garth, Bryant G. (1996). *Dealing in Virtue: International Commercial Arbitration and the Construction of a Transnational Legal Order*. Chicago: University of Chicago Press.

Donahey, M. Scott (1996). 'From *The Bremen* to *Mitsubishi* (and Beyond): International Arbitration Adrift in U.S. Waters'. *American Journal of International Arbitration*, 7: 149.

Drobnig, Ulrich (1998). 'Assessing Arbitral Autonomy in European Statutory Law', in Thomas E. Carbonneau (ed.), *Lex Mercatoria and Arbitration: A Discussion of the New Law Merchant*. Yonkers, N.Y.: Juris.

Dror, Yehezkel (1950). 'Probabilistic Logic and the Synthesis of Reliable Organisms from Unreliable Components', in C. Shanoon and J. McCarthy (eds), *Automata Studies*. Princeton: Princeton University Press.

—— (1968). *Public Policy Making Reexamined*. Chicago: Chandler.

Dyson, Kenneth (1982). 'West Germany: In Search of a Rational Consensus', in J. Richardson (ed.), *Policy Styles in Western Europe*. London: Allen and Unwin.

Eckstein, Harry (1973). 'Authority Relations: A Structural Basis for Political Inquiry'. *American Political Science Review*, 67: 1142.

—— (1975). 'Case Studies and Theory in Political Science', in F. Greenstein and N. Polsby (eds), *Handbook of Political Science*, vii. Reading: Addison-Wesley.

—— (1988). 'A Culturalist Theory of Political Change'. *American Political Science Review*, 82: 789.

Eisenberg, Melvin (1976). 'Private Ordering Through Negotiations: Dispute Settlement and Rulemaking'. *Harvard Law Review*, 89: 637.

—— (1997). 'The World of Contract and the World of Gift'. *California Law Review*, 85: 821.

Ellickson, Robert C. (1991). *Order Without Law: How Neighbors Settle Disputes*. Cambridge, MA: Harvard University Press.

Ellis, Evelyn (1991). *European Community Sex Equality Law*. Oxford: Oxford University Press.

Ely, John Hart (1980). *Democracy and Distrust*. Cambridge, MA: Harvard University Press.

Eurostat (1995). *External Trade, 1958–93*. Brussels: EC Publications.

Evans, Peter, Rueschemeyer, Dietrich, and Skocpol, Theda (eds) (1985). *Bringing the State Back In*. Cambridge: Cambridge University Press.

—— Jacobson, Harold K., and Putnam, Robert D. (1993). *Double-Edged Diplomacy*. Berkeley: University of California Press.

Farnsworth, Allan (1985). 'Conflict of Laws: Problems that Face Transnational Business and How to Avoid Them', in Beverly A. Allen and Christian S. Ward (eds), *The United States, Transnational Business, and the Law*. New York: Oceana.

Favoreu, Louis (1982a). 'Décentralisation et Constitution'. *Revue du droit public*, 98: 1259.

—— (1982b). *Une Grande Decision*, in L. Favoreu, ed. *Nationalisation et Constitution*. Paris; Aix-en Provence: Economica.

—— (1986). *Europe occidentale* [Western Europe], in L. Favoreu and J. A. Jolowicz, eds. *Le contrôle juridictionnel des lois* [Constitutional review of legislation]. Paris; Aix-en-Provence: Economica.

—— (1988). *La politique saisie par le droit* [Politics captured by law]. Paris; Aix-en-Provence: Economica.

—— (1990). 'Le Droit Constitutionnel, Droit de la Constitution et Constitution du Droit'. *Revue Française de Droit Constitutionnel*, 1: 71–89.

—— (1996). 'La Notion de Cour Constitutionnelle', in P. Zen-Ruffinen and A. Auer (eds), *De la Constitution: Études en L'Honneur de Jean-François Aubert*. Bâle: Helbing and Lichtenhan.

—— and Philip, Loïc (1991). *Les grandes décisions du Conseil constitutionnel*. Paris; Aix-en-Provence: Sirey.

Federation Internationale des Ingenieurs – Consails (1987). *Conditions of Contract for Works of Civil Engineering Construction* (4th edn). Brussels: FIIC.

Fernandez Esteban, Maria Luisa (1994). 'La Noción de Constitución Europea en la Jurisprudecia del Tribunal de Justicia de las Comunidas Europeas' [The Notion of a European Constitution in the Case Law of the European Court of Justice]. *Revista Española de Derecho Constitucional*, 14/40: 241.

Ferrari, Franco (ed.) (1998). *The Unification of International Commercial Law*. Baden-Baden: Nomos.

Fisher, Louis (1978). *The Constitution Between Friends: Congress, the President, and the Law*. Princeton, NJ: Princeton University Press.

—— (1988). *Constitutional Dialogues*. Princeton, NJ: Princeton University Press.

Fishkin, James (1990). *Democracy and Deliberation*. Chicago: University of Chicago Press.

Fligstein, Neil. (2001). *The Architecture of Markets: An Economic Sociology of Twenty-First-Century Capitalist Societies*. Princeton: Princeton University Press.

—— and Stone Sweet, Alec (2001). 'Institutionalizing the Treaty of Rome', in A. Stone Sweet, W. Sandholtz, and N. Fligstein (eds), *The Institutionalization of Europe*. Oxford: Oxford University Press.

Foray, Dominique (1997). 'The Dynamic Implications of Increasing Returns: Technological Change and Path Dependent Inefficiency'. *International Journal of Industrial Organization*, 15: 733.

Foster, George M. (1977). 'The Dyadic Contract: A Model for the Social Structure of a Mexican Peasant Village', in S. W. Schmidt, J. C. Scott, C. Landé, and L. Guasti (eds), *Friends, Followers, and Factions*. Berkeley: University of California Press.

Frank, Jerome (1949). *Courts on Trial*. Princeton, NJ: Princeton University Press.

Friedman, Lawrence (1985). *Total Justice*. New York: Macmillan.

Friedman, W. (1967). *Legal Theory* (5th edn). New York: Columbia University Press.

Friedrich, Carl J. (1958). 'Authority, Reason, and Discretion', in C. J. Friedrich (ed.), *Authority 28*. Cambridge, MA: Harvard University Press.

Fudenberg, Drew and Maskin, Eric (1986). 'The Folk Theorem in Repeated Games with Discounting or with Incomplete Information'. *Econometrica*, 50: 533.

Garrett, Geoffrey (1992). 'International Cooperation and Institutional Choice: The European Community's Internal Market'. *International Organization*, 46: 533.

—— Keleman, R. Daniel, and Schultz, Heiner (1996). 'The European Court of Justice: Master or Servant? Legal Politics in the European Union'. Unpublished manuscript.

George, Alexander (1979). 'Case Studies and Theory Development: The Method of Structured, Focused Comparison', in P. Lauren (ed.), *Diplomacy: New Approaches in History, Theory, and Policy*. New York: Free Press.

Giddens, Anthony (1984). *The Constitution of Society: Outline of the Theory of Structuration*. Berkeley: University of California Press.

Gillette, Clayton P. (1998). 'Lock-In Effects in Law and Norms'. *Boston University Law Review*, 78: 813.

Gillman, Howard (1993). *The Constitution Besieged*. Durham, NC: University Presses of North Carolina.

Gilson, Ronald and Robert Mnookin (1989). 'Coming of Age in a Corporate Law Firm: The Economics of Associates Careers'. *Stanford Law Review*, 41: 567.

Goetz, Charles and Scott, Robert (1980). 'Enforcing Promises: An Examination of the Basis of Contract'. *Yale Law Journal*, 89: 1261.

Goldman, Berthold (1984). 'The Complementary Roles of Judges and Arbitrators in Ensuring That International Commercial Arbitration is Effective', in *International Chamber of Commerce, Sixty Years of ICC Arbitration*. Paris: ICC.

Goldsmith, Jack L. (ed.) (1997). *International Dispute Resolution: The Regulation of Forum Selection*. Irvington, NY: Transnational.

Goldstein, Judith, Kahler, M., Keohane, R., and Slaughter, A. (eds) (2000). 'Special Issue on Legalization of International Politics'. *International Organization*, 54.

Goldstein, Leslie Friedman (1994). 'Centrifugal States and Centripetal Courts: Early State Reaction to European Court of Justice (1958–1994) and U.S. Supreme Court (1789–1860)'. Unpublished manuscript.

—— (2001). *Constituting Federal Sovereignty: The European Union in Comparative Context*. Baltimore: Johns Hopkins University Press.

Goldstone, Jack A. (1998). 'Initial Conditions, General Laws, Path Dependence and Explanation in Historical Sociology'. *American Journal of Sociology*, 104: 829.

Golub, John (1996). 'The Politics of Judicial Discretion: Rethinking the Interaction between National Courts and the European Court of Justice'. *West European Politics* 19: 360.

Goodstein, Eban (1995). 'The Economic Roots of Environmental Decline: Property Rights or Path Dependence?'. *Journal of Economic Issues*, 29: 1029.

Gordon, Robert (1984). 'Critical Legal Histories'. *Stanford Law Review*, 36: 57.

Gormley, Laurence (1985). *Prohibiting Restrictions on Trade within the EEC*. North Holland, The Netherlands: Elsevier-TMC Asser Instituut.

Gouldner, Alvin W. (1977). 'The Norm of Reciprocity', in S. W. Schmidt, J. C. Scott, C. Landé, and L. Guasti (eds), *Friends, Followers, and Factions*. Berkeley: University of California Press.

Green, Leon (1959–60). 'Tort Law: Public Law in Disguise'. *Texas Law Review*, 38/1: 257.

Greif, Avner (1989). 'Reputation and Coalitions in Medieval Trade: Evidence on the Maghribi Traders'. *Journal of Economic History*, 49: 857.

—— (1993). 'Contract Enforceability and Economic Institutions in Early Trade: The Maghribi Trader's Coalition'. *American Economic Review*, 83: 425.

—— (1994). 'Cultural Beliefs and the Organization of Society: A Historical and Theoretical Reflection on Collectivist and Individualist Societies'. *Journal of Political Economy*, 102: 912.

—— Milgrom, Paul, and Weingast, Barry R. (1994). 'Coordination, Commitment, and Enforcement: The Case of the Merchant Guild'. *Journal of Political Economy*, 102: 745–76.

Grossman, Joel (1962). 'Role Playing and Analysis of Judicial Behavior'. *Journal of Public Law*, 11: 285.

Gusy, Christoph (1985). *Parlamentarischer Gesetzgeber und undesverfassungsgericht* [Parliamentary legislature and the Federal Constitutional Court]. Berlin: Duncker and Humblot.

Haas, Ernst B. (1958). *The Uniting of Europe: Political, Social, and Economic Forces, 1950–57*. Stanford, CA: Stanford University Press.

—— (1961). 'International Integration: The European and the Universal Process'. *International Organization*, 15: 366.

Hall, Peter and Taylor, Rosemary (1996). 'Political Science and the Three Institution-alisms'. *Political Studies*, 44: 936.

Hand, Learned (1958). *The Bill of Rights*. Cambridge, MA: Harvard University Press.

Hardin, Russell (1982). *Collective Action*. Baltimore: Johns Hopkins University Press.

Harlow, Carol and Rawlings, Richard (1984). *Law and Administration*. London: Weidenfeld and Nicolson.

Hart, H. L. A. (1994). *The Concept of Law*. Oxford: Clarendon Press.

Hartley, T.C. (1988). *The Foundations of European Community Law* (2nd edn). Oxford: Clarendon Press and Oxford University Press.

Harvey, Ruth A. (1990). 'Equal Treatment of Men and Women in the Workplace: The Implementation of the European Community's Equal Treatment Legislation in the Federal Republic of Germany'. *American Journal of Comparative Law*, 38: 31.

Hattam, Victoria (1992). 'Institutions and Political Change: Working-Class Formation in England and the United States, 1820–1896', in S. Steinmo, K. Thelen, and F. Langstreth (eds), *Structuring Politics: Historical Institutionalism in Comparative Analysis*. New York: Cambridge University Press.

Heiner, Ronald (1986). 'Imperfect Decisions and the Law: On the Evolution of Legal Precedent and Rules'. *Journal of Legal Studies*, 15: 227.

Helfer, Lawrence and Slaughter, Anne-Marie (1997). 'Toward a Theory of Effective Supranational Adjudication'. *Yale Law Journal*, 107: 273.

Hill, Jonathan (1997). 'Some Private International Law Aspects of the Arbitration Act 1996'. *International and Comparative Law Quarterly*, 46: 274.

Hobhouse, Leonard Trelawney (1906). *Morals in Evolution: A Study in Comparative Ethics*. New York: Holt Reprint: New York: Johnson 1968.

Hoffman, Daniel (1997). *Our Elusive Constitution*. Albany, NY: State University of New York Press.

Hoffmann, Stanley (1991). 'Ethics and the Rules of the Game between the Super-powers', in L. Henkin *et al.*, *Right v. Might: International Law and the Use of Force*. New York: Council on Foreign Relations.

—— Malzacher, S., and Ross, G. (eds) (1987). *The Mitterrand Experiment*. New York: Oxford University Press.

Holtzmann, Howard M. (1992). 'Balancing the Need for Certainty and Flexibility in International Arbitration Procedures', in Richard B. Lillich and Charles N. Brower (eds), *International Arbitration in the 21st Century: Towards 'Judicialization' and Conformity?* Irvington, NY: Transnational.

Holyoak, Keith and Thagard, Paul (1995). *Mental Leaps: Analogy in Creative Thought*. Cambridge, MA: MIT Press.

—— —— (1997). 'The Analogical Mind'. *American Psychologist*, 52: 35.

Horn, Robert (1960). 'The Warren Court and the Discretionary Power of the Executive'. *Minnesota Legal Review*, 44: 639.

Horwitz, Morton J. (1977). *The Transformation of American Law 1780-1860*. Cambridge, MA: Harvard University Press.

Huang, Philip C. C. (1996). *Civil Justice in China*. Stanford, CA: Stanford University Press.

Hudec, Robert E. (1992). 'The Judicialization of GATT Dispute Settlement', in M. H. Hart and D. Steger (eds), *In Whose Interest?: Due Process and Transparency in International Trade*. Ottawa: Center for Trade Policy and Law.

—— (1993). *Enforcing International Trade Law: The Evolution of the Modern GATT Legal System*. Salem, NH: Butterworth.

Hull, Adrian Prentice (1999). 'Comparative Political Science: An Inventory and Assessment Since the 1980s'. *PS*, 32: 117.

Hurst, Willard (1950). *The Growth of American Law: The Law Makers*. Boston: Little, Brown.

Hyneman, Charles S. (1963). *The Supreme Court on Trial*. New York: Atherton Press.

International Chamber of Commerce (1997). *The ICC Model International Sale Contract* (Pub. No. 556 (E)). Paris: ICC.

Irons, Peter (1982). *The New Deal Lawyers*. Princeton, NJ: Princeton University Press.

Jacob, Herbert and Vines, Kenneth (1963). 'The Role of the Judiciary in American State Politics', in G. Schubert (ed.), *Judicial Decision-Making*. New York: Free Press.

Jepperson, Ronald L. (1991). 'Institutions, Institutional Effects, and Institutionalism', in W. W. Powell and P. DiMaggio (eds), *The New Institutionalism in Organizational Analysis*. Chicago: University of Chicago Press.

—— (2001). *The Development and Application of Sociological Neo-Institutionalism* (Robert Schuman Centre Working Paper 2001/5). San Domenico di Fiesole: European University Institute.

Jin, Ning (1996). 'The Status of *Lex Mercatoria* in International Commercial Arbitration'. *American Journal of International Arbitration*, 7: 163–98.

Joerges, Christian (1995). 'The Europeanization of Private Law as a Rationalization Process and as a Contest of Disciplines—An Analysis of the Directives on Unfair Terms in Consumer Contracts'. *European Review of Private Law*, 3: 175.

Johnson, Jack (1997). 'Symbol and Strategy in Comparative Political Analysis'. *APSA-CP: Newsletter of the APSA Organized Section in Comparative Politics*, Summer.

Johnson, Nevil (1978). 'Law as the Articulation of the State in Western Germany: A German Tradition Seen from a British Perspective'. *West European Politics*, 1: 177.

—— (1982). 'The Interdependence of Law and Politics: Judges and the Constitution in Western Germany'. *West European Politics*, 5: 236.

Juenger, Friedrich K. (1998). 'The Lex Mercatoria and the Conflict of Laws', in Thomas E. Carbonneau (ed.), *Lex Mercatoria and Arbitration: A Discussion of the New Law Merchant*. Yonkers, N.Y.: Juris.

Kagan, Robert (1978). *Regulatory Justice*. New York: Russell Sage.

—— (1995). 'Adversarial Legalism and American Government', in M. Landy and M. Levin (eds), *The New Politics of Public Policy*. Baltimore: Johns Hopkins University.

—— (1997). 'Should Europe Worry About Adversarial Legalism?' *Oxford Journal of Legal Studies*, 17: 165–83.

—— and Rosen, Robert (1985). 'On the Social Significance of the Large Law Firm'. *Stanford Law Review*, 37: 399.

Kahn, Ronald (1994). *The Supreme Court and Constitutional Theory 1953–1993*. Lawrence: University of Kansas Press.

Kandori, Michihiro (1992). 'Social Norms and Community Enforcement'. *Review of Economic Studies*, 59: 63.

Katzenstein, Peter J. (1987). *Policy and Politics in West Germany: The Growth of a Semisovereign State*. Philadelphia: Temple University Press.

Keane, Mark (1988). *Analogical Problem Solving*. Chichester, UK: Ellis Horwood Ltd.

Keeler, John T. S. and Stone, Alec (1987). 'Judicial-Political Confrontation in Mitterrand's France: The Emergence of the Constitutional Council as a Major Actor in the Policy-Making Process'. In S. Hoffmann, S. Malzacher, and G. Ross (eds), *The Mitterrand Experiment*. New York: Oxford University Press.

Kelsen, Hans (1928). 'La Garantie Juridictionnel de la Constitution'. *Revue de Droit Public*, 44: 197.

Kenney, Sally J. (1992). *For Whose Protection? Reproductive Hazards and Exclusionary Policies in the United States and Britain*. Ann Arbor: University of Michigan Press.

—— (1994). 'Pregnancy and Disability: Comparing the United States and the European Community'. *The Disability Law Reporter Service*, 3: 8.

—— (1996). 'Pregnancy Discrimination: Toward Substantive Equality'. *Wisconsin Women's Law Journal*, 10: 351.

—— (1999). 'Beyond Principals and Agents: Seeing Courts as Organizations by Comparing Référendaires at the European Court of Justice and Law Clerks at the U.S. Supreme Court'. *Comparative Political Studies*, 33: 593.

—— Reisinger, William, and Reitz, John (eds) (1999). *Constitutional Dialogues in Comparative Perspective*. London: Macmillan; New York: St Martin's Press.

Keohane, Robert (1984). *After Hegemony: Cooperation and Discord in the World Political Economy*. Princeton: Princeton University Press.

—— and Hoffmann, Stanley (1991). 'Institutional Change in Europe in the 1980s', in Robert O. Keohane and Stanley Hoffmann (eds), *The New European Community*. Boulder, CO: Westview.

Key, V. O. (1961). *Public Opinion and American Democracy*. New York: Knopf.

Kiewiet, Roderick and McCubbins, Matthew D. (1991). *The Logic of Delegation: Congressional Parties and the Appropriations Process*. Chicago: University of Chicago Press.

Kilroy, Bernadette A. (1996). 'Member State Control or Judicial Independence?: The Integrative Role of the European Court of Justice, 1958–1994'. Unpublished manuscript.

King, Gary (1986). 'How Not to Lie with Statistics: Avoiding Common Mistakes in Quantitative Political Science'. *American Journal of Political Science*, 30: 666.

Kirchheimer, Otto (1966). 'Germany: The Vanishing Opposition', in R. A. Dahl (ed.), *Political Oppositions in Western democracies*. New Haven: Yale University Press.

Knight, Jack and Epstein, Lee (1996). 'The Norm of *Stare Decisis*'. *American Journal of Political Science*, 40: 1018.

Kommers, Donald P. (1976). *Judicial Politics in West Germany*. Beverley Hills, CA, and London: Sage.

—— (1989). *The Constitutional Jurisprudence of the Federal Republic of Germany*. Durham, NC: Duke University Press.

Kommers, Donald P. (1994). 'The Federal Constitutional Court in the German Political System'. *Comparative Political Studies*, 26: 470.

—— (1997). *The Constitutional Jurisprudence of the Federal Republic of Germany* (2nd edn). Durham, NC: Duke University Press.

Koppenol-Laforce, Marielle (1996). 'Contracts in Private International Law', in Marielle Koppenol-Laforce (ed.), *International Contracts: Aspects of Jurisdiction, Arbitration, and Private International Law*. London: Sweet and Maxwell.

Kornhauser, Lewis (1992*a*). 'Modeling Collegial Courts I: Path-Dependence'. *International Review of Law and Economics*, 12: 169.

—— (1992*b*). 'Modeling Collegial Courts II: Legal Doctrine'. *Journal of Law, Economics, and Organization*, 8: 441.

Kratochwil, Friedrich V. (1989). *Rules, Norms, and Decisions*. Cambridge: Cambridge University Press.

Kreps, David M. (1990). 'Corporate Culture and Economic Theory', in J. Alt and K. Shepsle (eds), *Perspectives on Positive Political Economy*. Cambridge: Cambridge University Press.

—— and Wilson, Robert (1982). 'Reputation and Imperfect Information'. *Journal of Economic Theory*, 27: 253.

Krislov, Samuel (1959). 'Constituency v. Constitutionalism: The Desegregation Issue and Tensions and Aspirations of Southern Attorney's General'. *Midwest Journal of Political Science*, 3: 75.

Kritzer, Herbert (1990). *The Justice Brokers: Lawyers and Ordinary Litigation*. New York: Oxford University Press.

Laing, E. A. (1993). 'Equal International Economic Access and Its Antidote: National Welfare As Legitimate Discrimination'. *Emory International Law Review*, 7: 337.

Landau, Martin (1969). 'Redundancy, Rationality, and the Problem of Duplication and Overlap'. *Public Administration Review*, 29: 346.

Landé, Carl H. (1977). 'The Dyadic Basis of Clientelism', in S. Schmidt, J. C. Scott, C. Landé, and L. Guasti (eds), *Friends, Followers, and Factions*. Berkeley: University of California Press.

Landfried, Christine (1984). *Bundesverfassungsgericht and Gesetzgeber* [The Federal Constitutional Court and the Legislature]. Baden-Baden, Germany: Nomos.

—— (1985). 'The Impact of the German Constitutional Court on Politics and Policy Outputs'. *Government and Opposition*, 20: 522.

—— (1989). 'Legislation and Judicial Review in the Federal Republic of Germany', in C. Landfried (ed.), *Constitutional Review and Legislation: An International Comparison*. Baden-Baden, Germany: Nomos.

—— (1992). 'Judicial Policymaking in Germany: The Federal Constitutional Court'. *West European Politics*, 15: 50.

Lando, Ole (1985). 'The Lex Mercatoria in International Commercial Arbitration'. *International and Comparative Law Quarterly*, 34: 747.

—— (1995). *Principles of European Contract Law*. Dordrecht: Kluwer.

—— (1998). 'Optional or Mandatory Europeanisation of Contract Law'. Paper presented at the Workshop, Private Law Adjudication in the European Multi-Level

System, 2-3 October. San Domenico di Fiesole: Robert Schuman Centre, European University Institute.

Lasswell, Harold (1930). *Psychopathology and Politics*. New Haven: Yale University Press.

Laycock, Douglas (1994). *Modern American Remedies*. Boston: Little, Brown.

Lehmbruch, Gerhard (1978). *Parteien Wettbewerb im Bundesstaat* [Party Struggle in the German Federal State]. Stuttgart, Germany: Kohlhammer.

Leibfried, Stephen and Pierson, P. (eds) (1995). *European Social Policy*. Washington, DC: Brookings Institution.

Leicht, Robert (1974). *Grundgesetz und politische Praxis* [The Constitution and Political Praxis]. Munich: Diæresis.

Lenaerts, Koen (1988). *Le Juge et la Constitution aux États-Unis D'Amérique et dans l'Ordre Juridique Européen*. Brussels: Bruylant.

—— (1990). 'Constitutionalism and the Many Faces of Federalism'. *American Journal of Comparative Law*, 38: 205.

Lepsius, Ranier (1982). 'Institutional Structures and Political Cultures', in H. During and G. Smith (eds), *Party Government and Political Culture in West Germany*. London: Macmillan.

Levitsky, Jonathan E. (1994). 'The Europeanization of the British Style'. *American Journal of Comparative Law*, 42: 347.

Levy, Edward (1988). *An Introduction to Legal Reasoning*. Chicago: University of Chicago Press.

Levy, Leonard (1960). 'Judicial Realism and Prospective Overruling'. *University of Pennsylvania Law Review*, 109: 1.

Liebowitz, S. J. and Margolis, Stephen E. (1995). 'Path Dependence, Lock-In and History'. *Journal of Law, Economics and Organization*, 11: 205.

Lillich, Richard B. and Brower, Charles N. (eds) (1992). *International Arbitration in the 21st Century: Towards 'Judicialization' and Conformity?* Irvington, NY: Transnational.

Lindblom, Charles (1977). *Politics and Markets*. New York: Basic Books.

Lipstein, K. (1981). *Principles of the Conflict of Laws, National and International*. The Hague: Martinus Nijhoff.

Long, Olivier (1985). *Law and its Limitations in the GATT Multilateral Trade System*. Boston: Martinus Nijhoff.

Lörchner, Gino (1998). 'The New German Arbitration Act'. *Journal of International Arbitration*, 15: 85-93.

Luchaire, François (1979). 'Le Conseil constitutionnel: Est-il une juridiction?' [Is the Constitutional Council a Jurisdiction?]. *Revue du droit public*, 95: 27.

Ludlow, Peter (1991). 'The European Commission', in R. O. Keohane and S. Hoffmann (eds), *The New European Community*. Boulder, CO: Westview.

Luker, Kristin (1984). *Abortion and the Politics of Motherhood*. Berkeley: University of California Press.

Maass, Arthur (1959). *Area and Power*. Glencoe, IL: Free Press.

Macauley, Melissa (1998). *Social Power and Legal Culture: Litigation Masters in Late Imperial China*. Stanford, CA: Stanford University Press.

McCann, Michael (1986). *Taking Reform Seriously: Perspectives on Public Interest Liberalism*. Ithaca, NY: Cornell University Press.

MacCormick, Neil (1978). *Legal Reasoning and Legal Theory*. Oxford: Clarendon Press.

—— (1989). 'Spontaneous Order and Rule of Law: Some Problems'. *Ratio Juris*, 41: 2.

McCubbins, Martin, Noll, Roger, and Weingast, Barry (1992). 'Positive Canons: The Role of Legislature Bargains in Statutory Interpretation;. *Georgetown Law Review*, 80: 705.

Macy, Josiah Jr. (1953). 'Coding Noise in a Task-Oriented Group'. *J. Abnor. Psychol.*, 48: 401.

Majone, Giandomenico (2001). 'Two Logics of Delegation: Agency and Fiduciary Relations in EU Governance'. *European Union Politics*, 2: 103.

Malinowski, Bronislaw (1932). *Crime and Custom in Savage Society*. London: Paul, Trench, and Trubner.

Mancini, Federico G. (1991). 'The Making of a Constitution for Europe', in R. O. Keohane and S. Hoffmann (eds), *The New European Community*. Boulder, CO: Westview.

Mansbridge, Jane (ed.) (1990). *Beyond Self-Interest*. Chicago: University of Chicago Press.

March, James G. and Olsen, Johan P. (1984). 'The New Institutionalism: Organizational Factors in Political Life'. *American Political Science Review*, 78: 734.

—— —— (1989). *Rediscovering Institutions*. New York: Free Press.

—— and Simon, Herbert (1958). *Organizations*. New York: Wiley

Marchant, Garry, Robinson, John, Anderson, Urton, and Schadewald, Michael (1991). 'Analogical Transfer and Expertise in Legal Reasoning'. *Organizational Behavior and Human Decision Processes*, 48: 272.

—— —— —— —— (1993). 'The Use of Analogy in Legal Argument: Problem Similarity, Precedent and Expertise'. *Organizational Behavior and Human Decision Processes*, 55: 95.

Markovits, Andrei (1986). *The Politics of the West German Trade Unions*. Cambridge, UK, and New York: Cambridge University Press.

Marks, Gary, Hooghe, Liesbet, and Blank, Kermit (1996). 'European Integration and the State'. *Journal of Common Market Studies*, 34: 341.

Mather, Lynn (1998). 'Theorizing About Trial Court Lawyers, Policy Making and Tobacco Litigation'. *Law and Social Inquiry*, 23: 897.

Mattli, Walter (1999). *The Logic of Regional Integration: Europe and Beyond*. New York: Cambridge University Press.

—— (2001). 'Private Justice in a Global Economy: From Litigation to Arbitration'. *International Organization*, 55: 919.

—— and Slaughter, Anne-Marie (1998). 'Revisiting the European Court of Justice'. *International Organization*, 52: 177.

Mayer, Richard (1992). *Thinking, Problem Solving and Cognition* (2nd edn). New York: W.H. Freeman & Co.

Mazey, Sonia (1998). 'The European Union and Women's Rights: From the Europeanization of National Agendas to the Nationalization of a European Agenda'. *Journal of European Public Policy*, 5: 131.

Mendelson, Wallace (1961). *Justices Black and Frankfurter: Conflict in the Court*. Chicago: University of Chicago Press.

Merryman, John (1985). *The Civil Law Tradition: An Introduction to the Legal Systems of Western Europe and Latin America* (2nd edn). Stanford, CA: Stanford University Press.

Milgrom, Paul R. and Roberts, John (1992). *Economics, Organization and Management*. Englewood Cliffs, NJ: Prentice Hall.

—— North, Douglass C., and Weingast, Barry R. (1990). 'The Role of Institutions in the Revival of Trade: The Law Merchant, Private Judges, and the Champagne Fairs. *Economics and Politics*, 2: 1.

Miller, Arthur (1961). 'A Note on Supreme Court Decisions'. *Journal of Public Law*, 10: 139.

—— and Howell, Ronald (1960). 'The Myth of Neutrality in Constitutional Adjudication'. *University Chicago Law Review*, 27: 661.

Mishkin, Paul (1965). 'The High Court, the Great Writ, and the Due Process of Time and Law'. *Harvard Law Review*, 79: 56.

Mnookin, Robert and Louis Kornhauser (1979). 'Bargaining in the Shadow of the Law: The Case of Divorce'. *Yale Law Journal*, 88: 950.

Moe, Terry (1987). 'An Assessment of the Positive Theory of Congressional Dominance'. *Legislative Studies Quarterly*, 12: 475.

Le Monde. (1984*a*). 24 January.

—— (1984*b*). 15 October.

Moravcsik, Andrew (1991). 'Negotiating the Single European Act: National Interests and Conventional Statecraft in the European Community'. *International Organization*, 45: 19.

—— (1993). 'Preferences and Power in the European Community: A Liberal Intergovernmentalist Approach'. *Journal of Common Market Studies*, 31: 473.

—— (1994). 'Why the European Community Strengthens the State'. Unpublished manuscript.

—— (1995). 'Liberal Intergovernmentalism and Integration: A Rejoinder'. *Journal of Common Market Studies*, 33: 61.

—— (1998). *The Choice for Europe: Social Purpose and State Power from Massina to Maastricht*. Ithaca, NY: Cornell University Press.

Mueller, Dennis C. (1997). 'First-Mover Advantages and Path Dependence'. *International Journal of Industrial Organization*, 15: 827.

Murphy, Walter (1959). 'Lower Court Checks on Supreme Court Power'. *American Political Science Review*, 53: 1017.

—— (1962*a*). *Congress and the Court*. Chicago: University of Chicago Press.

—— (1962*b*). 'Marshalling the Court: Leadership, Bargaining and the Judicial Process'. *University of Chicago Law Review*, 29: 640.

—— (1964). *Elements of Judicial Strategy*. Chicago: University of Chicago Press.

—— and Tanenhaus, Joseph (1977). *Comparative Constitutional Law*. New York: St Martin's Press.

Murray, James (1982). 'The Role of Analogy in Legal Reasoning'. *UCLA Law Review*, 29: 833.

Nagel, Stuart (1963). 'Off-the-Bench Attitudes', in Glendon Schubert (ed.), *Judicial Decision Making*. New York: Free Press.

Nehl, Hanns Peter (1999). *Principles of Administrative Procedure in E.C. Law*. Oxford: Hart Publishing Co.

Newland, Chester (1961). 'Personal Assistants to Supreme Court Justices: The Law Clerks'. *Oregon Law Review*, 40: 299.

Newman, Lawrence W. (1998). 'A Practical Assessment of Arbitral Dispute Resolution', in Thomas E. Carbonneau (ed.), *Lex Mercatoria and Arbitration: A Discussion of the New Law Merchant*. Yonkers, N.Y.: Juris.

Noonan, John (1976). *Persons and Masks of the Law*. New York: Farrar, Straus and Giroux.

Nordlinger, Eric, Lowi, Theodore, and Fabbrini, Sergio (1988). 'The Return to the State: Critiques'. *American Political Science Review*, 82, 875.

North, Douglass R. (1981). *Structure and Change in Economic History*. New York: Newton.

—— (1990). *Institutions, Institutional Change, and Economic Performance*. Cambridge: Cambridge University Press.

—— (1991). 'Institutions, Transaction Costs, and the Rise of Merchant Empires', in James D. Tracy (ed.), *The Political Economy of Merchant Empires*. Cambridge: Cambridge University Press.

Northrop, F. S. C. (1959). *The Complexities of Legal and Ethical Experience*. Boston: Little, Brown.

Note (1988). 'General Principles of Law in International Commercial Arbitration'. *Harvard Law Review*, 101: 1816.

Nyikos, Stacy (2000). 'The European Court, the National Courts and Strategic Interaction within the Preliminary Reference Procedure'. Dissertation. Charlottesville: University of Virginia.

Okekeifere, Andrew I. (1998). 'Commercial Arbitration As the Most Effective Dispute Resolution Method: Still a Fact or Now a Myth?' *Journal of International Arbitration*, 15: 81.

Oliver, Peter (1988). *Free Movement of Goods in the EEC*. London: European Law Centre.

Onuf, Nicholas (1989). *World of Our Making: Rules and Rule in Social Theory and International Relations*. Columbia, SC: University of South Carolina Press.

—— (1994). 'The Constitution of International Society'. *European Journal of International Law*, 5: 1.

O'Reilly, Dolores and Stone Sweet, Alec (1998). 'From National to Supranational Governance: The Liberalization and Reregulation of Air Transport'. *Journal of European Public Policy*, 5: 477.

Orrin, Karen (1996). 'The Emergence of an Authoritative International Court in the European Union'. *West European Politics*, 19: 458.

Parsons, Talcott and Shils, E. A. (eds) (1951). *A General Theory of Action*. Cambridge, MA: Harvard University Press.

Pechota, Vratislav (1998). 'The Future of the Law Governing the International Arbitral Process', in Thomas E. Carbonneau (ed.), *Lex Mercatoria and Arbitration: A Discussion of the New Law Merchant*. Yonkers, N.Y.: Juris.

Peltason, Jack (1955). *Federal Courts in the Federal System*. New York: Random House.

—— (1961). *Fifty Eight Lonely Men: Southern Federal Judges and School Desegregation*. Urbana: University of Illinois Press.

Peter, Wolfgang (1995). *Arbitration and Renegotiation of International Investment Agreements* (2nd edn). The Hague: Kleuwer.

Pierson, Paul (1993). 'When Effect Becomes Cause: Policy Feedback and Political Change'. *World Politics*, 45: 595.

—— (1996a). 'The Path to European Integration: A Historical Institutionalist Analysis'. *Comparative Political Studies*, 29: 123.

—— (1996b). 'Path Dependence and the Study of Politics'. Paper Presented at the Annual Meeting of the American Political Science Association, San Francisco.

—— (1997). *Path Dependence, Increasing Returns and the Study of Politics* (Study of Germany and Europe Working Paper No. 7.7). Cambridge, MA: Harvard University Center for European Studies.

—— (1998). 'The Path to European Integration: A Historical-Institutional Analysis', in W. Sandholtz and A. Stone Sweet (eds), *European Integration and Supranational Governance*. Oxford: Oxford University Press.

—— (2000). 'Increasing Returns, Path Dependence, and the Study of Politics'. *American Political Science Review*, 94: 251.

Pillinger, Jane (1992). *Feminising the Market*. London: Macmillan.

Poiares Maduro, Miguel (1997). 'Reforming the Market or the State? Art. 30 and the European Constitution: Economic Freedom and Political Rights'. *European Law Journal*, 3: 1.

Pollack, Mark (1997). 'Delegation, Agency, and Agenda Setting in the European Community'. *International Organization*, 51: 99.

Post, Robert (1995). *Constitutional Domains: Democracy, Community and Management*. Cambridge, MA: Harvard University Press.

Powell, Walter W. and DiMaggio, Paul J. (1991). 'Introduction', in W. Powell and P. DiMaggio (eds), *The New Institutionalism in Organizational Analysis*. Chicago: University of Chicago Press.

Powers, David (1992). 'On Judicial Review in Islamic Law'. *Law and Society Review*, 26: 315.

Prechal, Sacha and Burrows, Noreen (1990). *Gender Discrimination Law of the European Community*. Hants, UK: Gower-Dartmouth.

Pridham, Geoffrey (1975). 'The Ostpolitik and the Opposition in West Germany', in R. Tilford (ed.), *The Ostpolitik and Political Change in Germany*. Westmead, UK: Saxon House.

—— (1982). 'The Government/Opposition Dimension and the Development of the Party System in the 1970s: The Reappearance of Conflictual Politics', in H. Döring and G. Smith (eds), *Party Government and Political Culture in West Germany*. London: Macmillan.

Priest, George (1977). 'The Common Law Process and the Selection of Efficient Rules'. *Journal of Legal Studies*, 6: 65.

'Principles for International Commercial Contracts' (1992). *American Journal of Comparative Law*, 40: 705.

Pritchett, C. Herman (1948). *The Roosevelt Court, A Study in Judicial Politics and Values 1937–1947*. New York: Macmillan.

—— (1954). *Civil Liberties and the Vinson Court*. Chicago: University of Chicago Press.

Probert, Walter (1968). 'Law Through the Looking Glass of Language and Communicative Behavior'. *Journal of Legal Education*, 20: 253.

Pulzer, Peter (1978). 'Responsible Party Government and Stable Coalition: The Case of the German Federal Republic'. *Political Studies*, 26: 181.

Ramseyer, Mark (1994). 'The Puzzling (In)dependence of Courts: A Comparative Approach'. *Journal of Legal Studies*, 23: 721.

Rasmussen, Eric (1994). 'Judicial Legitimacy as a Repeated Game'. *Journal of Law, Economics, and Organization*, 10: 63.

Règlement de l'Assemblée nationale (1986). Paris: Assemblée nationale.

Renoux, Thierry and de Villiers, Michel (1994). *Code Constitutionnel*. Paris: Litec.

Rensmann, Thilo (1998). 'Anational Arbitral Awards: Legal Phenomenon or Academic Fiction'. *Journal of International Arbitration*, 15: 37.

Roe, Mark J. (1996). 'Chaos and Evolution in Law and Economics'. *Harvard Law Review*, 109: 641.

Rosenberg, Shawn W. (1995). 'Against Neoclassical Political Economy: A Political Psychological Critique'. *Political Psychology*, 16: 95.

Rosenblum, Victor (1955). *Law as a Political Instrument*. New York: Random House.

Rosett, Arthur (1992). 'Unification, Harmonization, Restatement, Codification, and Reform in International Commercial Law'. *American Journal of Comparative Law*, 40: 683

Rubin, Paul (1977). 'Why is the Common Law Efficient?' *Journal of Legal Studies*, 6: 51.

Rubino-Sammartano, Mauro (1995). 'New International Arbitration Legislation in Italy'. *Journal of International Arbitration*, 12: 77.

Rumble, Wilfred (1968). *American Legal Realism*. Ithaca, NY: Cornell University Press.

Russell, Peter H., Knopff, Rainer, and Morton, Ted (1989). *Federalism and the Charter*. Ottawa: Carleton University Press.

Safran, William (1988). 'Rights and Liberties under the Mitterrand Presidency: Socialist Innovations and Post-socialist Revisions'. *Contemporary French Civilization*, 12: 1.

Sandholtz, Wayne (1992). *High-Tech Europe: The Politics of International Cooperation*. Berkeley: University of California Press.

—— (1993). 'Choosing Union: Monetary Politics and Maastricht'. *International Organization*, 47: 1.

—— (1996). 'Membership Matters: Limits of the Functional Approach to European Institutions'. *Journal of Common Market Studies*, 34: 403.

—— (1998). 'The Emergence of a Supranational Telecommunications Regime', in W. Sandholtz and A. Stone Sweet (eds), *European Integration and Supranational Governance*. Oxford: Oxford University Press.

—— and Stone Sweet, A. (eds) (1998). *European Integration and Supranational Governance*. Oxford: Oxford University Press.

—— and Zysman, John (1989). 'Recasting the European Bargain'. *World Politics*, 42: 95.

Sarat, Austin and Felstiner, William (1995). *Divorce Lawyers and Their Clients*. New York: Oxford University Press.

Sartor, Giovanni (1994). 'A Formal Model of Legal Argumentation'. *Ratio Juris*, 7: 177.

Sayrs, Lois W. (1989). *Pooled, Time Series Analysis*. Newbury Park, CA: Sage.

Sbragia, Alberta M. (1993). 'The European Community: A Balancing Act'. *Publius*, 23: 23.

—— (1998). 'Institution-building from Below and Above: The European Community in Global Environmental Politics'. In W. Sandholtz and A. Stone Sweet (eds), *European Integration and Supranational Governance*. Oxford: Oxford University Press.

Schanze, Erick (1981). 'Forms of Agreement and the Joint Venture Practice', in Kirchner, Christian *et al.*, *Mining Ventures in Developing Cultures*, Part II. Frankfurt: Bender.

Scharpf, Fritz (1977). *Politischer immobilismus and ökonomische Krise* [Political Immobilism and Economic Crisis]. Kronburg, Germany: Athenäum.

Schattschneider, Elmer (1961). *The Semi-Sovereign People*. New York: Holt Reinhart and Winston.

Schenke, Wolf-Rüdiger (1986). 'Die Subsidiarität der Verfassungsbeschwerde gegen Gesetze'. *Neue Juristiche Wochenschrift*, 39: 1451.

Schindler, Peter. (1991). 'Der Deutscher Bundestag 1972/1990/91: Parliaments und Wahlstatistik'. *Zeitschrift für Parlamentsfragen*, 22: 344.

Schlink, Bernhard (1993). 'German Constitutional Culture in Transition'. *Cardozo Law Review*, 14: 711–36.

Schmidhauser, John (1959). 'The Justices of the Supreme Court: A Collective Portrait'. *Midwest Journal of Political Science*, 3: 1.

Schmidt, Manfred G. (1978). 'The Politics of Domestic Reform in the Federal Republic of Germany'. *Politics and Society*, 8: 131.

Schofeld, N. 1985. Anarchy, Altruism, and Cooperation. *Social Choice and Welfare* 2: 207.

Schubert, Glendon (1958). 'The Study of Judicial Decision Making As an Aspect of Political Behavior'. *American Political Science Review*, 53: 1007.

—— (1962). 'Policy Without Law: An Extension of the Certiorari Game'. *Stanford Law Review*, 14: 284.

—— (1963). *Judicial Decision Making*. New York: Free Press.

Schwarze, Jurgen (1992). *European Administrative Law*. London: Sweet and Maxwell.

Segal, Jeffrey and Spaeth, Harold (1993). *The Supreme Court and the Attitudinal Model*. Cambridge: Cambridge University Press.

—— —— (1996). 'The Influence of *Stare Decisis*'. *American Journal of Political Science*, 40: 975.

—— —— (1999). *Majority Rule or Minority Will: Adherence to Precedent on the U.S. Supreme Court*. Cambridge: Cambridge University Press.

Seitzer, Jeffrey (1999). 'Experimental Constitutionalism: A Comparative Analysis of the Institutional Bases of Rights Enforcement in Post-Communist Hungary', in Sally Kenney, William Reisinger, and John Reitz (eds), *Constitutional Dialogues in Comparative Perspective*. London: Macmillan and New York: St Martin's Press.

Seventh Geneva Global Arbitration Forum (1999). 'Reconsidering a Key Tenet of International Commercial Arbitration: Is Finality of Awards what Parties really

Need? Has the Time of an International Appellate Arbitral Body Arrived?' *Journal of International Arbitration*, 16: 57.

Shapiro, I. (ed.) (1994). *The Rule of Law: Nomos XXXVI*. New York: New York University Press.

Shapiro, Martin (1961). 'Morals and the Courts: The Reluctant Crusaders'. *Minnesota Law Review*, 45: 897.

—— (ed.) (1962). *The Supreme Court and Public Policy*. Glenview, IL: Scott, Foresman.

—— (1963). 'Judicial Modesty: Down with the Old——Up with the New?' *U.C.L.A. Law Review*, 10: 533.

—— (1964). *Law and Politics in the Supreme Court: Studies in Political Jurisprudence*. Glencoe, IL: Illinois Free Press.

—— (1965). 'Stability and Change in Judicial Decision-Making: Incrementalism or Stare Decisis'. *Law in Transition Quarterly*, 2: 134.

—— (1966a). 'Book Review: Walter Murphy, *Elements of Judicial Strategy*'. *Stanford Law Review*, 18: 544.

—— (1966b). *Freedom of Speech: The Supreme Court and Judicial Review*. Englewood Cliffs, NJ: Prentice-Hall.

—— (1968). *Supreme Court and Administrative Agencies*. New York: Free Press.

—— (1969). *The Supreme Court and Public Policy*. Glenview, IL: Scott, Foresman.

—— (1970). 'Decentralized Decision-Making in the Law of Torts', in S. Ulmer (ed.), *Political Decision-Making*. New York: Van Nostrand.

—— (1971a). 'Obscenity Law: A Public Policy Analysis'. *Journal of Public Law*, 20: 503.

—— (1971b). 'The Impact of the Supreme Court'. *Journal of Legal Education*, 23: 77.

—— (1972a). 'Toward a Theory of *Stare Decisis*'. *The Journal of Legal Studies*, 1: 125.

—— (1972b). 'From Public Law to Public Policy'. *PS*, Fall: 5.

—— (1975). 'Courts', in F. Greenstein and N. Polsby (eds), *Handbook of Political Science*. Reading, MA: Addison-Wesley.

—— (1978). 'The Supreme Court and Economic Rights', in M. Judd Harmon (ed.), *Essays on the Constitution of the United States*. Port Washington, NY: Kennikat Press.

—— (1979). 'Judicial Activism', in S. M. Lipset (ed.), *The Third Century*. Stanford, CA: Hoover Institution Press.

—— (1980). 'Appeal'. *Law and Society Review*, 14: 629.

—— (1981a). *Courts: A Comparative and Political Analysis*. Chicago: University of Chicago Press.

—— (1981b). 'On the Regrettable Decline of Law French: Or Shapiro Jettet Le Brickbat'. *Yale Law Journal*, 90: 1198.

—— (1982). 'Predicting the Future of Administrative Law'. *Regulation*, May/June: 18.

—— (1983). 'Administrative Discretion'. *Yale Law Journal*, 92: 1487.

—— (1986a). 'Fathers and Sons: The Court, the Commentators and the Search for Values', in V. Blasi (ed.), *The Burger Court*. New Haven: Yale University Press.

—— (1986b). 'The Supreme Court's "Return" to Economic Regulation'. *Studies in American Political Development*, 1: 91.

—— (1986c). 'Libel Regulatory Analysis'. *California Law Review*, 74: 883.

—— (1986d). 'Administrative Procedures Act: Past, Present, Future'. *Virginia Law Review*, 72: 447.

—— (1988). *Who Guards the Guardians: Judicial Control of Administration*. Athens, GA: University of Georgia Press.

—— (1989a). 'Political Jurisprudence, Public Law and Post-Consequentialist Ethics'. *Studies in American Political Development*, 3: 88.

—— (1989b). 'Morality and the Politics of Judging'. *Tulane Law Review*, 63: 1555.

—— (1990a). 'The Constitution, Economic Rights, and Social Justice', in Shalomo Slonin (ed.), *The Constitutional Bases of Political and Social Change in the United States*. New York: Praeger.

—— (1990b). 'Lawyers, Corporations and Knowledge: A Review Essay'. *American Journal of Comparative Law*, 38: 683.

—— (1992). 'The European Court of Justice', in A. Sbragia (ed.), *Euro-Politics*. Washington, DC: Brookings Institution.

—— (1993a). 'Public Law and Judicial Politics', in Ada W. Finifter (ed.), *Political Science: The State of Discipline II*. Washington, DC: American Political Science Association.

—— (1993b). 'Globalization of Law'. *Indiana Journal of Global Legal Studies*, 1: 37.

—— (1994). 'Judges As Liars'. *Harvard Journal of Law and Public Policy*, 17: 155.

—— (1995). 'Of Interests and Values: The New Politics and the New Political Science', in M. Landy and M. Levin (eds), *The New Politics of Public Policy*. Baltimore: Johns Hopkins Press.

—— (1996a). 'The Globalization of Judicial Review', in Lawrence Friedman and Harry Scheiber (eds), *Legal Culture and the Legal Profession*. Boulder, CO: Westview.

—— (1996b). 'Codification of the Administrative Law: The U.S. and the Union'. *European Law Review*, 2: 26.

—— (1997). 'The Problems of Independent Agencies in the United States and the European Union'. *Journal of European Public Policy*, 4: 276.

—— (1998a). 'The European Court of Justice: Of Institutions and Democracy'. *Israel Law Review*, 32: 3.

—— (1998b). 'The Politics of Information: U.S. Congress and the European Parliament', in Paul Craig and Carol Harlow (eds), *Lawmaking in the European Union*. Dublin: Round Hill, Sweet and Maxwell.

—— (1999a). 'The European Court of Justice', in P. Craig and G. de Burca (eds), *The Evolution of E.U. Law*. Oxford: Oxford University Press.

—— (1999b). 'The Success of Judicial Review', in Sally Kenny, William Reisinger, and John Reitz (eds), *Constitutional Dialogues in Comparative Perspective*. London: Macmillan; New York: St Martin's Press.

—— (2000). *The Common Core: Some Outside Comments, in Mauro Bussani and Ugo Mattei, Making European Law*. Trento: Universita Degli Studi Di Trento.

—— (2001a). 'The Politics and Policy of the Regulated Market, Efficiency-Constrained Welfare State', in M. Levin, M. Landy, and M. Shapiro (eds), *Seeking the Center: Politics and Policy Making at the New Century*. Washington, DC: Georgetown University Press.

Shapiro, Martin (2001b). 'The European Court of Justice', in P. Russell and D. O'Brien (eds), *Judicial Independence in the Age of Democracy*. Charlottesville, VA: University Press of Virginia.

—— (2001c). 'Two Transformations in Administrative Law: American and European?', in Karl-Heinz Ladeur (ed.), *The Europeanization of Administrative Law*. Aldershot: Ashgate Dartmouth.

—— (2001d). 'The Institutionalization of European Administrative Space', in W. Sandholtz, A. Stone Sweet, and N. Fligstein (eds), *The Institutionalization of Europe*. Oxford: Oxford University Press.

—— (2002). 'Judicial Delegation Doctrines: The US, Britain, and France'. *West European Politics*. 25: 173.

—— and Stone, Alec (eds) (1994). 'Special Issue: The New Constitutional Politics in Europe'. *Comparative Political Studies*, 26: 397.

Shklar, Judith (1957). *After Utopia*. Cambridge, MA: Harvard University Press.

Sigelman, Lee and Gadbois, George H. (1983). 'Contemporary Comparative Politics: An Inventory and Assessment'. *Comparative Political Studies*, 16: 275.

Sigler, Jay A (1968). 'Cybernetics Model of the Judicial System'. *Temple Law Quarterly*, 41: 398.

Simmel, Georg (1950). *The Sociology of Georg Simmel*. New York: Free Press.

Slaughter, Anne-Marie, Stone Sweet, Alec, and Weiler, Joseph (eds) (1998). *The European Court and the National Courts——Doctrine and Jurisprudence: Legal Change in its Social Context*. Oxford, UK, and Evanston, IL: Hart Press and Northwestern University Press.

Smith, David N. and Wells, Louis T. (1975). *Negotiating Third World Mineral Agreements*. Cambridge, MA: Ballinger.

Smith, Rogers (1988). 'Political Jurisprudence, the "New Institutionalism," and the Future of Public Law'. *American Political Science Review*, 82: 89.

Snyder, Helen (1958). 'The Supreme Court as a Small Group'. *Social Forces*, 36: 232.

Spaeth, Harold (1962). 'Judicial Power As a Variable Motivating Supreme Court Behavior'. *Midwest Journal of Politics*, 6: 54.

—— (1963a). *Warren Court Attitudes Toward Business: The 'B' Scale*, in Glendon Schubert (ed.), *Judicial Decision Making*. New York: Free Press.

—— (1963b). 'An Analysis of Judicial Attitudes in the Labor Relations Decisions of the Warren Court'. *Journal of Politics*, 25: 290 .

Spellman, Barbara and Holyoak, Keith (1992). 'If Saddam is Hitler then Who is George Bush?: Analogical Mapping Between Systems of Social Roles'. *Journal of Personality and Social Psychology*, 62: 913.

Der Spiegel (1978). Interview with judge Martin Hirsh. Vol. 48: 38.

Stearns, Maxwell (1995). 'Standing Back from the Forest: Justiciability and Social Choice'. *California Law Review*, 83: 1309.

Stein, Eric (1981). 'Lawyers, Judges, and the Making of a Transnational Constitution'. *American Journal of International Law*, 75: 1.

Steinmo, Sven, Thelen, Kathleen, and Longstreth, Frank (1992). *Structuring Politics: Historical Institutionalism in Comparative Analysis*. New York: Cambridge University Press.

Sterret, Susan (1997). *Creating Constitutionalism*. Ann Arbor, Mich.: University of Michigan Press

—— (1999). 'Judicial Review in England', in Sally Kenney, William Reisinger, and John Reitz (eds), *Constitutional Dialogues in Comparative Perspective*. London: Macmillan and New York: St Martin's Press.

Stewart, David P. (1992). 'National Enforcement of Arbitral Awards Under Treaties and Conventions', in Richard B. Lillich and Charles N. Brower (eds), *International Arbitration in the 21st Century: Towards 'Judicialization' and Conformity?* Irvington, NY: Transnational.

Stimson, James (1985). 'Regression Across Time and Space'. *American Journal of Political Science*, 29: 914.

Stone, Alec (1989a). 'In the Shadow of the Constitutional Council: The "Juridicisation" of the Legislative Process in France'. *West European Politics*, 12: 12.

—— (1989b). 'Legal Constraints to Policy-Making: The *Conseil constitutionnel* and the *Conseil d'état*', in P. Godt (ed.), *Policy-Making in France: From De Gaulle to Mitterrand*. New York: Columbia University Press.

—— (1990). 'The Birth and Development of Abstract Review: Constitutional Courts and Policy-making in Western Europe'. *Policy Studies Journal*, 19: 81.

—— (1992a). *The Birth of Judicial Politics in France*. New York: Oxford University Press.

—— (1992b). 'Where Judicial Politics Are Legislative Politics: The Impact of the French Constitutional Council'. *West European Politics*, 15: 29.

—— (1994). 'What is a Supranational Constitution?: An Essay in International Relations Theory'. *Review of Politics*, 56: 441.

—— (1996). 'The Constitutional Council, Constitutional Politics, and *Malaise*', in J. T. S. Keeler and M. Schain (eds), *New Patterns of Public Policy in France: State Responses to Social Change and European Integration*. New York: St Martins Press.

Stone Sweet, Alec (1997). 'The New GATT: Dispute Resolution and the Judicialization of the Trade Regime', in M. Volcansek (ed.), *Law Above Nations: Supranational Courts and the Legalization of Politics*. Gainesville, Fla.: University of Florida Press.

—— (1998a). 'Rules, Dispute Resolution, and Strategic Behavior: Reply to Vanberg'. *Journal of Theoretical Politics*, 10: 327–38.

—— (1998b). 'Qu'y a-t-il de concret dans le contrôle abstrait aux États-unis?' *Revue Française de Droit Constitutionnel*, 34: 227.

—— (1999a). 'Constitutional Dialogues: The Protection of Human Rights in France, Germany, Italy and Spain', in Sally Kenney, William Reisinger, and John Reitz (eds), *Constitutional Dialogues in Comparative Perspective*. London: Macmillan and New York: St Martin's Press.

—— (1999b). 'Judicialization and the Construction of Governance'. *Comparative Political Studies*, 31: 147–84.

—— (2000). *Governing with Judges: Constitutional Politics in Europe*. Oxford: Oxford University Press.

Stone Sweet, Alec (2002). 'Constitutional Courts and Parliamentary Democracy'. *West European Politics*, 25: 77–100.

—— and Brunell, Thomas L. (1998a). 'Constructing a Supranational Constitution: Dispute Resolution and Governance in the European Community'. *American Political Science Review*, 92: 63.

——— (1998b). 'The European Courts and the National Courts: A Statistical Analysis of Preliminary References, 1961–95'. *Journal of European Public Policy*, 5: 66.

——— (2000a). 'The European Court, National Judges and Legal Integration: A Researcher's Guide to the Data Base on Preliminary References in European Law, 1958–98'. *European Law Journal*, 6: 117.

——— (2000b). 'Researcher's Guide to the Data Base on Preliminary References in European Law'. *Särtryck ur Europarättslig Tidskrift* [Swedish Journal of European Law], 3: 179.

—— and Caporaso, James (1998a). 'From Free Trade to Supranational Polity: The European Court and Integration', in W. Sandholtz and A. Stone Sweet (eds), *European Integration and Supranational Governance*. Oxford: Oxford University Press.

——— (1998b). 'La Cour européenne et l'intégration' (The European Court and Integration). *Revue française de science politique*, 48: 195.

—— and McCown, Margaret (2000). 'Path Dependence, Precedent and Judicial Power'. Unpublished manuscript.

—— and Sandholtz, Wayne (1997). 'European Integration and Supranational Governance'. *Journal of European Public Policy*, 4: 297.

——— (1998). 'Integration, Supranational Governance, and the Institutionalization of the European Polity', in W. Sandholtz and A. Stone Sweet (eds), *European Integration and Supranational Governance*. Oxford: Oxford University Press.

——— and Fligstein, N. (eds) (2001). *The Institutionalization of Europe*. Oxford: Oxford University Press.

Stumph, Harry, Shapiro, Martin, Danelski, David, Sarat, Austin, and O'Brien, David (1983). 'Whither Political Jurisprudence: A Symposium'. *Western Political Quarterly*, 36: 533.

Sugden, Robert (1989). 'Spontaneous Order'. *Journal of Economic Perspectives*, 3: 85.

Summers, Robert S. and Taruffo, Michele (1991). 'Interpretation and Comparative Analysis', in N. MacCormick and R. Summers (eds), *Interpreting Statutes: A Comparative Study*. Brookfield, VT: Dartmouth.

Sunstein, Cass (1993). 'On Analogical Reasoning'. *Harvard Law Review*, 106: 741.

Swenson, Peter (1989). *Fair Shares: Unions, Pay, and Politics in Sweden and Germany*. Ithaca, NY: Cornell University Press.

'Symposium: Conflict of Laws in the Global Village' (1995). *Vanderbilt Journal of Transnational Law*, 28, 359.

'Symposium: Contract Law in a Changing World' (1992). *American Journal of Comparative Law*, 40, 541.

Tardan, Arnaud (1988). 'Le rôle législatif du sénat'. *Pouvoirs*, 44: 97.

Tate, C. Neal and Vallinder, T. (eds) (1995). *The Global Expansion of Judicial Power*. New York: New York University Press.

Taylor, Michael (1976). *Anarchy and Cooperation*. Cambridge: Cambridge University Press.

—— (1982). *Community, Anarchy, and Liberty*. Cambridge: Cambridge University Press.

—— (1989). 'Structure, Culture, and Action in the Explanation of Social Change'. *Politics and Society*, 17: 115.

Taylor, Paul (1983). *The Limits of European Integration*. New York: Columbia University Press.

Thatcher, Mark and Stone Sweet, A. (eds) (2002). 'Special Issue: The Politics of Delegation: Non-Majoritarian Institutions in Europe'. *West European Politics*, 25.

Thurstone, James and Egan, Walter (1951). 'A Factorial Study of the Supreme Court'. *Proceedings of the National Academy of Sciences*, 1951: 628.

Tilford, Roger (ed.) (1975). *The Ostpolitik and Political Change in Germany*. Westmead, England: Saxon House.

—— (1981). 'The State, University Reform, and the "Berufsverbot"'. *West European Politics*, 4: 149.

Trakman, Leon (1983). *The Law Merchant: the Evolution of Commercial Law*, Littleton, CO: Rothman.

Tribe, Laurence (1988). *American Constitutional Law*. Mineola, NY: Foundation Press.

Truman, David (1958). *The Governmental Process*. New York: Knopf.

Tsebelis, George (1990). *Nested Games: Rational Choice in Comparative Politics*. Berkeley: University of California Press.

—— (1994). 'The Power of the European Parliament as a Conditional Agenda Setter'. *American Political Science Review*, 88: 128.

—— (1999). 'Veto Players and Law Production in Parliamentary Democracies: An Empirical Analysis'. *American Political Science Review*, 93: 591.

Tsoukalis, L. (1993). *The New European Economy: The Politics and Economics of Integration* (2nd edn). Oxford: Oxford University Press.

Tushnet, Mark (1991). 'Critical Legal Studies: A Political History'. *Yale Law Journal*, 100: 1515.

Ulmer, Sidney (1959). 'An Empirical Analysis of Selected Aspects of Law Making of The United States Supreme Court'. *Journal of Public Law*, 8: 414.

—— (1960). 'Supreme Court Behavior and Civil Rights'. *Western Political Quarterly*, 13: 288.

—— (1961a). 'Scaling Judicial Cases: A Methodological Note'. *American Behavioral Scientist*, 4: 31.

—— (1961b). 'Homeostatic Tendencies in the United States Supreme Court', in S. Ulmer (ed.), *Introductory Readings in Political Behavior*. Chicago: Rand McNally Inc.

—— (1963). 'Leadership in the Michigan Supreme Court', in G. Schubert (ed.), *Judicial Decision Making*. New York: Free Press.

Vanberg, Georg (1998a). 'Abstract Judicial Review, Legislative Bargaining, and Policy Compromise'. *Journal of Theoretical Politics*, 3: 299.

—— (1998b). 'Reply to Stone Sweet'. *Journal of Theoretical Politics*, 3: 339.

Veitch, John M. (1986). 'Repudiations and Confiscations by the Medieval State'. *Journal of Economic History*, 46: 31-6.

Voigt, Stefan (1999). *Explaining Constitutional Change: A Positive Economics Approach*. Williston, VT: American International Distribution Corporation.

Volcansek, Mary L. (ed.) (1992). 'Special Issue: Judicial Politics in Western Europe'. *West European Politics*, 15.

Voltz J. L. and R. S. Haydock (1996). 'Foreign Arbitral Awards: Enforcing the Award Against the Recalcitrant Looser'. *William Mitchell Law Review*, 21: 867.

Von Beyme, Klaus (1983). *The Political System of the Federal Republic of Germany*. Hants, UK: Gower.

—— (1989). 'The Genesis of Constitutional Review in Parliamentary Systems', in C. Landfried (ed.), *Constitutional Review and Legislation: An International Comparison*. Baden-Baden: Nomos.

Vose, Clement (1959). *Caucasians Only: The Supreme Court, The National Association for the Advancement of Colored People and The Restrictive Covenant Cases*. Berkeley: University of California Press.

Vosniadou, S. and Ortony, A. (eds) (1989). *Similarity and Analogical Reasoning*. Cambridge: Cambridge University Press.

Waline, Marcel (1928). 'Éléments d'une théorie de la juridiction constitutionnelle'. *Revue du droit public*, 45: 441.

Waltz, Kenneth (1979). *Theory of International Politics*. New York: McGraw-Hill.

Weakland, John (1967). 'Communications and Behavior——An Introduction'. *Amer. Behav. Sci.*, 10: 1.

Weaver, Suzanne (1977). *Decision to Prosecute: Organization and Public Policy in the Anti-Trust Division*. Cambridge, MA: MIT Press.

Webb, Philip (1985). *The Conflict of Laws and Contract*. Auckland, NZ: Legal Research Foundation.

Webber, Douglas (1983). 'A Relationship of Critical Partnership? Capital and the Social-Liberal Coalition in West Germany'. *West European Politics*, 6: 61.

Weiler, Joseph (1981). 'The Community System: The Dual Character of Supranationalism'. *Yearbook of European Law*, 1: 268.

—— (1986). 'Eurocracy and Distrust'. *Washington Law Review*, 61: 1131.

—— (1987). 'The European Court, National Courts, and References for Preliminary Rulings—the Paradox of Success: A Revisionist View of Article 177 EEC', in H. Schermers, C. Timmermans, A. Kellerman, and J. Stewart Watson (eds), *Article 177 EEC: Experiences and Problems*. North Holland, the Netherlands: T. M. C. Asser Institute.

—— (1989). *Pride and Prejudice–Parliament v. Council*. Florence: European University Institute Studies.

—— (1991). 'The Transformation of Europe'. *Yale Law Journal*, 100: 2403.

—— (1993). 'Journey to an Unknown Destination: A Retrospective and Prospective of the European Court of Justice in the Area of Political Integration'. *Journal of Common Market Studies*, 31: 417.

—— (1994). 'A Quiet Revolution: The European Court and Its Interlocutors'. *Comparative Political Studies*, 26: 510.

—— (1999). *The Constitution of Europe: 'Do the New Clothes Have an Emperor?' and Other Essays on European Integration*. Cambridge: Cambridge University Press.

Wendt, Alexander (1992). 'Anarchy is What States Make of It: The Social Construction of Power Politics'. *International Organization*, 46: 391.

Werner, Jacques (1997). 'The Trade Explosion and Some Likely Effects on International Arbitration'. *Journal of International Arbitration*, 14: 2–15.

—— (1999). 'Reconsidering a Key Tenet of International Commercial Arbitration: is Finality of Awards What Parties Really Need? Has the Time for an International Appellate Arbitral Body Arrived?' *Journal of International Arbitration*, 16: 57–61.

Wessels, Wolfgang (1991). 'The EC Council: The Community's Decision-Making Center', in R. O. Keohane and S. Hoffmann (eds), *The New European Community*. Boulder, CO: Westview.

Westin, Alan (1958). 'The Supreme Court and Group Conflict: Thoughts on Seeing Burke Put Through the Mill'. *American Political Science Review*, 52: 665.

Wiegand, Wolfgang (1991). 'The Reception of American Law in Europe'. *American Journal of Comparative Law*, 39: 229.

—— (1996). 'Americanization of Law: Reception or Convergence', in Lawrence Friedman and Harry Scheiber (eds), *Legal Culture and the Legal Profession*. Boulder, CO: Westview Press.

Wildavsky, Aaron (1987). 'Choosing Preferences by Constructing Institutions: A Cultural Theory of Preference Formation'. *American Political Science Review*, 81: 3.

Wolfe, Christopher (1986). *The Rise of Modern Judicial Review*. New York: Basic Books.

World Bank (1990). *The World Tables of Economic and Social Indicators, 1950–1988* (2nd release) (Inter-university Consortium for Political and Social Research #9300). Washington, DC: World Bank.

—— (1995). *The World Tables of Economic and Social Indicators*. Washington, DC: World Bank.

Yu, Hong-lin (1998). 'Total Separation of International Commercial Arbitration and National Court Regime'. *Journal of International Arbitration*, 15: 145.

Index